ISBN 978-1-331-04321-8
PIBN 10137441

1 MONTH OF
FREE
READING

at

www.ForgottenBooks.com

By purchasing this book you are eligible for one month membership to ForgottenBooks.com, giving you unlimited access to our entire collection of over 700,000 titles via our web site and mobile apps.

To claim your free month visit:
www.forgottenbooks.com/free137441

English
Français
Deutsche
Italiano
Español
Português

www.forgottenbooks.com

Mythology Photography **Fiction**
Fishing Christianity **Art** Cooking
Essays Buddhism Freemasonry
Medicine **Biology** Music **Ancient**
Egypt Evolution Carpentry Physics
Dance Geology **Mathematics** Fitness
Shakespeare **Folklore** Yoga Marketing
Confidence Immortality Biographies
Poetry **Psychology** Witchcraft
Electronics Chemistry History **Law**
Accounting **Philosophy** Anthropology
Alchemy Drama Quantum Mechanics
Atheism Sexual Health **Ancient History**
Entrepreneurship Languages Sport
Paleontology Needlework Islam
Metaphysics Investment Archaeology
Parenting Statistics Criminology
Motivational

THE
LIFE OF GEORGE MASON

1725–1792

BY

KATE MASON ROWLAND

INCLUDING HIS SPEECHES, PUBLIC PAPERS, AND CORRE-
SPONDENCE; WITH AN INTRODUCTION BY
GENERAL FITZHUGH LEE

VOLUME I

> There is a time when men shape for their land
> Its institutions 'mid some tempest's roar,
> Just as the waves that thunder on the strand
> Shape out and round the shore.
>
> .   .   .   .
>
> These rise before me; and there Mason stands,
> The Constitution-maker, firm and bold,
> Like Bernal Diaz, planting with kind hands
> Fair trees to blaze in gold.
>
> *James Barron Hope*, "*Yorktown Centennial Ode.*"

G. P. PUTNAM'S SONS

NEW YORK   LONDON
27 WEST TWENTY-THIRD STREET   24 BEDFORD STREET, STRAND

𝕿𝔥𝔢 𝕶𝔫𝔦𝔠𝔨𝔢𝔯𝔟𝔬𝔠𝔨𝔢𝔯 𝕻𝔯𝔢𝔰𝔰
1892

COPYRIGHT, 1892
BY
KATE MASON ROWLAND

Electrotyped, Printed, and Bound by
The Knickerbocker Press, New York
G. P. Putnam's Sons

TO

VIRGINIA

THE ILLUSTRIOUS, THE DEARLY LOVED

OLD DOMINION

THIS MEMOIR OF ONE OF HER SONS

IS

DEDICATED

CONTENTS OF VOL. I.

CONTENTS.

INTRODUCTION.

Every fact bearing upon the character and service of the statesmen whose genius created a model form of human government should receive a warm greeting from those who are proud of the growth, progress, and prosperity of the republic. The harmonious working of the component parts which enter into the life of the country is to-day the result of the intelligent labors of a small group of men over a hundred years ago. Like the rays of the sun which give light to the world, a government which proves capable of maintaining the purpose for which it was established, and protects the liberties of its citizens, should be hailed and imitated by mankind in every clime.

The sword of Washington carved success upon the standards of the new republic. The pen of Jefferson declared in immortal phrase our independence of Great Britain. The young eagle was pluming for his flight among the nations of the globe. But how should he so adjust his wings as to carry with nice balance, upon pinions of freedom, the glorious mission of establishing a government of the people, to replace the power of the tyrant?

Among the eminent patriots of those days, whose minds grasped this great problem, the subject of this book stands out in bold relief. A most remarkable man was George Mason! His conception of the authority of the citizens to control the government, and that the government existed only by their will and consent, was thorough and complete.

His warning as to the exercise of undelegated powers by either Congress or the President was truly prophetic. He desired to erect a republic whose strength at the centre was only great enough to carry out the object for which it was created; while the creator—the States themselves—should be left undisturbed in the exercise of all power not specified as having been relinquished. He had a full appreciation that the safety of the States was indeed the safety of the Union. He was the champion of the States and of the people. His signature, as one of the delegates from Virginia, was not attached to the Constitution, as it came from the hands of its framers in 1787, only because, in his opinion, that instrument did not completely guard the safety of the States.

His great labors may not be as widely established in the public mind as those of some others of the same period, because he persistently declined public positions in the federal councils, where his conspicuous talents would easily have kept him in the front rank of public knowledge and esteem. In the hearts of the students of his country's history, his name and fame occupy a place second to none. He was indeed the people's man in a people's government. The tent of his faith was pitched upon the bed-rock of the freedom of the citizen. Great was his belief in the security of a purely republican form of government. Sublime was his reliance in the power of the people. If Madison was, as John Quincy Adams said, "the Father of the Constitution," to Mason we are certainly indebted for those features which embrace sovereignty of the States, and protect the inalienable rights of their inhabitants. He was at once "the Solon and the Cato, the law-giver and the stern patriot, of the age" in which he lived. Marvellous was his wisdom, and great his intellectual force and breadth; and both were exerted to form a constitution which should have, traversing its length and breadth, broad, clear, comprehensive lines, separating the delegated powers conferred on the general government from those reserved to the States.

In the great battle fought by learned opponents in the Convention called by Virginia to ratify this Constitution, it will be remembered that George Mason bore a most prominent part. He believed, with a great orator of American liberty, that this Constitution in its first principles, was "highly and dangerously oligarchic"; and that a government of the few is of all governments the worst. He insisted upon such amendments as would forever obliterate the "awful squint towards monarchy"; and so great was the effect of his arguments, that the wisdom of a John Marshall, the oratory of an Edmund Randolph, the persuasive grace of a Henry Lee, the logic of a Madison, supported by the great reserve force of Washington, could secure the ratification of the Constitution by Virginia, by a majority of only ten votes in some one hundred and sixty-eight cast; and then only after nine States (the number sufficient) had already endorsed it. Among the intellectual giants composing this Convention, Mason was in the ranks of the opposition, strongly favoring specific limitations to the powers conferred by the Constitution upon the Legislative, Executive, and Judicial departments of the government. By his side was Patrick Henry; and supporting these two leaders were such men as Benjamin Harrison, James Monroe, and William Grayson. Mason's power of expression, must also have deeply impressed his opinions upon the minds of some of the great leaders of that day. Madison pronounced him the ablest debater he had ever known; and Jefferson declared he was the wisest man of his generation. It is most significant, therefore, that the former in drafting the famous Virginia Resolutions of 1798, following the doctrines of Mason, laid down the principle that in case of a deliberate, palpable, and dangerous exercise of powers not granted by the Constitution, the States have the right, and are in duty bound, to interpose in arresting the progress of the evil; while Jefferson in the Kentucky Resolutions declared that no State was bound to tamely submit to undelegated and unlimited powers by any man or body of men on earth. Such were the views of the Father of the Constitution, and the author of the Declaration of Independence in 1798, some ten years after the adoption of the Federal Constitution. That a great majority of the people of the United States sustained these opinions of Mason, Jefferson, and Madison, is manifested by the fact that, after their expression, the two last named held for eight years, respectively, the office of Chief Magistrate by the people's suffrages.

Virginia was not the only State so construing the Constitution. It will be remembered that the Massachusetts Legislature condemned as unconstitutional the Embargo Act of 1807, just as Kentucky and Virginia had, the Alien and Sedition laws. The government of Connecticut had recommended nullification as being within the power and authority of the State, as did South Carolina; and we are told that the Hartford Convention of December 14, 1814, which was attended by delegates from Connecticut, New Hampshire, Rhode Island, Massachusetts, and Vermont, was prevented from recommending the secession of those States from the Union, only by the termination of the war with England, which was seriously damaging their commercial interests.

The withdrawal of some of the States from the Union in 1861 was in accordance with the theories of the Fathers of the Government, endorsed in the earlier history of the republic by the great masses of the people. If success crowns the efforts of a people struggling for their rights and liberties, the world applauds; if they are unsuccessful, the world frowns.

This life of Mason is proper and opportune. A period in our history has been selected, to which we ought more frequently to recur, by calling attention to the services of a man with whose career we should become more familiar. When Washington presented the Non-Importation Resolutions of 1769 to the Virginia Assembly, pledging the Virginia planters to purchase no slaves that should be brought into the country after the first of November of that year, Mason wrote them for him. He was the author, too, of the famous

Non-Intercourse Resolutions, which were reaffirmed by the Continental Congress in October, 1774, as well as by the Constitution of Virginia, with its Declaration of Rights. In regard to this celebrated bill, a wise writer has stated that there was more wisdom and concentration of thought in one sentence of it, than in all former writings on the subject.

We have before us the life of a patriot who labored by tongue and pen to erect a bulwark between Federal power and State rights, so strong, that the hand of an oppressor could never take away the liberties of the people. "The people should control the Government, not the Government the people," was his war-cry. If we strictly adhere to these safe principles of government, we shall discharge our whole duty to the republic, and make it what our forefathers intended it should be—"the glory of America, and a blessing to humanity."

FITZHUGH LEE.

AUTHOR'S PREFACE.

It had long been a cherished purpose among George Mason's descendants to write the memoirs of their illustrious ancestor, and in several instances collections of papers were made with this object in view. The Hon. James Murray Mason from the family manuscripts preserved by his father, Gen. John Mason, prepared a sketch of his grandfather which was never completed. Another grandson of George Mason, as far back as 1827, contemplated writing his biography, but never carried out the design. This gentleman's son, the late George Mason, of Alexandria, in a fire which consumed his dwelling-house some years ago, lost many of his father's papers. Those which remained, mostly transcripts from the original documents, were kindly given by him to the present writer, who also received copies of the letters and papers owned by Miss Virginia Mason, daughter of the Hon. James Murray Mason, and copies of the manuscripts owned by Mrs. St. George Tucker Campbell, granddaughter of Thomson Mason of " Hollin Hall." A copy of the manuscript reminiscences of Gen. John Mason was obtained from his daughter, the late Mrs. Gen. Samuel Cooper of Fairfax County, Virginia. From her own immediate family, and from other branches of the same stock, the descendants of George Mason's brother, Thomson Mason of " Raspberry Plain," additional material has been procured by the author, such as the Thomson wills ; the sketch of the family

copy of the will, with entries from the Family Bible of Thomson Mason, owned by Arthur Mason Chichester, of Loudoun County, Virginia. All letters or other documents now in possession of any members of the family are classed together as " Mason Papers," and so designated in the foot-notes to this biography.

Important data, throwing light on the family history, the writer owes to her more distant relatives, members of the Fitzhugh, Bronaugh, Mercer, and Fowke families. She would name gratefully, in this connection, the daughters of the late Rev. George Fitzhugh Worthington, and Mr. Henry M. Fitzhugh of Baltimore; George Carter of " Oatlands," Loudoun County, Virginia ; Mr. William R. Mercer, and Prof. James Mercer Garnett; the late R. M. Conway and his brother, Mr. Moncure D. Conway, Dr. Dinwiddie B. Phillips, of Orange County, Virginia, the Rev. Douglas French Forrest, Alexander H. Robertson, Esq., of Baltimore, Mr. Gerard Fowke, Sidney, Ohio, and Mr. Frank Rede Fowke, Department of Science and Art, South Kensington, London.

Through the courtesy of the Hon. Thomas F. Bayard, while Secretary of State, copies were obtained of the Mason letters and papers among the manuscripts of Washington, Madison, and Jefferson in the State Department. For assistance in supplying her with memoranda of various kinds, the author acknowledges her obligations to Mr. R. A. Brock, of the Virginia Historical Society ; to Mr. W. G. Stanard, Manchester, Va. ; to Mr. William Wirt Henry ; to Mr. Worthington C. Ford, and Mr. Paul L. Ford ; to Mr. C. F. Lee, Jr., of Alexandria ; to Prof. Lyon G. Tyler, President of William and Mary College, Williamsburg ; to the late Dr. Philip Slaughter, of Virginia ; to the Rev. Samuel A. Wallis, rector of Pohick Church ; to the Rev. Horace E. Hayden, Wilkesbarre, Penn.; to Mr. George W. Kirchwey, Albany, N. Y. (custodian of the Clinton papers); to Dr. John S. H. Fogg, Boston; to Dr. Joseph M. Toner, Washington, D. C.; to President Gilman and other gentlemen of the Johns

Hopkins University; to Mrs. S. L. Gouverneur (for a letter to Mason among the Monroe papers in her possession); to Mrs. Swann, *née* Alexander, of Alexandria, Va.; and to J. A. Weston, London, England; as also to the late Hon. Lyman C. Draper, of Wisconsin, for a copy of his valuable essay on the Autograph Collections of America. And she would acknowledge her indebtedness for ever ready assistance and courtesy, to the librarians of the Historical and Peabody Libraries of Baltimore, the State Library of Richmond, Virginia, and the Congressional Library in Washington.

BALTIMORE, December, 1891.

LIST OF PERSONS FROM WHOM THE AUTHOR HAS RECEIVED COPIES OF GEORGE MASON'S LETTERS.

William R. Mercer, Doylestown, Penn.; Jeremiah Colburn, Boston, Mass.; William Wirt Henry, Richmond, Va.; Dr. John S. H. Fogg, Boston; Charles Roberts, Philadelphia; Simon Gratz, Philadelphia; the late Dr. Robert C. Davis, Philadelphia; Charles C. Jones, Augusta, Georgia, Cassius F. Lee, Jr., Alexandria, Va.; Justin Winsor, Harvard University (from the Lee papers, Cambridge); James M. Garnett, University of Virginia (from the Lee papers, U. of V.); Mrs. John R. Joyner, Berlin, Maryland (a descendant of Richard Henry Lee, who presented the author with an autograph letter); D. McN. Stauffer, New York; W. D. Hixson, Maysville, Kentucky (copy of a land warrant); the late Joseph Horner, Warrenton, Virginia; J. B. Moore, of the New York Historical Society (Lamb papers); Charles P. Greenough, Boston; the late Benson J. Lossing, Dover Plains, New York; F. J. Dreer, Philadelphia; John M. Hale, Phillipsburg, Penn.; John Boyd Thacher, Albany, N. Y.; Stan. V. Henkels, of the firm of Thomas Birch's Sons, Philadelphia; Walter R. Benjamin, New York (from whom an autograph letter was received); Dr. Thomas Addis Emmet, New York; Fisher Howe, Jr., Boston; the collection of the late Professor Leffingwell, New Haven, Conn., lately dispersed by auction in Boston; and the collection of the late Conway Robinson, now in possession of the Virginia Historical Society.

BIBLIOGRAPHY—GEORGE MASON.

MAGAZINE ARTICLES.

"George Mason, of Virginia," by Judge Bland.—Niles' *Principles and Acts of the Revolution*, Baltimore, 1822.

"George Mason, of Virginia," by John Esten Cooke.—*New York Century* (weekly paper), 1859.

"Gunston Hall," by J. Esten Cooke.—*Appleton's Journal*, April 4, 1874.

"A Statesman of the Colonial Era," by General Richard Taylor.—*North American Review*, February, 1879.

"The Virginia Declaration of Independence—A Group of Virginia Statesmen," by J. E. Cooke.—*Magazine of American History*, May, 1884.

"George Mason," by Mason Graham Ellzey, M.D.—*Southern Bivouac*, August and September, 1885.

"The Mount Vernon Convention."—*The Penna. Magazine of History and Biography*, January, 1888.

"Gunston Hall, Virginia."—*The Home-Maker*, April, 1890.

Brief biographical sketches are found in Hugh Blair Grigsby's "Convention of 1776."

"Garland's Life of John Randolph," chap. 8, p. 35.

Mrs. Mary Lamb's "Homes of America" (which contains a view of "Gunston Hall").

Appleton's "Cyclopedia of American Biography."

ETC., ETC.

LIFE AND CORRESPONDENCE OF GEORGE MASON, OF VIRGINIA.

CHAPTER I.

ENGLISH AND VIRGINIAN ANCESTRY.

In September, 1651, the last battle of the English Civil War was fought and lost by the young Charles II., whose father had perished on the scaffold three years previously. The cavaliers, in their desperate fortunes, turned their faces, many of them, to Virginia, the far-off, faithful Dominion across the Atlantic. And as early as 1649, the year of the king's execution, one ship alone, we are told, brought over three hundred and thirty of his followers.[1] Many Virginia families trace their beginning in the New World to this period of the cavalier immigration. The ancestors of Washington, Madison, Monroe, Pendleton (and Jefferson on the maternal side) were among these royalist refugees. And such is the tradition concerning Col. George Mason, the great-grandfather of George Mason of Gunston, the revolutionary patriot. According to the account preserved in the family, Colonel Mason commanded a troop of horse at the battle of Worcester, and escaping from this fatal field disguised himself and was concealed by some peasants until an opportunity offered for him to embark to America.[2] A younger brother is said to have accompanied him to Vir-

---

[1] "Virginia," American Commonwealth Series, J. Esten Cooke, p. 192.
[2] Copy of old paper of 1793, by George Mason of "Lexington."

ginia. They landed at Norfolk, and George Mason's brother, William Mason, according to one version of the story, married and died at or near Norfolk.[1] George Mason " went up the Potomac River and settled at Accohick, near Pasby-tanzy, where he was buried," says the chronicle above quoted. Of the family of the Masons of Stratford-upon-Avon, Warwickshire, Colonel Mason himself is believed to have been born in Staffordshire and to have lived there until the time of his leaving England. In the Church of the Holy Trinity in Stratford-upon-Avon are the vault of the Mason family and a number of memorial tablets and monuments inscribed to its different members, beginning with Daniel Mason, who died in 1689, and closing with Thomas Mason, who died in 1869. " With him," as is recorded on his tomb-stone, " the family of Mason of this town becomes extinct."

With George Mason, or about the same time, there came to Virginia another Staffordshire gentleman, Col. Gerard Fowke, of the Fowkes of Brewood Hall and Gunston, an old county family still represented among the English gentry. Mason and Fowke were doubtless neighbors and friends in England and the two families were to be neighbors in Virginia, and by a marriage in the next generation connecting them together, Colonel Fowke became the maternal ancestor of George Mason of '76. Brewood is a small and very ancient town eleven miles from Stafford. And in the Brewood parish was, at one time, a hamlet called Gunston. The latter now consists of two farm-houses, one quite modern, and some laborers' cottages.[2] The older of these farm-houses, the original Gunston Hall, was visited and described by the Hon. James M. Mason in 1865, and it was then owned by the Giffard family.[3] The Giffards of Chillington in 1651 were among the royalists at Worcester, and it was at their place " Boscobel," that Charles II. was concealed after his defeat. " Chillington," " Boscobel," " Brewood " and " Guns-

[1] The Hon. John Y. Mason is believed to be descended from this William Mason. (See " Virginia Cousins," G. Brown Goode, p. 236.)
[2] Letter from the Vicar of Brewood, July, 1885.   [3] MS. letter, 1865.

ton " were all in the same vicinity, and at least one scion of
the Fowke family was in the battle of Worcester.[1] This
was also a Gerard Fowke, but not the one who came to Vir.
ginia. In Brewood Church there are a number of monuments
to the old families of the neighborhood, the Fowkes of Bre.
wood Hall and Gunston among others. But there are none
of the name living in Staffordshire at this time. " Brewood
Hall " still stands and is the seat of some of the Monckton
family.[2] The Hussey family of " Wyrley Grove," of which
there is a description and an engraving in Shaw's " Stafford.
shire," are the present representatives in that county of the
Fowkes of Brewood. According to the Virginia tradition,
Col. Gerard Fowke, the founder of the family in America,
was the sixth son of Roger Fowke of " Gunston Hall."[3] The
English pedigrees place this Gerard Fowke in " Port Mary.
land," Island of Tobago, and trace his descent back to
William Fowke of Staffordshire, 1403–1438, whose second
son, John, married Agnes, daughter and heiress of John
Newman of Gunston, and was known, in right of his wife, as
John Fowke of Gunston.[4] It is to be regretted that no list
of the royalists who fought at Worcester has been preserved, though there is a list of nearly all the prisoners taken
above the rank of private, in the British Museum collections.[5] The family tradition that Col. George Mason was a
member of Parliament seems to be without foundation, as
his name is not in the published records.[6] In the second
Parliament of Charles I., 1625, a William Mason represented
Aldborough, Suffolk, while in the Parliament of 1628, Robert Mason represented Winchester, Southampton County.
He it was, evidently, who in the debate on the Petition of
Right " in a long and able speech," writes Creasy,[7] contended

[1] Calendar of State Papers, November, 1663.
[2] Murray's " Hand-Book for Stafford."
[3] Old MS. of the Fowke family in Virginia.
[4] Data furnished by Frank Rede Fowke.
[5] *Notes and Queries*, January 17, 1885.
[6] " Notitiae Parliamentaria," Browne Willis.
[7] " Rise and Progress of the English Constitution," p. 258.

against extending the king's prerogative, as likely to endanger the liberties of the people. This was, in all probability, the same Robert Mason who was Master of the Requests to Charles I., and Chancellor of the Diocese of Winchester. A portrait of him was on sale some three years ago at a London auction. It would be interesting, if it were possible, to trace a relationship between this champion of liberty in England's Parliament, and the Virginia family, whose most distinguished representative was to formulate in the New World a later and more decided Petition of Right, carrying out the same principles.

Among the adventurers in the London Company, 1609, is found the name of "Captain Mason," and in 1620, "George Mason," doubtless the same person, is an adventurer to the extent of twelve pounds ten shillings.[1] The identity in the Christian name, which will be seen to descend in Virginia from father to son down to the present day, and the interest in the colony that would naturally have been transmitted from the sire of 1620 to the son of 1651, make it seem not unlikely that the George Mason of the Virginia Company was the father of the cavalier emigrant.[2]

The first mention of George Mason, the founder of the Virginia family, in the colonial records, occurs in the patent of land obtained by him in March, 1655, "said land being due unto the said George Mason by and for the transportation of eighteen persons into this colony."[3] The names of these eighteen persons, "Head Rights," as they were called, are not given, and it is not known, therefore, whether they included any of Captain Mason's family. This tract of nine hundred acres, fifty acres for each one of those who were brought over at Captain Mason's expense, was in Northumberland County, or, more properly, Westmoreland, which

---

[1] Smith's "History of Virginia," p. 52 ; Force, vol. iii., tract v.

[2] Mr. Alexander Brown in "The Genesis of the United States," gives George Mason as one of the leading men interested in the American enterprise during 1606–16. He thinks "Captain Mason" was Capt. John Mason, the founder of New Hampshire.

[3] Westmoreland Court-House and Virginia Land Registry Office.

was cut off from the former county in 1653, and extended northward "to the falls of the great river Pawtomake, above the Necostin's towne." [1]   In other words, Westmoreland County included the land on the Virginia side of the river from the northern boundary of Northumberland County as far up as the site of the present city of Georgetown in the District of Columbia.

The patent provides "that if said Captain George Mason, his heirs and assigns, doe not plant or seat or cause to be planted or seated upon the said land within three years ensuing, that then it shall and may be lawful for any adventurer or planter to make choice and seat thereon." In 1658, Captain Mason disposed of five hundred acres of this land to Mr. John Leare for "five cows with calves and two thousand five hundred pounds of tobacco." In this transaction "Gerrard Fowke" is Leare's attorney. [2]   With the land sold to Mr. Leare George Mason transferred "all privileges of hawking, fishing, and fowling." We can fancy Captain Mason at this time fairly established in his settlement in the wilderness, with some of his old comrades near him, Colonel Fowke and Sir Thomas Lunsford, the latter on the Rappahannock on the other side of the Northern Neck, among them.   These, with Capt. Giles Brent, who had moved from Maryland to Virginia some years previously, made up a group of stout borderers and gallant gentlemen. Captain Mason was a married man at this time, as we know through the mention of his wife Mary, who gives her consent to the sale of land in 1658.   Whether his family followed him from England, or his marriage took place after his settlement in Virginia, we have no means of knowing.   But he must have been a young man in all probability as he is seen to be active in the colony at a much later period, and he led now necessarily a rough and adventurous life, being called on frequently with his neighbors to defend his frontier home against the unruly aborigines.   Meanwhile the

[1] Act of Assembly, July, 1653.
[2] Westmoreland Court-House Records.

days of the English Commonwealth came to an end, and in
1660 the hearts of all good cavaliers rejoiced over the restoration of church and king.

Sir William Berkeley, who had lived quietly in Virginia
all this time, returned to his place as governor, and all
seemed to promise well for the "Old Dominion." But
though battle and bloodshed were well over in England,
in Virginia there were enemies at the planters' doors, not to
be dealt with always after the slow methods of civilized
communities. Some of the Indians were friendly, but over
others it was necessary to exercise a strict supervision. And
the dwellers on the borders, especially, were subject to frequent alarms and forced to take justice into their own hands.
So we find our friends on the Potomac having their own
private feud with the Indian chief here, and the House of
Burgesses not approving of their proceedings. At their session, 1661–2, a charge of high treason and murder was
brought by Capt. Giles Brent against the king of the Potomac Indians. He was acquitted by the committee, and it
was ordered by the Assembly, upon the report of the committee to inquire into the differences between the English
and the Indians: "That in satisfaction of the several injuries
and affronts done to Wahanganoche, King of the Potowmack
Indians, by Capt. Giles Brent, Col. Gerard Fowke, Mr. John
Lord, and Capt. George Mason that the said Capt. Brent
pay the said Wahanganoche two hundred arms length of
roanoke, and that Col. Fowke, Mr. Lord, and Capt. Mason
pay him one hundred arms length apiece, or that they
pay and deliver him presently matchcoates for the said
roanoke of two arms length each, at twenty arms length
every coate." [1] At the same time Colonel Fowke was fined
for permitting the murderer of an Indian to escape; and
Captain Brent and Colonel Fowke were fined and declared
incapable of holding any office and compelled to give security for good behavior, for illegally imprisoning the "King
of Potowmack," Captain Brent to pay the whole charge of

[1] Hening's "Statutes," vol. ii., 1661–2.

the witnesses. Furthermore, John Lord and Capt. George Mason were ordered to " pay to the public two thousand pounds of tobacco apiece for their contempt of the right honorable governor's warrant, unless they show cause to the contrary at next quarter court; that they be both sus- pended from all civil and military power till they have cleared themselves from the King of Potowmack's charge against them and give bond with good security to such per- son as the honorable governor shall appoint for their good behavior towards the said King, his and all other Indians." But the Assembly confessed that with Brent, Fowke, Mason, and Lord deprived of office there was no one in Westmoreland County able to conduct its affairs, and they proposed to join it to Northumberland County, or else ask the governor to send some persons there " capable and fit " to govern it.[1] In April, 1664, Captain Mason is found to be buying more land, six hundred and fifty acres in Westmoreland County, from Col. Valentine Peyton, for which he paid " a valuable consid- eration " but the sum is not named.[2] At the General Court in October, 1669, George Mason petitioned for and obtained five hundred additional acres, part of the same tract, which had been deserted by the original patentee.

About this time the Dutch, Lord Baltimore, and the Indians were all giving the Old Dominion some trouble. So the Grand Assembly proclaimed a fast on account of the dis- turbed state of the country, and furthermore voted for five forts, one of which was to be on the Potomac. Now then were the proscribed soldier-planters to come again into the public service. George Mason appears to have held the office of sheriff of Stafford County in 1670, and is called in the MS. records of the General Court for that year, Major George Mason.[3] The sheriff was the executive officer of the county court. The judges in this court were called Jus-

---

[1] *Ibid.*

[2] Westmoreland Court-House Records.

[3] " Virginia Carolorum," p. 344 (note). (From a MS. owned by the Virginia Historical Society.)

tices of the Peace, and they had almost entire control of the affairs of the county.   They were chosen from the principal gentlemen of the neighborhood and received their commissions from the governor with the advice of the council.   They received no compensation for their services, the office being considered one of honor not of emolument, and thus a high standard was obtained.   In 1673, and perhaps earlier, George Mason was clerk of the court of Stafford County.[1]   The Stafford county records are so incomplete it is impossible to determine when the appointment was made, or how long any of these appointments continued.   Both offices were held by the second George Mason many years later.   Some time between 1673 and 1675 apparently, Captain Mason received the highest office in the county of Stafford, that of its County Lieutenant.   Stafford was cut off from Westmoreland probably in 1666–7, when it is first mentioned as sending a delegate to the Assembly.   A tradition in the Mason family, found in the old paper before quoted, asserts that George Mason gave the county its name, calling it after his native shire in England.   The County Lieutenant in the early records is called " Commander of Plantations."   The office, which in England was held generally by a knight, was conferred always in Virginia on the class of " gentlemen," and they were chosen usually from the large landholders.   The County Lieutenant commanded the militia with the rank of colonel, was entitled to a seat in the council, and as such was a judge of the General Court, was appointed directly by the governor, and was the possessor of very large powers in the civil and military control of the county.   He presided over the county courts at the head of the justices.   The MS. records of the General Court, of which only two fragments now remain, for this period, show Col. George Mason to have been successful in a suit in which he was the defendant in March, 1675–6, upon an appeal from

[1] Old deed in the Brent family.

In the interesting " Memorials of Old Virginia Clerks," F. Johnston, none are given for Stafford previous to the Revolution.

Stafford County court. The decision of the Stafford court was confirmed, but the amount of damages does nor appear.[1]

In this same month, March, 1675, Colonel Mason's name appears in an act of Assembly, in connection with the defence of the country against the Indians. Lieut.-Col. John Washington is named among the commissioners appointed for Westmoreland. And the act specifies that " Col. George Mason and Mr. James Austin or one of them in Stafford county be further commissionated when occasion shall be to use Indians in the war, and require and receive hostages from them, also to provide one hundred yards of trading cloth to each respective fort, that it be ready to reward the service of Indians as hereafter in and by this act shall be provided." [2] And then we learn of a special service of Colonel Mason's by which he had taken the lead in the negotiations with the friendly Indians. The act continues:

" And whereas Coll. George Mason exhibited to this Grand Assembly a certain agreement by him made with certain Indians, vizt. : that the young men shall go in search of all murderers and all other Indian enemies to the English to be paid three matchcoates for every prisoner they bring in alive, and one matchcoate for the head of every one they kill ; Bee it enacted by the authority aforesaid, that the said agreement shall be well and truly observed on our parts, and that those commissioners, herebefore in this act named to take hostages may make the like agreement (if they can) with all other the neighboring Indians.'

We have now arrived at an important period in Virginia's colonial history, when occurs the episode of Bacon's Rebellion in 1676, the prototype *in parvo* of the later " Rebellion " of 1776. There are several contemporary accounts of this affair, and one of them is particularly interesting in itself, and is furthermore valuable for our purpose, as it makes mention of Col. George Mason. This is the paper signed " T. M.," which was written by a colleague of Colonel Mason

---

[1] MS. owned by the Virginia Historical Society.

[2] Hening's " Statutes," vol. ii.

in the Assembly.[1] " My dwelling-house," he says, "was in Northumberland, the lowest county on the Potomack river, Stafford being the upmost." Here also in Stafford " T. M." had a plantation, with servants and cattle, and his overseer had engaged for him in this county a herdsman who was killed a short time after by the Doegs, an Indian tribe in the vicinity. " From this Englishman's blood did (by degrees) arise Bacon's Rebellion," as our narrator explains.

" Of this horrid action Col. Mason who commanded the militia regiment of foot and Capt. Brent the troop of horse in that county (both dwelling six or eight miles downwards), having speedy notice raised 30 or more men and pursued those Indians 20 miles up and 4 miles over that river [the Potomac] into Maryland, where landing at dawn of day they found two small paths. Each leader with his party took a separate path and in less than a furlong either found a cabin, which they (silently) surrounded. Capt. Brent went to the Doegs cabin (as it proved to be) who speaking the Indian tongue called to have a ' matchacomichaweeokio,' *i. e.*, a council, called presently, such being the usual manner with Indians. The king came trembling forth, and would have fled when Capt. Brent catching hold of his twisted lock (which was all the hair he wore) told him he was come for the murderer of Robert Hen. The King pleaded ignorance and slipt loose, whom Brent shot dead with his pistol. The Indians shot two or three guns out of the cabin, the English shot into it, the Indians thronged out of the door and fled. The English shot as many as they could so that they killed ten, as Capt. Brent told me, and brought away the King's son of about 8 years old, concerning whom is an observable passage at the end of this expedition. The noise of this shooting awakened the Indians in the cabin which Col. Mason had encompassed, who likewise rushed out and fled, of whom his company (supposing from that noise of shooting Brent's party to be engaged) shot (as the Colonel informed me) 14, before an Indian came who with both hands shook him (friendly) by one arm, saying 'Susquehanoughs netoughs,' *i. e.*, 'Susquehanaugh

---

[1] Force's " Tracts," vol. i., tract viii.

friends,' and fled. Whereupon he (Col. Mason) ran amongst his men, crying out, ' For the Lord's sake, shoot no more ; these are our friends, the Susquehanaughs.' This unhappy scene ended ; Col. Mason took the King of the Doegs son home with him, who lay ten days in bed as one dead, with eyes and mouth shut, no breath discovered, but his body continuing warm, they believed him yet alive. The aforenamed Capt. Brent (a papist) coming thither on a visit, and seeing his little prisoner thus languishing, said, ' perhaps he is *paweward*,' *i. e.*, bewitched, and that he had heard baptism was an effectual remedy against witchcraft, wherefore advised to baptise him. Col. Mason answered no minister could be had in many miles ; Brent replied, 'your clerk, Mr. Dobson, may do that office,' which was done by the Church of England liturgy, Col. Mason with Capt. Brent godfathers, and Mrs. Mason godmother, my overseer Mr. Pimet being present, from whom I first heard it, and which all the other persons (afterwards) affirmed to me. The four men returned to drinking punch, but Mrs. Mason staying looking on the child, it opened the eyes, and breathed, whereat she ran for a cordial, which he took from a spoon, gaping for more, and so (by degrees) recovered, tho' before his baptism they had often tried the same means but could not by no endeavours wrench open his teeth." [1]

This little incident puts very vivedly before us the manners of the time, with its odd combination of piety and superstition. The whole scene stands out distinctly from its seventeenth century background in the Virginia wilderness; the small Indian prisoner, unconscious on his couch, the stern and resolute, but kindhearted planter-soldiers, seeking to restore their young captive from his uncanny trance by the use of the church's sacrament. Then the men going back to their punch and their discourse over the late bloody affair, while the lady of the house bends over the child with anxious womanly ministrations, assisting the miraculous recovery by her timely watch.

This expedition of Colonel Mason's and Capt. George Brent's proved indeed, as has been said, to be the occasion of

_____
[1] *Ibid.*

the Indian war that soon disturbed the colony. Colonel Mason, by his unfortunate mistake in attacking the friendly Susquehannocks, incited them to acts of retaliation. The murders that were committed soon after both in Maryland and Virginia were attributed to this tribe, and the Marylanders determined to rid themselves of such dangerous neighbors. They invited the Virginians to co-operate with them, and Col. John Washington, Col. George Mason, and Major Allerton commanded the body of Virginia militia that was sent over to Maryland for this purpose. The Indians in their strong fort, built for the protection of the frontier, held out for six weeks, and then, under cover of the night, marched out, murdering the sleeping guards, and making their way across the Potomac, devastated the country in their path as far as the York and James rivers. They had met with a cruel provocation, it must be admitted, for six of their chiefs had been put to death by the Marylanders and Virginians in retaliation for murders they were accused of committing. No doubt it was difficult for these early colonists, who had so often suffered from Indian treachery and barbarity, to extend to their foes the laws which govern warfare between civilized races. But the Maryland Assembly condemned this action of their militia, and not without reason. In the Indian warfare which followed the massacres perpetrated to avenge the Susquehannock chiefs, Bacon, whose overseer was one of the victims, took a sweeping revenge. Under his command the Virginians were completely successful against the allied Indians, and the brave Susquehannocks themselves were almost annihilated.[1]

This affair of the fort occurred in September and October, 1675, and in the following spring Colonel Mason was elected to the Assembly from Stafford County. Of this Assembly "T. M." also gives some account. " In March, 1675–6," he writes, "writs came up to Stafford to choose their two members for an Assembly to meet in May ; when Col. Mason, Capt. Brent, and other gentlemen of that county,

[1] *Historical Magazine*, vol. i., p. 65, " The Fall of the Susquehannocks."

invited me to stand a candidate—a matter I little dreampt
of. . . . They pressed several cogent arguments, and I
having considerable debts in that county, besides my plantation concerns, (in one and the other) I had much more
severely suffered, than any of themselves, by the Indian
disturbances in the summer and winter foregoing, I held it
not (then) discreet to disoblige the rulers of it; so Col.
Mason, with myself, were elected without objection. He at
time convenient went on horseback; I took my sloop, and
the morning I arrived to Jamestown, after a week's voyage,
was welcomed with the strange acclamations of 'All's over—
Bacon is taken,' having not heard at home these Southern
commotions, other than rumors like idle tales of one Bacon
risen up in rebellion, nobody knew for what, concerning the
Indians." Bacon, however, not satisfied with Governor
Berkeley's fair promises, soon after made his escape and
next appeared in the capitol at the head of his armed followers. Bacon demanded a commission from the Assembly
as general of the forces, which they replied they had not the
power to give him. It being rumored later that Governor
Berkeley had bestowed upon him the coveted command,
" T. M." visited Bacon to consult with him on the interests
of the frontier counties. He assured " T. M." that "the like
care should be taken of the remotest corners in the land as
of his own dwelling-house." Bacon then wished to know
"what persons in those parts were most fit to bear commands." " T. M." gives it as his opinion that the commanders of the militia should be appointed, "wherewith he was
well pleased, and himself wrote a list of those nominated.
That evening I made known what had past with Mr. Bacon
to my colleague, Col. Mason (whose bottle attendance
doubled my task); the matter he liked well, but questioned
the governor's approbation of it. I confess the case required
sedate thoughts, reasoning that he and such like gentlemen
must either command or be commanded, and if on their
denials Mr. Bacon should take distaste, and be constrained
to appoint commanders out of the rabble, the governor him-

self, with the persons and estates of all in the land, would be at their dispose, whereby their own ruin might be owing to themselves.   In this he [Colonel Mason] agreed, and said: ' If the governor would give his own commission he would be content to serve under General Bacon (as now he began to be entitled), but first would consult other gentlemen in the same circumstances,' who all concurred 't was the most safe barrier in view against pernicious designs, if such should be put in practise.   With this I acquainted Mr. Lawrence, who went (rejoicing) to Mr. Bacon with the good tidings that the militia commanders were inclined to serve under him as their general, in case the governor would please to give them his own commissions."[1]   " T. M.'s " disrespectful allusion to his colleague in the above extract may be taken, probably, *cum grano salis;* though hard drinking was characteristic of the times, and we have not forgotten the bowl of punch at the baptism.   " T. M.," who has been identified by recent historians with Thomas Matthews, son of one of the Commonwealth governors, evidently wished to take all the credit to himself for sobriety and attention to business at the expense of his deceased colleague, for Colonel Mason was not living at the time this tract was written.   But the latter was too important a figure in his county, by " T. M.'s " own showing, for him to have been other than the habitually cool, clear-headed man of affairs that his several public trusts demanded.

The Assembly of 1676 has been called Bacon's Assembly, as he is seen to have inspired its proceedings.   It was Bacon against Berkeley in the legislative halls as in the armed field. Berkeley's Assembly, as it might be called, had lasted sixteen years, there having been no election of burgesses since 1660, the year of the Restoration.   Col. George Mason, it is noteworthy, was one of the new assemblymen in this the reforming House of 1676.   Not much was really accomplished, but the burgesses made protest against abuses, anticipating in their " rebellious " designs the Assembly of

[1] Force's " Tracts," vol. i., tract viii.

1776, where a greater George Mason was also prominent. "T. M." tells how when directed by Berkeley to consider Indian affairs they took the "opportunity to endeavor the redressing several grievances the country was then laboring under; and motions were made for inspecting the public revenues, the collector's accounts, etc." The governor interfered and these projects were not carried out. Another demonstration was made in the same direction when the Baconians demurred to the motion made by one of the governor's party, that two members of the council should be asked to sit with them and assist in their debates as had been usual. One of the burgesses raised a laugh by replying: "'T is true it has been customary, but if we have any bad customs among us we are come here to mend 'em." Little was done, however, beyond passing a law to extend the suffrage, and evincing the wish to go further had they felt themselves strong enough. But it was a time of public commotions, and civil war was at their doors. Soon the indignant young General Bacon left the Assembly in disgust and Governor Berkeley declared war against him and his supporters.

Colonel Mason is heard of again in connection with Indian affairs in 1679, when the Assembly ordered four garrison houses for stores to be built on the four great rivers. Maj. Isaac Allerton, Col. St. Leger Codd, and Col. George Mason were the gentlemen appointed to provide for the storehouse on the Potomac.[1] In 1681 and 1683, Colonel Mason's name occurs in the letters of William Fitzhugh in connection with certain lawsuits.[2] In the latter year Fitzhugh writes to an English correspondent: "All affairs stand just as you left them. . Neither have I heard any fighting news lately of Col. Mason, which gives me occasion to believe his stock is pretty well exhausted." Colonel Mason's reputation as a "fighting" man was not confined to Indian war-

[1] Hening's "Statutes," vol. ii.
[2] Fitzhugh Letters, Virginia Historical Society. (The original MS. is at Harvard University.)

fare apparently, if we have interpreted correctly the above allusion. His name is met with again, and for the last time, in the acts of the Assembly in 1684. At the April session it was provided that when the militia were to be called out, " for the more easy and expeditious performing of any ser. vices hereby injoyned, or to be injoyned to the officers and soldiers aforesaid, be it enacted, that there be deposited into the hands of Collonel George Mason [and three other gentlemen who are named] the sum of 1200 pounds of tobacco each. To the end the said Col. Mason etc. shall each of them buy, build or provide an able boat for the transporting the soldiers and horses over the several rivers and places hereafter mentioned." [1] Colonel Mason was to provide a boat for the Occoquan River in Stafford County. This river is now the dividing line between Fairfax and Prince William counties.

Colonel Mason's death occurred probably in 1686. A will of this date, believed to have been his, was at Stafford Court- House in 1840, and doubtless was there also in 1861. It was, it may be presumed, either carried away or destroyed, with other valuable papers, at the sack of Stafford Court-House by Federal soldiers in 1862. Unfortunately no copy of it is extant. The tomb of Colonel Mason in the family " Bury. ing Place," at Accokeek, and all traces of the graveyard itself had disappeared as far back as 1845.

In the Fitzhugh Letters mention is made of both " Captain Mason " and " Colonel Mason." And George Fitzhugh, the antiquarian, seems to take for granted that the allusions all point to the elder George Mason, whom he describes as " a justice of the peace, a commander of one of the forts, a great Indian fighter, always a favorite with the people, and under the government of William and Mary, which was somewhat republican, a favorite with the court." [2] The first Colonel Mason is here confounded with his son, who bore the same name and succeeded to the same county offices and

[1] Hening's " Statutes," vol. iii.

[2] *De Bow's Review*, vol. xxvii. and vol. xxx.   Articles by George Fitzhugh.

titles. Both were "great Indian fighters" and men of mark in the community, and while Colonel Mason, the elder, was a true cavalier, he appears to have inclined to the popu_ lar side in the contest between Berkeley and Bacon. The second George Mason proved himself a decided whig, as we learn from the correspondence of the zealous tory Colonel Fitzhugh.

Lord Howard of Effingham had made himself very un_ popular in Virginia, in advancing the bigoted views of James II. And when the Revolution of 1688 took place, while the council leaned to the Stuart cause and supported the governor, the Assembly welcomed the accession of the new dynasty. Great excitement prevailed and it was said in Virginia that the "papists" in Maryland were going to bring in Indians to destroy " the Protestants of both Do_ minions." In the Maryland Council pains were taken to contradict those extravagant rumors, raised, as was report- ed, "by Mr. Burr Harris [son] of Virginia and several evil disposed persons to this [the Maryland] government."[1] Colonel Spencer, Colonel Lee, and Colonel Allerton of the Virginia Council exerted themselves successfully in the effort to allay the excitement. Captain Brent, as a Roman Catholic, was an object of persecution by the more ignorant and fanatical of his neighbors in Stafford County, the seat of the disturbances, and he was advised to take refuge from the mob at " Mr. Fitzhugh's or Captain Mason's." In the con- flict between whig and tory in Stafford County, the leader of the whigs was the Rev. John Waugh, a non-conformist clergyman. Crowds flocked to his eloquent ministry and his denunciations of the government of Lord Howard and his royal master inflamed the people, and produced disturb- ances of the peace approaching to a rebellion.[2] Three of the councillors were sent to Stafford, Spencer, Lee, and Allerton, to quiet the county. Colonel Fitzhugh asso-

[1] Archives of Maryland. Proceedings of the Council, 1687–8–1693. (Mary- land Historical Society, 1890.)

[2] Burk's " History of Virginia," vol. ii., p. 305.

2

ciates George Mason with the Rev. Mr. Waugh in his denunciations of the latter. He wrote from Jamestown to his brother-in-law, Mr. Luke, then in England, on the 27th of October, 1690, and betrays a very sore feeling against these gentlemen, who had evidently found favor in high places for their political principles, whatever penalties it had been thought necessary to prescribe in the first instance against the over-zealous clerical partisan. " The conclusion of Parson Waugh's business is," writes Fitzhugh, " he has made a public and humble acknowledgment in the general court, by a set form drawn up by the court and ordered there to be recorded ; and is appointed to do the same in our court, as soon as I come home, with a hearty penitence for his former faults and a promised obedience for the future, which he sincerely prays for the accomplishment of, and for the sake of his coat I do too. .   I stood in the gap and kept off an approaching rebellion (Waugh's), to my no small charge and trouble, as you fully know, being sending almost every day for five months together, and writing with mine own hand above three quires of paper to quash the raised stories and settle the panic fears ; having my house most part of the time constantly thronged, and in daily expectation of being treacherously murdered ; for all which charge and trouble I being out, as you know, above £25 sterling, particularly for messengers sent severally up and down, besides the purchasing the powder and shot for our men in arms ; for all which I thought at least I deserved thanks, if no retaliation, but, thank God, I have missed them both, and can do it with cheerfulness too ; but to be disre_ garded, nay, and slighted too, and to see those mischievous, active instruments, as you well know Waugh and Mason, · · · the only men in favor and the only men taken notice of, grates harder than the non-payment for shot and other disbursements. I thought good to intimate this to you, that you may give my Lord [Howard] a particular account of that whole affair wherein his Lordship, as you know from these persons [Waugh, Mason, etc.] missed not his share of the scandal, . and fully set forth the wickedness of Waugh and Mason, . . . the at present grand favorites, but I hope, upon his Lordship's arrival, the scene of affairs may be changed "[1] It is evident that the tories were down at this time and the whigs uppermost. And in Stafford the leaders of the late "rebellion" were enjoying the favor of the new government. Waugh and Mason were, no doubt, among those who signed the "association" for the defence of King William after the Jacobite plot of Barclay's in 1696.[2] Virginia and New York were the only two colonies, apparently, that testified their loyalty in this way. The Rev. John Waugh (or Wough, as the name is spelt in the old record) had charge of two churches in 1680, Stafford Parish and Chontanck [Chotank].[3] And in 1691 he patented six thousand, three hundred and fifty acres of land in Stafford. His friend, George Mason, became his son-in-law, as will be seen later.

Colonel Fitzhugh had been engaged in lawsuits with Colonel Mason which apparently descended to the son, and may have helped to embitter the political animosity which subsisted between Fitzhugh and the younger Mason. The former wrote to George Luke in regard to one of these suits: "Mason's business appeared with such a report from the referees Allerton and Lee (back friends to us both as this court then found) that there was neither word nor argument to be used. When I see you I shall be more full."[4] This Lee was Col. Richard Lee of the council, whose daughter Mary was to marry the younger William Fitzhugh. Colonel Fitzhugh seems to have considered Colonel Lee a "back friend" and Captain Mason an open enemy at this time. But these legal animosities, not less than the political ones, were apparently assuaged subsequently. At least the unfriendliness between these neighbor families gave place in the next

[1] Fitzhugh Letters, Virginia Historical Society.
[2] *The London Gazette*, August 27, 1696.
[3] Colonial Records of Virginia.
[4] Fitzhugh Letters, Virginia Historical Society.

generation to the amenities of kinship. At a court held for Stafford County on the 9th of October, 1689, Lieut.-Col. Fitzhugh and Capt. George Mason head the list of justices. On this occasion George Brent laid before the court the case of a disputed patent which he had surveyed "in obedience to an order of the worshipful court of Stafford."[1] In 1691 the town of Marlboro', on Potomac Neck was appointed to be laid off by act of Assembly, on fifty acres of land surveyed by Theodorick Bland. The first "feoffees" of the town granted thirty of the ninety odd lots into which the town was divided to different persons, of whom Captain Mason was one, the deeds conveying these lots to him being dated February, 1691-2.[2] Captain Mason's plantation, inherited from his father, it will be remembered, was in this same neck of land in Stafford County. There is reason to believe, however, that Captain Mason was not living at "Aquaceek," which may have been occupied by his mother or other members of the family, if, as is probable, he had brothers and sisters; and that he had fixed his residence near "Pohike" Creek, or Pohick as it is called at the present day, in Dogue Neck, much nearer the northern boundary of the county. Such, at least, is the inference to be drawn from the notices of him in the quaint journal kept by one of the Potomac Rangers in 1692. These rangers were appointed by the governor for frontier duty, and according to one of the acts of the Assembly regulating this service, a lieutenant or commander of rangers was to have under him eleven men with horses, arms, etc.[3] These men were to reside as near as might be to the station, and the County Lieutenant, as commander-in-chief of the county militia, was empowered to impress men for rangers. George Mason seems to have been one of the Stafford rangers, deriving his military title, as is likely, from this service. The paper alluded to is dated October 31, 1692.

[1] Mercer Land Book.
[2] *Ibid.*
[3] Hening's "Statutes," vol. ii.

"A Journiall of our Ranging, Given by me David Strahan, Lieutenant of ye Rangers of Pottomack. June 9th .   June, the 17th ; We ranged over Ackoquane, and so we Ranged Round persi-Neck and ther we lay that night.   And on ye 18th came to Pohike, and ther we heard that Capt. Mason's Servt-man was missing.   Then we went to see if we could find him, and we followed his foot abut half a mile, to a house that is deserted, and we took ye tract of a great many Indians and we followed it about 10 miles, and having no provisions we was forced to return.   June the 26th : We Ranged up to Jonathan Matthews hs. along with Capt. Masone, and ther we met with Capt. Houseley, and we sent over for the Emperour, but he would not come, and we went over to ye towne, and they held a Masocomacko (?) and ordered 20 of their Indians to goe after ye Indians that carried away Capt. Masone's man, and so we returned.   July the 3[d] . . July 11th ; We ranged up to Brenttowne and ther we lay.
The 19th we ranged up to Ackotink, and discovered nothing. . . So we Ranged once in ye Neck till ye 20th Sept[br], then we mercht to Capt. Masone's, and ther we met with Capt. Houseley and his men ; so we draved out 12 of our best horses, and so we ranged up Ackotink, and ther we lay that night.   Sept. 22[d]
Sept 23[d] We marcht to the Suggar Land . . And the 24th We Ranged about to see if we could find ye tract of any Indians, but we could not see any fresh signe . . ; the 26th marcht. to Capt. Masone's, and ther I dismissed my men till ye next March.[1] "

"Suggar Land" is supposed to be identical with Fairfax and Loudoun counties and the opposite shores of Maryland, and its name was derived from the sugar maple tree, though there are none now in that locality.[2]

The Northern Neck, or the country between the Potomac and Rappahannock rivers, had been granted by Charles II. to Lord Culpepper in 1683. But the colonists here had objected to this arrangement, and in memorials to the Assembly prayed that they might have their lands secured to them by patent as was the case elsewhere in Virginia.

1 "Virginia Calendar Papers," vol. i., p. 44.
2 *Ibid.*, p. xlvi.

In 1692, George Mason being at this time sheriff of Stafford, there were disturbances in the Neck, growing out of alleged abuses in the proprietary government, and a council was held at James City, April 25th, when complaints were laid before it respecting "unfair and illegal proceedings" in the Northern Neck, "the Proprietors granting the escheats of lands in that neck to several persons, without finding any office, as the law directs, to the great dissatisfaction of divers of the inhabitants." And to obtain a full account of these escheats and determine the remedies for this discontent, it was ordered: "that the sheriffs of the respective counties in the said Neck do forthwith give public notice at the next courts to be held for the said counties, and in each of their parish churches, that all persons who have had any land granted them in the said Neck by escheats, since the proprietors' office was first set up there, do immediately give the said sheriffs copies of the grants for the same to be trans-mitted by them to the council." The copy of this paper sent to the sheriff of Stafford is thus endorsed by him:

"This warrant was Published in open Cort, being read every day dureing ye Cort-Setting ; the Cort holding 4 days, and then I made demand in Generall—

"Given un^{dr} my hand
"Geo. Mason, Sheriff
"of Stafford County." [1]

Captain Mason in 1694 sold "Accokeek" "being the late mansion house of Col. George Mason deceased," to Robert Wright of Stafford County. While disposing of all the "houses, outhouses, barns, stables, tobacco houses and all other edifices" on the place, and every thing pertaining to the plantation, the deed of sale reserves "the Tomb of the said Col. George Mason and the Burying Place in which it stands . . . to be and to remain to the said George Mason and his heirs forever." [2] This estate of Accokeek, after passing through other hands, finally came into possession

[1] *Ibid.*, p. 38.   [2] Mercer Land Book.

of Nathaniel Hedgman in 1707, and as late as 1862, it was owned by his descendants. It lies in Potomac or Marlboro' Neck, the peninsula formed by Aquia and Potomac creeks, Accokeek Creek running into Potomac Creek, and has been identified as one of the plantations now known as "The Cottage" and "Rose Hill." This sale took place in September, and in October, 1694, Capt. George Mason received a patent from the proprietors of the Northern Neck, Lady Culpepper, Lord Fairfax and his wife, and Alexander Culpepper, for the eleven hundred and fifty acres upon Accokeek Creek which he had inherited from his father. This included the hundred and fifty acres he had just sold,[1] Two years later, in 1696, George Mason bought of William Sherwood, James City County, two thousand one hundred and nine acres of land lying in Stafford County between the Potomac and Occoquan rivers, called "Doeg's Island."[2] As he was living in this locality some years before, apparently, he must have made an earlier purchase of land of which no record remains. The earliest books at the Court-House, Stafford County, are in a very imperfect condition, the leaves having been wantonly torn out in many instances, while other volumes are altogether missing.

"Doeg's Island" was, no doubt, a part of Dogue Neck or Mason's Neck, as it was afterwards called, when the whole of it came into the possession of the family. Bishop Meade, in his invaluable chronicles of the old Virginia parishes and families, notices the circumstance that peninsulas were sometimes called islands by the early settlers, as was the case with Farrar's Island on James River and the neck of land on which Jamestown was built. On the 17th of November, 1699, George Mason bought two hundred acres of land near Little Hunting Creek, in what is now Fairfax County, and the tract is described in the deed as "next to land late of Harper sold to Mason."[3] "Mount Vernon" is between Dogue Neck Creek and Little Hunting Creek, as marked on the map of Fry and Jefferson, 1751; Doag Creek the former is called in the

---

[1] *Ibid.*   [2] Records at Stafford Court-House.   [3] *Ibid.*

coast-survey maps at the present day.   But the neck of land bounded on the north side by Doag Creek is not the same as Mason's Neck.   It is much smaller than the latter, yet apparently both of these peninsulas were at one time called by the same Indian name.   In 1698, the Stafford County gentlemen send a letter of "grievances" to Governor Nicholson, the Council and Assembly, asking that the "bloody villain, Squire Tom, a convict upon record," be demanded from the "Emperor of Piscataway," who was then protecting him from punishment.[1]   "G. Mason" is one of the signatures to this communication.   The following year Governor Nicholson wrote to the people of Stafford in regard to the Indian emperor above mentioned, who had fled from Maryland to Virginia with his nation.   The governor wishes the emperor and some of his great men to come to the meeting of the Assembly in April, and the Stafford gentlemen are required to send one or more messengers to the Indians with this message., George Mason heads the list of names signed to the letter of the Stafford justices replying to the governor.[2] It would appear that Captain Mason received the appointment of County Lieutenant of Stafford about this time, and a letter from him to Governor Nicholson is extant, dated the 9th of November, 1699, relating to this embassy.[3]   There was a George Mason in this year, clerk of the court, and this was in all probability, Colonel Mason's eldest son.   He gave in a list of tobacco tenders for 1699.   "Between the South-side of Potomack and ye Lower End of Overwharton p'ish."[4]

In the following letter to Governor Nicholson, which is modernized in its orthography and capitalization as reproduced here, Colonel Mason gives a graphic account of an Indian outrage perpetrated in his county in 1700:

STAFFORD COUNTY, June 18, 1700.

May it please your Excellency :

I got my letters ready to send your Excellency on Monday early, but on Sunday, late in the night, came a post to give an

---

[1] "Virginia Calendar Papers," vol. i., p. 60.

[2] *Ibid.*, p. 62.   [3] *Ibid.*, p. 68.   [4] *Ibid.*

account of a murder done in these parts, so hindered my then desire.

SIR : On Sunday the sixteenth, about three of the clock in the afternoon, came about twenty or thirty Indians to Thomas Barton, about twenty miles above my house. The man and his wife and brother, being abroad, and left his three children and an orphan boy at home, and had got a man and his wife and three children from a plantation of mine, about two miles from him, to stay to look after his house until they came home. The Indians fell on them and killed Barton's three children, the man and his wife and his three children. The orphan boy ran away, he being out at play, blessed be God, got to a neighbor's house and is safe. They killed them with arrows and wooden tomahawks, plundered all the house and carried every thing away ; killed a mare of the man's that was tied to a door. We took up about the house and pulled out of the people and the mare sixty-nine arrows. They left ugly wooden tomahawks five. On the news, I went immediately with a small parcel of men and buried the poor people. This murder was the horriblest that ever was in Stafford, and I thank God we have not had the least harm on this side of Occoquan since I have been in the freshes, and have kept the people bravely on their plantations, but God knows what I shall do now, for this has almost frighted our people out of their lives and interests, and besides the Emperor and his Indians being still out, which did as surely done the murder as God is in heaven. The man himself coming home, called at a mill and took a bag of meal with him, and about four hundred yards from his house, about twenty Indians as he guesses, started up and immediately had him in a half-moon ; he well-mounted, put on endeavoring for his house, but he being loaded, they had like to have got him, but with great difficulty [he] got his bag off, and broke through the woods and got safe to a neighbor's house. I am of opinion they had done all the murder before, for undoubtedly they would have killed him but had no arms, for he saith they never fired neither shot nor arrow, neither had they any lodges with them, but naked. So I am of opinion that they had another party besides. If they had had arrows, they would have killed him, for their arrows was of great force, for they have made holes in the roof of the house as big as swan shot, and [he] believes there was at least forty by their several great tracks, and [I] am of opinion that great part of them is gone to Maryland and the rest back.

SIR : I have raised twelve men, and have sent every way to search our frontiers and back forest plantations, and intend, God willing, to keep constantly moving myself with them until [I] have your Excellency's commands, then trust in God shall be able to give our people better satisfaction than at present can, for I am afraid that we shall have a bad summer, but if, please God, [I] can but keep them upon their plantations, it will be some discouragement to the enemy, but those two are deserted for this year.   I do not doubt your Excellency's Christian care for the good of his Majesty's subjects, for without immediate care I shall have but few plantations in Stafford.   Not [nought] to add, but my humble services to your Excellency, conclude, as in duty, I am your Excellency's most humble servant.

G. MASON.[1]

The handsome red wax seal attached to this letter is in a perfect state of preservation.   The device is a heart pierced with two arrows, surmounted by a crown.   And it seems probable that this impression was taken from a seal ring, which coming, as is likely, to Colonel Mason's grandson, George Mason of Gunston, was chosen by him as a model for a beautiful ring given by him to one of his daughters.   This last, which is now in possession of one of her descendants, is set with rubies and diamonds in the shape of a heart with a crown above it.

The Emperor of Piscataway disclaimed any connection with the late murders, and consented to remove his family and property back to Maryland.   But the people of Stafford evidently distrusted his intentions, and they sent an " humble petition " to the executive begging that he would provide more fully for the safety of the frontier.   George Mason signed this petition, and on the same day, July 10th, he wrote to Governor Nicholson, giving him an official account of the state of affairs :

[1] *Ibid.*, p. 69.

STAFFORD, C. H., July 10, 1700.

May it please your Excellency :

Your Excellency's commands from Colonel Fitzhugh have received, and shall be carefully observed. The Rangers continue their duty according to your Excellency's commands, and I have upon the request of the frontiers placed six men and Ensign Giles Vandecastiall officer to range upon the heads of the river ; that is I have raised them from Giles Vandicasteall's house up to the uppermost plantation. They [the ?] neighbors having fitted out their sons and other young men well acquaint, so their ranging is as low as my Plantation at Pohick, so round all the necks, up to the uppermost Inhabitants, so down upon the back plantations ; and Cornet Burr Harrison, from Occoquan down to Potomack Creek with two officers and men doth give good content. They range each party four days a week, which is as hard duty as can be performed ; with said officers is the best to content in our upper parts. If your Excellency think fit so they may act, as they are cornet and ensign of the militia, but leave it to your Excellency's consideration.

The Inhabitants still continue from their houses, but abundance better satisfied since part of the Rangers is constantly ranging among them. Sir, I find it will be of great disservice to our county business to have Captain Hooe out of the commission ; most humbly beg leave to conclude, Sir, your Excellency's most humble servant,

G. MASON.[1]

An order was issued from Jamestown, July 10, 1700, to " Lieut.-Coll. George Mason, made commander-in-chief of the militia," requiring him to raise twelve men, with two officers over them, to range in the county for its further security. And we find the council again in the fall of this same year sending a fresh order to Colonel Mason. This time it is dated from the new capital, Williamsburg, and authorizes the County Lieutenant to continue the same rangers as heretofore, until the next session of the General

[1] *Ibid.*, p. 71.

Assembly.[1]   Colonel Mason patented seventy-nine acres of land in 1704, part of it being the tract on which the present village of Occoquan now stands.[2]   He held at this time 1703-4, divers tracts in the county, amounting in all to 8,000 acres, and his "home seat" was "Dogue's Island."[3]   He bought of Joseph Waugh 1,085 acres of land in Overwharton parish at a little later period; and on the 11th of June, 1707, he patented seventy-nine acres on the Occoquan River, which last, however, he soon sold.[4]   The feoffees of the incipient town of Marlborough at this time were George Mason and William Fitzhugh.[5]   Col. George Mason, whose unmistakable autograph identifies him with the writer of the letters of 1699-1700, sent a communication to Governor Spotswood, in 1713, asking that his son, who had been nominated for that office by the justices of Stafford, might be made sheriff.[6]   The last purchase of land made by Colonel Mason was on the 4th of January, 1714.   He obtained, in partnership with James Hereford, 2,244 acres in Stafford County, a rude plat of which tract is found on the deed.   It is described as situated between the main run of Accotink and Dogue Run, being commonly called "Hereford Manor."[7]   It seems to be part of the neck of land on which "Belvoir," the Fairfax estate, was afterward situated.   In the plat, "Mrs. West's land" is seen on the left of Accotink Run, and to the left of Dogue Run is situated the "Chaple land," with a building on it representing the "Chaple."   This was doubtless one of the Rev. Mr. Waugh's churches.   The "county main road" runs south of Hereford Manor.   In the will of Colonel Mason he bequeathed this property to two of his daughters, and the same tract is mentioned in the will of George Mason of Gunston.   On the 5th of January, the day after this purchase, "Mr. George Mason, jun.," is seen to have patented 1,930 acres of land in Stafford.[8]

[1] *Ibid.*, p. 72.   [2] Virginia Land Registry Office, Richmond.
[3] Records of Stafford Court-House.   [4] *Ibid.*
[5] Journal of the Virginia Assembly, October, 1748.
[6] "Virginia Calendar Papers," vol. i., p. 166.
[7] Virginia Land Registry Office.   [8] *Ibid.*

Colonel Mason, as appears in his will, bought land of a number of private individuals, and apparently was a large property holder at the time of his death, which occurred in 1716.[1] He had been married three times, and a large family had gathered around him. The first wife of Colonel Mason, to whom he had been married some time previous to 1694, was Mary, daughter of Gerard Fowke, the second of the name in Virginia. This Gerard Fowke, removing from Pasbytanzy, near the early Mason homestead, settled in Charles County, Maryland, where he built a substantial mansion, which he called " Gunston Hall," and which is still owned by some of his descendants. The children of this marriage, named in Colonel Mason's will are George, French, Nicholson, Elizabeth, and Simpha Rosa. The second wife of Colonel Mason was Elizabeth, daughter of the Rev. John Waugh, and she had one child named Catherine. The Christian name of the third Mrs. Mason was Sarah, as appears by her will, but her surname is not known. Her children were Francis, Thomas, aud Sarah. There appears to have been a son Gerard,[2] not living at the time of his father's will, and two married daughters, whom he does not name in this instrument. These were Anne and Mary, the first of whom was married three times and the second twice, and their first husbands are mentioned in Colonel Mason's will as his sons-in-law. Anne's second and Mary's first husband were sons of William Fitzhugh, the founder of the Fitzhugh family of Virginia, and the writer of the letters above quoted. Simpha Rosa Enfield was married twice also, first to John Dinwiddie, a brother of Governor Dinwiddie, and secondly to Colonel Jeremiah Bronaugh, of King George County, and her descendants by both husbands are numerous.[3] Catherine Mason married John Mercer of Marlboro',[4] who came into possession of the whole " town " of that name on Potomac Neck, or Marlboro' Neck, as it was afterwards called. And it is to John Mercer that we owe the preservation of

[1] Appendix I.
[2] Fowke Family MS.
[3] Bronaugh Family Bible, etc., etc.
[4] Mercer Family Bible.

his father-in-law's will.[1] Elizabeth Mason married William
Roy. Of the sons of Colonel Mason only two, George and
French, married and left descendants.

George Mason, the third of the name and line in Virginia,
the father of George Mason of Gunston, like his predecessors, was prominent in the affairs of the colony. He was a
justice of the peace in 1713, and probably sheriff of Stafford
soon after. When next we hear of him it is in the gallant
expedition of the "Knights of the Golden Horse-shoe," as
we may reasonably infer.

In 1716, Governor Spotswood made his famous passage
over the Blue Ridge Mountains, instituting his knightly
order of the Golden Horse-shoe—an incident in Virginia's
early eighteenth-century history over which there has always
rested a glamour of romance, and which has captivated the
imagination of both poet and novelist. In the small party of
gay and gallant gentlemen who formed the governor's escort
there was one by the name of Mason, and there seems every
probability that this was George Mason of Stafford County.
One of the gentlemen of the company, Robert Brooke,
afterwards surveyor of the colony, was living on the Rappa-
bannock, in very much the same part of the Northern Neck
as George Mason, and in his family the gold horse-shoe "set
with garnets and worn as a brooch," given to him by Governor Spotswood, was long preserved as an interesting relic.[2]
Beverley, the historian of Virginia, was also of the party.
In the brief account of this expedition by the Rev. Hugh
Jones, chaplain to the General Assembly, written a few years
after it had taken place, we are told that the golden horse-
shoes were "studded with valuable stones resembling the
heads of nails, with this inscription on the one side: *Sic
juvat transcendere montes*."[3] They were given to his com-
panions by the governor, in commemoration of their success,

---

[1] Mercer Land Book. (A copy of it is owned by the Va. Hist. Society.)
[2] "Narrative of My Life," p. 6, by Judge Francis T. Brooke.
[3] Hugh Jones' "Present State of Virginia," p. 14.

and the horse-shoe was selected as a symbol because of its being an unusual requirement in the lower part of the country, whereas for this mountain exploration a large quantity were needed. One of the party, John Fontaine, a Huguenot refugee, several of whose brothers settled in Virginia later and left descendants, wrote a journal of the expedition, from which the fuller details are gathered, and it is a lively and picturesque narrative.[1] The party numbered about fifty persons in all, including pioneers, Indian servants, and rangers. The several camps or stopping-places along the route were named after the gentlemen of the governor's staff, and one of them was called "Mason's Camp." On the return, when they reached Germanna on the Rappahannock, the journalist says: "Mr. Mason left us here." He took his way, doubtless, across the Neck to his home on the Potomac, carrying with him pleasant memories of the novel expedition and its harmless adventures.

But in the paternal household there was sickness and death about this time, Colonel Mason, his wife, and his son Nicholson all dying within a few weeks of each other apparently, leading to the inference that they were carried off by some epidemic. And on November 14, 1716, George Mason appeared at the Stafford Court as the sole executor of the wills of his father and step-mother. In 1717 George Mason and his brother French both patent some land in Stafford. George Mason gets his, a tract of 534 acres, in partnership with "Colonel Robinson, of Richmond."[2] This was one of the gentlemen who went over the Blue Ridge Mountains with Governor Spotswood the year previously.

In 1718, George Mason made his first appearance in the Assembly, he and his brother-in-law, George Fitzhugh representing Stafford County. A seat in the House of Burgesses was always an object of ambition to the colonial gentry, and this mark of popular favor continued to be held in great esteem after the Revolution, only declining in importance

[1] "Memoirs of a Huguenot Family," New York, 1853, p. 281.
[2] Virginia Land Registry Office.

upon the adoption of the Federal Constitution.   In the early part of the eighteenth century the power of the Assembly, though much hampered by the Executive, was not to be despised, as Governor Spotswood found out.   He had a high sense of his prerogative, and the burgesses were equally convinced of their rights and desirous to maintain them. In 1715, he found the Assembly intractable, and they had censured him in some resolutions which had been sent on to the Lords of Trade in London, who had control of colonial affairs.   The new Assembly of April, 1718, it was hoped would meet him in a better spirit.   But the people had their grievances, which the fair words of the governor could not make them forget.[1]   And not the burgesses only, but some of the council were opposed to the executive, in his rather autocratic administration of the government.   Col. William Byrd of Westover, Colonel Ludwell, and Commissary Blair were among these independent councillors.   The last named the founder and president of William and Mary College, led the minority of the clergy who upheld the position of the Assembly against the executive in the Church Convention which took place at Williamsburg in April, 1719.[2]   One of the prerogatives which the Virginians were striving against at this time was the claim of the royal governors to collate to ecclesiastical benefices, as representatives of the Crown.   On the other hand, the vestries maintained the right to select their own rectors.   Bishop Meade points out how closely the principle in question approximated to the one at issue in 1776.   "The vestries," he writes, "had been fighting the battles of the Revolution for a hundred and fifty years. Taxation and representation were only other words for support and election of ministers."[3]   Governor Spotswood, however, was accounted, on the whole, a public-spirited and upright governor.   He made up his differences later with

---

[1] "Virginia Historical Register," vol. iv., pp. 11–17; Spotswood Letters, Virginia Historical Society, vol. ii., pp. 299–306.

[2] "Old Churches and Families of Virginia," vol. ii., appendix i.

[3] *Ibid.*, vol. i., p. 151.

the burgesses and the council, and one of the latter, Colonel Byrd, his sworn foe in 1718–19, visited him in after years in his home in Northern Virginia, and has left on record a genial picture of him as he appeared in the softer atmosphere of domestic life.

George Mason in July, 1719, was commissioned County Lieutenant of Stafford, succeeding his father and grand-father in this important office. The original commission, with the large official seal attached to it, is in possession of one of his descendants. Some of the words have become illegible in the lapse of time, and it has been thought best to supply them, from other papers of the same character which are extant.

Alexander Spotswood, His Majesty's Lieut.-Governor and Vice-Admiral of His Colony of Virginia, and Commander-in-Chief of the Same Dominion :

To GEORGE MASON, Esquire.

By virtue of the authority and power to me given by His Majesty as Commander-in-chief of this His Colony and Do-minion, I, relying upon and reposing all trust and confidence in your Loyalty, Courage, and Conduct, Do hereby constitute and appoint you, the said George Mason, to be Lieutenant of the County of Stafford, Virginia, and Chief Commander of all His Majesty's Militia, Horse and Foot, in the said County of Stafford, Virginia, and I do give unto you full power and authority to Command, Levy, Arm, and Muster all per-sons which are or shall be liable to be levied and listed in the said County. You are therefore carefully and dili-gently to discharge the Duty of Lieutenant and Chief Com-mander of the Militia by doing and performing as allowed all manner of Things thereunto belonging, particularly by taking care that the said Militia be well provided with Arms and Am-munition as the law of this Colony directs, and that all Officers and Soldiers be duly exercised and kept in good Order and Dis-cipline, And in case of any sudden Disturbance or Invasion I do likewise Impower you to raise, order, and march all or such part of the said Militia as to you shall seem meet for resisting and

3

subduing the enemy ; and I do hereby Command all the Officers and Soldiers of His Majesty's Militia in the said County to obey you as their Lieutenant or Chief Commander, and you are to approve [observe ?] and follow such Orders and Directions from Time to Time as you shall receive from me or the Commander-in-Chief of this Colony for the time being or from any other your superior Officer, according to the Rules and Discipline of War. Given under my Hand, and the Seal of the Colony at Williamsburgh this Second Day of July, 1719 in the Fifth Year of His Majesty's Reign, A. D.

A. Spotswood.[1]

Colonel Mason's "loyalty, courage, and conduct," as this paper phrases it, had been manifested, perhaps, in defence of the frontiers which still required protection against the Indian foe ; and it may be these attributes had been shown upon other occasions, as in the tramontane expedition. In the recent Assembly, George Mason could not have made himself conspicuous in opposition to the governor, or his "loyalty" would not have been so apparent to his Excellency. Colonel Mason's courage and conduct commended themselves to others also about this time. The Scotch merchants, in their trade with the planters on the Potomac, were brought into close relations with the County Lieutenant of Stafford, it seems, and he had it in his power to extend them courtesies for which, as a mark of their appreciation, he was given, in 1720, the freedom of the city of Glasgow. As a large landholder and tobacco-planter himself, Colonel Mason would have, it is probable, extensive transactions with the merchants of the mother country on his own account. The old parchment "Burgess Ticket" is still preserved by Colonel Mason's descendants. It is endorsed on the outside, "Collonell George Mason, his booke of Glasgow 1720." The border is illuminated in red and blue, and the arms of the city, with its motto, "Let Glasgow flourish," are found at the top of the paper, which reads as follows:

[1] This interesting relic was taken out of its glass case during the late war and carried for safe-keeping to Canada by the late Hon. James M. Mason. whose daughter now owns it.

"At Glasgow, the second day of March, one Thousand, Seven hundred and Twenty years. The which day in presence of the Rt. Honble. John Bowman, Provost of the City of Glasgow, Peter Murdoch, Mr. John Orr, and Stephen Crowford, Baillies thereof, James Peadie, Dean of the Gild, and several of the Gild Council of the said city, the Honble. George Mason, Esqr., Collonel of the County of Stafford in Potomack River, Virginia, is Admitted and Received Burgess and Gild Brother of this city : and the Whole Liberties, privileges, and immunities, belonging to a Burgess and Gild brother thereof are granted to him in most ample Form : Who gives his oath of Fidelity as Use is. Extracted furth of the Gild Books of the sd. City by mee.

"J°. Mc. Gilchrist, *Clk.*"

The following letter accompanied the Burgess ticket :

Glasgow, March 3, 1720.

Having received certain Information of the many Extraordinary Favours you have done to our merch^ts. or their agents in Virginia we thought ourselves obliged in the name of our City to acknowledge your Goodness, and in Testimony hereof we do send you the compliment of the City a Burgess Ticket by which you are entitled to all the Rights and privileges and Immunities of a Burgess or Citizen of Glasgow.

Hitherto your Favours to our people have flowed from the wider motives of Hospitality, in time coming you will if possible multiply your goodness towards them when you can consider them not only as strangers but as Fellow Citizens with yourself. We wish you all happiness and prosperity and do most earnestly recommend you to the protection of the Almighty.

To the Hon. George Mason, Esq :
Colon^l. in Stafford Co., Pottomack River, Virginia.

A Virginian who was in Glasgow in 1848, tells of the pleasure he felt in finding a street there named " Virginia "; and he adds, " We listened with interest to an intelligent Scotchman, who related anecdotes of the days when Virginia merchants thronged that street, and were regarded with such respect that other men gave way that they might pass. He referred with pride to the beginning of the eighteenth century, when our ports were thrown open to Scotch adventure, and Glasgow, becoming the great *entrepôt* whence the farmers-general of France derived their supplies of tobacco from Virginia, received her first impulse towards that high state of prosperity she has since enjoyed." [1]

In 1721 Colonel Mason was married to Ann Thomson, daughter of Stevens Thomson, Attorney-General of Virginia for some years during the reign of Queen Anne. Governor Spotswood went to Albany in 1722 to confer with the Five Nations, taking with him a member of the council and Col. William Robinson, who at this time represented Stafford County with George Mason in the Assembly. In the propositions made to the Five Nations, relating to the boundaries "between the Indians subject to the Dominion of Virginia and the Indians belonging to and depending upon the Five Nations," a stipulation was made in regard to the return of runaway slaves belonging to Virginia, "That if any such negro or slave shall hereafter fall into your hands, you shall straightway conduct 'em to Col°. George Mason's House on Potowmack River." And the governor promised them upon "the delivery of every such runaway, one good gun and two blankets, or the value thereof." The Indians agree to the demand, and upon the final settlement of this treaty with the Five Nations, Governor Spotswood finds a novel use for the horse-shoe badge of the tramontane order. He "told them he must take particular notice of their Speaker and give him a Golden Horse-shoe which he wore at his breast, and bid the Interpreter tell him there was an Inscription upon it which signified that it would help to pass over the mountains; and that when any of their people should come to Virginia with a pass, they should bring that with them." [2]

The inconspicuous administration of Hugh Drysdale succeeded that of Governor Spotswood in 1723. The latter held his last Assembly in May, 1722, and this was the second session of one convened in November, 1720. An Assembly

---

[1] Address of Rev. Phillip Slaughter before the Va. Hist. Society, Jan., 1850.
[2] " Byrd Manuscripts," vol. ii., p. 262.

was called by Governor Drysdale soon after he had entered
upon his office, in which George Mason again, with William
Robinson, represented Stafford County. Colonel Mason
patented a tract of land adjoining the estate of Col. Thomas
Lee in Stafford, in January, 1724. It consisted of two hundred and fifty acres, and was about two miles below the falls
of Potomac. In the same month George Mason patented
over four hundred acres on the north side of Dogue Run.[1]

The Assembly met again in May, 1726, this being the
second session of the Assembly of 1723, and Colonel Mason
was doubtless present as one of the Stafford burgesses. The
governor in his opening address tells the burgesses that they
"laid a duty last session on liquors and slaves imported
as had been done by a former Assembly with very good
effect, lessening the levy per poll. The interfering interest
of the African Company has deprived us of that advantage
and has obtained a repeal of that law."[2] Here was another
grievance which was to grow in weight and significance.
From 1710 to 1718, the Virginians had taxed slaves imported
into the colony. But in this latter year the tax had been
repealed by royal authority, and vainly in 1723 and 1726, did
the colonists seek to restore it, renewing the effort fruitlessly
at later periods. In 1727, the first year of the reign of
George II., a new Assembly was called, which held sessions
also in 1730, 1732 and 1734. But it is not known whether
Colonel Mason was elected a delegate. If such was the case,
it is not likely he was present except at the first session, in
February, 1727, as he moved to Maryland to live in 1730,
though whether before or after the meeting of the Assembly
in May does not appear.

An old paper has been preserved copied from the Stafford
County records, dated August, 1729, showing Colonel Mason
to have bought two hundred and thirteen acres of land
at this time from Robert Hedges " for four thousand pounds
of tobacco and cash." The deed from Robert Hedges to

<hr />

[1] Virginia Land Registry Office.
[2] "Virginia Historical Register," vol. iv., p. 67.

George Mason was sealed and delivered in presence of John Mercer.[1] This land adjoined that of the Alexanders. In 1730 the county of Prince William was formed from the upper portions of Stafford and King George. And it was about this time that Colonel Mason moved from Virginia to one of his Maryland plantations. He took up his residence at Chickamuxon Creek, Charles County, opposite the new county of Prince William. And we find him on the 15th of June, 1731, leasing the plantation of Occoquan to his brother-in-law John Mercer, for one year.[2] At the same time he leased to John Mercer certain lots in Marlborough as the following paper testifies:

" Col. George Mason to John Mercer—Release, June 16, 1731,— 3 lots.
    " This indenture etc., etc., Between George Mason, late of the County of Stafford, in the Colony of Virginia, but now of Charles County, in the Province of Maryland, of the one part, and John Mercer of the said County of Stafford and Colony of Virginia aforesaid, on the other part.
    " Whereas, Matthew Thompson and John Withers, Gents., and feoffees of and for the town of Marlborough in Potomac Neck, in the County of Stafford, by their deed or deeds dated the 11th February, 1691-2, and now remaining enrolled among the records of Stafford, did grant, sell and convey unto George Mason, late of the said County of Stafford, Gentlemen, deceased (father of the said George Mason party to these presents) all the land those the several and respective lots of land situate and lying in the said town of Marlborough. And, whereas, by the death of the father, George Mason, the said lots descended to and upon the son George Mason, party to these presents as heir of his said father, etc., etc.   [Signed]
                              " GEORGE MASON."[3]

An act of the Virginia Assembly passed in May, 1732, for settling new ferries on the Potomac River, establishes one

[1] MSS. of the Alexander Family.
[2] Mercer Land Book.
                                        [3] *Ibid.*

" Just below the mouth of Quantico Creek, over the river, to the landing-place at Colonel George Mason's in Maryland, the price for a man one shilling and sixpence and for an horse one shilling and sixpence." [1] Quantico Creek or Run, passes through Dumfries and enters the river about three miles below.

Colonel Mason, tradition says, was married twice, but his first wife died early, leaving no children. By his marriage with Ann Thomson he had six or seven children, though three only lived to maturity. Three little daughters died of an eruptive disease, supposed to have been small-pox, and were buried in the same coffin. Colonel Mason's death took place in 1735. While crossing the Potomac from Virginia to Maryland, he was drowned by the upsetting of a sail-boat. It was said he was buried at " New Town," the seat of his brother-in-law, Mr. Bronaugh. But it is probable his remains were afterwards removed to " Gunston " to be placed by those of his widow.

While George Mason's paternal ancestors were prominent for several generations in Virginia as men of affairs, colonial burgesses, and county lieutenants, the family of his mother, the Thomsons, bore a distinguished record, two of them in England and one in Virginia, as members of one of the learned professions. The first of the family of whom any thing is known, Henry Thomson or Thompson of Yorkshire, purchased the estate of " Hollin Hall," near Ripon, in 1658, from the Markinfields, and this place was sold by the Thomsons to the Woods in 1718–19,[2] who have owned it ever since.

William, eldest son of Henry Thomson, George Mason's great-grandfather, was born about the year 1644, was admitted to the Middle Temple November 24, 1664, where he is entered as " son and heir of Henry Thomson of Hollinghose, [sic] in the parish of Ripon, co. York, Gentleman "; took his degree of A. B. at Cambridge, it would

[1] Hening's " Statutes," vol. iv., p. 362.
[2] Memoranda kindly furnished by Mrs. Grace Wood of " Hollin Hall," Ripon, Yorkshire.

seem, in 1670 and of A. M. in 1674; was made a Serjeant-at-Law on the 18th of June, 1688, and was knighted at Whitehall on the 31st of October, 1689.[1] The order of Serjeants-at-Law, or the order of the Coif as it is called, was an old and honorable one in England. It was confined to a small number, seldom exceeding forty or forty-five members. And for a long time the King's Council embraced only the Serjeants-at-Law and the Attorney- and Solicitor-General. Sir William Thomson appears to have filled his office with dignity and prudence, attaining to eminence in its ranks. In the biographical sketch of him compiled by Woolrych, some of the more noted cases in which he was concerned are briefly cited. In 1680, says this writer:

" The tide was about to turn against the Popish plot. Nevertheless it was thought expedient to prosecute John Tasborough and Anne Price, for an offence, which in law is called subordination of perjury; an attempt to persuade a person to forswear himself. The particular charge was an alleged conspiracy to persuade the notorious Dugdale first—not to give evidence against, among others, Langhorne, the Jesuit; and secondly to retract and deny all the evidence he had given. He was to keep himself away in secret, and to sign a note, acknowledging that he had been in error."

Sir William Thomson was one of the counsel for the defendants, and was associated with Pollexfen, afterwards Chief-Justice of the Common Pleas. In the extracts from the trial given by Woolrych, the justices on the side of the prosecution are seen to be somewhat lacking in temper and good manners; while Sir William Thomson's urbanity appears to be unruffled by the attacks upon him. One of them says to him, " You toss great names about and make great noise with them, when you know they are not here," and another rejoins: " It is a fine thing thus to make a long

---

[1] Admissions to the Middle Temple. Graduati Cantabrigienses. Haydn's " Book of Dignities." " Lives of Eminent Serjeants-at-Law," Woolrych, vol. i., p. 447.

brief with to no purpose." Then there was a passage of
arms between the Bench and the defendant Mrs. Price,
"who spoke up like a woman, the counsel keeping warily
out of the scuffle." A verdict of guilty was brought in
as was to be expected, and Tasborough was fined £100 and
Anne Price £200.

In this same year, 1680, Sir William was counsel for the
prosecution against Giles for the attempt to murder Mr.
Arnold. This was a very mysterious affair, and excited
much attention. Arnold was a justice of the peace, and was
known to be zealous against the Popish Plot, so it was not
difficult to assign a cause for the murderous attack. He was
passing through a lane in London on a dark night when he
was suddenly seized by two men, badly wounded, and otherwise maltreated. "Mr. Thompson," says Woolrych, "appeared to lead the prosecution, and conducted the case with
prudence and fairness." Giles was found guilty, and was
sentenced to the pillory and also to pay a heavy fine. Sir
William Thomson in 1681 defended Slingsby Bethel, Esq.,
for an assault upon Robert Mason, at the election in Southwark, and made an able speech in his behalf. But though
Bethel, who was sheriff of Southwark, was acting in the line
of his duty, it was thought he had exceeded it in this case,
and he was fined five marks. Not long afterwards Sir William was made King's Serjeant. A famous case in which
he was engaged in 1691 was that of John Ashton, who was
charged with high treason. Sir William was leading advo-
cate for the prosecution, and the crime alleged was that
Ashton had sought to inform the French King of the number and strength of the English men-of-war and the best
means to surprise them, and so facilitate an invasion of
Great Britain. "The King's Serjeant opened the case with
much moderation," writes Woolrych.

"He continued the same patience throughout the evidence. It
had been supposed that Mr. Ashton was a papist; but the
Serjeant interfered, and said, 'We have not objected anything
as to his religion at all.' And again, 'My Lord, I would not

press anything further than the nature of the thing would bear.' Chief-Justice Holt replied, ' Pray go on, brother, we are only talking among ourselves.' "

The prisoner was found guilty and executed. In the following year Sir William Thomson assisted in the prosecution in the case of the Duke of Norfolk and Mr. Germaine. He also appeared as King's Serjeant on the trial of Lord Mohun for the murder of Mr. Mountford.[1]

In Foster's " London Marriage Licenses " is the following notice of Sir William Thomson's marriage :

" William Thompson, of the Middle Temple, gent, bachelor, about 24, and Mary Stephens, of St. Mary Magdalene, Bermondsey, Surrey, spinster, about 23, and at [her] own dispose, at St. Mary, Savoy, St. Giles, Cripplegate, St. Alphage, St. Mary, Islington, or St. Martin-in-the-fields, Co. Middlesex, 5 May, 1668."

Le Neve gives Sir William Thomson's residence as Middlesex,[2] and it is known that his son William had a country-seat there. He died some time before 1700. The will of his widow, " Dame Mary Thompson," dated 1706, has been preserved by some of her descendants in Virginia.[3] In it she requests to be buried " in the Temple Church," by the side of her late husband.

Stevens Thomson, eldest son of Sir William Thomson, was born probably in 1670, was a student at Cambridge in 1688, and was in this year admitted, with his brother William, to the Society of the Middle Temple, where the entry appears as follows :

" June 12, 1688,
Stephens Thomson, son and heir of William Thomson, one of the Masters of the Utter Bar "

After fifteen years' practice of his profession he had attained such distinction as to be named for the important

[1] " Lives of Eminent Serjeants-at-Law of the English Bar," Woolrych, vol. i., p. 447.

[2] " Pedigree of Knights of Queen Anne."

[3] Mason Papers.

office of Attorney-General of Virginia. Through the corre.
spondence of the Lords of Trade we learn the particulars as
to his appointment and other items concerning him. Gov.
ernor Nicholson wrote to the Board of Trade in March, 1703,
asking that an Attorney-General might be sent to Virginia.
Benjamin Harrison (this was Benjamin Harrison of " Berke.
ley," the third of the name in Virginia), who had officiated
as her Majesty's Council-at-Law, lived forty miles from the
capital of the colony, and his salary of £40 a year was
so small that he would not consent to retain the office.
In July the Lords of Trade represent the matter to the
Queen, and " having been recommended by the Attorney.
General to nominate Stephens Thomson as a person fit for
that employment, and that he have a salary of £100 per
annum, payable out of her Majesty's revenue in Virginia,
humbly submit that he may be appointed for that service,
and that the Governor of Virginia may be authorized to
constitute him Attorney-General in like manner as the late
Earl of Bellomont constituted Mr. Broughton the present
Attorney-General of New York." Sir Edward Northey, the
Attorney-General, in his letter to the Lords of Trade says,
in obedience to their commands, he recommends Stephens
Thomson, Esq., who was the eldest son of Sir William
Thomson, one of his late Majesty's Serjeants-at-Law. He,
Stephens Thomson, was educated first at the University
and afterwards in the study of the law in the Middle
Temple, where he is of fifteen years' standing, and Sir
Edward thinks him a fit person to serve as Attorney-Gen-
eral in Virginia. And he incloses a certificate in his favor,
signed by all the magnates of the law, Sir J. Holt, Chief-
Justice of the Queen's Bench, the Chief-Justice of Common
Pleas, and seven others whose names are given. Finally,
after further preliminaries, the order of the Queen in Council
appears, authorizing Governor Nicholson to appoint Stephens
Thomson as her Majesty's Attorney-General in Virginia,
provided he be obliged to make his ordinary residence at
Williamsburg, where her Majesty's service will chiefly require

his presence. On the 6th of August Stephens Thomson wrote his acknowledgments to the Lords of Trade for their favorable recommendation. He says that nothing shall be wanting on his part to make good the character they have given him. And he begs a recommendation to the Admiralty that himself and family may have passage in one of the men-of-war now bound to Virginia. A letter was then written by the Lords of Trade asking of his Royal Highness Prince George of Denmark, Lord High Admiral of England, that Mr. Stephens Thomson may have such accommodation for himself and family as has been usual on the like occasion. It seems, however, from a memorandum appended, that Mr. Thomson did not make use of this letter but went in a merchant ship. On the 10th of August he waited on the Board of Trade at Whitehall to receive their commands, and they gave him a letter recommending him to the governor's protection and encouragement in the execution of the Attorney-General's office.[1] From a letter of his daughter's, Mrs. Mason, we learn that Stevens Thomson (as the name is now spelt in the family) brought with him to Virginia his wife, Dorothea, and five children, Mary, Elizabeth, William, Ann, and Stevens. He had a son born later, in Virginia, named Taunton. Elizabeth, William, Stevens, and Taunton all died under age. Mary married twice, but left no children, so that Ann became her father's sole heir.[2]

Little can be learned now of the public life of Stevens Thomson, as the records of the General Court preserved at Richmond were destroyed by the burning of the Court-House, April 3, 1865. One memorial of his decisions has come down to us, and it is in connection with the famous case of witchcraft in Princess Anne County—Virginia's solitary instance of the sort. A certain unfortunate Grace Sherwood living in Princess Anne County was accused of being a witch and put in the river to see if she would sink or swim. It was

[1] Sainsbury MSS., Virginia State Library, pp. 29, 46, 77, 81, 83, 84.
[2] Mason Papers.

in 1705 that she was first charged with this crime, and the case was brought before the August council at Williamsburg the following spring. Luke Hill presented the petition and it was referred to the Attorney-General, who was to consider it and give his opinion. This he did on the first day of the General Court, April 15, 1706. He thought that the county court ought to have made a fuller examination of the matter of fact, and to have proceeded thereon " according to the directions and powers to county courts given by a late Act of Assembly in criminal cases, and if they thought 'here was sufficient cause, to have committed her to prison, whereby it would have come regularly before the General Court. And whereupon," he adds, " I should have prepared a Bill for the Grand Jury, and if they had found it I should have prosecuted." The opinion then concludes in these words: " I therefore with humble submission, offer and conceive it proper, that the said County Court do make a further enquiry into the matter, and that if they are of opinion that there be a cause, they act according to the above said law. And I shall accordingly be ready to present a Bill, and if found proceed thereon.—S. THOMSON, A. G." [1]

A recent writer has said of this opinion of Virginia's astute Attorney-General, that it is " in its way as sagacious as the utterance of the Delphian oracle." [2] Luke Hill could not justly complain of it, nor could it have been very alarming to the friends of poor Grace Sherwood. And it is satisfactory to know that the matter ended here. The legend still lingers in the locality where Grace Sherwood lived and suffered her petty persecution, and the spot is pointed out as the " Witch Duck."

The time of Stevens Thomson's death is determined by the following notice in one of Governor Spotswood's letters. He is writing to the Lords of Trade, " March 9, 1713–14," and says: " Mr. Thompson, who was for some years past Attorney General of this Colony, died in ye beginning

[1] " Virginia Calendar Papers," vol. i., p. 100.
[2] *Magazine of American History*, vol. x. ; " A Virginia Witch." p. 425.

of last Mo., and I have commissioned in his place Mr. John Clayton, an English gentleman, a Barrister-at-Law." [1] Stevens Thomson's will was probably to be found before the late war among the records at Williamsburg. No copy of it is extant. The wife of Attorney-General Thomson is said to have been a niece of Sir William Temple, and tradition asserts that Ann Mason as a child was a great favorite with her maternal great-uncle. "There is still preserved," writes one of her descendants, "in one branch of our family, as a cherished relic, a gift from him to her, being the Lord's Prayer written legibly and tastefully upon a circle of parchment, the size of a quarter of a dollar.[2] The name of William Temple was given by the younger of Ann Mason's sons to one of his children, whose place in Loudoun County was called "Temple Hall."

The younger brother of Stevens Thomson remaining in England, attained there a position of considerable eminence. This Sir William Thomson (2d) was admitted to the Middle Temple in the same year with his brother Stevens, but was not called to the bar until 1698. He soon afterwards entered Parliament where he represented first Orford, Suffolk and then Ipswich, for a great many years. He was Recorder of Ipswich from 1707 up to the time of his death in 1739, and he held the offices of Recorder of the City of London, Solicitor-General, and Baron of the Exchequer. He was knighted, probably in 1714. While in Parliament, Sir William Thomson took a prominent part in the impeachment by the Whig party of the tory Dr. Sachavarel, in the reign of Queen Anne, 1709, a famous case which excited much popular commotion, and brought on riots that led to further judicial proceedings, when William Thomson was also employed as junior counsel against the rioters. Upon him it devolved, in his office of Recorder of London, to read the address of congratulation from the city to both

[1] "Spotswood Letters," vol. ii., p. 61.
[2] MS., "Sketch of the Mason Family," by the late Judge John Thomson Mason, of Annapolis, Md.

George I. and George II. on their accession to the throne. Sir William Thomson married in 1711, Julia, daughter of Sir Christopher Conyers and widow of Sir William Blacket, Bart. His country seat "Osterly Park," was in Heston, Middlesex.[1] Dying childless at Bath in 1739, he left his property to his sister Sarah Thomson, with bequests to his step-children and others. After the fashion of the period, he left mourning rings to a number of persons. Among others, one to each of the Aldermen of London and the three other officers of that court, and he left a ring also to each of the postmen of Ipswich. The bequest of his portrait was made by Sir William to the Court of Aldermen of the City of London, and the testator adds:

"I desire it may be accepted by the said court as a token of my respect and grateful sense of the kindness and regard shown to me by the City of London, whose welfare and prosperity I heartily wish and have always endeavored to promote to the best of my capacity, and have the satisfaction of being conscious that I have served the city faithfully and with integrity, and hope to be remembered accordingly."[2]

This portrait now hangs in the Guildhall, London, and is considered a fine picture. In 1743, there was a suit in chancery for the sale of Sir William Thomson's estate, and his cousin and executor, John Thomson, Esq., of the Exchequer Office, made inquiries in Virginia for the heirs of his brother Stevens Thomson.[3]

[1] "Recorders of London," Frith ; "Lives of the Judges of England," Foss ; etc., etc.
[2] Copy of will of Sir William Thomson.—Mason Papers.
[3] Letters of Ann Thomson Mason.—Mason Papers.

CHAPTER II.

THE VIRGINIA PLANTER.

1725–1764.

George Mason of Gunston, the patriot and statesman, was born in 1725, as we know from an entry in the Family Bible, recording his age at the time of his marriage. He was probably born in the dwelling-house at Dogue's Neck, or Mason's Neck as it came to be called, which had been the residence of his father and grandfather. There was also a mansion-house at the plantation of Chappawamsic, in which his grandfather had lived at one time, and where his aunt, Mrs. Mercer, had been born. This estate came later to Mrs. Ann Thomson Mason as her dower, and she was living there apparently at the time of her death. The old house at Chappawamsic, which was built of stone and situated on a hill, is not now standing. George Mason was ten years old at the time of his father's death, in 1735, and his brother Thomson was but an infant of two years, while the only daughter, Mary Thomson Mason, was a child of four. The two guardians of George Mason and his brother and sister were their mother, Mrs. Mason, and their uncle-in-law, John Mercer of Marlboro'. From 1730 to 1742, Dogue's Neck was in Prince William County, and Dumfries was the county-seat at this time, though this honor was afterwards transferred to Brentsville, doubtless the " Brenttown " of the earlier annals. Here may be seen, at Brentsville, between the years 1732 and 1735, numerous deeds and leases to and

Charles County in the province of Maryland. There is preserved here also the record of the administration on the
estate of Colonel Mason in 1735 by his widow, who gives
bond and passes her accounts. The following is the guardian's bond.

"Know all men by these presents that we, Ann Mason, John
Mercer, John Gregg, James Baxter, and Catesby Cocke, are held
and firmly bound unto the worshipful Justices of Prince William
County, their heirs, executors, and administrators, in the sum of
five thousand pounds, to the true payment whereof we bind ourselves, our heirs, executors, and administrators, jointly and severally, firmly by these presents, as witness our hands and seals
this 21st day of May, 1735.

"The condition of the above obligation is such that, if the
above bound Ann Mason and John Mercer, guardians of George,
Mary and Thomson Mason, their heirs, ex$^{r.'s}$ and adm$^{r.'s}$ do and
shall well and truly pay, or cause to be well and truly paid, unto
the said orphans all such estate or estates that now is or hereafter
shall come to the hands of the said Ann Mason and John Mercer
as soon as the said orphans shall attain to lawful age, or when
thereunto required by the Justices of the Peace of Prince William
County Court, and also to save and keep harmless the said Justices, their heirs and successors, from all trouble and damage
that shall or may arise about the said estate, then this obligation
to be void or else to remain in full force and virtue.

Signed, sealed, and delivered
in the presence of
THOS. ROBINSON.

{ ANN MASON,
  J. MERCER,
  JOHN GREGG,
  JAMES BAXTER,
  CATESBY COCKE.

"At a Court held for Prince William County the 21st day of
May, 1735, Ann Mason, John Mercer, John Gregg, James Baxter, and Catesby Cocke acknowledge this bond in open court,
and it is ordered that the same be recorded.

Teste = CATESBY COCKE,
  Clk. Ct." [1]

[1] Prince William County Records.

4

Ann Mason's accounts as guardian give in great detail the expenses of the three children, George, Mary, and Thomson. Each child is charged for board and other items one thousand pounds of tobacco yearly. Thomson, on one occasion, is charged with linen and making three ruffled shirts, so many shillings; while Mary is charged with wooden-heeled shoes, petticoats, one hoop petticoat, and linen.[1] Two years after her husband's death, Mrs. Mason leased to John Mercer the same plantation of Occoquan that Colonel Mason had leased to him for a year in 1731. It would appear to have included more than one house, being, in fact, a small settlement with court-house and prison upon the place, besides the ferry. These three things are reserved in the lease, and a room also in the mansion-house is to be for Mrs. Mason's use when she has occasion for it.

"Occoquan Plantation, Mrs. Ann Mason, widow of George Mason, lease to John Mercer, September 23d, 1737. This indenture between Ann Mason of Stafford Co., Va., widow and relict of George Mason, Gent., late of Charles Co., Maryland, deceased, guardian and next friend of George Mason, eldest son of the above George Mason, deceased, an infant under the age of twenty-one years, of the one part and John Mercer of Stafford, Va., of the other part. Witnesseth that the said Ann Mason hath devised, let, and to farm to John Mercer all that messuage, tenement, and plantation of land on the south side of Occoquan River, and now in the possession of Thos. Dent, to contain one hundred and fifty acres, with all the houses, outhouses, gardens, woods, etc., appertaining to the same, Except the Court-House and Prison, and reserving one room upstairs, with a fireplace, when the said Ann Mason shall have occasion to make use of the same. Also excepting the Ferry, with the profits thereon. To the said John Mercer from the 3d October next ensuing for and during the term of nine years from thence next ensuing, paying the yearly rent of twenty pounds current money of Virginia to Ann Mason or such person as she shall authorize, &c., &c.

ANN MASON."[2]

---

[1] *Ibid.*   [2] Mercer Land Book.

The lease was for nine years, at the end of which time George Mason would have attained his majority. This ferry over the Occoquan River is thus mentioned in the will of George Mason of Gunston, who left the Occoquan plantation, afterwards known as "Woodbridge," to his youngest son. With it he was to have "the right and benefit of keeping the ferry over Occoquan from both sides of the river, which has been vested in me and my ancestors from the first settlement of this part of the country, and long before the land there was taken up or patented."

Mrs. Ann Mason proved herself a very careful and prudent guardian. Her husband left no will, and under the then existing laws of primogeniture his whole estate vested in his eldest son. "At this early period," to quote from the manuscript sketch of the family by the late Judge Mason, "there had already sprung up a strong opposition to this system, and in this Mrs. Mason participated, on the ground of its manifest injustice as was especially developed in the case of her own children. Her younger children were left without a farthing. To remedy this inequality she directed all her energies and talents towards the accumulation of the means to place them, as near as possible, upon an equal footing with their elder brother. Their mother appropriated all the money she should gather, whether from economy or otherwise, to the purchase of ten thousand acres of what was then called 'wild lands' in Loudoun County, for which she paid only a few shillings per acre. No sooner had she completed the purchase than she divided the land between her younger children. She did not delay this until her death, for the reason assigned by her that she did not wish her children to grow up with any sense of inequality among them in regard to fortune. The investment turned out a most fortunate one, and she thereby unwittingly made her two younger children wealthier than their elder brother." Ann Mason, yet a young and beautiful woman when left a widow by her husband's untimely death, never married again, though tradition reports that her hand was sought by numerous suitors.

She devoted herself to her children, and her sons owed much to this wise and affectionate parent. She is said to have possessed all the brilliant intellectual qualities of her father, Stevens Thomson, and she was also a woman of great personal charms and most amiable and domestic disposition.

But while George Mason's youth was indebted much to his mother's judicious training, doubtless, there was another influence not to be overlooked. His early years must have felt the impress of John Mercer's mind. For it was to him the youth would have turned as to a second father for direction in his studies and for guidance, later, in the management of his affairs. The considerable difference in the ages of the two brothers, felt in childhood and youth, though lost sight of in maturer years, left the eldest son without a companion in his own family during his minority. He would naturally find associates in the household of his uncle and guardian, and the latter must have regarded with special solicitude the ward who was in the position of the heir to his father's property, with all the responsibilities this entailed. John Mercer was a man of fine talents and attainments. As a lawyer he stood in the foremost rank of his profession. And as a patriot he was among the first to raise his voice against the aggressions of Great Britain. He was the owner of one of the best private libraries in the colony, and some of his books, having his heraldic book-plate in them, are still to be found in the collections of Virginia bibliophiles. George Mason must have enjoyed the advantages of this library and the benefits of his uncle's scholarship. Whether he received his early education, technically speaking, at a school kept by one of the clergy, as was common about this time, or whether he had a private tutor, cannot now be determined. It is certain from an item in his will that he had at one time others associated with him in his studies ; for he speaks in this instrument of a " Mr. Richard Hewit, my old schoolfellow and acquaintance from my childhood." Be that as it may, there is no evidence of his having been sent to college, and it seems likely that his tuition was mostly received at home, as was the case with many of the Virginia gentlemen of his time. There is testimony from George Mason's writings and speeches that he was a classical scholar, and his well-filled library in later years attested his wide and solid reading in the literature of his own tongue. His father is said to have been a man of scholarly tastes, and he may have had some share in forming the mind of his young son, as far as that was possible at the latter's tender age, for he had seen but one decade when this parent was taken from him. The brother of George Mason adopted the profession of the law, and was sent to London to study at the Temple, where his maternal grandfather and great-grandfather had left honorable records before him. His admission to the Middle Temple is found on its books in these words : " August 14, 1751. Thomson Mason, 3rd son of George Mason of Virginia in America, Esquire." This was the year after George Mason's marriage, and we learn from George Mason's will that he advanced money to Thomson Mason for his use at this time, which he is careful to state was a free gift, and not to be claimed as a debt by his heirs.

The early years of George Mason must have been passed, from the time of his father's death, in his country home in Virginia, Mrs. Mason having evidently left the Maryland plantation after the catastrophe which made her a widow. His studies were varied, doubtless, by the amusements of shooting, fishing, and sailing, and his associates were found in the families of the gentry scattered throughout the neighborhood, among whom were the Mercer, Fitzhugh, and Bronaugh cousins. With his namesake, George Mercer, a lasting intimacy was formed subsequently, but the latter, born in 1733, was just the age of his cousin, Thomson Mason. John Mercer jotted down in a diary the names of some of his neighbors, and the distances they lived from " Marlboro'," and these families were Mrs. Mason's neighbors also, and some of them kinspeople of hers. " Marlboro' " was at the extreme end of Potomac

Neck, it will be remembered; eight miles from Potomac Church and sixteen from Aquia Church—both of which were in Overwharton Parish. Capt. Peter Hedgman's, the old Mason place, known subsequently as "The Cottage," was six miles from "Marlboro'," and at a distance of three miles only lived Captain Fowke, one of the Mason cousins. His plantation, "Pasbytansy," was on the creek of this name. Mrs. Mason's place, apparently the Chappawamsic plantation, was sixteen miles from "Marlboro'." And Mrs. Washington, the mother of George Washington, a widow like Mrs. Mason, lived also sixteen miles from the Mercers. Mrs. Washington did not move into Fredericksburg until 1750, when George Washington was about eighteen years old, for he was some seven years the junior of George Mason. And while still a youth, Washington lived with his elder brother at Mount Vernon, and was then a near neighbor of George Mason's. But it was probably at this earlier period that the acquaintance and friendship between Washington and George Mason commenced, a friendship of which the latter speaks towards the close of his life as dating from his youth. John Mercer names as within visiting distance, seventeen miles and more, as neighborhoods were reckoned in those days, the Carters of "Clives," the Taliaferros, Moncures, Mountjoys, and Travers' families, the latter being only two miles from "Marlboro'." [1] Besides these we know there lived in this vicinity the Brents of "Woodstock" and of "Richland," the Fitzhughs, some of whom were George Mason's relatives, and the Bronaughs, who were also allied to him. There were also sons and daughters in the latter family, who were doubtless his associates in childhood, as we know they were the friends of his maturer years.

Two letters of Mrs. Ann Mason, written in 1743, have come down to us, through copies preserved by her descendants, showing that at this time she had some prospect of inheriting property in England through her uncle, Sir William Thomson. His death, at Bath, in England, had

[1] Mercer Land Book.

occurred in 1739, and his estate was at this time, in 1743, the subject of a suit in chancery. Mr. Ambler and the Nelsons, Thomas and William Nelson at Yorktown, had, in response to inquiries from London in regard to the heirs of Stevens Thomson, interested themselves in Mrs. Mason's behalf, and her friend and " relation," as she describes him, John Mercer, was active in forwarding her interests. Ann Mason's letters to her cousin and her uncle's executor, John Thomson, and to the merchants, Haswell and Hunt, London, on this subject are well written and give evidence of her business capacity. Incidentally they are of much value in elucidating the family history. Whether anything was ever realized for her out of the suit is not known.

In 1746 George Mason attained his majority, and a few years subsequently we may surmise he left his mother's house and went to reside on his estates in Dogue's Neck. In 1748, a ferry was established " from the plantation of George Mason, opposite to Rock Creek, over to Maryland." [1] And this ferry across the Potomac has an historic interest. Rock Creek runs between Georgetown and Washington, and the land opposite in Virginia was a tract patented by George Mason's father, and lies a short distance above " Arlington." Near here in 1738, a ferry had been established across the Potomac on the land of Francis Awbrey, and it was now removed to George Mason's place, about half a mile higher up the river. And about this time it may have been that George Mason obtained by patent from Lord Baltimore the island opposite Rock Creek, called Analostan or Mason's Island, though it was called at one time, as we learn by George Mason's will, Barbadoes. The island and ferry both came later to one of George Mason's sons. And for more than a century the ferry continued in existence, to be replaced at length by a toll bridge. Finally, in April, 1888, a free bridge was inaugurated at this point, and for the first time in a century and a half the traveller could cross the Potomac at Rock Creek without paying toll or fee.

[1] Hening's " Statutes."

In 1748, when George Mason was but twenty-three, he was one of five candidates balloted for at the election of burgesses in Fairfax County, and he received ninety-three votes. The most important event of his domestic life, his marriage, took place in 1750. Young, wealthy, handsome, and talented, he must have been at this time a distinguished figure among the *jeunesse dorée* of the Northern Neck. Doubtless he went to balls and races, and met there the belles of the country-side, both of Maryland and Virginia. But it was probably at her father's house, which was near property of his own in Charles County, Maryland, that George Mason made the acquaintance of his future bride, Anne Eilbeck. She was an only child and an heiress, and very lovely both in person and disposition. Her father, Col. William Eilbeck, was a wealthy planter and merchant, and had removed, in early manhood it seems, from Whitehaven, Cumberland County, England, to the province of Maryland. His wife was a Miss Edgar, of Maryland. Their country home, " Mattawoman," on the Potomac, adjoined the plantation where George Mason's father lived at the time of his death, and where his son had spent some years of his boyhood. The little Anne was but a year old in 1735, however, and no playmate then for the boy of ten. She grew up a belle and beauty, and a vague tradition associates her with young Washington as the veritable " lowland beauty " for whom he sighed in 1746. He was then but fourteen, and she two years younger. Her youthful charms, no doubt, made havoc in more than one susceptible heart. But at sixteen she became the wife of the stately, young planter of Dogue's Neck. It was a love match, and proved to be a very happy union. In the Gun-ston Bible there is to be found, as the first entry, in George Mason's own clear calligraphy, the record of this marriage:

" George Mason, of Stafford County, Virginia, aged about twenty-five years, and Ann Eilbeck, the daughter of William Eilbeck, of Charles County, Maryland, merchant, aged about sixteen years, were married on Wednesday, the 4th day of April, in the year 1750, by the Rev. Mr. John Moncure, Rector of Over-wharton parish, Stafford County, Virginia."

Soon after their marriage the portraits of Mr. and Mrs. Mason were taken by Hesselius, the early instructor of Charles Wilson Peale, and thus have been transmitted to us the features and appearance of George Mason in his early prime, with those of his lovely girl-wife. The picture of George Mason represents him in the fashionable short wig of the day, which effectually conceals his own dark hair. His features are regular, the eyes hazel and full of expression, the complexion clear and dark. The broad, firm brow betokens intellectual ability, while the chin in its firm, strong contour, is indicative of character and will power. Lace ruffles fall over his well-shaped hand, in the picture, as it is thrust through an opening in the embroidered waistcoat. One of the handsomest young men of his day, he is said to have been, with a dignified and attractive bearing, graceful and prepossessing ; an expert horseman, and doubtless not inexpert as a partner in the minuet and country dance of the period. Mrs. Mason, as the old canvas portrays her, had small, delicate features, black eyes, auburn hair, and the fair pink and white complexion that is so often found with it. She was as charming in character as she was in appearance. One of her descendants wrote of her: " She was remarkable for the great beauty of her person, her good intelligence, and the sweet mildness of her disposition." It was doubtless soon after his marriage that George Mason projected the building of " Gunston Hall," which received its name from the old home in Staffordshire of his Fowke ancestry.

According to one account, the mansion-house of Gunston was erected in 1755. But this is evidently a mistake, or if the building was commenced at this time, it was not completed until the spring of 1758. George Mason's letters, such as have been preserved, are dated " Dogues Neck," until May, 1758 ; and the entries in the Family Bible record the births of the elder children, invariably as in " Dogues Neck," until in 1759 Thomson Mason's birth is set down as at " Gunston Hall." The eldest son, George, was born in in 1753, and was baptized by the Rev. Charles Green, rector of Truro parish, Fairfax County.   William, the second son, was born in 1756, and his godfathers were the Rev. John Moncure and Thomson Mason.   The latter, the child's uncle, was then a young man of twenty-three, and had probably just returned from his legal studies across the water.   Five sons and four daughters, who lived to maturity, were born at length in the Gunston household, and were baptized severally in the large silver bowl of which George Mason makes mention in his will as that " in which all my children have been christened, and which I desire may remain in the family unaltered for that purpose."   And no doubt on these festal occasions the christening cake provided for the guests was put on the " large silver salver " of which the will also speaks as " an old piece of family plate " that is likewise to remain unaltered.   The early years of George Mason's married life appear to have been years of quiet, domestic happiness, with no greater calls to public duty than those embraced in the offices of vestryman or justice of the peace.   He did not, like his predecessors, become County Lieutenant, it would seem, though he is always given the title of " Colonel" by his contemporaries.

The first time that George Mason's name comes before us in any published records, associating him with matters outside of his county, is in connection with the Ohio Company of which he was a member.   The Ohio Company, consisting of twenty shareholders and having their agent in London, a prominent merchant there, was organized in 1749, and had for its object the colonization of Virginia's western territory and the promotion of trade with the Indians on the Ohio. They obtained a grant of six hundred thousand acres of land, lying mostly west of the mountains and south of the Ohio ; and they sent out Christopher Gist as their agent to build a road and survey the ground for a town and fort, which were to be situated near the present site of Pittsburg.   Gist was the first white settler west of the Alleghany Mountains, and the Ohio Company made the first road in this locality. Eleven families settled around Gist, and there was a plan at one time for inducing German settlers to take up the lands. The chief promoter of the Ohio Company's scheme at its out-set was the venerable Thomas Lee, President of the Council. Lawrence Washington succeeded Lee as the head of the Company, and interested his half-brother George Washington in the undertaking. John Mercer of Marlboro' was the secretary of the Company, and his son George became later its agent in England. Governor Dinwiddie was also a member. The Company had been incorporated the year after the treaty of peace between England and France in 1748, and these countries had not yet settled the disputed question as to their respective boundaries in America, so that the Ohio Company in its pioneer work came in contact with the pretensions of the French government in this quarter. In 1752 a treaty was made at Logstown with the western Indians, in which the Ohio Company had its commissioner present in the person of Christopher Gist, and the Dominion of Virginia was represented by three gentlemen, one of whom was Colonel Fry, who died in 1754 at Will's Creek, where the Company had established its storehouse. Col. Thomas Cresap with an Indian guide had marked out the Company's road to Will's Creek in 1748, and he was living, as an agent of the Company, on some of its land when Governor Dinwiddie, the newly appointed Virginia Executive, wrote to him January, 1752, in regard to its affairs : " I have the success and prosperity of the Ohio Company much at heart," he says, " though I have not a line from any concerned since my arrival, but this from you. There is a cargo for the concerned come in the ship with me ; it now lies at Colo. Hunter's, the severity of the weather prevented his sending the goods to Colo. Mason's." [1]

This mention of Colonel Mason shows him as active in aiding the transmission of the supplies procured for the settlers on the Ohio Company's lands. Colonel Hunter's house was near Hampton, where the ship from England probably anchored, and a cargo of goods sent from

[1] " Dinwiddie Papers," vol. i., p. 18.

there to Dogue's Neck on the Potomac would be conveyed
by George Mason to the landing in Virginia, opposite
Rock Creek, where was the plantation and ferry before
referred to, and from here it would go direct to Will's
Creek. The French in Canada had taken the alarm, as has
been said, and troops were sent out by them to garrison the
posts along the route of the disputed western boundary.
This measure was calculated to disturb the operations of the
Company, and the Virginia enterprise had also to contend
with the jealousy of the Pennsylvania traders, who feared
any interruption to their profits in the Indian traffic.

Such was the condition of affairs when in 1753 Governor Dinwiddie sent George Washington out as a commissioner to confer with the French commandant on the Ohio.
Washington took the road over the Alleghanies which had
been opened by the Ohio Company, and was afterwards
used by Braddock, and hence called " Braddock's Road."
This journey had taken him up the Potomac to Will's Creek,
where he crossed the mountains at Fort Cumberland.[1] It
is not unlikely that Washington's account of the country
about Will's Creek, given to his friend George Mason, on
his return may have led the latter to patent lands in Hampshire County at this time. The Northern Neck had been
construed to embrace Hampshire County and much more
than was strictly in its bounds, and George Mason's patent
from the proprietor is dated in October, 1754. It included five tracts of " waste and ungranted lands," amounting
in all to one thousand four hundred and thirty-five acres.
The boundary of one of these tracts begins " at a white oak
standing upon the edge of the Potomac river," and ends at
" a red oak standing upon the edge of said river opposite to
the mouth of Will's Creek." Another one begins " at a sugar
tree standing on the edge of Potomac river right against
George's Creek "; and the last tract beginning at a black
walnut on the edge of the river, goes down the same and

---

[1] Washington's report in regard to extending the navigation of the Potomac,
written at this time, was given by him, in his last years, with other papers, to
Gen. John Mason. (See Stewart's report. First Session 19th Congress.)

"thence into the mountain east."[1] The proprietor's office was in Fairfax County at this time, and Lord Fairfax's agent was William Fairfax of "Belvoir" on the Potomac, the founder of the Fairfax family of Virginia. He was a near neighbor of George Mason. And George Washington spent much of his time at "Belvoir," the Washington and Fairfax families being connected by marriage.

Washington was stationed in Alexandria in the early part of 1754, and was busily employed in getting ready for his first campaign in the French war, a struggle which had been precipitated, it will be seen, in the interest of the Ohio Company. He remained until April getting in recruits and supplies. And doubtless his friend at Dogue's Neck was keenly interested in these operations. Leaving Alexandria with two companies, Washington went out to Will's Creek with the object of strengthening the Ohio Company's fort at the junction of the Alleghany and Monongahela. He arrived too late, the French commandant having already possessed himself of the post and named it Fort Duquesne. The young Virginia officer threw up defences, but was compelled finally to surrender. In this expedition Capt. George Mercer was engaged, as was also another cousin of George Mason's, William Bronaugh. In the following spring a portion of Braddock's two regiments enlivened Alexandria with the bustle of military parade. And here the ill-fated general held a consultation with the governors of five colonies before going out to meet his doom at the disastrous battle of the Monongahela. George Mason must have mixed in this military and civic gathering, and made the acquaintance of the prominent men there assembled, among whom was the Deputy Postmaster-General of the colonies, Benjamin Franklin, who accompanied Governor Shirley to Alexandria. The Braddock House, dating from 1733, is still standing on Fairfax Street, and the Blue Room is pointed out to visitors as that in which Washington received his first commission. Maj. John Carlyle, who had married a daughter of William Fairfax, owned this old dwelling in 1755, and it was then known as the Cary House, having been built by

[1] Virginia Land Registry Office.

Jonathan Cary, one of the Fairfax connections. Among the letters of George Mason that have come down to us, letters, in Carlyle's phrase, " selected not by the Genius of History, but by blind accident, which has saved them hitherto and destroyed the rest," is one to George Washington written at this time. A month had elapsed after the battle in which Braddock had lost his life and Washington had won his first honors, and the latter was back again in Virginia, and not at " Mount Vernon," but staying apparently at " Belvoir " on a visit, to which place George Mason sends his letter, or note, as it might be more properly termed.

DEAR SIR :   DOGUES NECK, August 1st, 1755.

I fully intended to have waited on you this evening at Belvoir, but find myself so very unwell after my ride from court that I am not able to stir abroad.

I have taken the liberty to enclose you two bills for £300 stirling, drawn by Mr. paymaster Genl. Johnston on Col. Hunter, and an order on Govr. Dobbs from his son for £18 . . 15 . stir :, also a letter for Colo : Hunter and another for his Honor our Governor. If Colo. Hunter should be in town whilst you stay there, I should esteem it a particular favor if you'll be so kind to negotiate the affair with him. It is indifferent to me whether he pays cash or bills, payable in London, at the prevailing exchange at the time ; 't is probable it may suit him to take up the order on Governor Dobbs. If you should not see Colo : Hunter please to leave the bills with Governor Dinwiddie.

I beg you'll excuse the trouble I have taken the liberty to give you on this occasion, and give me leave to assure you that nothing would give me more sensible pleasure than an opportunity of rendering you any acceptable service.

I heartily wish you health and every felicity, and that you may find the new Regulations in our military affairs agreeable to your wishes, and such as will enable you to accept the command of our troops with honor.

I am, with my compliments to all at Belvoir,

Dear Sir, Your most obdt. hub. sert.

G. MASON.[1]

[1] Washington MSS., State Department.

In the "Dinwiddie Papers" there is mention of Colonel Mason at this time, in connection apparently with the matters forming the subject of the above letter. On the 28th of June, 1755, Governor Dinwiddie writes to Major Carlyle: "I answered Mr. Mason's letter by Mr. Alexander, and sent him a bill of exchange for the goods sent to the General." And again he writes to this same correspondent, July 9th: "Yours of the 20th June I should have answered before now, but have been much hurried. Mr. Mason's letter to me was to send him money or a bill for his account. The last I complied with, so he will have no demand against you, sir."[1] In this same letter Governor Dinwiddie calls Colonel Hunter "Mr. Hunter," as he at one time speaks of George Mason as "Colonel Mason," and again as "Mr. Mason." It would seem that George Mason had been engaged in supplying the commissariat of General Braddock. Colonel John Hunter was commissary of the army at this time, and Major Carlyle was his agent in Alexandria. Governor Dobbs, of North Carolina, had a son in the service, who is evidently the one referred to in George Mason's letter. Colonel Fry's regiment, which was after his death commanded by Colonel Washington, was to have a "magazine" of supplies provided for it by Major Carlyle. Two of the companies were applied for by "young Mr. Mercer and Mr. Bronaugh." The former was John Fenton Mercer, a brother of George Mercer. He was killed by the Indians in the spring of 1756 when but twenty-one. William Bronaugh, saved from the arrows of the Indians and from French bullets, lived to receive in 1771 his allotment of six thousand acres of land under Governor Dinwiddie's proclamation of 1754. A hospital was established in Alexandria, and French prisoners were quartered there in 1755, and the little town, with its commissary department and its importance as a military depot, must have been full of unwonted life. Twenty years later its pulses were stirred anew by the drum-beat of war, and this time the French were friends and allies, and the Virginia

[1] "Dinwiddie Papers," vol. ii. pp. 79, 97.

provincials were contending against the British regulars. Colonel Washington, who was now in command of the Virginia forces, was in Winchester in October, 1755, from which place he writes to Governor Dinwiddie of the distress of the inhabitants from the incursions of the Indians, and urges him to hurry the "militia from Fairfax, Prince William, etc., which Lord Fairfax had ordered." In January Colonel Washington is back again in Alexandria, but in the following summer, while at Winchester, George Mason writes to him, this time not on business of his own, but in behalf of one of his neighbors, an old schoolfellow of Washington's, who after enlisting in the army is desirous of returning to his farm.

DOGUES NECK, June 12th, 1756.

DEAR SIR

I take the liberty to address you on behalf of my neighbor and your old schoolfellow, Mr. Piper, who without duly considering the consequences, when he was at Winchester enlisted as a serjeant in Captain Mercer's company. He has been down to consult his father upon it, and finds him excessively averse to it, and as his principal dependence is upon the old man (besides the duty naturally due to a parent) his disobliging him in an affair of this nature cannot but be highly detrimental to him. I need not then say that it would be an act of humanity in Colo. Washington to discharge him. Mr. Piper tells me that he has never yet been attested, which seems so essential a part of the enlisting that I conceive he could not be legally detained against his will, but has still a right to depart upon returning whatever money he may have received; this I only hint and submit it to your better judgment. Be that as it will Mr. Piper would much rather choose to receive his discharge from you as a favor than insist upon it as a matter of right. It would be superfluous to add that your good offices to Mr. Piper on this occasion will ever be esteemed the greatest obligation on

Dear Sir
Your most obd. Servt.
G. MASON.[1]

[1] Washington MSS., State Department.

Efforts were being made at this time to enlist the Cherokee and Catawba Indians in the service of the Americans against the French, and in November, 1755, commissioners were sent from Virginia to negotiate an alliance. A treaty was concluded with them in the summer of 1756, and they promised to send a number of warriors to Washington's aid, forty of the Catawbas and a hundred Cherokees. Governor Dinwiddie wrote to Major Lewis on the 23d of August that he had given orders to provide provisions for them on their march to Winchester. He was expecting ships from England with guns for the Indians, but they had not arrived, and he was sending all over the country to purchase blankets, leggings, and other things for them. " I have wrote to Col. Washington," he adds, " to endeavour to purchase guns for them from Col. Mason, or any other person." [1] Washington, it seems, wrote to Colonel Mason five days later, and received the following reply, in which, however, there is no allusion to the guns.

DOGUES NECK, September 13th, 1756.

DEAR SIR :

Your favor of the 29th August did not come to my hands till yesterday, as I did not see the messenger who brought it, who, I understand, called at my building on his way to Fredericksburg, I shall keep this a day or two, to see if he will call for an answer as he returns from thence, if he does not I shall send it to Mount Vernon, and beg the favour of your brother to convey it by the first safe hand to Winchester.

By the enclosed list you will be able to judge whether we can furnish such goods as will be necessary for our friends the Catawba and Cherokee Indians. The principal articles wanting are kettles and striped Duffields ; I much doubt whether they can be got on this side Philadelphia, and perhaps not there, as the Indian trade has been at a stand a good while.

The goods are all charged at the genuine first cost and shop notes, upon which I think we cannot afford to take less than one hundred per cent. Virginia currency which I hope will not be

---

[1] " Dinwiddie Papers," vol. ii., p. 487.

thought unreasonable, considering the height of freight and in-surance, and the high exchange we shall be obliged to pay in paper currency for bills to make a remittance.

I hope I shall not have anything to do with the C——l or C——m, for though I have no objection to any of the gentlemen in their private, yet they are the last people in the world I should choose to have any concern with—in their public capacity ! An uncontrollable power of delaying, altering, or rejecting the ac-counts of private persons, for articles furnished, or services done by their own orders, is a very discouraging circumstance. 'T is a power which I dare say none of the government's officers in England would offer to assume, and I am mistaken if the fre-quent exercise of it here has not been highly detrimental to the public, as well as greatly injurious to many private people.

My friend Captain Mercer gave me reason to flatter myself with the thoughts of having your company in Dogues Neck some time this month, but I am afraid if you wait the arrival of the warriors of the South, I shall not have the pleasure of seeing you a long time. We have been often made to expect great matters from these Cherokees, and yet I steadfastly believe they have no thoughts of giving themselves any further trouble than to get what they can from us by amusing us with fair promises '

I very sincerely wish you health. success, and every felicity, and am

Dear Sir

Your most obedient

Humble Servant

G. Mason. '

The "C——l " and the " C——m " evidently signify the Council and the Committee of the House, powers which Colonel Washington had been obliged to consult, sometimes somewhat to his discomfort, and George Mason, as a private citizen, did not wish to come under their sway. The Captain Mercer of this letter was George Mercer, a member at this time of Washington's staff. Washington paid a short visit later to " Mount Vernon," but was back again at Winchester by the last of September, from which place he made, soon

<hr />

' Sparks MSS., Harvard College Library.

after, a seven-days' tour to Augusta and Halifax, examining the forts and the condition of the country. On this expedition he met with Major Lewis returning from the Cherokees with only seven men. Colonel Mason's skepticism concerning the "warriors of the South" would seem to have been justified. However, Washington did not lose faith in them, and some of these Indians came to his assistance eventually, performing much-needed services, for which Colonel Washington complained they received very inadequate compensation.

In 1757 Washington was obliged to leave the army on account of his health, and he was for several months seriously ill at "Mount Vernon." George Mason wrote to him on the 4th of January, 1758, sending the letter by his cousin, French Mason, the son, probably, of George Mason's uncle of the same name. Colonel Mason's sister was at this time, as we learn from this letter, lying at the point of death at her mother's place, "Chappawamsic." Mary Thomson Mason had married, April 11, 1751, Colonel Samuel Selden of "Salvington" in Stafford County, near Fredericksburg. Of her two children, Samuel, born in 1756, and Mary Mason Selden, born in 1754, the latter only lived to maturity. She married Mann Page of "North End," and her descendants are found among the Pages, Swanns, and other prominent families of Virginia and Maryland. Mrs. Selden's portrait, which has been preserved, shows her to have inherited her mother's beauty. She died January 5, 1758.

DEAR SIR :   DOGUES NECK, 4th Jany., 1758.

The bearer (my cousin French Mason) waits on you with an account I received from Captain Trent, amounting to £165-12-2¾. As I have an immediate call for a pretty large sum, you will particularly oblige me in sending the cash per this bearer who will give a receipt for what he receives. If you happen not to have the cash at home, I must beg the favor of you to order it for me by the first safe hand from Winchester.

I intended to have waited on you myself this day or tomorrow with this account, but am prevented by an express this morning from Chappawamsic, to acquaint me that my Sister Selden (who has been ill a long time) is now given over by her physician, and not expected to live many hours, and I am just setting off upon the melancholy errand of taking my last leave of her !—

I hope you will comply with the opinion and advice of all your friends, and not risk a journey to Winchester till a more favorable season of the year, or a better state of health will permit you to do it with safety. And give me leave, Sir, to mention another consideration, which I am sure will have weight with you, in attempting to attend the duties of your post at a season of the year when there is no room to expect an alarm, or anything extraordinary to require your presence, you will, in all probability, bring on a relapse, and render yourself incapable of serving the public at a time when there may be the utmost occasion. And there is nothing more certain than that a gentleman in your station owes the care of his health and life not only to himself and his friends, but to his country. If you continue any time at Mount Vernon, I will do myself the pleasure of spending a day or two with you very soon.

I am, with Mrs. Mason's compliments and my own to your brother, his lady, and yourself

Dear Sir

Your affectionate humble servant

G. MASON. [1]

How little did either Washington or Mason then dream of that " utmost occasion " which would demand the services of both of them in the future ! The next letters preserved of this correspondence were written by Colonel Mason to Washington at Fort Loudoun, to recommend his cousin, French Mason, for an appointment in the army.

RACE GROUND AT BOGGES'S,
Saturday, 6th May, 1758, 5 o'clock P.M.

DEAR SIR :

The bearer, French Mason, a relation of mine, has an inclination to serve his country upon the intended expedition. I recommended him to the president for a lieutenancy in the

[1] Washington MSS., State Department. Sparks publishes an extract from this letter.

regiment now raising, but unfortunately before he reached Wil.
liamsburg every commission was disposed of, otherwise he was
sure of succeeding, as the president would have done him any
service in his power. As there are some vacancies in your regi.
ment, his honor has been so kind to give him a letter of recom.
mendation to you. Had I known of these vacancies I should
have taken the liberty of applying to you sooner on his behalf ;
for as he purposes to continue longer in the service than this
campaign and push his fortune in that way of life, he would
prefer a commission in your regiment, and it would give me great
satisfaction that he was under the immediate command of a gen.
tleman for whom I have so high an esteem.

You may be assured, Sir, that I would not recommend a person
to your favor whom I did not from my own knowledge believe to
be a young fellow of spirit and integrity. He has lived a good
while with me, and, if I am not greatly deceived, he has personal
bravery that will carry him through any danger with reputation,
and this opinion I am the more confirmed in as he never was a
flashy fellow. He has been but little in company, and has not
that address which is requisite to set a man in an advantageous
light at first, but he is a very modest lad, and does not want parts,
and I am confident will endeavour to deserve your good opinion,
as well as to support the character I have given him. He this
moment came up from Williamsburg and found me here, and as
I thought there was no time to be lost I advised him to set off
instantly for Winchester, as soon as I could procure this scrap of
paper, and get a place in the crowd to sit down to write. If he
fails in a commission he had thoughts of going out a volunteer,
but as he has but a small fortune I advised him against it. Whatever you are so kind to do for him on this occasion I shall always
regard as a particular obligation to me. I beg you 'll excuse this
trouble and believe [me] on all occasions, very sincerely

Dear Sir

Your most obedient humble servant,

G. Mason.

I have really wrote this in such a hurry, that I am afraid it is
hardly intelligible.[1]

---

[1] *Ibid.*

The president of the council and acting governor at this time was John Blair, and evidently he was a good friend of George Mason's. The " Race Ground at Bogges's," from which this letter is dated, is pointed out to-day as near the present Pohick Church. And the race of the Bogges has disappeared as completely as the race-course itself, though the older inhabitants in the neighborhood still recall the name. It is difficult now in driving over this quiet, rather deserted locality, to picture the gay scenes of these early days, when the gentry of the country, the Fairfaxes, Lees, Washingtons, Masons, and others indulged in one of their favorite amusements on this old race-ground. The yellow manuscript with its faintly traced characters, penned by Colonel Mason in such haste, amidst the crowd and confusion of that May afternoon in 1758, still seems, however, to carry with it a suggestion of the genial, stirring, eighteenth-century life of which it was once a part. George Mason wrote again to Colonel Washington ten days later ·

DOGUES NECK, 16th May, 1758.

DEAR SIR :

I am favored with yours of the 8th inst. per French Mason and am perfectly satisfied with the justice of your reasons for not providing for him in your regiment at this time. I am convinced, from your state of the case, that it could not well have been done without prejudicing the service. He tells me you were kind enough to promise him a commission the next vacancy that happens. I should have been very glad his fortune would have supported him as a volunteer. Both he and I were very fond of his entering as such in your regiment ; but I really did not think it advisable that he should run his own little estate in debt upon the occasion. You know what kind of an establishment our Virginia troops are on. Nobody can tell how soon they may all be disbanded, without any provision for a broken leg or a shortened arm ! Or if they should happen to be kept up for a good many years, how possible is it for an officer to be reduced without being guilty, or so much as accused of any misbehaviour ? Faith, these are discouraging circumstances. On the British establish-

ment a young fellow may venture to dip his estate a little on the
road to preferment, where he is sure, if he behaves well, that a
commission is some sort of a provision for life ; but I really think
a young man who enters into the service and has but a small
estate of his own, ought if possible to preserve it unimpaired, to
return to in case of a disappointment or an accident. These
reasons have influenced me to dissuade French Mason from entering as a volunteer, and as he is very fond of trying a soldier's
life, and indeed I found it absolutely necessary that he should do
so, as the only means of getting clear of a very foolish affair he is
likely to fall into with a girl in this neighborhood, I have advised
him to enlist in the new regiment, if he can be made a serjeant.
My reason for advising him to enlist in that regiment is, that if he
should be disappointed in getting a commission, he may, if he
pleases, quit the service the first of December next ; whereas
from the Act of Assembly it appears to me that the men who enlist in the old regiment may be detained as long as any troops are
kept up in the pay of this government ; at least it may admit of
a dispute.   I speak to you only as my own private opinion, without any intention of making it public to the prejudice of the
recruiting service.   If he should have the good fortune to get a
commission, though he will accept of the first that offers in either
regiment, he will prefer an ensigncy in your regiment to a lieutenancy in the other ; and I have advised him if he should get a
commission in Colonel Byrd's regiment to exchange it if he can
by any means for one in yours.   I shall rely, sir, on your good
offices in his favor whenever a vacancy happens, and I flatter
myself that, by a strict adherence to his duty, he will strive to
deserve your good opinion.

I very sincerely wish you health and every felicity, and am,

Dear Sir,

Your most obedient servant,

G. Mason.[1]

Whether French Mason, this " young fellow of spirit and
integrity," a " modest lad " who did not " want parts," ever
obtained his coveted commission is not made apparent. His
name drops out of the family history at this point.

[1] *Ibid.*

The above letter of George Mason is the last that has been preserved that is dated from "Dogues Neck." "Gunston Hall," as we have said, was probably completed about this time, and the family moved into it from the older plantation. Colonel Mason made more purchases of land in 1757. He patented three tracts of land in Fairfax County in July, and one in September of this year; in all they amounted to 3,641 acres. One of these tracts adjoined some of George Mason's property on the branches of Accotink and Difficult Run. One was on the south branch of Little Hunting Creek, and a third was on Dogue's Neck, "being marsh and sunken ground upon Potomac River, adjoining to his own land, opposite to Crane Island." [1] In 1758 Colonel Washington, after the capture of Fort Duquesne (Fort Pitt), resigned his commission, and was married in the following year to the young widow of the "White House." Governor Dinwiddie had sailed for Europe in January, 1758, and it was the president of the council, as we have seen, who had promised French Mason a commission. Governor Fauquier was to arrive a little later.

At the Assembly in this year the town of Leesburg, in Loudoun County, was incorporated, and received its name from the Lees, who were extensive landholders in Loudoun at this time. Thomson Mason, whose estates in Loudoun gave him large interests in the county, was appointed, with Thomas Lightfoot and Philip Ludwell Lee, and others, a trustee of the newly established town. [2] It was at this session, September, 1758, that Thomson Mason's name first appears in the Assembly as one of the burgesses from Stafford, a county which had been represented by his ancestors for three generations. George Mason was to be identified in the Assembly with Fairfax County, which was, of course, a part of the original Stafford. Thomson Mason was probably living at this time in Dumfries, or at "Chappa-

[1] Virginia Land Registry Office.
[2] Hening's "Statutes," vol. vii. In the printed Statute "Francis Mason" is evidently a misprint for Thomson Mason.

wamsic" with his mother. His marriage must have occurred in 1758 or 1759, and his eldest son, Stevens Thomson Mason, was born at "Chappawamsic" in 1760. The Assembly in 1758 increased the Virginia army for the French war, and Colonel Washington visited Williamsburg to consult with the executive on military affairs. In the meagre journal of the Assembly Thomson Mason's name occurs only twice. Once this is in connection with the petition of a certain John Smith, captain of a company that had been engaged in an unfortunate expedition against the Shawnese Indians in 1756. He had been degraded from the service and his pay stopped, without opportunity of clearing his character, and Thomson Mason was a member of the committee appointed to inquire into his case. The single other legislative act reported of the future jurist and statesman was the preparation of a bill *for killing crows and squirrels.*[1] There was one important law passed by this Assembly for which one would rather not hold Thomson Mason in any way responsible. This was the famous act which reduced the salaries of the clergy and brought on a controversy between them and the Assembly and vestries which had far-reaching consequences. Bishop Meade speaks of this Option Law, or Two-penny Act, as it was called, as " a deep stain on the legislature of that day."[2] A second session of this Assembly was held in November, when the act was passed for defending the frontiers. And on the 22d of February, 1759, this Assembly held its third session.

It is on this occasion that George Mason's name is first met with in the journals of the burgesses. He may, however, have been in the Assembly earlier. It is impossible to obtain a complete list of the burgesses in Virginia previous to the Revolution. He represented Fairfax County, and apparently did not take his seat until March. On the 6th of this month he was added to the Committee of Privileges and Elections, and two days afterwards he was put on the Com-

[1] Journal of the Assembly.
[2] "Old Churches and Families of Virginia," vol. i., p. 225.

mittee of Propositions and Grievances. The House at this time had quite an exciting affair on hand, Mr. Thomas Walker having to defend himself against charges brought by Thomas Johnson, a member of the burgesses, as to his contract with the government in 1757 to supply the troops with provisions. This was Dr. Thomas Walker of " Castle Hill," one of the eminent Virginians of his day, and a man of ability and integrity. The House took his part, and he was kept in office as Commissary-General of the Virginia troops ; " courted and caressed by the Assembly," complains the irate Mr. Johnson. When the latter was asked how he could be thus sustained if he had cheated the country, the reply was : " You know very little of the schemes, plots, and contrivances that are carried on in the House of Burgesses ; in short, one holds the lamb while another skins ; and it would surprise any man to see in what manner the country's money is squandered away, which I have used my utmost endeavours to prevent, in which I could never succeed but once, and that to a trifling amount." Further iniquities of the House are thus unfolded by this professed reformer of the Civil Service. He says, " that when the clerk's salary was proposed to be settled, Mr. Randolph [John], the clerk, got up, and walking through the Burgesses, gave a nod to his creatures on each side, who all followed him out of the House and promised to be for the largest sum proposed." All this matter is referred to the Committee of Privileges and Elections.

On the 14th of March the Committee of Propositions and Grievances made a report, and different petitions as to warehouses, the dissolution of vestries, establishment of ferries, and other subjects were considered, and it was ordered that bills be prepared by the committee in the several cases. A petition of the justices and others of the county of Fairfax was read and referred to the Committee of Propositions and Grievances. It was in opposition to a scheme for making the justices pay the twenty-two thousand pounds of tobacco levied by them on the inhabitants of the county for building a wharf at Alexandria. And no doubt George Mason saw this matter rightly adjudicated. The following day this same committee made several reports, and bills were ordered to be prepared for establishing towns, lessening the duty on slaves, regulating the fees of pilots, etc. On the 17th this committee made a report on various subjects, and the question of the wharf in Alexandria was disposed of. It was agreed " that the said wharf ought to be vested in trustees of the said town of Alexandria, and they be impowered to take wharfage, and out of the money arising thereby to pay the said Justices the moneys by them to be refunded, and to apply the over-plus towards keeping the said wharf in repair."

There were petitions and counter-petitions before the House on the subject of adding a part of Prince William County to the county of Fairfax, and otherwise altering the boundaries of these two counties and that of Loudoun. The treasurer's accounts were referred to a committee to examine into, and George Mason was one of their number. On the 3d of April the Committee of Propositions and Grievances administered a rebuke to Mr. Johnson by a resolve that his remarks were " false, scandalous, and malicious." But there was evidently a strong party behind him, as in the vote of the House on the resolution of censure it was agreed to by thirty-seven yeas against thirty-two nays. On the 10th of April the House resolved that two hundred out of the five hundred men to be raised for the protection of the frontiers should be employed as artificers, and joined to the regiment now in the pay of the colony ; and that an additional bounty of five pounds be paid to the persons who shall enlist in the said companies. George Mason was one of the committee appointed to prepare the necessary bills.[1] George Washington was also in the Assembly, for the first time, in February, 1759. And he received the thanks of this body for his services on the frontier. The excitement aroused in certain counties of the Northern Neck on the

[1] Journal of the Assembly, February, 1759.

question of their boundary lines must have communicated itself to the Assembly at this session. And though the journal does not give us any clew to Colonel Mason's views, it is evident, from a letter that has been preserved, written by Lord Fairfax to his cousin, George William Fairfax, of " Belvoir," that George Mason had been active in urging a project that did not commend itself to the Lord Proprietor. Colonel Mason must have met Lord Fairfax often at " Belvoir," and it is very probable he visited " Greenway Court " at one time, as in a recently published, undated letter from Lord Fairfax to Charles Lee of Alexandria, the writer says he had sent his correspondent some money due him by the hands of " Col. George Mason," who " will deliver the letter himself." [1] Lord Fairfax, a short time before the Assembly met, wrote as follows :

" February 16, 1759.

" DEAR GEORGE :

" Yours I this evening received and shall be very sorry if Mr. Mason should be able to carry a point so prejudicial to the three counties of Fairfax, Loudon, and Prince William. If the Lees and Custis should join in the affair I doubt they with the assistance of James River will carry it in the House of Assembly. I will therefore write to Col. Philip Lee and Col. Tayloe and try what we can do in the upper House." [2]

The Assembly passed an act for dividing the county of Prince William and forming the county of Fauquier. And probably this is what Lord Fairfax has reference to. There were five other sessions of this Assembly ; one more in 1759, three in 1760, and one in the spring of 1761, but it does not appear that George Mason attended any of them, or that he was a candidate for the next Assembly, which met in the fall of 1761. It would seem that this was his first and only experience of political life previous to the Revolution, and that it had not impressed him favorably. In the famous

[1] *Magazine of American History,* February, 1886.
[2] " The Fairfaxes of England and America," p. 111. E. D. Neill.

passage in his will, drawn up in 1773, Colonel Mason gives his own " experience in life," as that which led him to urge upon his sons " to prefer the happiness of independence and a private station to the troubles and vexation of public business." This contest with Lord Fairfax may have been one of these vexations. And the independent spirit of the future patriot, perhaps, felt too sensibly the irksomeness of constraints imposed upon the colonial burgess by the ever potent prerogative of the governor and council. These and other considerations may have combined to keep the scholarly country gentleman away from the halls of legislation in the busy little capitol of Williamsburg. It was no inconsiderable journey, at that time, either. We learn from an act passed by the Assembly a few years later, regulating the pay of the burgesses, that it took five days to go from Fairfax County to Williamsburg, and four days from Stafford County. And the candidate was put to no little trouble and expense in securing his election. Colonel Washington, who proposed himself to the electors of Frederick County in 1758, expended thirty-nine pounds and six shillings on the poll. As those were not the days of Local Option or High License, thirty-six gallons of wine, forty-three gallons of strong beer, and a hogshead and barrel of punch, were supplied to the enthusiastic constituency, and the candidate's personal friends had cider and dinner provided them.[1]

George Mason was for many years a member of the Board of Trustees of the town of Alexandria, having been first elected to this office at a meeting of the board in June, 1754, when a vacancy was created by the death of Philip Alexander. Colonel Mason was one of the first purchasers of lots when the town was laid out in 1749. It is probable that he built a house on the lot at the southwest corner of King and Fairfax streets, or one on the southwest corner of King and Royal streets, where he owned the quarter squares. The trustees began in the summer of 1754 to enforce the law which required those who had lots to build upon them or

[1] Sparks' " Washington," vol. ii., p. 297.

forfeit the property.   George Mason and George Mercer each bought one of these forfeited lots at this time.[1]

In 1761, we find Colonel Mason, with other members of the Ohio Company, writing to Governor Dinwiddie, then in London, asking his interest in securing their rights to the lands granted them.   This letter is dated the 9th of September, and is in these words :

" As we may expect a peace next winter, and have no doubt North America will be secured to the British government and liberty will then be granted to his Majesty's subjects in these colonies to settle on the lands on the Ohio, we the committee of the Ohio Company think it a proper time as soon as peace is concluded to apply for a grant of the lands intended us by his Majesty's instructions to Sir William Gooch, and have for that purpose sent over a petition to his Majesty and a large and full state of our case ; and have employed Mr. Charles Palmer, a man we are informed of great capacity and diligence, to solicit our cause, and to endeavor by all means to get us a patent in England.   He will be directed to apply to our members in London, for their advice and assistance ; and as no person knows the affair better than Mr. Dinwiddie, nor can it be imagined any of the Company have such an acquaintance or interest with persons in power, let us beg you will please to exert yourself in getting us a patent by natural bounds, on the best terms possible ; for rather than be remitted to the government here, who from jealousy or some other cause have ever endeavored to disappoint us in every design we could form to settle and improve the lands, we will agree to any reasonable consideration for such a deed from England.   But if this cannot be obtained that the most plain and positive instructions to the Governor of Virginia be procured on terms the most advantageous to the Company.

" We are, Sir, &c.

> JAMES SCOTT,
> J. MERCER,
> G. MASON,
> THOS. LUDWELL LEE,
> PHILIP LUDWELL LEE."[2]

---

[1] " Colonial Alexandria," chap. iv., v., by William F. Carne, Alexandria.

[2] " Plain Facts," etc., Philadelphia, 1781, p. 120.

The French war had interfered with the operations of the Ohio Company, and now their title was in dispute. They never succeeded in recovering their former prosperity, though the struggle was kept up until the Revolution altered the conditions of all parties.

In 1762, George Mason was to suffer that memorable loss in the lives of most men, the loss of a mother. Mrs. Mason died the 13th of November of this year, leaving a reputation among her connections and neighbors for great prudence and business capacity, united to the charms of an amiable, womanly character. "She was a good woman, a great woman, and a lovely woman," was said of her with the pardonable pride of affection by the Rev. John Moncure, her friend and connection, and for many years her pastor. She appointed Mr. Moncure her executor, in her will drawn up the 25th of August, 1760, to which was added a codicil in November, 1762. It was produced in court by "John Moncure, Clerk" on the 14th of December in the latter year. Mrs. Mason's will, which she drew up for herself, opens with the words:

"In the name of God. Amen. I, Ann Mason of the county of Stafford, in the colony of Virginia, being at present in perfect health and of sound mind and memory, have thought fit, before age or infirmities impair them, to make this my last will and testament, etc. My soul I leave to God who gave it hoping for remission of all my sins through the merits and mediation of my Redeemer Jesus Christ."

She gave to her son George Mason the "land lying on Goose Bay in Charles County in Maryland," and also nine slaves whose names are enumerated, also her "largest silver salver." To her son Thomson Mason she gave the following articles of plate: "My ring and castors, two salts, my soup spoons and all the rest of my silver spoons, large and small." She makes a bequest to one of her nephews, who must have been a favorite, leaving "to John Bronaugh the son of my sister Bronaugh of Fairfax County and his heirs forever five hundred acres of land lying in Loudon County." Mrs. Mason then directs that two negroes each be purchased for her grandchildren Samuel Selden and Mary Selden, and she gives to the latter a large bay mare to be kept for her use, and also some articles of household furniture and table linen. She gives Mary Selden "a small silver cann," and all the rest of her silver plate not before disposed of is to be divided between this grandson and granddaughter. But it is enjoined that her "two small silver dishes be kept in the same form they are without change or alteration." All the rest of the estate not required to pay debts or legacies is to devolve to Samuel and Mary Selden, and if these are not needed for the above purposes, all the "stock of horses, cattle, sheep, and hogs shall be equally divided" between these grandchildren, "and settled upon the lands where the negroes belonging to the said Samuel Selden and Mary Selden are respectively worked and kept for their use and benefit." The wives of her sons George and Thomson are each remembered by the bequest of a slave to be purchased for them severally. Mrs. Mason names her two sons with Mr. Moncure her executors. Hannah Hedgman and Helen Scott are two of the witnesses ; the latter was very probably the wife of the Rev. James Scott, who was a sister of Mrs. Moncure.

In a memorandum to her will Mrs. Mason makes the following disposition of her daughter's portrait :

" It is my will and desire that my cousin Frances Moncure, the wife of John Moncure, Clerk, take care of my daughter Mary Thompson Selden's picture now in my hall and give it to my grandson Samuel Selden when he comes of age, but if he should die before he becomes of age that then it be given to my granddaughter Mary Selden."

In the case of the death of the latter during her minority the portrait was to go to Col. George Mason. In the codicil to her will, Mrs. Mason makes it her "earnest request that the mulatto wench named Nan Old Gate," who had been "a useful slave in the family, may not be sold or exposed to hardship," and she wishes, if possible, that this old servant "may be allowed to live with my son George, who I hope will use her with humanity." No doubt she was well taken care of at "Gunston Hall" for the rest of her days. Mrs. Mason left some personal property to her grandsons George, William, and Thomson Mason, Jr., and to her granddaughter Ann Eilbeck Mason. Her personal estate was appraised in Fairfax County, January 10, 1763, and amongst the list of things is one boat at Occoquan, showing that she still retained the estate and ferry at "Woodbridge," or received the benefits of it, though it was her son's property. In 1760, the same year that Mrs. Mason made her will, the Rev. John Moncure made his. He had succeeded the Rev. Alexander Scott as rector of Overwharton parish in Stafford County. Mr. Moncure was a Scotchman by birth, though of Huguenot ancestry. He married Frances Brown, the daughter of Dr. Gustavus Brown, of Port Tobacco, Maryland, by his first wife, Frances Fowke. Dr. Brown styles himself in his will as "Laird of Wainside and House Byres and of Stone Middleton, Scotland, and of Rose and Rich Hills, Maryland." Mr. Moncure appointed as the guardian of his children "George Mason, Gentleman," of whom he speaks as "my good friend." And he mentions in his will a negro girl as having been presented to his daughter Frances by her "Godfather George Mason."[1] No letters of Colonel Mason written in 1762 or 1763 have been preserved, and there is nothing to witness of the grief that must have filled his life at the loss of his admirable mother.

In 1764 his good friend Mr. Moncure died, and Colonel Mason, as the guardian of the orphaned children, the trusted friend and relative of the bereaved family, made the necessary arrangements for the funeral, writing to Mrs. Moncure the following letter on the occasion :

[1] Data furnished by the late Richard Moncure Conway, Virginia.

6

GUNSTON, 12th March, 1764.

DEAR MADAM :

I have your letter by Peter yesterday, and the day before I had one from Mr. Scott, who sent up Gustin Brown on purpose with it. I entirely agree with Mr. Scott in preferring a funeral sermon at Aquia Church, without any invitation to the house. Mr. Moncure's character and general acquaintance will draw together much company, besides a great part of his parishioners, and I am sure you are not in a condition to bear such a scene ; and it would be very inconvenient for a number of people to come so far from church in the afternoon after the sermon. As Mr. Moncure did not desire to be buried in any particular place, and as it is usual to bury clergymen in their own churches, I think the corpse being deposited in the church where he so long preached is both decent and proper, and it is probable, could he have chosen himself, he would have preferred it. Mr. Scott writes to me that it is intended Mr. Green shall preach the funeral sermon on the 20th of this month, if fair ; if not, the next fair day ; and I shall write to Mr. Green to-morrow to that purpose, and inform him that you expect Mrs. Green and him at your house on the day before ; and if God grants me strength sufficient either to ride on horseback or in a chair, I will certainly attend to pay the last duty to the memory of my friend ; but I am really so weak at present that I can't walk without crutches and very little with them, and have never been out of the house but once or twice, and then, though I stayed but two or three minutes at a time, it gave me such a cold as greatly to increase my disorder. Mr. Green has lately been very sick, and was not able to attend his church yesterday, (which I did not know when I wrote to Mr. Scott ;) if he should not recover soon, so as to be able to come down, I will inform you or Mr. Scott in time, that some other clergyman may be applied to.

I beseech you, dear madam, not to give way to melancholy reflections, or to think that you are without friends. I know nobody that has reason to expect more, and those that will not be friends to you and your children now Mr. Moncure is gone were not friends to him when he was living, let their professions be what they would. If, therefore, you should find any such, you have no cause to lament the loss, for such friendship is not worth anybody's concern.

I am very glad to hear that Mr. Scott purposes to apply for Overwharton parish. It will be a great comfort to you and your sister to be so near one another, and I know the goodness of Mr. Scott's heart so well, that I am sure he will take a pleasure in doing you every good office in his power, and I had much rather he should succeed Mr. Moncure than any other person. I hope you will not impute my not visiting you to any coldness or disrespect. It gives me great concern that I am not able to see you. You may depend upon my coming down as soon as my disorder will permit, and I hope you know me too well to need any assurance that I shall gladly embrace all opportunities of testifying my regard to my deceased friend by doing every good office in my power to his family.

I am, with my wife's kindest respects and my own, dear madam,

Your most affectionate kinsman,
GEORGE MASON.[1]

It seems probable that Colonel Mason was suffering at that time from his lifelong enemy, the gout, from what he says of his health in this letter. He gives testimony in his own will, written nine years later, of the affection he had felt for good Mr. Moncure. He therein says: "I give to Mr. John Moncure a mourning ring of three guineas value which I desire him to wear in memory of my esteem for my much lamented friend his deceased father."

[1] Meade's "Old Churches and Families of Virginia," vol. ii., p. 201.

CHAPTER III.

"GUNSTON HALL" AND ITS NEIGHBORHOOD.

1745–1769–1772.

George Mason's early church associations must have been
with Overwharton parish and its two church buildings,
"Aquia" and "Old Potomac," as they were called. And
he may also have attended sometimes the ministry of the
Rev. James Scott, Dettingen parish, Prince William County.
This was the brother of the Rev. Alexander Scott, of Overwharton parish. His wife, as has been said, was one of Colonel
Mason's cousins, and a sister of Mrs. Moncure. He lived at
his glebe on Quantico Creek, and officiated also in two
churches, one at Broad Run and one near Dumfries.

We first hear of George Mason in connection with parish
affairs in 1749 when at twenty-four, in the year previous to
his marriage, he was elected vestryman of Truro parish,
Pohick church, in Fairfax County. There was some objection to him then, it was said on the ground that "he did not
reside in the parish, but this was overlooked."[1] He was
probably living with his mother at "Chappawamsic." The
Rev. Charles Green was at this time the rector of Pohick
church. Mr. Green was succeeded in Truro parish by the
Rev. Lee Massey, whose third wife, Miss Bronaugh, was also
a cousin of Colonel Mason's. The ministry of the former
incumbent had lasted until 1765, and a list of the vestry-
men of the parish was preserved by Washington, with the
number of votes given for each one.[2] George Mason heads

[1] Meade's "Old Churches and Families of Virginia," vol. ii., appendix xx.

[2] Sparks' "Life of Washington," appendix iv. At an earlier election in this
same year Colonel Mason received 210 votes.

the list of twelve members, with two hundred and eighty-two votes, while Washington comes third on the list with two hundred and fifty-nine votes. Daniel McCarty and George William Fairfax were also among the vestry of this year. Washington was in this same year elected vestryman for Fairfax parish, Alexandria. One of the old churches of Overwharton parish, Potomac church, half-way between Aquia Creek and Fredericksburg, was visited by Benson J. Lossing in 1850, and it was then almost a ruin.[1] He describes it as "more than half concealed by a thicket of trees, dwarf cedars, and brambles. The windows were now gone, so also were the pews and the pulpit. The roof, which was supported by columns painted in imitation of variegated marbles, had partly fallen in, but the Law, the Creed, and the Prayer upon its walls seemed almost as fresh as when the old Virginians worshipped there."

Aquia church, which is not far from the former, when visited by Bishop Meade in 1837, is thus described[2]: "The church had a noble exterior, being a high two-story house, of the figure of the cross. On its top was an observatory, which you reached by a flight of stairs leading from the gallery, and from which the Potomac and Rappahannock rivers, which are not far distant from each other, and much of the surrounding country, might be seen." The names of the rector, the Rev. John Moncure, and his vestry for the year 1757, are still to be seen painted on the panels of the gallery. The vestry included John Mercer, of Marlboro', John Lee, William Mountjoy, Thomas and John Fitzhugh, Peter Daniel, and Travers Cooke. Mrs. Wood, a daughter of the Rev. Mr. Moncure, in her account of her parents, contributed to Bishop Meade's chronicles, tells of the experiences of the young couple in their country parish where they lived their early married life in quite Arcadian simplicity and bliss. During their first year in the parish,

[1] *Potter's American Monthly*, March, 1875: "The Historic Buildings of America."

[2] "Old Churches and Families of Virginia," vol. ii., p. 203.

which was some time earlier than 1750, when Mr. Moncure officiated at the marriage of George Mason, they knew few persons, though the Masons doubtless had not neglected them. But soon after, adds Mrs. Wood, " the neighboring gentry found out the value of their minister and his wife, and contended for their society by soliciting visits and making them presents of many comforts. Frequently these grandees would come in their splendid equipages to spend a day at the glebe, and bring everything requisite to prevent trouble or expense to its owners—merely for the enjoyment of the society of the humble inhabitants of this humble dwelling. In the lapse of a few years, by frugality and industry in the management of a good salary, these dear parents became quite easy in their circumstances. My father purchased a large tract of land on the river Potomac. He settled this principally by tenants, but on the most beautiful eminence that I ever beheld he built a good house, and soon improved it into a very sweet establishment." [1] Mrs. Wood goes on to describe the happy life of the good pastor and his family, which came to an end at last by the death of the former in 1764. The Overwharton parish register records the circumstance that George Mason was godfather to three of Mr. Moncure's children : Frances, who was baptized in September, 1745 ; and Ann,—Mary Mason, his sister, being one of the godmothers—and lastly John, the second son, who was baptized in 1747. Frances married Travers Daniel and Ann married Walker Conway. [2] Aquia church is in good repair at the present day, and many of the descendants of its old rector still worship there.

Before proceeding in the chronological survey of Colonel Mason's life, it may be interesting to give some further account of the neighborhood in which he lived, that we may picture, as far as possible, his social environment, and ascertain the names, if nothing more, of his immediate friends and associates. And materials are not wanting for a sketch

[1] *Ibid.,* vol. ii., p. 201.

[2] Ancestors of Moncure Daniel Conway.

of his country home and the plantation life of which it was the centre, in the papers of his son, General John Mason. The James River and its ancient, historic seats, " Shirley," " Westover," " Berkeley," and " Brandon," and the many others which the annals of an earlier day celebrate as abodes of colonial wealth and hospitality, is better known to us, perhaps, in our visions of pre-Revolutionary Virginia than that other and northernmost of the four great Virginia rivers, the broad Potomac. Yet the latter, associated as it is with Washington and the Lees, and preserving on its banks " Stratford," if " Chantilly " is no longer standing, and " Mount Vernon," if the birth-place of Washington at the junction of Pope's Creek and the Potomac has long since disappeared, is scarcely behind the older locality in objects of Revolutionary and colonial interest. And in our own day the Potomac has gained a new title to our veneration in its memories of Robert E. Lee, whose home and birthplace were both on its borders. But the names of neither Washington, Lee, nor Mason are found to-day in the old mansions that once were theirs. And though " Gunston Hall " still stands on its high banks much the same as it was a hundred years ago, with a few exceptions, the old places that made up its neighborhood have now either gone to decay or entirely disappeared.

An Englishman travelling in America at the close of the Revolution took note of the gentlemen who were then living on the Virginia side of the Potomac, not far from Alexandria or Belhaven, as it was once called: " Mr. Alexander, General Washington, Colonel Martin, Colonel Fairfax, Mr. Lawson, near the mouth of Oquaquon; Colonel Mason, Mr. Lee, near the mouth of Quantico; Mr. Brent (house burnt by the enemy during the war), Mr. Mercer, Mr. Fitzhugh, Mr. Alexander, of Boyd Hole and all Chotank; Colonel Frank Thornton, on Marchodock; Mr. Thacker Washington, Mrs. Blair, Mr. McCarty, Col. Phil. Lee, of Nominey." Our traveller grows eloquent over the beauties of the scenery, and says of the Potomac it " is certainly the most noble, excellent and beautiful river I ever saw, indeed it can be excelled by no other river in the universe." And he adds: "The situations and gentlemen's seats on this river are beyond comparison or description beautiful."[1] A neighborhood very much the same as this one is described in the recollections of Judge Daniel whose fathers lived in the Stafford of George Mason's ancestry. And it will be observed how the same families were found for generations in the same spot, as in England. Raleigh Travers, from whom the Colonel Mason of 1715 bought some of his land, was Judge Daniel's great-grandfather. He was said to be of the same family as Sir Walter Raleigh. One of the largest landed proprietors in Stafford, and a prominent planter and burgess of his day, he married the half-sister of Mary Ball, the mother of Washington. One of his daughters, Elizabeth, married Sir John Cooke, an Irish baronet; the other, Sarah, married Colonel Peter Daniel, of the "Crow's Nest," two or three miles from John Mercer of Marlboro'. Travers Daniel, who married Frances Moncure, was the only son of Colonel Peter Daniel. The nearest neighbors to Travers Daniel after John Mercer (whose son, the future governor of Maryland, lived at "Marlboro'" in Judge Daniel's boyhood), to name only those most prominent, were John Hedgman, Thomas, William, and John Mountjoy, one of whose places went later into the Brooke family. The glebe of the Rev. Robert Buchan was not far off, and adjoining it, in the immediate vicinity of the church, was "Berry Hill," the residence of Colonel Thomas Ludwell Lee. He possessed another plantation on the opposite side of Potomac Creek called "Bellevue." One of his daughters married Daniel Carroll Brent, of "Richland," in Stafford County. After passing "Berry Hill," and crossing Potomac Creek, adds Judge Daniel, you came to the plantations of John, James, and Thomas Fitzhugh, the latter living at "Boscobel." Major Henry Fitzhugh resided near, at "Belle Air." Then came Samuel Selden, of "Salvington," who had married

[1] Smyth's "Tour in the United States," vol. ii., p. 144.

as his second wife Ann Mercer, and lastly "Belle Plaine," the estate of Gaury Waugh, and after his death, of his sons George Lee Waugh and Robert Waugh. All these places were in a "space of some eight or ten square miles."[1] Most of these families were connected by marriages between their members in successive generations.

Very much the same circle of neighbors is to be met with, though our glance extends beyond it into Westmoreland, lower down the Potomac, as we read the "Journal" written by a young daughter of the Lees, who visited about among these country-seats soon after the Revolution.[2] She has something to tell us of "Belleview" and "Berry Hill" as well as of "Stratford" and "Chantilly," the latter place made gay at that time by the fair daughters of Richard Henry Lee, one of whom had recently married Corbin Washington. The diary, a girlish chronicle of country merry-making, was meant only for the eyes of the writer's bosom friend—a daughter of Daniel Brent, of "Richland." The writer, while staying at "Bellevue," meets at church, old Aquia church, no doubt, "Mrs. Brook, Mrs. Selden, and Nancy," who are very civil to her and press her to dine at "Salvington." This "Nancy" was Ann Mercer Selden, who married John T. Brooke, of Stafford County, a twin brother of Judge Brooke, of Fredericksburg. Mrs. William Fitzhugh, of "Chatham," invites our young lady to go from there to the races with her. William Fitzhugh, the grandfather of Mrs. General Robert E. Lee, lived later at "Ravensworth," in Fairfax County. While in Westmoreland, "Bushfield" is visited, the home of John Augustine Washington, one of General Washington's brothers. His daughter, "Milly," then a young belle, marries later Thomas Lee, a son of Richard Henry Lee. One day they dine at "Lee Hall," the whole pleasure-loving party, whose vivacious life is photographed in the little volume under review. At "Lee Hall" lived Richard Lee, the uncle of "Light-Horse Harry," whose

[1] "Old Churches and Families of Virginia," vol. ii., p. 204.
[2] "Journal of a Young Lady of Virginia," Baltimore, 1871.

father's place, "Leesylvania," was also on the Potomac, a
few miles above Dumfries. "Blenheim," the home of William Washington, one of General Washington's nephews, is
included in this catalogue of country-seats, with "Menokin"
(Manokin), on the Rappahannock, the residence of Francis
Lightfoot Lee; "Marmion," one of the McCarty places,
and "Peccatone," the home of the Turbervilles. Other
country-seats in the Northern Neck were "Nomini," on
the Potomac, below "Stratford," the residence of Robert
Carter, called Counsellor Carter; and on the Rappahannock,
"Sabine Hall," the home of Landon Carter; "Mount Airy,"
the Tayloe place; "Port Tobago," which was part of the
large tract of land patented by the gallant Sir Thomas
Lunsford, and which came into the Lomax family through
the marriage of Elizabeth Wormeley, daughter of Catherine
Lunsford to John Lomax; "Blandfield," the Beverley place,
and "Rosegill," the seat of the Wormeleys. Robert Carter
owned land also in Prince William County, as did Colonel
John Tayloe, who was also a member of the council, and
these were both friends and correspondents of George
Mason. In the sketch of his grandfather by Benjamin
Ogle Tayloe, mention is made of the fashionable race meet.
ings in Alexandria between 1750 and 1770. Colonel Byrd,
of "Westover," was with Colonel Tayloe at the head of the
turf in Virginia. Colonel Tasker, of Maryland, son of President Tasker, with his famous "Selima," beat them both, how.
ever, in 1752, but a few years later Colonel Tayloe's "Yorick"
was not to be excelled.[1]

One receives the impression in reading of colonial Virginia
that all the world lived in country-houses, on the banks of
rivers. And the Virginia world did live very much in this
way. In Smyth's enumeration of gentlemen's seats on the
Potomac, it will be noticed that Mr. Alexander is named as
of "Boyd Hole and all Chotank." Elsewhere Smyth says:
"After we had passed this noble river [the Potomac] we en.

[1] "In Memoriam Benjamin Ogle Tayloe," Washington, 1872. (Privately
printed.)

tered one of the most agreeable as well as respectable settle_
ments in Virginia, named Chotank." And he goes on to
tell us that George Washington, of whom by the way as a
loyal Briton he has a very poor opinion, was born in Cho_
tank. In General Washington's will he leaves certain sou_
venirs "to the acquaintances and friends" of his "juvenile
years," Lawrence and Robert Washington of Chotank. The
original estate that went by this name had belonged to the
Withers family and was devised by will in 1698 to one of the
name in England, William Withers, private secretary to Gov_
ernor Dinwiddie. He came to Virginia in 1754 to find that
Chotank had been sold by the daughter of John Withers,
from whom he should have inherited it, to Augustine Wash_
ington and been left by him to his son Samuel. A lawsuit of
course followed, which resulted in the Washingtons retaining
Chotank after paying a considerable sum to William With_
ers.[1] The name Chotank, however, came to be applied to a
whole neighborhood, though it is used here also at different
periods in a somewhat elastic sense. George Fitzhugh, writing of Chotank in 1861 says : " The neighborhood lies on the
Potomac and takes its name from a little creek of some two
miles in length. When we first remember the place the
creek and all its tributaries were included within the farms
of Richard Stuart of ' Cedar Grove,' Needham L. Washington of ' Waterloo,' and Henry Fitzhugh of ' Bedford.' "

But Chotank in its larger signification embraced, according
to Fitzhugh, all " the country on the Virginia side of the
Potomac, beginning ten miles below Chotank Creek, and
extending up the river about forty miles to Occoquhan
Creek, and out from the river a distance about five miles."[2]
It was, adds this writer, the tract of a hundred thousand
acres settled by the cavaliers of 1651, the right to and rents
of which William Fitzhugh wished to buy out from Lord
Fairfax. The opposite shore of Maryland was also, by courtesy, included in Chotank, the river in those earlier years

[1] " Dinwiddie Papers," vol. i., p. 441. Note by the Editor.
[2] *DeBow's Review*, vol. xxx., p. 77.

uniting instead of separating the two colonies. This fellow ship between the borderers on both shores of the Potomac reached down into Colonel Mason's day, marriages being common, as Fitzhugh notes, between the two communities. And it is observable that both George and Thomson Mason married Maryland wives. George Fitzhugh, himself a " Chotanker," as he boasted, writes of the people of this section that they preserved unimpaired, in his day, the characteristics of their progenitors: " They are the same people in disposition, manners, temper, and blood, that they were two hundred years ago." Mrs. George N. Grymes, a granddaughter of George Mason, and Daingerfield Lewis of " Marmion," a nephew of Washington, were two of the oldest living Chotankers in 1861. And the Alexanders were represented there by Gustavus B. Alexander who lived at " Caledon " on the Potomac River near Chotank Creek, on land belonging to them from the earliest settlement of the country. Dr. Abram Barnes Hooe belonged at this time to Chotank, and several branches of the Washington family had lived there, among whom, at the time of the Revolution, was Samuel Washington, a brother of George Washington.

The ancestors of Colonel William Washington of the Revolution, so famous in the Southern campaign, lived at " Hilton " on Chotank Creek. Bailie Washington, his father, was a friend of Thomson Mason's, and named by him one of the executors of his will. Among those who came to Chotank after the earliest settlement, Fitzhugh names the Masseys, a Huguenot family, and still later the Grymes and Lewis families. Lawrence Lewis, a nephew of Washington's lived at " Woodlawn," a few miles from " Mount Vernon," and the house, though it has passed into the hands of strangers, still remains a landmark of the olden time. The Stuarts, a Jacobite family, who followed the elder Pretender, fled from Scotland to Chotank in 1715. Dr. David Stuart of " Hope Park " and " Ossian Hall " married the widow Custis, daughter-in-law of Mrs. Washington. Other families in Fairfax County were the Fairfaxes at " Belvoir," the Chichesters at "Newington," and the Wests. Hugh West is enumerated with the Alexanders, Fairfaxes, and Lawrence Washington in the act incorporating Alexandria in 1748, and the town was built on land of Hugh West and John and Philip Alexander. One family of the Wests in Virginia is descended from a brother of Lord Delaware whose family name it was. Among the Fitzhughs who lived in this neighborhood in George Mason's day, was his cousin Col. William Fitzhugh, a son of George Fitzhugh and Mary Mason. Col. William Fitzhugh married Martha Lee, and left but one son, George Lee Fitzhugh. Colonel Fitzhugh was an officer in the French and Indian war, and removed before the Revolution to Maryland, where he had a beautiful estate, "Rousby Hall," in Calvert County. He was a friend and correspondent of General Washington. And he was probably a frequent visitor at "Gunston Hall." Another neighbor and friend of Colonel Mason's was Colonel Blackburn of "Rippon Lodge," near Dumfries. He married a cousin of George Mason, a daughter of the Rev. James Scott, pastor of the church in Prince William. One of his daughters became the wife of Bushrod Washington.

On the James, the Appomattox, the Rappahannock, and the Potomac, with their creeks and bays, clustered these early Virginians, at a period when, as has been said, the rivers were Virginia's highways, like the canals of Venice. Of the region which has been described as "Chotank" an enthusiastic visitor there published his "recollections" in 1834, in the time-honored *Gazette* of Alexandria. The writer begins by wishing the land "from the Pasbytansy swells to the Neck levels," peace in all its borders. He recalls the happy days and nights spent among "the hills and flats, the forests and swamps of old Chotank—the ardent fox-hunt with whoop and hallo and winding horn," the houses with their cool porticos shaded by the Lombardy poplar, "the proper tree, let them say what they will, to surround a gentleman's mansion," with its old-fashioned stateliness and grace. The breeze on the height, the white sails of the vessels seen through the trees on the bank, to be traced up and down as far as the eye can reach, the "slopes of the fields in Maryland cultivated to the water's edge, fill up a picture surpassingly beautiful" These recollections go back fifteen or twenty years, but even in 1834 a change had come to Chotank, according to this writer: "The ancient seats of generous hospitality are still there, but their former possessors, so free of heart, so liberal, and blessed with all the means of being free and liberal, where are they?"[1] Yet, though times had changed somewhat, the sons of the old magnates still lived, for the most part, on their fathers' lands, and the "merry Chotankers" led scarcely less easy, hospitable lives than in the earlier days. Down to George Fitzhugh's time in 1861, before the great cataclysm of the War between the States, with its radical results to the South in breaking up the foundations of its old social system, Virginia and Chotank remained indeed, in all essentials, much the same as of yore.

The recollections of George Mason's son, General John Mason, written in old age, preserve some account of the "Gunston Hall" neighborhood as it was in his boyhood and youth, and give us welcome glimpses into the patriot's household. He describes "Gunston Hall" as situated "about four miles from the great public road from North to South, by which all communication in those days from North to South, or one end of the Union to the other, was held; for there was no western country in those days, and no steamboats. At that time all the best families of the State were located on the tide-waters of the rivers. Great hospitality reigned everywhere, and besides the social and friendly intercourse of the immediate neighborhood, the habit was for families who were connected or on friendly terms to visit each other and spend several days or weeks at the respective mansions, in a circuit of fifty or a hundred miles. And, moreover, it was the habit for travellers of distinction to call and pass a night or several days at the houses of the Virginia gentlemen

---

[1] *Southern Literary Messenger*, vol. i., p. 43.

near the public roads. And during the Revolutionary war particularly, the officers of the different army corps passing from North to South, knowing how welcome they would always be, very often took up their quarters at these houses for a night at least and sometimes for some days. From my earliest days I saw all these visitors at my father's house. His neighborhood was an excellent one in those times, and he was, as I can affirm with truth, greatly beloved and admired by it.

"Our nearest neighbor was Mr. Cockburn, living within one mile. He was an English gentleman from Jamaica, who had settled here to enjoy life, and had married a Miss Bronaugh, a relation of my father's (before my memory). He was an excellent man, of some singular traits too. And his wife, with fine talents, was one of the best women and the most notable housekeeper in the world. They made a part of our family, and the children of our family—they had no children—made a part of theirs by the most intimate and constant intercourse. The household establishment at my father's was conducted with great regularity and system, and I believe though large and expensive, [here the pencilled manuscript is illegible,] of my revered parents while my mother lived. After her death, my sisters being young and housekeepers employed, the interior [establishment] I presume was not conducted with so much regularity. My father being an active politician and decided in his opposition to the measures of the mother country, his house was frequented by the leading men of the State. Among the first things I can remember were discussions and conversations upon the high-handed, tyrannical conduct of the king towards his colonial subjects in this country; for in those days the government was designated by the name of the king in all conversations. And so universal was the idea that it was treason and death to speak ill of the king that I even now remember a scene in the garden at Springfield [the Cockburn place] when my father's family were spending the day there on a certain Sunday when I must have been very small. Several of the children having collected in the garden, after hearing in the house among our elders many complaints and distressing forebodings as to this oppressive course towards our country, we were talking the matter over in our own way and I *cursed the king*, but immediately begged and obtained the promise of the others not to tell on me." This little incident gives one a graphic impression of the power the monarchical idea must have had over our forefathers—as indeed it was then dominant throughout the civilized world—when a little child could be thus afraid of committing high treason !

It is related of Martin Cockburn, George Mason's friend and neighbor, that it was while travelling in this country, a youth of eighteen, with his father that he met Miss Bronaugh and fell in love with her. His father promised that if he would wait until he was of age he should have his bride. The three years of probation over, the lover returned to claim the lady, but finding that she could not be prevailed on to go so far from her family as the West Indies, he pur- chased a place near her relatives in Virginia, where he and his wife lived in the quiet enjoyment of rural life to an ad- vanced age. The Rev. Lee Massey, his brother-in-law, said of Mr. Cockburn and his wife that they were the only couple he believed who had lived fifty years together without a moment's disturbance of their domestic harmony, so entire was their mutual affection. Martin Cockburn was a fine scholar, as well as a courteous and amiable gentleman, and no doubt was a most congenial neighbor to the studious planter at Gunston. It will be seen that on the questions at issue with the mother country their sympathy was complete. It was a nephew of Martin Cockburn who, as an admiral in the British navy, led the fleet of England against America in the war of 1812. But to return from this digression to the Mason manuscript :

" There being but few public schools in the country in those days, my father, as was the case with most of the gentlemen of landed estates in Virginia, kept a private tutor for the education of his family. And the Revolutionary war occurring, and all of the tide-water country of that State being invaded, harassed, and plundered from time to time by the enemy, while most of the children of this family were yet under age, it made it very difficult to arrange for their education. I believe none of them were sent from home for that purpose but myself and my brother Thomas, who, being the youngest sons, were approaching to manhood about the conclusion of that war. We were both sent about that time to an academy in Stafford County, Virginia, kept by the Rev. Mr. Buchan, a Scotchman by birth, then the rector of two adjoining parishes in Stafford, one of which was in the lower part of the county on Potomac Creek [Potomac church] and the other in the upper part of the county on Aquia Creek [Aquia church], at which he preached on alternate Sundays. He enjoyed in the right of his curacy and lived on the glebe of the lower parish. There the academy was kept. He was a pious man and a profound classical scholar. We remained with him about two years. I was then sent to a Mr. Hunter, a Scotchman also, and quite a recluse, who kept a small school in a retired place in Calvert County, Maryland. I was sent there to study mathematics, in which Mr. Hunter was well versed. I remained something less than a year at this school. Thomas was about the same time removed to an academy in Fredericksburg, Virginia, where he remained about two years. The private tutors in my father's family, as far back as I can remember, were first a Mr. McPherson, of Maryland, next a Mr. Davidson, and then a Mr. Constable, of Scotland. Both of the two last were especially engaged in that country to come to America (as was the practice in those times with families who had means) by my father to live in his house and educate the children. I remember that I was so small when the first of these three gentlemen took charge of the school that I was permitted to be rather an occasional visitor than a regular attendant. The tutoress of my sisters was a Mrs. Newman. She remained in the family for some time."

Another unfinished manuscript of General Mason's preserves for us some details of the plantation life at "Gunston Hall," with a brief description of the house and grounds:

" Gunston Hall is situated on a height on the right bank of the Potomac river within a short walk of the shores, and commanding a full view of it, about five miles above the mouth of that branch of it on the same side called the Occoquan. When I can first remember it, it was in a state of high improvement and carefully kept. The south front looked to the river ; from an elevated little portico on this front you descended directly into an extensive garden, touching the house on one side and reduced from the natural irregularity of the hill top to a perfect level platform, the southern extremity of which was bounded by a spacious walk running eastwardly and westwardly, from which there was by the natural and sudden declivity of the hill a rapid descent to the plain considerably below it. On this plain adjoining the margin of the hill, opposite to and in full view from the garden, was a deer park, studded with trees, kept well fenced and stocked with native deer domesticated. On the north front by which was the principal approach, was an extensive lawn kept closely pastured, through the midst of which led a spacious avenue, girded by long double ranges of that hardy and stately cherry tree, the common black heart, raised from the stone, and so the more fair and uniform in their growth, commencing at about two hundred feet from the house and extending thence for about twelve hundred feet ; the carriage way being in the centre and the footways on either side, between the two rows, forming each double range of trees, and under their shade.

" But what was remarkable and most imposing in this avenue was that the four rows of trees being to be so alligned as to counteract that deception in our vision which, in looking down long parallel lines makes them seem to approach as they recede ; advantage was taken of the circumstance and another very pleasant delusion was effected. A common centre was established exactly in the middle of the outer doorway of the mansion, on that front, from which were made to diverge at a certain angle the four lines on which these trees were planted, the plantation not commencing but at a considerable distance therefrom (about two hundred feet as before mentioned) and so carefully and accurately had they been planted, and trained and dressed in accordance each with the others, as they progressed in their growth, that from the point described as taken for the common centre, and when they had got to a great size, only the first four trees were visible. More than once have I known my father, under whose special care this singular and beautiful display of trees had been arranged and preserved, and who set great value on them, amuse his friends by inviting some gentleman or lady (who visiting Gunston for the first time, may have happened to arrive after night, or may have come by the way of the river and entered by the other front, and so not have seen the avenue) to the north front to see the grounds, and then by placing them exactly in the middle of the doorway and asking 'how many trees do you see before you?' 'four' would necessarily be the answer because the fact was that those at the end of the four rows next the house completely, and especially when in full leaf, concealed from that view, body and top, all the others, though more than fifty in each row. Then came the request, 'Be good enough to place yourself now close to either side of the doorway, and then tell us how many you see?' The answer would now be with delight and surprise, but as necessarily, 'A great number, and to a vast extent, but how many it is impossible to say!' And in truth to the eye placed at only about two feet to the right or left of the first position, there were presented, as if by magic, four long, and apparently close walls of wood made up of the bodies of the trees, and above, as many of rich foliage constituted by their boughs stretching, as seemed to an immeasurable distance.

"To the west of the main building were first the school-house, and then at a little distance, masked by a row of large English walnut trees, were the stables. To the east was a high paled yard, adjoining the house, into which opened an outer door from the private front, within, or connected with which yard, were the kitchen, well, poultry houses, and other domestic arrangements ; and beyond it on the same side, were the corn house and granary, servants houses (in those days called negro quarters) hay yard and cattle pens, all of which were masked by rows of large cherry and mulberry trees. And adjoining the enclosed grounds on which stood the mansion and all these appendages on the eastern side was an extensive pasture for stock of all kinds running down to the river, through which led the road to the Landing, emphatically so called, where all persons or things water borne, were landed or taken off, and where were kept the boats, pettiangers and canoes of which there were always several for business transportation, fishing and hunting belonging to the establishment. Farther north and on the same side was an extensive orchard of fine fruit trees of a variety of kinds. Beyond this was a small and highly fenced pasture devoted to a single brood horse. The occupant in my early days was named Vulcan, of the best stock in the country and a direct descendant of the celebrated Old James.[1] The west side of the lawn or enclosed grounds was skirted by a wood, just far enough within which to be out of sight, was a little village called Log-Town, so-called because most of the houses were built of hewn pine logs. Here lived several families of the slaves serving about the mansion house ; among them were my father's body-servant James, a mulatto man and his family, and those of several negro carpenters.

"The heights on which the mansion house stood extended in an east and west direction across an isthmus and were at the northern extremity of the estate to which it belonged. This contained something more than five thousand acres, and was called Dogue's Neck (I believe after the tribe of Indians which had inhabited this and the neighboring country), water-locked by the Potomac on the south, the Occoquan on the west, and Pohick Creek (a bold and navigable branch of the Potomac) on the east, and again by Holt's Creek, a branch of the Occoquan, that stretches for some distance across from that river in an easterly direction. The isthmus on the northern boundary is narrow and the whole estate was kept completely enclosed by a fence on that side of about one mile in length running from the head of Holt's to the margin of Pohick Creek. This fence was maintained with great care and in good repair in my father's time, in order to secure to his own stock the exclusive range within it, and made of uncommon height, to keep in the native deer which had been preserved there in abundance from the first settlement of the country and indeed are yet there [1832] in considerable numbers. The land south of the heights and comprising more than nine tenths of the estate was an uniform level elevated some twenty

[1] Perhaps this is meant for "Old Janus" an imported horse, described in the *Am. Turf Register* and owned by a gentleman in North Carolina at the time of his death.

feet above the surface of the river, with the exception of one ex-tensive marsh and three or four water courses, which were accom-panied by some ravines and undulations of minor character—and about two thirds of it were yet clothed with the primitive wood ; the whole of this level tract was embraced in one view from the mansion house. In different parts of this tract and detached from each other, my father worked four plantations with his own slaves, each under an overseer ; and containing four or five hundred acres of open land. The crops were principally Indian corn and tobacco ; the corn for the support of the plantations and the home house, and the tobacco for sale. There was but little small grain made in that part of the country in those days. He had also another plantation worked in the same manner, on an estate he had in Charles County, Maryland, on the Potomac about twenty miles lower down, at a place called Stump Neck.

" It was very much the practise with gentlemen of landed and slave estates in the interior of Virginia, so to organize them as to have considerable resources within themselves ; to employ and pay but few tradesmen and to buy little or none of the coarse stuffs and materials used by them, and this practise became stronger and more general during the long period of the Revolutionary War which in great measure cut off the means of supply from elsewhere. Thus my father had among his slaves carpenters, coopers, sawyers, blacksmiths, tanners, curriers, shoemakers, spinners, weavers and knitters, and even a distiller. His woods furnished timber and plank for the carpenters and coopers, and charcoal for the blacksmith ; his cattle killed for his own con-sumption and for sale supplied skins for the tanners, curriers and shoemakers, and his sheep gave wool and his fields produced cot-ton and flax for the weavers and spinners, and his orchards fruit for the distiller. His carpenters and sawyers built and kept in repair all the dwelling-houses, barns, stables, ploughs, harrows, gates &c., on the plantations and the outhouses at the home house. His coopers made the hogsheads the tobacco was prized in and the tight casks to hold the cider and other liquors. The tanners and curriers with the proper vats &c., tanned and dressed the skins as well for upper as for lower leather to the full amount of the consumption of the estate, and the shoemakers made them into shoes for the negroes. A professed shoemaker was hired for three or four months in the year to come and make up the shoes for the white part of the family. The blacksmiths did all the iron work required by the establishment, as making and re-pairing ploughs, harrows, teeth chains, bolts &c., &c. The spin-ners, weavers and knitters made all the coarse cloths and stockings used by the negroes, and some of finer texture worn by the white family, nearly all worn by the children of it. The distiller made every fall a good deal of apple, peach and persimmon brandy. The art of distilling from grain was not then among us, and but few public distilleries. All these operations were carried on at the home house, and their results distributed as occasion required to the different plantations. Moreover all the beeves and hogs for consumption or sale were driven up and slaughtered there at the proper seasons, and whatever was to be preserved was salted and packed away for after distribution.

"My father kept no steward or clerk about him. He kept his own books and superintended, with the assistance of a trusty slave or two, and occasionally of some of his sons, all the operations at or about the home house above described ; except that during the Revolutionary War and when it was necessary to do a great deal in that way to clothe all his slaves, he had in his service a white man, a weaver of the finer stuffs, to weave himself and superin-tend the black weavers, and a white woman to superintend the negro spinning-women. To carry on these operations to the ex-tent required, it will be seen that a considerable force was neces-sary, besides the house servants, who for such a household, a large family and entertaining a great deal of company, must be numerous—and such a force was constantly kept there, inde-pendently of any of the plantations, and besides occasional drafts from them of labor for particular occasions. As I had during my youth constant intercourse with all these people, I remember them all and their several employments, as if it was yesterday. As it will convey a better idea of the state of the family and the habits of the times, I will describe them all."[1]

Unfortunately the manuscript ends abruptly just at this point. "Gunston Hall," as has been said, was about four miles

[1] There are said to have been five hundred persons on the estate, including the several quarters. And Colonel Mason is reported to have shipped from his own wharf at one time twenty-three thousand bushels of wheat.

from the stage road, the public route between Richmond and Philadelphia. The old Virginia almanacs give the distances between the several stopping-places, towns and taverns, on the way. Dumfries and Colchester were both on this road, and the distance between them was eighteen miles, while from Colchester to Alexandria the distance was twelve miles. Dumfries received its Scotch name from its principal settlers, the Scotch merchants who made it the thriving little place that it long remained. Doubtless among them were some of the merchants of this nationality who had acknowledged their obligations to the County Lieutenant of Stafford, Col. George Mason of 1720. Large vessels came to the wharfs of Dumfries with the luxuries of other lands, for which they received in return Virginia tobacco. The latter was sent in such quantities, we are told, that one merchant alone in Dumfries, the agent for the firm of Morris & Nicholson, Philadelphia, built three large warehouses to contain his purchases.[1] This was Richard Graham who became a large landed proprietor in Virginia, Kentucky, and Ohio. His eldest son, George Graham, a lawyer in Dumfries, married the widow of George Mason of " Lexington," Colonel Mason's eldest son. Thomson Mason practised law in Dumfries for some years, as did also his son Stevens Thomson Mason. But while merchants and lawyers are to be in some degree associated with town life, even with them the plantation was usually the home, and the town was resorted to for business purposes only. With the planter, as can be readily understood, there was little occasion for leaving his estates when, as was the case at " Gunston Hall," the slaves were taught all needful trades, and the master's wines and broadcloth were imported from abroad with the silk dresses and jewels of the mistress. George Mason in his peninsula principality was a fair type of his class in colonial Virginia. With his village of negro artisans, his flocks and herds and broad, teeming fields, he led a busy life. And his wife with her spinning-women, knitters, and weavers,—and the domestic

[1] *Alexandria Gazette*, Sept. 22, 1879. Article on " Old Families," etc.

cares of the plantation,—must have fully shared his responsibilities.

It is difficult too, at this day, to realize the caste feeling that then prevailed, separating the rich white proprietor from his poor white neighbor. The Rev. Devereux Jarratt, who was born in Virginia in 1732, and was the son of a carpenter, gives a curious account of his own early years in this connection : " We were accustomed to look upon *gentle folks*, as beings of a superior order," he writes. "For my part I was quite shy of them, and kept off at a humble distance. A periwig in those days was a distinguishing badge of gentlefolk, and when I saw a man riding the road, near our house with a wig on, it would so alarm my fears and give me such a disagreeable feeling, that I dare say I would run off as for my life "[1] The gentlefolks in their wigs, with their humble white neighbors bowing down before them, their white indented servants and negro slaves, had every temptation to pride and arrogance. But the situation had its ennobling influences, and made of the Southern gentry the foremost champions of the Revolution. Burke noticed that as in the ancient commonwealths, among the Goths, and later among the Poles, the spirit of liberty is more high and haughty, where freedom " is not only an enjoyment but a kind of rank and privilege. In such a people the haughtiness of domination combines with the spirit of freedom, fortifies it, and renders it invincible." [2]

Dogue's Neck was long famous for its game, the native deer, turkeys, and wild fowl. And Colonel Mason was considered one of the best shots and keenest sportsmen of his day. "General Washington, Governor Sharpe of Maryland, Colonel Fairfax, Colonel Blackburn, and other distinguished men, before and after the Revolution," says a writer in the *American Turf Register* "were often the guests of his hospitable mansion and associates in the hunt on his grounds in Dogue Neck, then, as now, remarkable for quantity and vari-

---

[1] " Life of Rev. Devereux Jarratt," p. 14. Baltimore, 1806.
[2] " Conciliation with America," March, 1775.

ety of game, and his favorite rifle, along with the elbow chair
of his study, are yet [1830] relics in the hands of one of his
immediate descendants."[1]   These relics, unhappily, are no
longer to be found.   In the collection of the Virginia Historical Society is a pistol, once the property of Colonel Mason.
It is said to have belonged originally to Captain John Smith,
and is marked with the initials "I. S."   In 1818 the "Rules
adopted by the Proprietors, to be observed for the increase and
preservation of the Game in Dogue's Neck," were published
in the *Turf Register*, the proprietors being John, George, and
William Mason, the son and two grandsons of Colonel
Mason. "Gunston Hall" is about half a mile from the
Potomac.   Pohick _Bay, put down on the modern coast-
survey maps as Gunston Cove, is the sheet of water just
opposite the Hall, and across this bay or cove stood the old
Fairfax place, "Belvoir," on what is known as Fairfax Point.
Four or five miles away, on still another point or peninsula,
is "Mount Vernon."

At "Belvoir" lived George William Fairfax, Colonel
Mason's frequent companion in the deer hunts on Dogue's
Neck.   Like "Gunston Hall," "Belvoir" was on a peninsula, surrounded almost by navigable water. The tract of
land consisted of two thousand acres, with its valuable
fisheries, its handsome brick mansion-house — built somewhat in the style of "Gunston Hall," as would appear from
a description of it in the *Virginia Gazette*,—its servants'
hall and cellars, offices, stables, and coach-house, its large
garden and valuable fruit trees.   It was the scene of wealth
and hospitality in the later colonial days, but the house was
destroyed by fire, and its master an exile in England, during
the Revolution.   On the same peninsula with Colonel Mason,
but beyond the Neck proper, lived his neighbors and connections the Cockburns at "Springfield," the Masseys at
"Bradley" and the Bronaughs at "New Town." The
Occoquan estate of Colonel Mason, "Woodbridge," where in
later years he established one of his sons, was in Prince

[1] *American Turf Register and Sporting Magazine*, vol. i., p. 400.

William County, opposite the picturesque little town of Colchester. And in Fairfax County, north of " Mount Vernon," about three miles from Hunting Creek, was " Hollin Hall," built for another son of Colonel Mason. One of the nearest and most intimate of the " Gunston Hall " neighbors was Col. Daniel McCarty, who lived at " Cedar Grove," between Pohick and Accotink creeks. His son, of the same name, married one of George Mason's daughters. The Chichesters, who also intermarried later with the Masons, lived in Fairfax County at " Newington," and were among George Mason's friends and associates.

" Gunston Hall," though no longer in the Mason family, has been well preserved, and the ravages of time, with the more fatal devastations of war, have so slightly affected it that it may be taken to-day as one of the best types of the Virginia colonial mansion. It is much superior to " Mount Vernon " in solidity, and in the character of its material and finish. The cellars are as substantial as when first built, and extend under the whole house. They consist of four rooms, with a passage-way between them. The wine-vault, op. posite the staircase leading up into the first floor, has been closed up. Here was stored the old Madeira, the favorite imported wine of the early Virginian, with native vintages, and the heavier beverages produced from the home distillery. A large oven is in one of these cellar-rooms, and in the others are alcoves, used in former days for keeping wines and other stores which it was desirable to place in their cool recesses. One of these cellars was used at one time as a winter dairy. The house has been freshly painted in recent years, and its bright-red brick walls with cut-stone facings at each angle, its steep roof and tall chimneys, present to the eye of the visitor a quaint and attractive appearance. From the front entrance, opposite the old road, there was, as has been described, an avenue of cherry trees, reaching to the gate, " the white gate," as it was called. Then an English haw. thorn hedge led up to the " red gate," which opened out on the public road. You enter the house on this side, through a square porch with four pillars and an arched doorway, by a flight of broad steps, the old free-stone blocks now cracked and uneven. This porch was once plastered, and remains of the old cement are still to be seen. On the front door also may be traced the mark on the wood where the old brass knocker, a lion's head, once rested. This was probably stolen during the late war. A window on each side of the door looks out on the porch, and both door and windows are broad and low, the latter having deep window seats. The wide, handsome hall, however, is high, and the general effect of the house on the first floor is airy and spacious. The hall is wainscoted and panelled in North Carolina pine, and the woodwork is elaborately carved—every door, window, and cornice. The wide staircase leading up to the second floor has a baluster of mahogany, also ornamented in the same manner. And the doors, it should be said, are likewise of mahogany. In the centre of the hall is a carved arch with a huge acorn as a pendant in the middle, and this is also elaborately carved. The hall opens out on a pentagonal porch at the river-front of the house, and on the left of this entrance is the drawing-room. Here the woodwork is exquisitely carved—doors, windows, and mantel,—the cornices almost reaching to the high ceiling. All this hand carving is reported to have been the work of convicts sent from England.[1] "The style of these decorations," writes John Esten Cooke, in his description of " Gunston Hall," "is said to be a combination of the Corinthian and the flower-and-scroll work of the old French architecture."

The great wide fire-places of the olden time have been altered in conformity with modern ideas of comfort, and the superb mantel-piece that was once to be seen in the drawing-room has long since disappeared. On each side of the chimney in this room is a carved alcove reaching to the level of the cornices over the doors and windows. These alcoves, with shelves, held old china, silver,

---

[1] " Historic Houses of Virginia." John Esten Cooke in *Appleton's Journal*, April 4, 1874.

and bric-a-brac. A space was left over the mantel, framed in the woodwork, to hold a mirror or a picture. The drawing-room was formerly handsomely wainscoted in walnut and mahogany, but during the Civil War much of the wainscoting was injured, and the walls have since been patched up and papered, unfortunately the old, rich, carved woodwork having been painted white to contrast with the dark papering used there. The woodwork elsewhere has been given a soberer hue more in harmony with the original coloring. The dining-room, as it was presumably in Colonel Mason's time, since it was so used by his descendants, opens into the parlor or drawing-room, and is of the same size. The wainscoting and cornices here are less elaborate, and on each side of the mantel is a deep closet instead of an alcove. The two corresponding rooms across the hall are separated by a narrow passage, and at the end of the latter was the back staircase leading into the second floor and the stairs leading down into the cellars. Both of these stairways have been closed up within recent years. The passage opened out on a little porch with an arched doorway, and this too has disappeared. Of the two rooms on this side of the hall, the one opposite the drawing-room was occupied by Colonel Mason and his wife, and was called, in the old Virginia parlance, "the chamber." The other room was the "nursery" in the days of Colonel Mason's grandchildren, and in all probability it was used for the same purpose by the earlier Gunston household.[1] In both of these rooms are deep closets like those in the dining-room.

Ascending the wide staircase in the hall, half-way up, over the first landing, is a window in the wall, corresponding to one over the front door. At the head of the stairs there are three arches supported on four pillars, one on each side against the wall and two in the centre. Between these middle pillars a lamp may be suspended. The arches and pillars are of dark,

---

[1] It seems likely, however, that this room was the guest-chamber at one period, as tradition avers that Washington, Jefferson, Richard Henry Lee, and others of the eminent men of the time have slept in this room.

old carved wood. The rooms on the second floor open on each side of a hall which runs at right angles to the hall below, and terminates at each gable-end of the house. These rooms are small and low-pitched, with dormer-windows and wide, low window seats. A steep staircase leads up from one of these rooms into the attics, where were kept, fifty years ago, old disused spinning-wheels and spinning-machines that had doubtless seen good service in colonial days. A round window at each end of the house lights this upper region; and by a ladder-like staircase one ascends now to a sort of villa-tower placed on the roof for viewing the landscape. This is a modern addition, scarcely in keeping with the old mansion, though the beautiful views of the river that it affords would almost reconcile one to the innovation. The tall outside chimneys at the Hall make a noticeable feature in its appearance, but, as has been said, the old-fashioned, huge fire-places and tall mantels that should be found with them have disappeared. On the river front of the house one descends the steps from the pretty pentagonal porch, with its carved red and white pillars and lattice-work, its benches on the four enclosed sides, the fifth being the doorway, into what was once a well-kept lawn. The porches on both sides of the house are embowered in fragrant rose-bushes, so venerable from their size that they look as though they might have flourished here a hundred years ago. A box-hedge, its bushes grown now to the stature of small trees, on either side of the path, leads from the lawn to what was called the " falls "—terraces which formed the old garden as described in General Mason's reminiscences. And one looks down here, from a considerable elevation, on the beautiful river, on wood, and field, and pastures dotted with sheep, an altogether enchanting prospect. White sails pass and repass on the blue sparkling waters, and it is not difficult in the stillness and solitude to imagine that the years have rolled back to the days of which we write. The old public road has long been disused, with its chariots and horsemen, making the long overland journey north and south, but the river is changeless, an immortal highway, though steamboats have superseded the slow barges and vessels of our forefathers. The railroad, that obtrusive element of modern civilization, is still four miles or more from " Gunston Hall," and the steamboat that takes the traveller from Washington to " Mount Vernon " on its return goes into Gunston Cove, where you land within a short drive of the Hall. It is not the old landing used in Colonel Mason's time, but it is very near it. Among the out-buildings at " Gunston Hall " that yet remain is the old school-house. And one may still drink at the venerable well-curb of ancient gray stone with its " old oaken bucket."

" Springfield," the home of Martin Cockburn, is still standing, though its marble mantels and other interior embellishments are no longer to be seen. It is a long, low frame building; the rooms all on one floor, and most of them communicating, while they are divided by wooden panels instead of plastered walls. It was said that having lived in the West Indies, the master of " Springfield " built his house after a fashion brought from his early home—and he would have it but one-story high for fear of earthquakes. In the little graveyard at " Springfield " are two unmarked mounds which tradition points out as the last resting-places of Martin Cockburn and his wife. On the death of the childless pair " Springfield " was left to Mrs. Cockburn's relatives, the Masseys; and Mrs. Nancy Triplett, a daughter of the Rev. Lee Massey, was the last one of the family to live at " Springfield." [1] At " Bradley," Mr. Massey's place, the dwelling-house has long since disappeared. The graveyard here is all that remains to remind one of its former associations. This little plot of ground is beautifully situated on a slope of the hill overlooking Occoquan Bay, and

---

[1] A great-nephew of Mrs. Triplett's sold the old house after his aunt's death, and with it many of the books, family portraits, and other interesting memorials of the Cockburns and Masseys. The diary of the Rev. Lee Massey, at this sale, came into possession of a gentleman in the neighborhood, but it cannot now be found.

marble tombstones here mark the graves of the good pastor and his wife Elizabeth. "New Town," the old Bronaugh place, where Mrs. Cockburn and Mrs. Massey spent their girlhood, has passed away utterly; the very name of it is unknown in the neighborhood at this day. And recent owners of the land have ruthlessly ploughed up the old graveyard, one of the old tombstones having been left leaning against a tree in one of the fields. "Cedar Grove," the McCarty place, like all those we have named, has gone out of the family of its original owners. It is beautifully situated on Pohick Creek, and is a low, rambling frame building, now much out of repair though still habitable. Its lovely water views, from its commanding position on high ground almost entirely surrounded by the creek, are its chief attraction now, but in former days, with its lawns, its orchards, and its shrubberies, it must have made a delightful residence. The family burying-ground at "Cedar Grove" is, perhaps, a half mile from the house, in a dense grove of oaks and poplars. Bending back the thick branches in this Druid-like solitude, and stooping over fallen trees, one finds three graves, with their gray, moss-covered stones, marking the spots where rest Dennis McCarty and his grandson, Daniel McCarty, with the wife of the latter, who was a daughter of Colonel Mason. Col. Daniel McCarty, the elder, the friend and contemporary of George Mason, was buried at "Mount Airy," another family seat of the McCartys.

All that remains of the famous old town of Colchester are a few straggling houses, several of them showing marks of great antiquity, and here and there a broken wall with its tall outside chimneys. And turning to the beach one is brought back from the past to the present, for here, instead of the famous arches which reminded the English traveller of London, a railroad bridge is to be found spanning the Occoquan River. Gone forever is the old inn of colonial days, with its highly praised wines, and every other vestige of the old gay life of the last century. Colchester is indeed a deserted village, with only its picturesque situation and its dim traditions left to interest the passing visitor. Directly opposite Colchester, in Prince William County, is "Woodbridge," the old Occoquan plantation, where the ferry was in former times. The railroad bridge now connects the two places, and the railroad station on the north side still bears the name of Woodbridge. A store and two or three houses are found there now, though the old mansion-house seems to have disappeared. "Hollin Hall," named by George Mason after the old Thomson place in England, is four miles from Alexandria, in Fairfax County, on what is known as the Accotink pike. The mansion-house at "Lexington" was destroyed a few years ago by fire. And this is the only one of George Mason's Virginia estates that remains in the hands of any of his descendants. Be. yond Mason's Neck, which is in Truro parish, and to the right or north of Pohick Creek on the Colchester road, is Pohick church. It is about five miles from "Gunston Hall." Very recently the old vestry-book of Truro parish, which had been unaccountably missing for about half a century, was found, and it affords valuable information in regard to the church and its vestry.

It was in 1772 that the new Pohick, or Mount Vernon church as it was sometimes called, was built. The old church, as Bishop Meade tells us, was a frame building, and was on the south side of Pohick Creek, two miles from the site of the new church. The parish was founded in 1732, and the first vestry-meeting was held on the seventh of November in that year. Dennis McCarty, whose grave lies at "Cedar Grove," was the first vestryman on the list. He was at this time twenty-eight, and died ten years later. The old church had been but three miles from "Gunston Hall," and the site is still pointed out. It is related that when the parishioners were called together to determine on the site of the new church, George Mason, who was the senior vestryman, strongly advocated remaining in the old locality, as the spot where their fathers had worshipped, and where many of their graves were to be found. His eloquent appeal to the sensibilities of his hearers proved convincing, it seemed. But Washington, who lead the opposition, argued in favor of a more convenient and central situation, and the meeting finally adjourned without coming to any decision. Before the day arrived, however, when the subject was to be definitely decided, Washington had made a survey of the whole ground, measured the distances, and marked down all the houses of the parishioners, and, producing his map, was able to give such cogent reasons for the change of site that his point was gained.[1] The church stands midway between "Gunston Hall" and "Mount Vernon." The old vestry-book gives full details as to its construction. It was built on ground given by Daniel French. The building committee were George William Fairfax, George Washington, George Mason, Capt. Daniel McCarty, and Edward Payne. We are told the size of the bricks, and how the materials of which they were made were to be mixed, so circumstantial are the old entries. On the death of Daniel French, George Mason was appointed his executor, and the contract for building the church was under his supervision. Washington was requested by the vestry to import cushions for the pulpit and a cloth for the desk, and one for the communion-table of crimson velvet with gold fringe. He was to provide also two folio prayer-books covered with blue Turkey leather, with the name of the parish thereon in gold letters. The pews of the church were disposed of to the parishioners on the 20th of November, 1772. Colonel Mason bought two, pews Nos. 3 and 4, joining the south wall of the church. He paid for them fourteen pounds eleven shillings eight pence each. Pew No. 13 was taken by Martin Cockburn, and No. 14 by Daniel McCarty. This last adjoined the rector's pew, No. 15, which was vested in him " and his successors for ever accordingly." In the centre of the church, pew No. 28, adjoining the north aisle, next the communion-table, was bought by George Washington for sixteen pounds. No 29 was taken

[1] "Old Churches and Families of Virginia," vol. ii., p. 227 ; Sparks' "Washington," chap. vi., p. 106.

8

by Lund Washington, but was afterwards bought from him by George Washington. In the vestry-book is the order for making the stone font. When the church was restored within recent years, nothing was known of this font, but it was found later in possession of one of the neighbors, who, in all ignorance of its sacred character, it may charitably be hoped, had used it as a *horse-trough.* It was restored to the church, and is preserved there as a relic. The rector of the church, in 1772, was the Rev. Lee Massey, George Mason's friend and connection. He had been a lawyer in his youth, and was induced to study for the ministry, which he adorned by his learning and ability, at the instance of his neighbors and personal friends, Washington, Mason, Fairfax, and McCarty, who wished him to become their pastor, and he went over to London to be ordained in 1766. Later, his infirmities obliging him to give up his charge, he studied medicine, which he practised, without fee, amongst the poor of his former parish. The names of the vestry of Pohick Church for 1773 have been preserved. George Washington heads the list, George Mason coming next, and among the rest were Daniel McCarty, Alexander Henderson, and Martin Cockburn. A description of the old Truro parish church, as it appeared to an English traveller in the latter part of the eighteenth century, has been preserved. The writer, Davis, gives us also a glimpse of the neighborhood at this time. On the piazza of the country tavern he writes that he found " a party of gentlemen from the neighboring plantations carous. ing over a bowl of toddy and smoking cigars." And he adds :

"No people could excel these men in politeness. On my ascending the steps to the piazza every countenance seemed to say, this man has a double claim to our attention, for he is a stranger in the place. In a moment there was room made for me to sit down ; a new bowl was called for, and every one who addressed me did it with a smile of conciliation. But no man asked me where I had come from, or whither I was going."

Our traveller then says of the scenery

"No walk could be more delightful than that from Occoquan to Colchester, when the moon was above the mountains. You traverse the bank of a placid stream, over which impend rocks, in some places bare, but more frequently covered with a odiferous plant that regales the traveller with its fragrance. [Could this have been mint, the herb of the Virginian's julep ?]
After climbing over mountains, almost inaccessible to human toil, you come to the junction of the Occoquan with the noble river of the Potomac, and behold a bridge, whose semi-elliptical arches are scarcely inferior to those of princely London. And on the side of the bridge stands a tavern where every luxury that money can purchase is to be obtained at first summons ; where the richest viands cover the table, and where ice cooled the Madeira that had been thrice across the ocean.   About eight miles from the Occoquan mills is a house of worship, called Pohick Church, a name it claims from a run that flows near its walls. Hither I rode on Sunday and joined the congregation of parson Weems, a minister of the Episcopal persuasion, who was cheerful in his mien that he might win men to religion. A Virginian church-yard on a Sunday resembles rather a race-course than a sepulchral ground ; the ladies come to it in carriages, and the men after dismounting from their horses make them fast to the trees. But the steeples to the Virginia churches were designed not for utility but ornament ; for the bell is always suspended to a tree a few yards from the church. . . . I was confounded on first entering the church-yard at Pohick to hear

' Steed threaten steed with high and boastful neigh.'

Nor was I less stunned with the rattling of carriage-wheels, the cracking of whips, and the vociferations of the gentlemen to the negroes who accompanied them."[1]

The eccentric Mr. Weems, Washington's imaginative biographer, was never rector of Pohick church, though he sometimes officiated there. Regular services ceased at Pohick after Mr. Massey's incumbency, as the church in Alexandria

[1] Howe's " Historic Collections," p. 255.

had taken a number of its parishioners, including General Washington. Many of the old families had left the neighborhood after the Revolution, and then, for obvious reasons, this was a period of depression for the Episcopal Church, which was associated in many minds with the British supremacy. Pohick church and Truro parish revived at a later period, and services were held there with more or less regularity down to the time of the late war. When Bishop Meade wrote of the church in 1857, many of the doors of the pews were gone, including those of Washington and Mason. Those of George William Fairfax, Martin Cockburn, Daniel McCarty, William Payne, and the rector's were still there, and the names on them legible. Benjamin Ogle Tayloe, writing in 1851, tells of the fate of Washington's pew door. A friend of his, a few years before, sought it as a valuable relic; "it was traced to an old negro's hovel, where it had been used as a hen-coop, but not found." The church, then, in 1860 could not have been in very good repair, though it was habitable. The ravages of war completed the desolation of the historic edifice. It was held alternately as an outpost by the pickets of the contending armies, and the soldiers, either for their value as relics or from sheer vandalism, carried off or destroyed all the interior work except the cornices and the roof. Floor, doors, and windows entirely disappeared, and the substantial brick walls, with roof and cornice, alone remained.

Chiefly through the liberality of Mr. Theodore B. Wetmore, of New York, the church was restored in 1871. The roof was then found to be very much out of repair, but the walls so substantially built in 1772, a hundred years before, were as stout and strong as ever. Unfortunately the church was not remodelled on the old plan. The floor was laid entirely in wood, and the pews built in the modern fashion. The position of the chancel was altered also, so that the appearance of the walls and cornice is all of the interior that remains the same. The tile floor, the high-back pews, the old-fashioned pulpit and reading-desk of colonial days are

all things of the past.   The present rector is the first one
that this old church has had for a period of over forty years.
The last one of ante-bellum days was the Rev. Mr. Johnson,
whose wife was a Miss Washington, of " Mount Zephyr,"
and he lived for some little time at " Gunston Hall " with
Mrs. Mason, the widow of Colonel Mason's grandson.

Colonel Mason, like General Washington, was fond of
buying land, and we find him in 1763 making purchases in
Maryland.   Two patents are preserved by one of his descendants of tracts in Frederick County, acquired by him at that
time.   One of them, containing 260 acres, bears date March
25th, and is called " The Welshman's Conquest "; the other,
containing 510 acres, and dated June 24th, is called " The
Cove."   The books of the proprietors of the Northern Neck
show that Colonel Mason, in September, 1767, had a re-survey made of several of the tracts of land he had inherited in
Fairfax County.   And he also patented at this time a piece
of waste and ungranted land on the Potomac, consisting of
$100\frac{1}{2}$ acres.   The re-survey of the land patented by George
Mason's father in 1724 showed that what was then supposed
to be 250 acres was only 118.   Another tract lying opposite
Georgetown proved to contain sixty-five acres of surplus
land, the deed of the old survey containing 650 acres, and
the new deed embracing 705 acres.   This land is described
as " beginning at the upper side of the mouth of a small run
called Rocky Run, opposite the middle of an island formerly
called Anacostin, alias My Lord's Island, but now called
Barbadoes."   This island became Colonel Mason's property
by a patent from Lord Baltimore, and is mentioned in his
will as " Barbadoes."   It is put down on Fry and Jefferson's
map of Virginia as " Mason's Island," but is now known
again by its Indian name, though Anacostin is changed to
Analostan.   Both words are corruptions of the name of the
Necostins, one of the early Indian tribes of this locality.
Surplus land was also found by Colonel Mason's re-survey
in a tract of his on the Potomac River below the falls.   This
was patented originally as 653 acres, but proved to contain

672.[1] A curious bit of testimony has been preserved in connection with one of these land purchases, showing the power of George Mason's name at this time, in his own section, though he had not as yet come prominently before the public. In a suit where Charles Alexander was plaintiff against William Bryan and others defendants, in ejectment, it is said :

"George Mason being seized of Going's and Houseley's patents which interfered with each other, as Houseley's had been laid off prior to 1767, laid him off differently, and run him upon Streetfield. Thereby he purchased Streetfield on easy terms, for though Streetfield might have been otherwise held till this time, viz., 1767, the proprietors might have been disposed not to have any contention with an adversary so potent in mind and [*word illegible*] as Col. G. Mason."[2]

Evidently Colonel Mason had impressed his neighbors as a person whom it was not expedient to go to law with.

One of Washington's letters, written in 1767, makes mention of George Mason in connection with a land purchase he was contemplating at this time. Washington is writing to Capt. John Posey, who was in some financial straits, and having borrowed all he could from Washington, now proposed to borrow from Colonel Mason. But the latter would soon want his money again, and so Posey would be as badly off as before. "He tells you," writes Washington, "in express terms and with candor that he is waiting for an opportunity to make a purchase which, when accomplished, he must have his money again, giving you three or four months' notice. It is likely, therefore, that he may call for it in six months as in a longer time, because the distress of the country and number of estates which are daily advertising afford great prospect of purchasing to advantage."[3] Capt. John Posey was one of George Mason's neighbors, and the latter

---

[1] Virginia Land Registry Office, Richmond.
[2] Old MSS. belonging to the Alexander family.
[3] "Writings of Washington," Ford, vol. ii., p. 226.

voted for him at an election for burgesses two years before. Gen. Thomas Posey, of this same family, was on General Washington's staff during the Revolution. The Poseys intermarried with the Thorntons of "Rumford," an estate in Stafford County, on the Rappahannock River. Major George Thornton, who served in the Stafford militia during the Revolution, "was at the bombardment of Marlboro', the seat of Judge Mercer, on the Potomac."[1] And one of the Thorntons, it will be seen later, married a daughter of Colo-nel Mason.

In 1769 George Mason seems to have come into possession of two thousand acres of land in the district of Kentucky, the land being due him for the importation of forty persons into the colony. Fifty acres constituted the head rights for each person, as established by the early Virginia law. The following is a copy of the land warrant for this tract.

Land Office Warrant, No. 10.
To the Principal Surveyor of any county within the common-wealth of Virginia.

This shall be your warrant to survey and lay off in one SEAL. or more surveys for George Mason, of the county of Fairfax, Esq. : his heirs and assigns, the quantity of two thousand acres of land, due unto the said George Mason for the importation of forty persons, the certificates of which have been duly presented and received into the Land Office. Given under my hand and the seal of the said office on this 12th day of July, one thousand seven hundred and sixty-nine.

JOHN HARVIE.[2]

Washington's private journals for this period contain fre-quent mention of Colonel Mason's name. As he relates, though with undue brevity, "where and how my time is spent," we learn in some degree of Colonel Mason's movements also. A vestry meeting at Pohick church, which Washington attended on the 28th of November, 1768, no doubt brought the

[1] "Virginia Cousins," p. 213, G. Brown Goode.
[2] Mason County Historical Society, Maysville, Kentucky.

friends together, and they must have discussed at this time the approaching election for burgesses.   After a hunt with Lord Fairfax on the 29th, Washington spent the following day at home, and in the evening George Mason and Martin Cockburn came over together from " Gunston Hall " and " Springfield," spent the night at " Mt. Vernon," and went with Washington to Alexandria where the election took place December 1st.   Washington and Colonel West were the successful candidates, and the event was celebrated by a ball, which they all attended, apparently.   After dinner on the 2d Washington returned to " Mt. Vernon," carrying back with him Mason and Cockburn and three other gentlemen.   It was a pleasant, easy, hospitable life, friends meeting first at one house then at another for long visits of several days at a time.   They rode to the hunt with the hounds on one day ; on the next, perhaps, they met at a vestry meeting or at court ; they had the occasional excitement of an election and its attendant festivities ; and they had, as yet, though political grievances sorely vexed them, no presage of the coming war, its hardships, and its glories.   Colonel Mason made another visit to " Mt. Vernon " in April, 1769.   Washington went to a meeting of the court on the 18th, and brought back several of his friends, George Mason among them.   At this time the latter seems to have come on the business of settling with Washington the bounds of their adjacent lands.[1] The two following days were spent by them in the woods surveying, and after a morning together in the house, Colonel Mason went home on the afternoon of the 21st.   The subject of the non-importation resolutions which George Mason had prepared for Washington to carry with him to the May Assembly must have been a topic of their conversation at this time.   And two days later George Mason was writing to his friend a final word on the subject.   The Assembly having been abruptly dissolved, Washington was back again

[1] A letter of George Mason to Washington in reference to this subject, dated the 9th of April, 1768, is extant, and at the end of it the latter has written that the lines were settled on the 19th of April, 1769.

at "Mt. Vernon" sooner than he could have anticipated. On the 20th of June he went up to court, returning in the evening with several of his fellow-justices, Bryan Fairfax, Mr. Scott, and Colonel Mason. The latter remained two days at "Mt. Vernon," discussing, doubtless, the serious political outlook with his friend. In October Colonel Mason was again at "Mt. Vernon." Washington, on the 23d of this month, went to a sale of Captain Posey's land, which he purchased. Here he met George Mason, who, with his son George and other gentlemen, returned home with him. In the following March Colonel Mason visited Washington with Mr. Christian, spending a day and night at "Mt. Vernon." There was a dancing-school in this year, 1770, for the young people of the neighborhood, and it met by turns at the different country-places, or perhaps alternately at "Mt. Vernon" and "Gunston Hall." Mr. Christian was the dancing-teacher, it would appear. Washington records on the 18th of April: "Patsy Custis and Milly Posey went to Colo. Mason's to the Dancing School." Martha Custis, the lovely young daughter of Mrs. Washington, was then about thirteen years old. One day in July Mr. Christian and all his scholars came to the dancing at "Mt. Vernon." Early in 1771 we hear of the two friends, Washington and Mason, meeting at Colchester, January 23d, and going together to Dumfries on some law business. At night Washington went to see the play of "The Recruiting Officers," most probably in company with Colonel Mason. Three weeks later they were again together at the court-house on this case. Thomson Mason and James Mercer were the lawyers, and George Mason was one of the arbitrators. In the fall of 1771, Washington records a visit of his to "Gunston Hall." He set off, the 27th of October, "before sunrise with John Custis for Colo. Mason's." After breakfast they went hunting in Mason's Neck, and killed two deer. They hunted again the next day, but killed nothing; and on the 29th they went to the vestry meeting at Pohick church, Washington returning to "Mount Vernon" that evening. They were building the new church at Pohick about this time, and Washington and Mason must have met frequently at conferences of the Building Committee.   In May of the following year Colonel Mason spent a night and day at "Mount Vernon," dining there on the 15th with his friend, Capt. Daniel McCarty. And on the 5th of June Washington "met the vestry at our New Church."[1]   Washington frequently received additions to his fruits and flowers from his friend at "Gunston Hall." In 1763 he tells in his journal of grafting cherries, apples, pears, and plums, the cherries and plums coming from Colonel Mason's, and the "Bergamy Pears and New Town pippins" also, the latter having had them "from Mr. President Blair."

[1] Washington's Private Journals (extracts from the transcripts of Dr. Toner).

CHAPTER IV.

FIRST POLITICAL PAPERS.

1764–1773.

The twelve years of British oppression which brought on the Revolution date from 1764, when in March of this year Parliament passed the Declaratory Act, asserting the principle which was felt at once to sap the foundations of political freedom in the colonies, the principle of taxation without representation. By this act it was maintained "to be proper to impose certain stamp duties in the colonies for the purpose of raising a revenue in America payable into the British exchequer." The Stamp Act itself, universally denounced by the free-spirited colonists, north, south, and east, was passed in the winter of 1765–6, to come into operation some months later. At the May session of the Virginia House of Burgesses in this year Patrick Henry thrilled the continent with his eloquence in his famous protest againt the Stamp Act, and "gave the first impulse," as was justly said by Jefferson, "to the ball of the Revolution." And Edmund Randolph rightly characterizes this era as an illustrious one in the annals of Virginia.

"Without an immediate oppression, without a cause depending so much on hasty feeling as theoretic reasoning ; without a distaste for monarchy ; with loyalty to the reigning prince ; with fraternal attachment to the transatlantic members of the empire ; with an admiration of their genius, learning and virtues ; with a subserviency in cultivating their manners and their fashions ; in

venerable; the house of burgesses in the year 1765 gave utterance to principles which within two years were to expand into a revolution."[1]

William Wirt in his life of Patrick Henry brings before us the prominent figures of this Assembly: Richard Bland, the Virginia antiquary, who wrote the first pamphlet of the many that the crisis was to call forth on the relations between the colonies and the parent state; Edmund Pendleton, the profound lawyer and able statesman; George Wythe, the elegant classical scholar and learned jurist, of whom Jefferson left a eulogistic sketch among his papers; Richard Henry Lee, "the Cicero of the House," and Patrick Henry, its most persuasive orator. These were some of the eminent names that were to be enrolled later among Virginia's leaders and law-makers in the new epoch that was dawning upon her. Jefferson had just attained his majority in 1764, and was at this time studying law under Wythe at Williamsburg and dancing with "Belinda" in the gay balls at the Apollo Room of the Raleigh tavern, so soon to be consecrated to sterner uses. The two brothers, George and Thomson Mason were not idle at this time. Thomson Mason's name will be seen among the signatures to the Westmoreland Resolutions drawn up by Richard Henry Lee in February, 1765, in which the prominent citizens of Westmoreland and the adjoining counties recorded their protest against the Stamp Act.[2] There were a hundred and fifteen members of the association, including several of the Lees and Washingtons, with other names more or less conspicuous, among whom was Samuel Selden, Thomson Mason's brother-in-law. This is said to have been the first public association in opposition to the Stamp Act that was organized in the colonies, and it antedated the meeting of the Virginia Assembly by three months. The justices of Stafford County in the following October resigned in a body rather

---

[1] MS. History of Virginia, Virginia Historical Society.
[2] Original in possession of the Va. Hist. Society.

than execute the new law. They sent to Governor Fau. quier an address, which was written by John Mercer of Marlboro', in which they quote the motto of their county seal, from Magna Charta, " We will deny or delay no man justice," which, they add, " we are firmly persuaded is incon. sistent with the Stamp Act." This paper is signed by Peter and Travers Daniel, William Bronaugh, John Alexander, William Brent, John Mercer, Thomas Ludwell Lee, Samuel Selden, Gowry Waugh, Thomas Fitzhugh of " Boscobel," and Robert Washington of " Chotank." These were all friends and some of them were connections of George Mason's and their noble act must have commended itself to his patriotic spirit.

In the meantime Colonel George Mercer, while his father was taking this decided stand in Stafford against the Stamp Act, arrived at Hampton in the odious character of a stamp distributor. It is evident that he did not realize the condition of affairs or he would not have put himself in such a false position. A soldier by profession and not a politician, he had not entered into the merits of the case, and as he was coming over to America on business of his own, or in the interests of the Ohio Company, he undertook at the request of the Stamp Office commissioners to carry over with him the stamps intended for three of the colonies. He was confronted by an excited mob at Hampton and only protected from violence through the influence of prominent gentlemen of the town. At Williamsburg he was met by several members of the General Court then in session, and required to say if he intended to enter on the duties of the office. They went with him to the coffee-house where the governor, most of the council, and other gentlemen were assembled, and here a crowd collected outside and could only be dispersed when it was known that Colonel Mercer would give an answer the next day at a stated hour. At five o'clock the following afternoon, according to promise, he met the citizens and the various prominent merchants of the colony then in Williamsburg, and engaged not to execute the Stamp Act without the consent of the Virginia Assembly. He was then carried from the capitol to the coffee-house with great rejoicing and an elegant supper was given him. Music, drums, and horns, and the ringing of the bells demonstrated the popular satisfaction, while at night the town was illuminated. [1]

Colonel Mercer wrote to Governor Sharpe of Maryland on the 10th of November saying that he had been entrusted with the stamps for Maryland and had promised to forward them to Annapolis, but on his arrival in Virginia found he could not comply with his engagement. He could not procure a conveyance for them at any price, and after all that he had heard of the reception of the distributors, he feared it would not be safe to trust them on shore at Annapolis without protection, and here in Williamsburg, he added, they were in no less danger. His duty to his royal master, he thought, obliged him to use every effort for their protection, and he had obtained permission to put them on the royal ship *The Rainbow*, where they awaited Governor Sharpe's orders. This had relieved him from the most disagreeable commission he has ever undertaken, he writes. He dared not let any one know where the stamps were, and feared all the time an attempt would be made to force the discovery from him. Although the season was so far advanced, and he had not been more than ten days in America, he found himself "under a necessity of returning immediately to England." [2] And Colonel Mercer went back to London a wiser man no doubt, and concerned himself no more with troubled semi-political missions to his irate countrymen.

George Mason, as has been said, was not idle at this time, Though not in the Assembly, he was ready as always to help his friends there; and the Fairfax representatives, George Fairfax and George Washington, called on him for assistance at this crisis. And we find him making his protest against the Stamp Act, in the scheme which he drew up for altering

[1] Campbell's "Virginia," p. 543.
[2] MS. Letter, Maryland Historical Society.

the method of replevying goods under distress for rent.[1] In it Colonel Mason explains the landlord's right by the common law, and he advocates very strongly the employment of free labor instead of slave labor, citing the experience of the Romans as an example and a warning to Virginia. African slavery at this time was considered by many as one of the grievances entailed upon the colonies by the mother country. Virginia had protested, as we have seen, more than once unavailingly against the system, and the crown had forced the slaves upon her. But in the lapse of years slave labor had become a part of the life of the State, and it could not be easily set aside. There was no question then as to its rightfulness, but among many thoughtful minds there was much doubt of its expediency.

Letter to Col. George Fairfax and Col. George Washington enclosing a scheme for replevying goods under distress for rent.

GUNSTON HALL, 23d December, 1765.

GENTLEMEN :

Inclosed is the scheme I promised you for altering the method of replevying goods under distress for rent. I thought it necessary to explain fully the landlord's right by the common law, to shew that our Act of Assembly was a mere matter of indulgence, and that an alteration of it now will be no encroachment upon the tenant. The first part of it has very little to do with the alteration proposed, and only inculcates a doctrine I was always fond of promoting and which I could wish to see more generally adopted than it is like to be. The whole is, indeed, much longer than it might have been, but that you will excuse as the natural effect of the very idle life I am forced to lead. I beg you will alter such parts of it as either of you think exceptionable.

If I had the Act of Assembly obliging our vestry to pay for the glebe &c, I would prepare a petition for redress, and get it signed in time.

Wishing the families at Belvoir and Mt. Vernon all the mirth and happiness of the approaching festival, I am, Gentlemen,

Your most obedient humble Servant

G. MASON.[2]

[1] Appendix ii.
[2] Washington MSS., Department of State.

As Colonel Mason in this letter speaks of the idle life he is forced to lead, it seems probable he was suffering at this time with the gout. The scheme he formulated for his Assembly friends was meant to obviate a difficulty that had arisen upon the passage of the Stamp Act. The law of Virginia had allowed a debtor to replevy his goods under execution by bond to pay the debt and costs with interest in three months. The act of Assembly which made this provision Colonel Mason thought was not clearly expressed, and the method prescribed was somewhat impracticable. But he says:

"This has not hitherto been productive of much inconvenience, though contrary to the course and spirit of the common law ; the landlord may thereby be brought into a court of judicature before he can get the effect of a just and legal distress, but in our present circumstances it will occasion manifest injustice. If the officer making a distress upon being offered security refuses to take a bond for want of stamped paper, the goods of the tenant must be immediately exposed to sale, and he deprived of the indulgence intended by the Act of Assembly. If the officer takes a replevin bond as usual, the landlord will lose his rent, the tenant then having it in his power to keep him out of it as long as he pleases ; for in the present confusion and cessation of judicial proceedings the landlord will not have an opportunity of applying to court for an execution when the bond becomes payable, or if he does the clerk will not venture to issue one. In either case there is such a hardship as calls for the interposition of the legislature."

Colonel Mason's mention of the glebe for which the Assembly was about to oblige the vestry to pay, recalls the fact that there was a division of Truro parish about this time. It had originally embraced Fairfax, Prince William, and Loudoun counties, but in 1749 Cameron parish, afterwards a part of Loudoun County, was cut off from it, and in 1764 Fairfax parish was established, its vestry-book beginning in 1765. Its principal church was built in Alexandria, about the time of the construction of the new Pohick church.

The meeting of the first American or Continental Congress took place in October, 1765, at New York, in which, how. ever, only nine colonies were represented. Virginia was one of the three colonies which did not send delegates. This was owing to the action of the executive in each case. A declaration of the rights and liberties of the colonies was drawn up at this Congress, and a committee was appointed to prepare addresses to the Commons, the King, and the House of Lords. The Virginia Assembly, to show its sym. pathy with the action of the Congress, drew up similar papers to be sent to the King and to the Houses of Parlia. ment. Colonel Mason's fourth son was born in the spring of 1766, the little boy whose earliest recollections were to be of the heated political discussions at " Gunston Hall " and " Springfield," calling forth his infantile bursts of treason, so vividly remembered in later years. The first of George Mason's political writings dates from this year, and attacked the theory involved in the Stamp Act, for though the ob- noxious measure had been repealed, the principle was still asserted by Parliament. The patriots throughout the coun- try at this time were writing letters and pamphlets stating the case between Great Britain and the colonies, and advo- cating this and that remedy for their grievances. The celebrated " Farmer's Letters," by John Dickinson, of Penn- sylvania, were attracting much attention in England and America : and Arthur Lee, while in London in 1769, wrote " The Monitor's Letters " in defence of his native land. His brother, Richard Henry Lee, addressed the " good people of Virginia " as " A Virginia Planter," explaining the injustice of the Stamp Act and the evils it would entail on the colo- nists if not stoutly resisted. In 1766 Richard Bland pub- lished his " Inquiry into the Rights of the British Colonies "; and John Mercer, as has been seen, as the spokesman of the Stafford justices in 1765, had been one of the first in Vir- ginia to take ground against the infringement of colonial

9

rights. Doubtless he exchanged views with his nephew and whilom ward, George Mason, and the latter in 1766 came before the public in the same good cause.

The London merchants, after the repeal of the Stamp Act, wrote an address to the planters of Virginia, and George Mason wrote a letter in response, signing himself "A Virginia Planter," as one of the class addressed by the English merchants. This paper was dated "Virginia, Potomac River, June 6th, 1766," and it appeared in the *London Public Ledger* of that year. The repeal of the Stamp Act was considered as a great act of grace on the part of the government, and was so represented in the letter of the merchants. The occasion was one in which simple justice was made to pass current as special favor, and the discontent of the colonists, it was argued, should be forever stifled. But as Parliament had not abandoned the principle of taxing the colonies, there was no security for the future. George Mason's letter, full of spirit and clear-sighted wisdom, laid bare the true aspect of the matter. In the following passage the writer warned the British public of the results that would follow any system of coercion :

"If the ministerial party could influence the legislature to make so cruel and dangerous an experiment as to attempt to enforce the Stamp Act by military power, would the nation have heartily engaged in such an execrable cause, and would there have been no difficulty in raising and transporting a body of troops sufficient to occupy a country of two thousand miles in extent ? Would they have had no danger to encounter in the midst of the wilds of America ? Three million of people driven to desperation are not an object of contempt."

Colonel Mason thus alludes to himself and his pursuits: " These are the sentiments of a man who spends most of his time in retirement, and has seldom meddled in public affairs ; who enjoys a modest but independent fortune, and content with the blessings of a private station, equally disregards the smiles and favors of the great."[1]

[1] Appendix iii.

The Revenue Act, laying duties on tea, glass, paper, and painters' colors, passed the British Parliament in 1767, and fanned the patriotic elements into a fresh flame. In a short time all were repealed except the duty on tea, but a tempest lurked in the teapot, as England was soon to learn. And the disturbances at Boston and other places with the suc-ceeding retaliatory acts of the government brought to a crisis the growing antagonism between the colonies and the mother country.

One letter of George Mason's, written in 1768, has been preserved, and has reference to the Ohio Company, which had had its claims referred back from the government in England to the government in Virginia. This letter is writ-ten to Robert Carter of " Nomini," Westmoreland County, a member of the council for many years, and usually called, from this circumstance, and to distinguish him from others of the family, " Councillor Carter."

GUNSTON HALL, January 23d, 1768.

DEAR SIR :

The Ohio Company, being informed that their case is referred by order of his Majesty and Council to the consideration of the Governor and Council of Virginia, who are to make a report thereon, I have, at the instance of several members, wrote to his Honor the Governor, to desire the favor of him to inform us of the purport of this order &c.; what is expected from the Company in consequence thereof. I have taken the liberty, Sir, to enclose the letter under cover to you and must beg the favor of you to make such inquiries and procure such copies as you think neces-sary for the Company's information, as well as forward any answer the Governor may think fit to favor us with.

There is to be a meeting of the Company at Stafford Court House on Tuesday, the 23d of February next, where we expect to have the pleasure of your company. I enclose an advertise-ment to give notice of it, which you will please to have inserted in the *Virginia Gazette*. One is already sent to the printer at Annapolis.

I received your favor of the 11th December last and wished it was in my power to oblige you with the sum you desire, but I had some little time before let out what cash I had by me upon Maryland bonds, with a promise to the gentleman who borrowed it not to call for it soon. I made some large purchase. If I should be lucky enough to receive any considerable sum next summer, I will let you know it.   '

I beg my compliments to your lady, and am, Sir,
                    Your most obedient humble servant,
                                                G. MASON.
To the Hon. Robert Carter, Esq. ·
Williamsburg.[1]

Lord Botetourt arrived in Virginia in 1768, and much was expected from his gracious manners, his good sense and native kindness of heart. A letter from Col. George Mercer to one of his brothers in Virginia, written just before Lord Botetourt's departure from London, gives an interesting account of him, and presents a hopeful view of the political situation, while it touches upon other matters which are not without value as illustrating the period and its manners.

                              " LONDON, August 16th, 1768.
" DEAR BROTHER .
      "   I have been long under orders to cross the Welsh mountains for the benefit of goat's milk, but have always met with some accident to disappoint the prosecution of that scheme, and though I will allow very readily every other consideration ought to yield to health, yet I have permitted some political and worldly ones to counteract them. Lord Hillsborough has really detained me here for some weeks, and though I cannot exactly tell you what I am at present, yet I am—something indeed, perhaps I may be able to tell you what before I close my letter, or you may even hear it from the public. Suffice it at present to tell you I have actually and *bona fide* been appointed a Lt. Govr. and that nothing prevents the publication of this news, but the very great probability that I may be superseded immediately. Don't stop long at the last line of the page, for when you turn over to this I shall tell you,—the risk I run of losing my present commission is very great, but to be sure not very alarming or disagreeable, as it will be changed for that of Captain General

¹ MS. Letter.

and Commander-in-chief in and over, etc., but if you have no authentic advices of this change, keep both circumstances to yourself till I clear up the point to you. . . .

"I congratulate you and my country on the appointment of Lord Botetourt to the government of Virginia. Lord Hillsborough, who is indefatigable in his endeavour to do good to the colonies, and be made acquainted with their real situation and complaints—I believe has determined no longer to allow posts in America, but especially governments, to be enjoyed by non-residents, and I know it was the first thing he thought of on entering into his office, to reform this terrible abuse in Virginia. At last thank Heaven he has effected the great work, and surely has given us a strong proof of his opinion of the consequence of an American government, by his appointment of Lord Botetourt ; a man of a very amiable character here, remarkable for his very great attention to business, as he was said never to be absent from the House of Commons during twenty years he was a member of it, at reading of prayers or when the house was adjourned, and he has been as remarkable since he came to the House of Peers for his close attendance there. He never was married, has been ever commended for his hospitality and affability, has, I believe, a very independant fortune, and, I know, one of the prettiest seats in England, as I have often visited it with great pleasure. You'll find his Lordship's title a very old one, though he was long kept out of it. He is one of the Lords of the King's Bed Chamber, and has always sat in the chair, since his title was acknowledged, when the Lords have been in a committee. Upon my honor I think from his general character and the small acquaintance I have the honor of with him, no man is more likely to make the people of Virginia happy, nor scarce any one who will be able more and essentially to serve them here, and I do most sincerely rejoice at his appointment.

"His Lordship has employed me as his councillor as to the first arrangement of his family affairs in Virginia, and I have given him the best [advice] I could, and such as indeed it is impossible any one about him could have given. I wrote to your landlord Mr. Nicholson to take the conduct and direction of his Lordship's household till he arrives, and have told him his character. I wish he may be of use to him, however he will satisfy him genteelly for his trouble now, and will use him in his way of business for the future.   I have told his Lordship that it was not impossible but you may have purchased a set of horses for me.   If you have he will take them off my hands, and I shall be well quit of that expense.   I presume you will of course take the first opportunity of waiting on your new governor, and I have promised for you, even at this distance, that you will cheerfully render him any service, but perhaps he will be more convinced of it, if you tell him so yourself.   If you have any worthy industrious young man to recommend as a clerk to the Governor,—he must not be a gentleman above his business— perhaps you may get the berth for him.   I have told his Lordship that Mr. Walthoe and you will be able to furnish him with one immediately.   Remember if you choose to be concerned in the recommendation, that his Lordship is a man of business, and employ no fine, proud young gentleman who will be above his employment.

"I presume you will meet with no opposition in your election, but it may perhaps assist your interest if the people are informed that I have a promise that the accounts due them, since the campaign under General Braddock, and all claims on the Crown shall be paid them.   Lord Botetourt can tell you the steps I have taken in that business.   .   .   .

"The resolutions in the House of Burgesses, and Council in Virginia, puzzle the great ones much.   Lord Hillsborough has talked to me very often on the subject, and says he doubts they will draw the resentment of Parliament on themselves, and wished frequently to be directed from Virginia not to present them, which he must do if they do not cancel them.   I mentioned to his Lordship the unanimity with which they had passed, as he showed me the journals of the House where it was resolved *nem. con.;* and that no doubt they had maturely weighed the subject before they determined; that none but those who had made the resolutions could withdraw them, and I thought it very improbable a step which had been taken with general consent should be so soon cancelled.   I said I would mention his wish if he desired it, but that I had not interest, provided I was inclined to do so, to assist him in obtaining it.   But he still persisted after my saying this to him, to declare his desire of their retracting, and recommended it as the most prudent and salutary step that could now be taken. He has very frequently mentioned his astonishment at the council joining in these representations, as they are all appointed by the King : 'To do justice, my Lord, I hope,' added I. It has been so often reported here that the council were to be dismissed, that I make no doubt it will be wrote over as news to Virginia, but I know from authority no such step has even been thought of yet.

" You mention the difficulty you were in about fixing the price of the Shenandoah land, which from my father's letter I think may very easily be got over. Colonel Lewis, he writes me, was to purchase it.

" As I know your election will carry you to Hampshire, I enclose you Major Livingston's power of attorney and his papers ; it may perhaps fall in your way to talk to some of the people about them, and get some money for him, which you are to reserve for my orders. As we are come to elections, you may from me, and by my authority and request, decline any offer that may be made of electing me in Frederick. I would not serve a set who had showed so little regard for me in my absence, though they were more indebted to me than any man that ever was in their county, not even were they to elect me without a dissenting voice in the county, and of this I beg you will take the trouble to inform them, for I am as fixed as fate, and therefore will in time save all expense and the chance of an opposition.

" If you receive any money for me it will not be disagreeable to me to have it remitted, as the difficulty of getting money here is inconceivable. If a gentleman merchant lends you, after begging, praying, beseeching, importuning, etc., etc., he is sure to tell it to all the trades, and though you tell him you cannot pay him under six months, he will be sure to ask you for it every week of the time. Thank my God I owe none of the gentry, and it would distress me more to fall in debt to one of them again, than thrice the sum would in the hands of a real gentleman. I should hope I have had the good luck to make some tobacco ; it surely bears a good price in Virginia, if not there, it gives a very good one here, but I would rather take a good Virginia price than run the risk of the danger of the seas and the merchant's honesty."[1]

[1] MS. Letter owned by Wm. R. Mercer.

The appointment which he had received through the influence of Lord Hillsborough, to which Colonel Mercer refers so mysteriously, was that of Governor of North Carolina. He was appointed in 1769 to succeed Governor Tryon, who was sent to New York. But Colonel Mercer did not go to North Carolina after all, and Major Martin, a British officer, became governor of that colony in 1771. The resolutions of the Virginia Assembly which puzzled the great ones in England, were those passed in March, 1768, against the duties on glass, tea, etc. Governor Fauquier had summoned this Assembly, but his death occurring in the meantime, President Blair, of the council, presided over its deliberations, and countenanced its determined action in condemning the duties.

Arthur Lee wrote to his brother from London the year after Lord Botetourt's arrival : " Your governor is becoming very popular, as we are told here, and I have the worst proof of it in the increased orders for fineries from the ladies at this time of general distress in their families. . If his Excellency introduce such a spirit, I am sure his popularity will be ill-founded." Whether his Excellency was responsible or not for the reported extravagance of the Virginia ladies, he was soon to find the Virginia legislators not as complaisant as he could desire. Their resolutions in the spring session of the Assembly for this year, 1769, denying the right of England to tax the colonies, and denouncing the act for transporting colonial offenders to England for trial, so alarmed the good Botetourt, that he incontinently dissolved the House. The delegates then adjourned to the house of Mr. Anthony Hay, in Williamsburg, and passed the " Non-importation resolutions of the Association at Williamsburg." [1] These were offered by George Washington, either in person or by deputy, and they were written by his friend and neighbor, the retired planter of " Gunston Hall." Thomson Mason who had been constantly a member of the As-

---

[1] "Writings of Washington," W. C. Ford, vol. ii., p. 263. Mr. Ford thinks it doubtful that Washington was present.

sembly, representing Stafford County since 1758, was present at the May session of 1769, and he is named with Edmund Pendleton, Richard Bland, Robert Carter Nicholas, Richard Henry Lee, Peyton Randolph, and Thomas Jefferson, as the committee to draw up an address to the governor. The four important resolutions prepared in committee of the whole house, protested against taxation by any but the House of Burgesses, declaring it their privilege to petition for redress of grievances, giving their opinion that all trials for treason ought to be held within the colonies, and protesting against sending persons suspected of such a crime to be tried beyond the sea. The fourth resolve declared their intention of presenting a dutiful address to the king asking him to " avert from them those dangers and miseries which will ensue, from the seizing, and carrying beyond sea, any persons residing in America, suspected of any crime whatsoever, to be tried in any other manner than by the ancient and long-established course of proceeding." The speaker of the House was instructed to transmit these resolves to the several Houses of Assembly on the continent. A committee of six, of whom Thomson Mason was one, was appointed to draw up an address to the king on the fourth resolution. The address, which was reported the following day, May 17th, closed with wishing the king a prosperous reign ; "and that after death your Majesty may taste the fullest fruition of eternal bliss, and that a descendant of your illustrious house may reign over the extended British empire until time shall be no more."

A message was shortly after received from the governor commanding their attendance in the council chamber. His speech was brief and to the point: " Mr. Speaker, &c., I have heard of your Resolves and argue ill of their effect. You have made it my duty to dissolve you, and you are dissolved accordingly." [1] Then followed the meeting above referred to and the formation of the non-importation association.

[1] Journal of the Virginia Assembly.

Jefferson, who had but recently entered the Assembly, comments on the circumscribed condition of the minds of the colonial burgesses, at this time, accustomed as they had been to consider it their duty to study in everything the interests of the mother country: " Experience," he adds, " soon proved that they could bring their minds to rights, on the first summons of their attention." The first summons, as we have seen, had been given by Patrick Henry, and Jefferson was to do much, later, in the work of leading and moulding public opinion. But on this occasion, in 1769, the summons was to come from Washington and George Mason, the one in his official position as a member of the House, the other as the unseen but potent ally of his friend, whose thoughtful mind and vigorous pen were to be ever henceforth at his country's service. The following correspondence between Washington and Mason will explain the views of each on this subject of non-importation. The resolutions, in the handwriting of George Mason, were found among Washington's papers by the latter's biographer. They were evidently written out at the suggestion of Washington, as these letters show. Washington took the paper with him to the Assembly, and the burgesses, at their informal session after the dissolution, apparently adopted its principles with one accord :

MOUNT VERNON, 5th April, 1769,

DEAR SIR :

Herewith you will receive a letter and sundry papers [containing resolves of the merchants of Philadelphia, respecting the non-importation of articles of British manufacture] which were forwarded to me a day or two ago by Dr. Ross of Bladensburg. I transmit them with the greater pleasure, as my own desire of knowing your sentiments upon a matter of this importance exactly coincides with the doctor's inclinations.

At a time when our lordly masters in Great Britain will be satisfied with nothing less than the deprivation of American freedom, it seems highly necessary that something should be done to avert the stroke, and maintain the liberty, which we have derived from our ancestors. But the manner of doing it, to answer the purpose effectually, is the point in question. That no man should scruple or hesitate a moment, to use arms in defence of so valuable a blessing, is clearly my opinion. Yet arms, I would beg leave to add, should be the last resource, the *dernier resort.* We have already, it is said, proved the inefficacy of addresses to the throne, and remonstrances to parliament. How far, then, their attention to our rights and privileges is to be awakened or alarmed, by starving their trade and manufactures, remains to be tried.

The northern colonies, it appears, are endeavoring to adopt this scheme. In my opinion it is a good one and must be attended with salutary effects, provided it can be carried generally into execution. But to what extent it is practicable to do so, I will not take upon me to determine. That there will be a difficulty attending the execution of it everywhere, from clashing interests and selfish, designing men, ever attentive to their own gain, and watchful of every turn, that can assist their lucrative views, cannot be denied ; and in the tobacco colonies, where the trade is so diffused, and in a manner wholly conducted by factors for their principals at home, these difficulties are certainly enhanced, but I think not insurmountably increased if the gentlemen in their several counties will be at some pains to explain matters to the people, and stimulate them to cordial agreements to purchase none but certain enumerated articles out of any of the stores after a definite period, and neither import nor purchase any themselves. This, if it should not effectually withdraw the factors from their importations would at least make them extremely cautious in doing it, as the prohibited goods could be vended to none but the non-associators, or those who would pay no regard to their association ; both of whom ought to be stigmatized, and made the objects of public reproach.

The more I consider a scheme of this sort, the more ardently I wish success to it, because I think there are private as well as public advantages to result from it,—the former certain, however precarious the other may prove. In respect to the latter, I have always thought that by virtue of the same power, which assumes the right of taxation, the Parliament may attempt at least to restrain our manufactures, especially those of a public nature, the same equity and justice prevailing in the one case as the other, it being no greater hardship to forbid my manufacturing, than it is to order me to buy goods loaded with duties, for the express purpose of raising a revenue. But as a measure of this sort would be an additional exertion of arbitrary power, we cannot be placed in a worse condition, I think, by putting it to the test.

On the one hand, that the colonies are considerably indebted to Great Britain, is a truth universally acknowledged. That many families are reduced almost, if not quite, to penury and want by the low ebb of their fortunes, and that estates are daily selling for the discharge of debts, the public papers furnish too many melancholy proofs. That a scheme of this sort will contribute more effectually than any other that can be devised to extricate the country from the distress it at present labors under, I most firmly believe, if it can be generally adopted. And I can see but one class of people, the merchants excepted, who will not, or ought not, to wish well to the scheme—namely, they who live genteelly and hospitably on clear estates. Such as these, were they not to consider the valuable object in view, and the good of others, might think it hard to be curtailed in their living and enjoyments. As to the penurious man, he would thereby save his money and his credit, having the best plea for doing that which before, perhaps, he had the most violent struggles to refrain from doing. The extravagant and expensive man has the same good plea to retrench his expenses. He would be furnished with a pretext to live within bounds, and embrace it. Prudence dictated economy before, but his resolution was too weak to put it in practice. "For how can I," says he, "who have lived in such and such a manner, change my method? I am ashamed to do it, and besides, such an alteration in the system of my living will create suspicions of the decay of my fortune, and such a thought the world must not harbour." He continues his course, till at last his estate comes to an end, a sale of it being the consequence of his perseverance in error. This I am satisfied is the way that many, who have set out in the wrong track, have reasoned, till ruin has stared them in the face. And in respect of the needy man, he is only left in the same situation he was found in,—better I may say, because, as he judges from comparison, his condition is amended in proportion as it approaches nearer to those above him.

Upon the whole, therefore, I think the scheme a good one, and that it ought to be tried here, with such alterations as our circumstances render absolutely necessary. But in what manner to begin the work is a matter worthy of consideration. Whether it can be attempted with propriety or efficacy, further than a communication of sentiments to one another, before May, when the Court and Assembly will meet at Williamsburg, and a uniform plan can be concerted, and sent into the different counties to operate at the same time and in the same manner everywhere, is a thing upon which I am somewhat in doubt, and I should be glad to know your opinion. I am, &c.,

GEORGE WASHINGTON.

To Col. GEORGE MASON.[1]

Colonel Mason wrote on the same day to Washington, sending him later the Resolutions he had prepared. He says :

" I entirely agree with you, that no regular plan of the sort proposed can be entered into here, before the meeting of the General Court at least, if not of the Assembly. In the meantime it may be necessary to publish something preparatory to it in our gazettes, to warn the people of the impending danger, and induce them the more readily and cheerfully to concur in the proposed measures to avert it ; and something of this sort I had begun, but am unluckily stopped by a disorder, which affects my head and eyes. As soon as I am able I shall resume it and then write you more fully, or endeavour to see you. In the meantime pray commit to writing such hints as may occur.

" Our all is at stake, and the little conveniences and comforts of life, when set in competition with our liberty, ought to be rejected, not with reluctance, but with pleasure. Yet it is plain, that in the tobacco colonies we cannot at present confine our importations within such narrow bounds as the northern colonies, A plan of this kind, to be practicable, must be adapted to our circumstances ; for if not steadily executed, it had better have remained unattempted. We may retrench all manner of superfluities, finery of all descriptions, and confine ourselves to linens,

---

1 Sparks' " Life and Writings of Washington," vol. ii., p. 351.

woollens, &c., not exceeding a certain price. It is amazing how much this practice, if adopted in all the colonies, would lessen the American imports, and distress the various trades and manufactures in Great Britain.

"This would waken their attention. They would see, they would feel, the oppressions we groan under, and exert themselves to procure us redress. This once obtained, we should no longer discontinue our importations, confining ourselves still not to import any article that should hereafter be taxed by Act of Parliament for raising a revenue in America ; for, however singular I may be in my opinion, I am thoroughly convinced that justice and harmony happily restored, it is not the interest of these colonies to refuse British manufactures. Our supplying our mother country with gross materials and taking her manufactures in return, is the true chain of connexion between us. These are the bands, which, if not broken by oppression, must long hold us together, by maintaining a constant reciprocation of interest. Proper caution should, therefore, be used in drawing up the proposed plan of association. It may not be amiss to let the ministry understand that, until we obtain a redress of grievances, we will withhold from them our commodities, and particularly refrain from making tobacco, by which the revenue would lose fifty times more than all their oppressions could raise here.

"Had the hint which I have given with regard to taxation of goods imported into America, been thought of by our merchants before the repeal of the Stamp Act, the late American revenue acts would probably never have been attempted." [1]

Colonel Mason reminds Washington, in a postscript, that "next Friday is appointed for the meeting of the vestry."

There were interviews between the two friends, as has been elsewhere noted, after this letter was written, and they saw each other doubtless at the vestry-meeting and talked over the politics of the hour. Another letter, a brief one, of Colonel Mason's, on the subject of their conferences, has been preserved :

[1] *Ibid. ;* also Washington MSS., State Department.

GUNSTON HALL, 23 April, 1769.

DEAR SIR :

Upon looking over the Association, of which I sent you a copy, I have made some few alterations in it, as per memorandum on the other side.

I beg your care of the enclosed letters ; and heartily wishing you (what I fear you will not have) an agreeable session, I am,

Dear Sir,

Your most obedient servant,

G. MASON.

P. S.—I shall take it as a particular favor if you 'll be kind enough to get me two pairs of gold snaps made at Williamsburg, for my little girls.   They are small rings with a joint in them, to wear in the ears instead of ear-rings ; also a pair of toupee-tongs.'

The fashions were not to be neglected at "Gunston Hall" any more than at gay little Williamsburg, and the young daughters of Colonel Mason must, if possible, have their "gold snaps" for the ears and the tongs with which to curl the *toupee*, the little tuft of hair that was worn on the forehead.   But jewelry and other vanities were soon to be on the proscribed list with Virginia patriots, and the ladies were not behindhand after all in their support of the law-makers.   The gazettes of the period contain occasional letters from them in Virginia, as in the other colonies, declaring their determination to abstain from luxuries, and especially to banish "India tea" from their tables.   The draft of the Non-Importation Resolutions adopted at Williamsburg corresponds exactly with the one written by George Mason, except that two short articles were added and one of Mason's omitted.'   This last was a resolution advocating non-exportation of certain enumerated articles. Two letters of interest, written by George Mason in 1770, have been preserved.   One of them is unsigned, as part of it has been lost, and the other is without an address, though we

---

¹ Washington MSS., State Department.
² Burk's "History of Virginia," vol. iii., p. 345.   Appendix iv.

learn from the context that it was written to a young rela-
tive in England. The former letter was written to Richard
Henry Lee, and has reference chiefly to the Non-Importation
Association.

GUNSTON HALL, June 7, 1770.

DEAR SIR :

Your favor of the 26th May did not come to hand till the
5th instant, or I should have answered it sooner. I now enclose
you the abstract of [paper torn] of Act of Parliament in the 4th
year of his present Majesty's reign, with some remarks thereon, to
which I beg leave to refer you, and think you will find them
worthy of consideration, as the said Act of Parliament has never
been totally repealed.

I am glad to hear that the members below intend to establish
some farther regulations to render the Association effectual, and
I know of none that will answer the end proposed, but preventing
by all legal and peaceable means in our power (for we must avoid
even the appearance of violence) the importation of the enumerated goods; experience having too fully proved that when the
goods are here many of our people will purchase, even some who
effect to be called gentlemen. For this purpose the sense of
shame and the fear of reproach must be inculcated and enforced
in the strongest manner, and if that can be done properly it has
a much greater influence upon the actions of mankind than is
generally imagined. Nature has impressed this useful principle
upon every breast ; it is a just observation that if shame was ban-
ished out of the world, she would carry away with her what little
virtue is left in it.

The names of such persons as purchase or import goods
contrary to the Association should be published, and themselves
stigmatized as enemies to their country. We should resolve not
to associate or keep company with them in public places, and
they should be loaded with every mark of infamy and reproach.
The interest, too, of the importer may be made subservient to our
purpose, for if the principal people renounce all connection and
commerce forever with such merchants, their agents and factors,
who shall import goods contrary to the tenor of the Association,
they will hardly venture to supply their worst customers with
such articles at the hazard of losing their best. But I don't see

how these regulations can be affected by any other means than appointing committees in the counties to examine from time to time into the imports and to convey an account of any violation of the Association to the Moderator, to be by him published, or by a committee appointed for that purpose in Williamsburg, or in such other manner as shall be judged best, for without such committees in the country, I am convinced we shall once more fail of carrying the plan into execution. As it is of great conse-quence to have these committees composed of the most respecta-ble men [paper illegible] ; it will be best that one committee be appointed for two or more counties, as the circumstances of particular parts of the country may require, and such of the merchants as are members of the Association ought by all means to be of these committees. It is true in Maryland there is a committee in every county, but their counties are generally larger than two of ours. The committees, whenever there is an im-portation of goods within their respective districts, should convene themselves and in a civil manner apply to the mer-chants or importers concerned, and desire to see the invoyces and papers respecting such importation, and if they find any goods therein contrary to the Association, let the importers know that it is the opinion and request of the country that such goods shall not be opened or stored, but reshipped to the places from whence they came, and in case of refusal, without any manner of violence, inform them of the consequences, and proceed to publish an account of their conduct. I am persuaded there are few importers who would persist in refusing to comply with such a request, and proper resolution in the Association, with one or two public examples, would quickly put an end to it. The objection that this would be infringing the right of others while we are contending for liberty ourselves is ill founded. Every member of society is in duty bound to contribute to the safety and good of the whole ; and when the subject is of such importance as the liberty and happiness of a country, every inferior consideration, as well as the inconvenience to a few individuals, must give place to it ; nor is this any hardship upon them, as themselves and their posterity are to partake of the benefits resulting from it. Objections of the same kind might be made to the most useful civil institutions.

10

It may perhaps be proposed to have such goods as are imported contrary to the Association stored here unopened, instead of re-shipping them. But besides the risk of having such goods privately sold, storing them would by no means answer the same purposes as reshipping them, for if the goods are reshipped they will most of them be returned to the wholesale dealers and shop-keepers, and occasion an immediate stagnation of business between them and the manufacturers ; this would be practice, not theory, and beyond anything else convince the people of Great Britain that we are [paper torn] by an appeal to their own senses. I am at a loss to determine, even in my own mind, whether these proposed regulations ought to have retrospect, so as to require the reshipping of goods that were already imported before the 14th of this month. Not that I think there is any in-justice in it, because all such persons as have imported goods contrary to the Association, have done it with their eyes open, and at their own peril, with a view to private gain, which deserves no countenance from the public ; and those merchants who have conformed themselves to the opinion and interest of the country have some right to expect that [paper torn] of the Association should [paper torn] upon the occasion. The principal objection is the seeming impracticability of such a measure, which would put the committees upon very minute and difficult inquiries ; on the other hand, there are some strong reasons for such retrospect. There is great cause to believe that most of the cargoes refused to be received in the other colonies have been sent to this. I will mention some recent instances, particularly a ship a few weeks ago from Baltimore, in Maryland, with a cargo of about £3,000. And a committee which sat a few days ago in Port Tobacco, after examining a merchant's imports there, and finding nothing contrary to Association, at last accidentally stumbled upon an invoyce of eight or nine hundred pounds of anti Association goods ; the nest was there, but the birds were flown—no such goods could be found ; they had been privately sent to Virginia. Unless these machinations can be counteracted, and their contrivers effectually disappointed, Virginia will become the receptacle of all the goods refused by the other colonies, and from hence they will be sent again privately, in small quantities at a time, to frustrate the Associa-tions of the other parts of the continent ; to our everlasting scandal and to the weakening of that mutual confidence, which in these oppressive and dangerous times should be so carefully cherished and preserved. Suppose (to observe a sort of medium) that all goods imported contrary to the Association which now remain unopened, or uncut, should be directed to be reshipped ; or, if this is thought too much, the retrospect may be limited to a certain time, so as to include the goods that shall come from the neighboring colonies, which I believe is but a late practice. I have had some conversation with the neighboring merchants upon the subject ; they profess themselves ready to acquiesce in whatever shall be thought the interest of the country. Mr. Henderson, in particular, declares that he will cheerfully order to be packed up such goods as are contrary to the Association in any of the stores he has the direction of (and you know he is concerned for one of the greatest houses in the tobacco trade), and either store them until our grievances are redressed, or reship them if the gentlemen of the Association shall require it. In his own store he says there are no goods contrary to the Association. In this I think he [paper torn] well ; it is not the interest of his owner to forfeit the esteem and good will of the people of this colony. To do the merchants in this neighborhood justice, they have, so far as I have been able to observe, behaved in a very becoming manner, and have all along testified their willingness to accede to any measure that shall be judged conducive to the public good.

Whoever looks over with attention the proceedings of the ministerial party in the H——e of C——ns will be convinced that the late vote for a partial instead of a total repeal of the revenue act complained of was founded upon an opinion that the Americans could not persevere in their Associations. The custom-house books showed that the exports to Virginia in particular were very little if at all lessened ; and that the exports to this colony are of greater importance to Great Britain than to any other on this continent, will not be denied by any man acquainted with the subject ; this shows the necessity of our exerting ourselves effectually upon the present occasion. Our sister colonies all expect it from us, our interest and our liberty and happiness, as well as that of our posterity, everything that is near and dear to us in this world requires it. [GEORGE MASON.][1]

[1] MS. Letter.

GUNSTON HALL, Dec. 6, 1770.

DEAR SIR :

I have your favor of the 7th July, which is the third you have obliged me with since you left Virginia. That I have not answered them sooner, I hope you know is not owing to want of friendship ; it will always give me pleasure to hear of your welfare, and a young fellow of twenty must not stand upon ceremony with an old one of forty-five. I am much obliged to you for the pamphlets you sent me ; we have had them in detached pieces in the public papers, but there is no judging of such performances by scraps. Junius's letters are certainly superior to anything of the kind that ever appeared in our language. The most remarkable periods for party-writing were about the change of the ministry in Queen Anne's time, and the latter end of Sir Robert Walpole's ministry in the late King's reign, and although the ablest men in the nation then entered the lists their performances fell far short of Junius. Most of our best writers have imitated the florid Ciceronian style, but this author is really an original. Learned and elegant without the vanity of seeming so, his manner of expression, though new and almost peculiar to himself, is yet free from the affectation of singularity, bold and nervous like the genius of the nation he writes for.

The non-importation associations here are at present in a very languid state. Most people seem inclined to try what the Parliament will do this winter towards redressing the American grievances, as they showed some inclination last session to a reconciliation. We are not without hopes that when men's passions have had time to cool, and reason takes its place, that this most desirable end may be attained, and that happy harmony restored which for more than a century produced such mutual benefits to both countries. Perdition seize the man whose arbitrary maxims and short-sighted policy first interrupted it ! But should the oppressive system of taxing us without our consent be continued, the flame lowered now will break out with redoubled ardor, and the spirit of opposition (self-defence is its proper name) wear a more formidable shape than ever—more formidable because more natural and practicable. The associations, almost from one end of this continent to the other, were drawn up in a hurry and formed upon erroneous principles. It was imagined that they would occasion such a sudden stagnation in trade, and such murmurs among the manufacturers of Great Britain that the parliament would feel the necessity of immediately repealing the American revenue acts. One year would do the business, and for one year or two we could do without importing almost anything from Great Britain. Men sanguine in an interesting subject easily believe that must happen which they wish to happen ; thus the Americans entered into agreements which few were able to perform even for the short time at first thought necessary. Many circumstances have concurred to frustrate such a scheme, particularly the unusual demand for British goods from the northern part of Europe, and more than anything else the impracticability of the scheme itself, and the difference between the plans adopted in the different provinces. Time has pointed out our mistakes, and errors well known are more than half corrected. Had the subject been well digested and an association entered into which people would have felt themselves easy under and persevered in ; had one general plan been formed exactly the same for all the colonies (so as to have removed all cause of jealousy or danger of interfering with each other) in the nature of a sumptuary law, restraining only articles of luxury and ostentation together with the goods at any time taxed, and at the same time giving all encouragement to American manufacturers and invitations to manufacturers from Europe to remove hither and settle among us, and as these increased from time to time still decreasing our European imports ; an association being formed upon these principles would have gathered strength by execution, and however slow in its operation it would have been certain in its effects. It may perhaps be thought that the trade of Great Britain would be little affected by such restriction, but luxury and ostentation are comprehensive terms, and I will venture to affirm that it immediately would lessen the imports to this continent from Great Britain £300,000, and the government would lose more in one year on two articles only (manufactured tobacco and malt liquors) than it would gain in ten by the American revenue acts.

Such a plan as this is now in contemplation, God grant we may have no cause to carry it into practice. Had the colonies an intention of throwing off their dependence, was the sovereignty of

Great Britain really in dispute as the ministry affect to believe, administration would be right in asserting the authority of the mother country ; it would be highly culpable if it did not do so, but the wildest chimera that ever disturbed a madman's brain has not less foundation in truth than this opinion. The Americans have the warmest affection for the present royal family, the strongest attachment to the British government and constitution ; they have experienced its blessings and prefer it to any that does or ever did exist ; while they are protected in the enjoyment of its advantages they can never wish to change. There are not five men of sense in America who would accept of independence if it was offered ; we know our own circumstances too well ; we know that our own happiness, our very being, depends upon our being connected with our mother country. We have always acknowledged, we are always ready to recognize, the government of Great Britain, but we will not submit to have our own money taken out of our pockets without our consent, because, if any man or any set of men take from us without our consent or that of our representatives one shilling in the pound we have no security for the remaining nineteen. We owe our mother country the duty of subjects ; we will not pay her the submission of slaves. So long as Great Britain can preserve the vigor and spirit of her own free and happy constitution, so long may she, by a mild and equal government, preserve her sovereignty over these colonies. What may be the effect of violence and oppression no man can answer, but any man may venture to pronounce that they can never be productive of good.

In answer to your question about the subscription to Mr. Wilkes, there was a subscription set on foot to ship that gentleman forty-five hogsheads of tobacco as a small acknowledgment for his sufferings in the cause of liberty, which I believe would have been filled up but for the very Mr. Miles you mention. He very officiously contrived to get the subscription into his hands, and after collecting some of the tobacco and applying it to his own use, as soon as the matter took wind, fearing a little American discipline upon the occasion, he scampered off with the subscription papers and has never been heard of since. I do not tell you this of my own knowledge (for I never saw Miles), but I believe there is no doubt of the truth of the fact.

I received a letter from my kinsman, Col. Mercer, dated the 24th July, speaking very doubtfully of the Ohio Company's affairs in England. This is only the third letter from him which ever came into my hands since I saw him in Virginia until this very day, when I received a small packet from him containing some interesting intelligence, but of a very old date, so long ago as the 2d of last January. From what he says of the many letters he has wrote me, and from what I know of the number I have wrote him, I am convinced some s—l who knows our handwriting must have interrupted them, though I can't pretend even to guess at any particular person. He tells me in his letter of the 24th of July that he shall leave England in September, otherwise Mr. Macpherson's going to London would have afforded me a certain opportunity of assuring him that a few years' absence had neither erased him out of my memory or affection. As to the Ohio Company's affairs here I could have given him no satisfaction or information. It is absolutely more difficult to procure a meeting of our members than it is to assemble a German Diet ; notwithstanding appointments and advertisements without number, I really believe there has never been a meeting of the Company since he went from Virginia.

As your brother Robert goes to London in the same ship by which I write, he will inform you of the situation of our relatives and friends in Virginia and Maryland. All at Gunston Hall join in wishing you health and happiness with, dear sir,

Your affectionate kinsman and obedient servant,

G. MASON.[1]

A recent writer has noted the excellence of the "party writing" in one of the periods to which George Mason alludes "The age," he says of Queen Anne's time, "was prolific in pamphlets. . . . It would be difficult to find a period when pamphleteers were both so many and so brilliant. With more or less to say of the Sacheverell affair we have Swift, Defoe, Atterbury, Davenant, Mainwaring, Charles Leslie, Tom Brown, and William King."[2] As his mother's uncle had been engaged in the "Sacheverell affair," no

---

[1] Mason Papers.
[2] "Reign of Queen Anne," vol. ii., p. 273, J. Hill Burton.

doubt Colonel Mason had read of it with more than ordinary interest. In his discussion of the merits of Junius, George Mason evinces his appreciation of the caustic style of the great unknown, whose letters were eagerly read by the American patriots, the latter seeing in these trenchant attacks upon the ministry a justification of their own course. Arthur Lee in London was corresponding with their author and signing his own productions *Junius Americanus.* Wilkes too was a hero at this time in America as well as in England, among good whigs. The tribute of the tobacco-planters in Virginia to his services in the cause of liberalism would seem to have met with unmerited disaster. The second "Association" had been formed in Williamsburg in June, 1770, and it is significant to mark George Mason's fervent hope that nothing more would be needed, and his emphatic protest against the "chimera" of independence may be taken as a fair indication of the general sentiment on the subject at this period. William Lee was also in London in 1770, and was sheriff of the city at the time of Wilkes' mayoralty. He wrote home to his brother, Richard Henry Lee, on the 6th of February, giving a graphic account of the political situation:

"Lords Camden and Chatham are greater than ever ; the last is really divine. His sentiments and expressions of America are the same as before. The second instant the House of Lords sate from two in the evening till past two in the morning, later than ever was known. Lord Chatham astonished even those that had known him for near forty years, though he was laboring under a fit of the gout. Lords Mansfield, Marchmont, Egmont, and all the rest fell before him like grass before a keen scythe. But 't was all in vain—a question involving annihilation to the constitution was carried against him by a great majority."

In the hall of the Virginia House of Assembly hangs to-day the full-length portrait of Lord Chatham, painted in 1768, by Charles Wilson Peale, then a young artist just beginning his career. It was the gift of a Virginian living in London, to the gentlemen of Westmoreland

County. Richard Henry Lee wrote over on behalf of himself and his neighbors to order Lord Camden's portrait about this time. It was to have been painted by West, but the artist could never find the great man ready to give him a sitting, and finally, in 1769, Lord Camden frankly admit- ted that he deemed it inexpedient to gratify his American admirers.[1] William Lee describes also an episode in the House of Commons, when "Col. Barré and Mr. Burke made everybody laugh ready to die for near an hour with their comments on Lord Botetourt's two speeches to your Assembly; the last Col. Barré challenged the whole min- istry, and defied them to make common sense of."[2] But the Virginians loved and respected Lord Botetourt, believ- ing him to be at heart their friend. And after his death, which occurred in this same year, they placed a statue of him in Williamsburg, where it may still be seen.

Lord Fairfax's books show that in October, 1771, George Mason had a tract of land granted to his father in 1709 re-surveyed, as he thought it contained surplus land. This proved to be the case, and the re-survey reached "to the line of Nicholas Brent's now Col. George Washington's land."[3] In September, 1772, Colonel Mason was at "Mt. Eilbeck," in Charles County, Maryland, on a visit appa- rently to his wife's mother, then a widow.[4] Colonel Eilbeck died in 1765, and Mrs. Eilbeck in 1780.

Thomson Mason, who had removed from Stafford County to Loudoun, was in the February Assembly, 1772—taking his seat, it would seem, on the 30th of March when he was placed immediately on the more important com- mittees. In April an address was drawn up to present to the king, protesting against the slave trade. It stated that "the importation of slaves into the colonies from the coast of Africa hath long been considered as a trade

---

[1] "Virginia Historical Register," vol. i., p. 68.
[2] "Lee's Campaigns of 1781," p. 63.
[3] Virginia Land Registry Office.
[4] MS. Letter.

of great inhumanity, and under its present encouragement we have too much reason to fear will endanger the
very existence of your Majesty's American dominions.
We are sensible that some of your Majesty's subjects in
Great Britain may reap emoluments from this sort of
traffic, but when we consider that it greatly retards the
settlement of the colonies with more useful inhabitants,
and may, in time, have the most destructive influence, we
presume to hope that the interest of a few will be disre-
garded when placed in competition with the security and
happiness of such numbers of your Majesty's dutiful and
loyal subjects" The petitioners besought the king to remove all those restraints on the governors of the colony,
"which inhibit their assenting to such laws as might check so
very pernicious a commerce."

A bill for opening and extending the navigation of the
Potomac River from Fort Cumberland to tide-water was committed to Thomson Mason, George Washington, and others.[1]
At this same session a law was passed making provision for
keeping in repair the roads leading to Alexandria and Colchester from the northwestern parts of the colony. They were
at this time, it is stated, owing to the large number of wagons
that used them, almost impassable. The county courts of
Fairfax, Loudoun, Berkeley, and Frederick, were required to
levy certain stipulated taxes for three years on the inhabitants of these counties, these sums to be paid by the respective
sheriffs to Thomson Mason, Francis Peyton, Bryan Fairfax,
Alexander Henderson, and others, who are appointed trustees
to carry the act into execution.[2]

In February, 1772, George Mason added two hundred
and fourteen acres to certain tracts in Hampshire that
he had bought in 1754.[3] The proprietor's office had been
removed from Fairfax to Frederick County. Washington
was having lands surveyed for himself at this time on
the Ohio, and he and George Mason, as members of

---

[1] Journal of the Virginia Assembly.   [2] Hening's "Statutes," vol. 8.
[3] Virginia Land Registry Office.

the Ohio Company, were interested in this locality. In a letter written to Washington, December 21st, 1773, by George Mason, the latter says: " I am much obliged to you for your information concerning the land upon the western waters. I long to have a little chat with you upon the subject." [1] William Crawford had been commissioned by the College of William and Mary as surveyor of the Ohio Company in 1773, in place of Christopher Gist, who was now dead. Crawford was Washington's friend and his agent in the western-land purchases, and he writes to Washington in the fall of this year: " I waited on Colonel Mason on my return home, and have agreed with him to survey the Ohio land as soon as the land for the soldiers is done." [2]

The affairs of the Ohio Company had reached a disastrous crisis in 1773. As early as 1765 there had been a project set on foot by Sir William Johnson, Governor Franklin, and others, to establish a colony in the Illinois country, on land which was within Virginia's chartered territory. This was revived in 1769 by Thomas Walpole, Samuel Wharton, Benjamin Franklin, and others, who formed what was called the Grand Company. The new colony was to be named Vandalia. In 1772, Lord Hillsborough reported adversely on the Walpole petition: " A measure which we conceive is altogether as unnecessary as it is impolitic, as we see nothing to hinder the government of Virginia from extending the laws and constitution of that colony to such persons as may have already settled there under legal titles." [3] Dr. Franklin made an elaborate and specious reply to Lord Hillsborough, in which he denied Virginia's title to the land, assuming that it had belonged to the Six Nations, from whom it was purchased for the king in 1768, at Fort Stanwix. Walpole's petition was granted, and Col. George Mercer, entirely without the consent of its members in Virginia, agreed to merge the Ohio Company in the Grand

---

[1] Washington MSS., State Department.
[2] " Washington–Crawford Letters," p. 36.
[3] " Works of Franklin," Sparks, vol. iv., p. 302.

Company. A letter of Colonel Mercer's, however, written in 1767, shows that he was then working diligently to secure the rights of the Virginia enterprise, the Ohio Company of 1748, whose grant was made to it as a part of Virginia, and whose members had no disloyal intention of setting up a separate government from that of the Old Dominion. He is writing to the company from London, November 21st. He speaks of the project of establishing new governments as no longer a secret, and he tells of his interviews with the Board of Trade, where he was examined on the subject of their practicability, expense, etc. He says:

"I took an opportunity in the course of my examination to mention the disappointments of the Ohio Company, to shew the use and necessity of their scheme of settlement, etc. . . And at the same time I thought it hard treatment to the Ohio Company that a set of gentlemen just informed of the fertility of that world, should be allowed to settle it, and have all the advantages which the first execution of a settlement there must at first enjoy over a later one, while the Ohio Company were restrained from what they esteemed a right, and for which they had paid very heavily ; while these Adventurers acknowledge themselves, not only indebted to the discoveries made at the expence of the Company, for part of their information, but for the passage they had at a great expence too, opened for them through the mountains, as they should always use the Company's road to convey everything and their settlers to their government. Indeed I complained as much as I thought I dared to do, of the delays the Company had met with, and especially in the last reference of their claim to the governor of Virginia." [1]

And he urges that the governor's report be sent over as soon as possible to re-enforce the company's claim. In August, 1771, Colonel Mercer wrote to the Ohio Company complaining that no instructions were sent him and no money, and that five letters he had written—one in 1767, and four in 1770—remained unanswered.[2] He tells of his admission to

---

[1] MS. Letter.

[2] Letter of Robert Carter, from the "Carter Letter-Books."

the Grand Company, and that " the whole claim of the Ohio Company is denominated two shares, which are entered on the minutes of the G. C. [to him] as agent for the Ohio Company." The difficulties in the way of correspondence between the company in Virginia and its agent in England were so remarkable as to lead to the inference that their mail was intercepted. Not hearing from any one in America, Colonel Mercer was won over to the Vandalia scheme, and he was promised the appointment of governor of the new colony. He wrote to George William Fairfax on the 2d of December, 1773, telling him of the compromise that was proposed, by which the two companies should be merged into one. But new scruples arose on the part of the English government : " I am not yet Governor," he adds, " and a fresh objection, the last I hope they have to offer, has arisen against the policy of the grant, so far as it relates to Britain." [1]

George Mason's correspondence with Colonel Mercer on this subject has not been preserved. But a valuable paper written by Colonel Mason in 1773, " Extracts from the Virginia Charters, with Some Remarks on Them," was evidently written to refute the arguments of Franklin and in support of the Ohio Company's claim. And the cause of the company was the cause of Virginia. This manuscript is referred to with commendation by both Bancroft and Grigsby. The latter says that it " was regarded as an unanswerable exposition of colonial rights under the charters," and " proved a rich mine of authority in the controversy then waging between the King and his colonies." [2] After a full discussion of the charters and quotations from acts of the Assembly under them, Colonel Mason goes on to say that these " demonstrate that the country to the westward of the Alleghany Mountains, on both sides of the Ohio River, is part of Virginia. And consequently that no new Government or Proprietary can legally be established there. Nor hath any attempt of that sort ever been made from the time of the

[1] " The Fairfaxes of England and America," p. 140
[2] " Virginia Convention of 1776," H. B. Grigsby.

said charter [the charter of King Charles II.] until the late extraordinary application of Mr. Walpole and his associates, to the Crown to grant them a Proprietary Charter and create a new government between the Alleghany mountains and the River Ohio (in direct violation of the Virginia Charters), which would not only have taken away great part of the territory of this colony, but would have removed from under the immediate protection of the Crown and the Government of Virginia several thousand inhabitants settled there under the faith of the said Charters, etc.   .   .   .   To this illegal and injurious attempt several Gentlemen in Virginia, the Ohio Company, were made in some measure accessory, without their knowledge and very contrary to their inclination ; but at the first general meeting after having received notice of it, they unanimously declared their disapprobation of the measure and their absolute refusal of having any concern in it, which regulation they not only entered in their own books and communicated to the member of their Company in England, but for their justification to posterity sent a copy thereof to the Governor and Council to be entered if they thought fit, on their journals." [1]

[1] Appendix v.

CHAPTER V.

THE FAIRFAX COUNTY COMMITTEE OF SAFETY.

1773–1775.

In 1773, the peaceful household at " Gunston Hall" was visited by a great affliction in the death of Mrs. Mason, the devoted wife and mother, the kind mistress, who for twenty-three years had been its presiding domestic genius. The eldest child at this time was a youth of twenty and the eldest daughter was a year or two younger. Thomas, the youngest son and child, was born in 1770, and was baptized, as the family Bible records, by the Rev. Lee Massey, Mr. Martin Cockburn and Capt. John Lee standing god-fathers and Mrs. Mary Massey and Mrs. Ann Cockburn god-mothers. The little Elizabeth, the youngest of four sisters, had been born two years previously. They were a happy united family, writes General Mason in his reminiscences. " Of my mother," he says, " being only seven years old at the time of her death, I have in most things but an imperfect recollection, but some matters relating to her of a domestic nature are yet perfectly written in my remembrance. As my father was spared until I had grown to manhood and indeed entered on the busy scenes of life, I of course remember much of him. We, the children, all lived together in great harmony at the paternal mansion, until the respective periods when each by marriage, or pursuits in business for themselves, were successively drawn off from that common home." The son's recollections of his mother's room are thus minutely detailed:

"I remember well the appearance and arrangement of her chamber. There stood, among other things, a large old chest of drawers so-called, which held the children's clothes, to which, little fellow as I was, I was often carried to get something, or would run there to rummage it without leave. The lower tier consisted of three drawers, the middle and larger of these was the [word illegible] drawer, that on the right and smaller was the [word illegible] drawer. Next above and the whole length of the case was the cap drawer, next above that, a deep one also and of the whole length, was the gown drawer. Next above was the shirt drawer, and next to that the jacket drawer. Then above all came the drawers, each of half length, which were kept locked. They were devoted to my mother's more private use and for matters of greater value. The other drawers were always unlocked and each was devoted to the purpose its name designated, and by that name it was known and used by all the family. There were also two large, deep closets, one on each side of the deep recess afforded by a spacious stack of chimnies. The one on the right of the chimney contained the current part of my mother's wardrobe and was called her closet, or, as the case might be by children or servants, ' mama's closet,' or ' mistress's closet.' The other, on the left, was emphatically designated *the* closet. It held the smaller or more precious stores for the table, and would now. I suppose, be called an upper pantry. I can't forget one of the articles deposited in my mother's closet. It was a small, green horsewhip, with a silver head and ring by which it was hung there against one of the walls, and which my mother used to carry when she rode on horseback, as she often did when in health. This little instrument was applied sometimes to other purposes as discipline required among the children, and we used to call it the ' green doctor.' "

Of Mrs. Mason's last illness we have this account :

" My revered mother was afflicted for a considerable time and confined to her room or bed for some months by the disease which terminated in her death. Long as that has been ago and young as I then was, yet I am confident in the recollection of her and of some of the scenes of her latter days, as well as of the furniture and structure of her room, and the more so that they have often since passed in review from time to time in my mind. She was attended during her illness by Dr. Craik, who lived in Charles County, Maryland, near my grandfather Eilbeck, and who was afterwards the surgeon-general of the Revolutionary army, and was the intimate and personal friend of General Wash. ington as he was of my father. Among his prescriptions for her was weak milk punch to be taken in bed in the morning. Little urchin as I was, it is yet fresh on my mind, that I was called sometimes by this beloved mother to her bedside to drink a little of this beverage, which I loved very much, from the bottom of the cup. The last that I remember, of that affectionate parent and excellent woman (for I know by the tradition of the surrounding country, among rich and poor, that she was beloved and admired by everybody for her virtues and charities), is that she took me one day in her arms on her sick bed, I believe it must have been but a few days before her death, told me she was soon going to leave us all, kissed me and gave me her blessing, and charged me to be a good boy, to love and obey my father, to love and never to quarrel with my brothers and sisters, to be kind to the servants, and if God spared me, when I grew up, to be an honest and useful man. The precise words in which this departing and all-affecting charge and blessing were conveyed, I, of course, cannot be certain about, but the substance of them I know I have retained ; and I well remember that I had intelligence and sensibility enough to be aware of the sacredness of the charge, and of the awful crisis in the family it foreboded, that I received it with a swollen heart and fell immediately into a hearty and long cry. It may be supposed that I have retained a perfect recollection of this scene when I say, as I can with truth, that I have been in the habit of often recalling it to my mind, with pious regard, as well in my younger as in latter days, and I believe and hope it has had its influence on my course of life. I ought not to omit to add that it was my mother's constant habit to make me and the other younger children, one or two at a time, kneel down before her, put our hands on her lap, and say our prayers every night before we went to bed. I remember well her funeral, that the whole family went into deep mourning suddenly prepared, that I was led clothed in black to her grave, that I saw her coffin lowered down into it by cords coverd with black cloth, and that there was a large assemblage of friends and neighbors of every class and of the slaves of the estate present ; that the house was in a state of desolation for a good while, that the children and servants passed each other in tears and silence or spoke in whispers, and that my father for some days, paced the rooms, or from the house to the grave (it was not far) alone." [1]

In the family Bible is preserved, in George Mason's own handwriting, the following tribute to the wife so sincerely loved and so deeply lamented :

" On Tuesday, the ninth of March, 1773, about three o'clock in the morning, died at Gunston Hall, of a slow fever, Mrs. Ann Mason, in the thirty-ninth year of her age, after a painful and tedious illness of more than nine months, which she bore with truly Christian patience and resignation, in faithful hope of eternal happiness in the world to come. She, it may be truthfully said, led a blameless and exemplary life. She retained, unimpaired her mental faculties to the last ; and spending her latest moments in prayer for those around her, seemed to expire without the usual pangs of dissolution. During the whole course of her illness, she was never heard to utter one peevish or fretful complaint, and wholly regardless of her own pain and danger, [she] endeavoured to administer hope and comfort to her friends, or inspire them with resignation like her own. For many days before her death she had lost all hopes of recovery, and endeavoured to wean herself from the affections of this life, saying that although it must cost her a hard struggle to reconcile herself to the thoughts of parting with her husband and children, she hoped God would enable her to accomplish it ; and after this, though she had always been the tenderest parent, she took little notice of her children, but still retained her usual serenity of mind.

" She was buried in the family burying-ground at Gunston Hall; but (at her own request) without the common parade and ceremony of a grand funeral. Her funeral sermon was preached in Pohick Church by the Rev. Mr. James Scott, rector of Dettingen

---

[1] MS. of Genl. John Mason.

Parish, in the county of Prince William, upon a text taken from the twenty-third, twenty-fourth, and twenty-fifth verses of the seventy-third Psalm.

"In the beauty of her person and the sweetness of her disposition, she was equalled by few and excelled by none of her sex. She was something taller than the middle size, and elegantly shaped. Her eyes were black, tender and lively ; her features regular and delicate ; her complexion remarkably fair and fresh, Lilies and roses (almost without a metaphor) were blended there, and a certain inexpressible air of cheerfulness and health. Innocence and sensibility diffused over her countenance formed a face the very reverse of what is generally called masculine. This is not an ideal but a real picture drawn from the life, nor was this beautiful outward form disgraced by an unworthy inhabitant.

> " ' Free from her sex's smallest faults,
> And fair as womankind can be.'

She was blessed with a clear and sound judgment, a gentle and benevolent heart, a sincere and an humble mind, with an even, calm and cheerful temper to a very unusual degree ; affable to all, but intimate with few. Her modest virtues shunned the public eye ; superior to the turbulent passions of pride and envy, a stranger to altercation of any kind, and content with the blessings of a private station, she placed all her happinness here, where only it is to be found, in her own family. Though she despised dress, she was always neat ; cheerful, but not gay ; serious, but not melancholy ; she never met me without a smile ! Though an only child, she was a remarkably dutiful one. An easy and agreeable companion, a kind neighbor, a steadfast friend, a humane mistress, a prudent and tender mother, a faithful, affectionate, and most obliging wife ; charitable to the poor, and pious to her Maker ; her virtue and religion were unmixed with hypocrisy or ostentation. Formed for domestic happiness, without one jarring atom in her frame ! Her irreparable loss I do and ever shall deplore, and though time I hope will soften my sad impressions, and restore me greater serenity of mind than I have lately enjoyed, I shall ever retain the most tender and melancholy remembrance of one so justly dear."

A handsome altar-shaped tomb was erected by Colonel Mason to his wife's memory. The four sides are of white marble, the base and upper portion of gray stone. On one side is the following inscription :

"Ann Mason Daughter of William Eilbeck
(of Charles County in Maryland Merchant
departed this Life on the 9th Day of March 1773
(in the 39th Year of her Age after a long and
painful illness, which she bore with uncommon
(Fortitude and Resignation.—

" Once She was all that cheers and sweetens Life ;
The tender Mother, Daughter, Friend, and Wife :
Once She was all that makes Mankind adore ;
Now view this Marble, and be vain no more." [1]

The following lines were found in Colonel Mason's pocket-book, after his death, and were preserved by his daughter, Mrs. McCarty, who believed them to have been written or copied shortly after her mother's death :

" Sweet were the halcyon hours when o'er my bed
Peace spread her opiate pinions, through the night ;
Love scattered roses gently round my head,
And morning waked me to increased delight ;
Yet every future hour resigned I 'd bear,
Oh could I but forget what once they were !
But nightly visions only keep alive
The fond remembrance of her much-loved form ;
And waking thoughts tend only to revive
The wreck of joys o'er which I mourn ;
Alas ! what can the honors of the world impart
To soothe the anguish of a bleeding heart."

Moved doubtless by the solemn warning of man's mortality given him through this bereavement, George Mason, on the 20th of March, 1773, eleven days after his wife's

---

[1] " Epistle to Mr. Jervas—with Mr. Dryden's Translation of Fresnoy's Art of Painting."—*Pope.* The epitaph on the wife of William Wirt—Sept. 17, 1799— is from the same poem. The lines in each case are slightly altered.

death, made his will. It was contained in fifteen pages and written with his own hand. He begins in the following manner:

" I, George Mason, of Gunston Hall, in the parish of Truro and county of Fairfax, being of perfect and sound mind and memory and in good health, but mindful of the uncertainty of human life and the imprudence of a man's leaving his affairs to be settled upon a death-bed, do make and appoint this my last will and tes- tament. My soul I resign into the hands of my Almighty Creator, whose tender mercies are over all his works, who hateth nothing that he hath made and to the Justice and Wisdom of whose dis- pensation I willingly and cheerfully submit, humbly hoping from his unbounded mercy and benevolence through the merits of my blessed Saviour, a remission of my sins."

He wishes to be buried by the side of his " dear and ever lamented wife." His eldest son George and his " good friend Mr. Martin Cockburn " were appointed executors of his will; and that no dispute or difficulty might arise to his executors or children about the division of his property among the residuary legatees, Colonel Mason appointed his " good friends the Rev. Mr. James Scott, the Rev. Mr. Lee Mas- sey, Mr. John West, Jun., Col. George Washington and Mr. Alexander Henderson," whenever it was necessary to make such division. And he adds: " I hope they will be so charitable as not to refuse undertaking this trouble for the sake of a friend who when living would cheerfully have done the many good office in his power." We learn who were Colonel Mason's intimate friends at this time by the trust here given, as well as by the bequests such as the following:

" I desire my old and long-tried friends the Rev. Mr. James Scott and Mr. John West, Junr., each of them to accept of a mourning ring. I leave to my friend and relation the Rev. Mr. Lee Massey a mourning ring . and I intreat the favor of him to advise and assist my Executors in the direc- tion and management of my affairs. I am encouraged to re- quest this of him from the experience I have had myself of his good offices that way and I am satisfied that both he and my worthy friend Mr. Cockburn will excuse the trouble I now give them when they reflect upon the necessity that dying men are under of thus employing the care and kindness of the living which must also one day be their own case. And as the most acceptable acknowledgment I can make them, desire them to receive out of the common stock of my estate the sum of ten pounds a year to be laid out by them in private charities upon such as they shall judge worthy objects."

Standing sadly by his wife's open grave George Mason spoke as a dying man. But life—public life—was just open- ing out before him. Three years before, to the boy of twenty, he had called himself an old man. He was then forty-five and now at forty-eight he doubtless felt that life had given him of its best. But in truth his talents and ener- gies were in their prime; and the blow that had fallen upon his domestic happiness may have been just the discipline of sorrow that was needed to brace his spirit—so enamoured of the sweets of a private station—for the performance of the grave public duties before him. And while he seemed to himself to put away the world and the world's work, in his noble exhortation to his sons the fires of patriotism are seen to glow as a flame within his soul. The charge to them was to be his own call to duty. In his will, while he recom- mends them to " prefer the happiness of a private station to the troubles and vexations of public business," he adds :

" If either their own inclination or the necessity of the times should engage them in public affairs, I charge them on a father's blessing never to let the motives of private interest or ambition induce them to betray, nor the terrors of poverty and disgrace, or the fear of dangers or of death, deter them from asserting the liberty of their country and endeavouring to transmit to their posterity those sacred rights to which themselves were born."

Mrs. Mason's funeral sermon was preached on the 27th of April, as we learn from Washington's diary. Mrs. Washing- ton drove to Pohick church to hear it, carrying with her

Mrs. Calvert and Mrs. William Augustine Washington, who, with their husbands, were on a visit to "Mt. Vernon." A few days later Washington went to see his sorrowing friend, taking dinner at "Gunston Hall," and returning home in the afternoon. Sorrow entered the "Mt. Vernon" household also in this year—lovely young Martha Custis dying on the 19th of June, 1773. Colonel Mason now in his turn visited the house of mourning. Meeting Washington at court the next day, he returned with him to "Mt. Vernon," where he remained overnight. Colonel Mason was not at "Mt. Vernon" again until the 16th of August, when he was there with his friend Major Jenifer, staying over until the eighteenth. In the spring of 1774, before the opening of the Assembly, which carried him to Williamsburg, Washington had another visit from George Mason, who probably wished to talk with him about the building of a vestry-house in the parish. The following advertisement on the subject appeared in *The Virginia Gazette*, on the 21st of April:

" To be let, on Friday the 22d of April, at the new church near Pohick, in Truro Parish, Fairfax Co., to the lowest bidder, by the vestry of the said Parish,

"The building of a Brick Vestry House 24 feet long and 18 feet wide, the enclosing of the said Churchyard 158 feet square, with posts and rails, the posts to be of sawed cedar, and the rails yellow pine, clear of sap, with three handsome palisade gates, the whole to be done in the neatest and most substantial manner.

"G. MASON
"THOMAZIN ELLZEY } Churchwardens."

In 1773 the movement for more combined action between the colonies received a stimulus by the origination in the Virginia House of Burgesses of Committees of Correspondence. Massachusetts soon after made a similar proposal. The resistance to the duty upon tea was more or less marked throughout all the colonies. But in Boston the signal action of its citizens, December, 1773, in throwing the tea overboard from the vessels in the harbor, brought down

upon them the vengeance of the administration in the Boston Port Bill, which threatened to destroy their commerce
and occasioned great distress to many of the poorer class of
the community.   This was in May, 1774, and the Virginia
Assembly was in session when the news reached Williamsburg.   A circular letter was sent from Boston, written by
Samuel Adams, to all the colonies, asking for their aid and
sympathy in this crisis.   The Virginia burgesses passed a
resolution on the 24th of May appointing the 1st of June,
the day on which the bill was to take effect, as a day of
fasting and prayer, in view of the distressed condition of
Boston.   And for this unequivocal expression of the light
in which they viewed the action of the government, Lord
Dunmore, on Thursday, the 26th of May, dissolved the
Assembly.   They adjourned to the Raleigh tavern, and
eighty-seven members of the " late house of burgesses," as
they styled themselves, put their names to an " Association "
expressive of sympathy with Boston, whose cause they considered as their own, and proposing that the Committee of
Correspondence should recommend to the other committees
of the colonies a general congress to concert united action.
This meeting at the Raleigh took place on the 27th of
May.   Colonel Mason, who was in Williamsburg at the time
on business of his own, wrote to his friend, Martin Cockburn,
at " Springfield," May 26th, the very day the House was
dissolved.   As he mentions in this letter, Mason had arrived
the Sunday before and had therefore been only four days in
town.

WILLIAMSBURG, May 26, 1774.

DEAR SIR ·

I arrived here on Sunday morning last, but found everbody's
attention so entirely engrossed by the Boston affair, that I have
as yet done nothing respecting my charter-rights, and, I am
afraid, shall not this week.

A dissolution of the House of Burgesses is generally expected ;
but I think will not happen before the house has gone through
the public business, which will be late in June.

Whatever resolves or measures are intended for the preservation of our rights and liberties, will be reserved for the conclusion of the session. Matters of that sort here are conducted and prepared with a great deal of privacy, and by very few members; of whom Patrick Henry is the principal. At the request of the gentlemen concerned, I have spent an evening with them upon the subject, where I had an opportunity of conversing with Mr. Henry, and knowing his sentiments; as well as hearing him speak in the house since, on different occasions. He is by far the most powerful speaker I ever heard. Every word he says not only engages but commands the attention; and your passions are no longer your own when he addresses them. But his eloquence is the smallest part of his merit. He is in my opinion the first man upon this continent, as well in abilities as public virtues, and had he lived in Rome about the time of the first Punic War, when the Roman people had arrived at their meridian glory, and their virtue not tarnished, Mr. Henry's talents must have put him at the head of that glorious commonwealth.

Enclosed you have the Boston Trade Act and a resolve of our House of Burgesses. You will observe that it is confined to the members of their own house; but they would wish to see the example followed through the country; for which purpose the members, at their own private expense, are sending expresses with the resolve to their respective counties. Mr. Massie (the minister at Fairfax) will receive a copy of the resolve from Col. Washington; and, should a day of prayer and fasting be appointed in our county, please to tell my dear little family that I charge them to pay a strict attention to it, and that I desire my three eldest sons and my two eldest daughters may attend church in mourning, if they have it, as I believe they have.

I begin to grow heartily tired of this town and hope to be able to leave it some time next week, but of this, I can't yet be certain. I beg to be tenderly remembered to my children, and am with my compliments to my cousins and yourself,

Dear Sir,

Your affectionate and obedient servant,

G. MASON.[1]

---

[1] "Virginia Historical Register," vol. iii., p. 27. The original, in 1850, was in the Alexandria Museum, afterwards destroyed by fire.

The governor's action in dissolving the Assembly evidently took them by surprise, as George Mason, who was in their counsels, writes so confidently of their business keeping them in session until the last of June. Through this letter we learn the date of George Mason's first acquaintance with Patrick Henry, to whose eloquence, ability, and public virtue, he here pays a glowing tribute. A mutual esteem and respect sprang up between these two leaders, and their accord on questions of public policy was never materially impaired throughout the momentous period that followed, in which they so often labored side by side. One can imagine the excitement in the small Virginia capital on those May days of 1774, as the news spread abroad of the events that were transpiring. Colonel Mason, after posting his letter, may have walked to the Assembly, and been present at its dissolution. He was doubtless among the spectators in the Apollo room the next day listening to the resolves of the Association. A Virginia historian has pictured him at the ball, given by the burgesses to Lady Dunmore, which took place the night of the twenty-seventh. [1] The polite Virginians, having made their preparations to entertain the governor's family, could not let this little political *contre-temps* interfere with their gallantry. Washington was present at this ball. But it is not likely the grave and sad-hearted visitor from " Gunston Hall," who had only the year before been made a widower, would appear on such an occasion. Rather sombre must have been the feeling of all thinking men and women among the guests at the festivities on this memorable night. Under the surface of their courtesy lurked latent embers of discontent not to be easily smothered. And Virginia had virtually seen the end of her royal Assemblies.

On the 29th of May, the delegates who were still in Williamsburg, met together to consider the propositions just received from Boston, advocating not only non-importation but non-exportation. The latter point called out a

[1] " Stories of the Old Dominion," J. Esten Cooke.

difference of opinion. A circular letter was sent by the deputies to their constituents, recommending a meeting of deputies, or a convention, to be held in Williamsburg the 1st of August, at which the sense of the colony on the subject under debate should be fully made known. The convention was also to appoint delegates to the Continental Congress, should the latter be resolved upon. Richard Henry Lee, in a letter to Samuel Adams, June 23d, gives an account of these proceedings at the capital. "The day before we were dissolved," he writes, " I had prepared a set of resolutions." They contained a protest against the blocking up of Boston harbor, and named delegates to meet with others from the several colonies to consider the means most effectual for stopping exports, etc., and "adopting other measures for securing the rights of America." He did not offer these resolutions, as it was urged public business should be finished first, and the burgesses "were inclined to believe from many conversations they had heard, that there was no danger of a dissolution before it had happened." Lee says that he then proposed to the dissolved Assembly the plan of a general congress, but they did not think they had the authority requisite, after their dissolution. And he adds: " Most of the members and myself among the rest, had left Williamsburg before your message from Boston had arrived. Twenty-five of them, however, were assembled to consider of that message, and they determined to invite a general meeting of the whole body to consider the measure of stopping the exports and imports." [1]

The "charter-rights" in regard to which Colonel Mason had come to Williamsburg at this time, related to lands which he had purchased in western Virginia. Among the Jefferson papers in the State Department, is to be found a copy of " The Memorial and Petition of George Mason, of the County of Fairfax, presented to the governor and council June, 1774, praying entrys or warrants for lands due for the importation of people, according to the royal charter."

[1] " American Archives," 4th series, vol. i., p. 446.

George Mason, in this paper, discussed the question of " Importation Rights," the ancient method of acquiring lands in the colony, and then describes the later method of " Treasury Rights," or purchase by money paid into the treasury, and he concludes in these words :

" That your petitioner confiding in, and upon the faith of the before mentioned royal charter laws and custom, hath been at great trouble and expence, and hath laid out considerable sums of money, in purchasing from the importers legal certificates of rights to large quantities of land, due for the importation of people from Great Britain and Ireland into this colony, and prays that he may be admitted to entrys for the said lands, upon the western waters in the County of Fincastle ; upon his producing the usual certificates and assignments, or that his Excellency, the Governor, will be pleased to grant your petitioner his warrant for surveying the same, etc." [1]

George Mason went back to Gunston, doubtless in company with some of the burgesses, discussing the serious aspect of political affairs.   During the summer, meetings were held in all the counties, at which resolutions were passed of the same general character, advocating a non-importation policy, and recommending a Continental Congress.   In Fairfax County, George Washington was chairman of the meeting, and one of the committee to prepare the resolutions. The work of drafting these resolves, however, was committed to George Mason.   They were twenty-four in number, and they set forth the grievances of the colonies, and mapped out a programme of non-intercourse with the mother country, while they advocated the necessity of calling a congress for the further guidance of the colonies in their just resistance to the usurpations of the crown.[2]   Sparks says of these Fairfax Resolves that "they constitute one of the ablest and most luminous expositions of the points at issue between Great Britain and the colonies which are to be found among the public documents of that period.   Embracing the great

---

[1] Appendix vi.   [2] Appendix vii.

principles and facts, clothed in a nervous and appropriate style, they are equally marked with dignity, firmness, intelligence and wisdom." [1] As a practical tribute to their value and efficiency it need only be stated that when the convention met in August, the Fairfax Resolves were taken as the basis of the association there entered upon, which association was in substance adopted by the general Congress at its first session in the following September. The meeting in Fairfax was held July 18th. Washington writes in his journal that Colonel Mason came to see him on the afternoon of the 17th, and stayed all night, and that he went up to Alexandria the next day "to a meeting of the county." On the 26th of the same month the freeholders of Albemarle held their meeting and Jefferson is believed to have been the author of the Albemarle Resolutions. His biographer Randall institutes the following comparison between the Albemarle Resolutions and those of the other counties, and he seeks out for special parallelism the Fairfax Resolves. In the former, he says, the ground is taken "that the colonists are subject to no laws but those of their own creation, that Parliament has no authority over them in any case, or on any subject, that they possess the power of self-government by 'natural right,' or 'the common rights of mankind,' that these rights have been invaded by Parliament, and particularly in the Boston Port Bill, that the inhabitants of Albemarle will ever be ready to join in executing and re-establishing these powers by whomsoever invaded." Of the Fairfax meeting, Randall says, it "took substantially the same positions" as those of Hanover, where Patrick Henry presided, and of the other counties, twenty-eight in all. Several of these, he adds, "deny the right of Parliament to *tax* the colonies under any circumstances; *but none other* contains a hint, or the shadow of a hint, that the colonies were wholly independent of Parliament— free, of natural right to enact all their own laws, and subject to none other. . . . The legal or constitutional right of

---

[1] " Life of Washington," chap. vi., p. 116.

Parliament to legislate for the general concerns of the colonies was nowhere denied, however bitterly the abuse of that right might be complained of." This doctrine of the Albemarle Resolutions, held by Jefferson, no one but Wythe shared with him, Randall asserts, and he quotes from Jefferson's memoir: "Our other patriots, the Lees, Nicholas, Pendleton, stopped at the half-way house of John Dickinson, who admitted that England had a right to regulate our commerce, and to lay duties for such purposes, but not for revenue."

Quoting from the Fairfax Resolves, Randall cites this clause, referring to the power of Parliament to regulate American trade and commerce · "Such a power directed with wisdom and moderation seems necessary for the general good of that great body politick of which we are a part, although in some degree repugnant to the principles of the constitution. Under this idea our ancestors submitted to it; the experience of more than a century, during the government of his Majesty's royal predecessors, has proved its utility." A doubt is here suggested, continues Randall, as to the "theoretical propriety of the Navigation Acts under the principles of the British Constitution, which is admitted paramount, but even this is waived on the plea of necessity and utility."[1] It would seem to amount to a "hint," and to something more than a hint, as to the illegality of the Navigation Acts. And it would be difficult for an unbiased mind to see the distinction in doctrine between the following declarations: "That no other Legislature [than that of the colony] can rightly exercise authority over them [the inhabitants]" (*Albemarle Resolutions*). "That the legislative power here can of right be exercised only by our provincial Assemblies or Parliaments" (*Fairfax Resolves*). The latter then continues: "But as it was thought just and reasonable that the people of Great Britain should reap advantages from the colonies adequate to the protection afforded them, the British Parliament have claimed and ex-

[1] Randall's "Life of Jefferson," vol. i., p. 86.

ercised the power of regulating our trade and commerce." Their ancestors, George Mason goes on to say, had submitted to this power, though it was capable of abuse and had been abused, "yet to avoid strife and contention with our fellow-subjects, and strongly impressed with the experience of mutual benefits, we always cheerfully acquiesced in it while the entire regulation of our internal policy, and giving and granting our own money, were preserved to our own Provincial Legislatures." Nothing could be clearer than this declaration of natural and constitutional right. There had been parliamentary usurpation, was the argument of the Fairfax Resolves, dating back for a century, but it was tolerated for obvious reasons. The new and distinct usurpations of Parliament, dating from 1764, were *not* to be tolerated, for reasons equally obvious.

While George Mason was thus occupied as the spokesman of his county in setting forth the rights and grievances of the colonists, his brother, Thomson Mason, was not idle in the same cause. The legal learning and ability for which he was conspicuous among his contemporaries, were brought to the service of his country in a series of letters written by him from Williamsburg in June and July of this year, under the signature of "A British American." [1] Six of these letters are preserved; three others had been published on the "long-litigated right of the British Parliament to tax the American colonies." He now wished to give his sentiments as to "what ought to be the conduct of the inhabitants of British America in the present alarming state of affairs." And he adds:

" I think it more peculiarly my duty to do so at this time, because (though one of the Representatives of the Colony of Virginia) I did not attend the last session of the Assembly ; indeed, as I live a very retired life, a great distance from Williamsburg, I did not hear of the Act of Parliament relative to Boston till after the Assembly was dissolved ; but I urge not this in justification, nor even in palliation of my offence, since nothing can excuse a

[1] " American Archives," 4th series, vol. i., pp. 647–653.

Representative of the people from constantly attending in Assembly ; and as I neither expect, or shall attempt to be chosen again, I take this as the only method left me of atoning to my country for having neglected my duty."

In the ninth and last of these letters, dated the 28th of July, ten days after the meeting in Fairfax and two days after the meeting in Albemarle, Thomson Mason enforces still more emphatically the view that his brother had expressed in the Resolves as above cited. He says, in regard to a plan he proposes for meeting the crisis :

" It is objected that this measure strikes at the Navigation Acts, which we have long submitted to. The very objection evinces the folly of trusting the decision of this dispute to posterity, who, familiarized to oppression, will never resist it, and who, by long use, will be accustomed to look upon every badge of slavery with as little horror as we do upon the Navigation Acts, which ought certainly to be considered as impositions of the strong upon the weak, and as such ought to be resisted as much as any of the other Acts we complain of ; nor will the dispute ever be ended till, by refusing submission to them, we remove so dangerous a precedent."

In this same letter is a passage, quoted by Rives in his " Life of Madison," where Thomson Mason tells his countrymen that, if all hope fails of a peaceful redress of grievances, there is but one alternative

" You must draw your swords in a just cause, and rely upon that God, who assists the righteous, to support your endeavors to preserve the liberty he gave, and the love of which he hath implanted in your hearts as essential to your nature."

In conclusion the writer avowed his authorship of the series in the following words :

" And now, my friends, fellow-citizens, and countrymen, to convince you that I am in earnest in the advice I have given you, notwithstanding the personal danger I expose myself to in so doing ; notwithstanding the threats thrown out by the British aristocracy of punishing in England those who shall dare to oppose them in America ; yet because I do not wish to survive the liberty of my country one single moment ; because I am de. termined to risk my all in supporting that liberty, and because I think it in some measure dishonest to skulk under a borrowed name upon such an occasion as this, I am neither afraid or ashamed to avow that the letters signed ' A British American ' were written by the hand and flowed from the heart of

" THOMSON MASON." [1]

Through a letter of Washington's to Bryan Fairfax, we learn that efforts were being made by Washington at this time to induce George Mason to re-enter the Assembly. The delegates from Fairfax were Washington and Colonel West, probably the father of John West, Jr., George Mason's friend mentioned in his will. Washington was ready to serve again, but Colonel West meant to withdraw, and Washington wished that either Bryan Fairfax or George Mason would come forward in his place, instead of Charles Broadwater, who eventually became the delegate. The members of the Assembly were to meet in convention the following March, the exigencies of the times calling for this measure, and it was important that Virginia should be represented by her best men. The eager politicians gathered in the churchyard, after the Sunday service, apparently to talk over the approaching election. It may have been at Christ Church, in Alexandria, which had been completed the year before, or at the new Pohick church, where the country gentlemen would doubtless assemble in goodly numbers, that the conferences Washington speaks of took place. He writes from " Mount Vernon " on the 4th of July, 1774 :

" I wished much to hear of your making an open declaration of taking a poll for this county, upon Colonel West's publicly declining last Sunday ; and I should have written to you on the

[1] Ibid.

12

subject, but for information then received from several gentlemen in the churchyard, of your having refused to do so, . . . upon which, as I think the country never stood more in need of men of abilities and liberal sentiments than now, I entreated several gentlemen at our church yesterday to press Colonel Mason to take a poll, as I really think Major Broadwater, though a good man, might do as well in the discharge of his domestic concerns, as in the capacity of a legislator. And therefore I again express my wish, that either you or Colonel Mason would offer. I can be of little assistance to either, because I early laid it down as a maxim not to propose myself, and solicit for a second." [1]

Edmund Randolph has left an interesting sketch of George Mason as he appeared to his contemporaries in 1774, before he had come prominently forward in political life. " Among the numbers," he writes, " who in their small circles were propagating with activity the American doctrines, was George Mason in the shade of retirement. He extended their grasp upon the opinions and affections of those with whom he conversed. How he learned his indifference for distinction, endowed as he was with ability to mount in any line; or whence he contracted his hatred for pomp, with a fortune competent to any expence, and a disposition not averse from hospitality, can be solved only from that philo-sophic spirit which despised the adulterated means of culti-vating happiness. He was behind none of the sons of Virginia in knowledge of her history and interest. At a glance he saw to the bottom of every proposition which affected her. His elocution was manly ; sometimes, but not wanton-ly, sarcastic." [2]

A subscription was started in Fairfax County for the poor of Boston, the sufferers from the Port Bill, and from Fairfax the undertaking spread through other portions of the colony. The Fairfax gentlemen, among whom doubtless were George Washington and George Mason, had subscribed by the 6th

[1] " Writings of Washington," Sparks, vol. ii., p. 388.
[2] MS. History of Virginia. (Virginia Historical Society.)

of July, after a few days' canvass of the county, two hundred and seventy-three pounds sterling in specie (about one thousand three hundred and sixty-five dollars), thirty-eight barrels of flour, and one hundred and fifty bushels of wheat.[1] The Continental Congress met in September, at Carpenter's Hall in Philadelphia. The delegates from Virginia, chosen by the convention in August, were carefully selected, and represented in Richard Henry Lee and Patrick Henry, as it has been said, oratory and eloquence, in George Washington the soldier, in Richard Bland the finished writer, in Edmund Pendleton the man of law, in Peyton Randolph solidity of character, in Benjamin Harrison the wealthy and influential planter. "There are some fine fellows come from Virginia," wrote Joseph Reed, "but they are very high. The Bostonians are mere milksops to them. We understand they are the capital men of the colony, both in fortune and understanding."[2] That the Virginians generally were "very high" in the expectations they had formed as to the future *rôle* of the Old Dominion and its sons may be inferred from what Edmund Randolph tells us of the election:

"Some of the tickets on the ballot assigned reasons for the choice expressed in them. These were that Randolph should preside in Congress ; that Lee and Henry should display the different kinds of eloquence, for which they were renowned ; that Washington should command the army, if an army should be raised ; that Bland should open the treasures of ancient colonial learning ; that Harrison should utter plain truths, and that Pendleton should be the penman for business."[3]

Edmund Pendleton and Patrick Henry stopped at "Mount Vernon" on their way to Congress. Colonel Mason came over from "Gunston Hall" and spent the night with them and the next day, the 31st of August, they went on to Philadelphia in company with Washington.

[1] "American Archives," 4th series, vol. i., p. 517.
[2] "Life of Reed," vol. i., p. 75.
[3] MS. History of Virginia.

The Congress decided upon a non-importation and non-exportation league.   The latter half of this self-denying measure had been advocated (with the former) as early as 1769 by George Mason, in the resolution which was rejected by the Association at Williamsburg.   He was thus five years in advance of the Congress, in the policy then, and long after, believed to be the surest way of averting war.   Certain modern writers, however, find the wisdom of the fathers folly in this respect.   And John Adams has been applauded because he endorsed but half of the measure, advocating non-exportation only.[1]   A congress would seem to have been needed to enable the hitherto disconnected colonial governments to inform themselves as to common needs and interests.   Two years before, Samuel Adams, writing to Richard Henry Lee, " having long wished a correspondence with some gentlemen in Virginia," shows incidentally how little this Northern commonwealth knew of its Southern neighbors : " We have heard," he says, " of bloodshed and even a civil war in our sister colony of North Carolina, and how strange is it that the best account we have of that tragical scene should be brought to us from England."   And William Wirt tells of the stories he had heard in his youth bearing on this point.   A soldier who went to Boston at the beginning of the Revolution entertained his neighbors with the marvels he had seen ; having gone " so far North that the North star was to the South."

The battle of Point Pleasant was fought on the 10th of October, 1774, in which General Andrew Lewis contended against the " Northern Confederacy of Indians," led by " Cornstalk," the Shawnese chief.   The Indians, it was believed, were instigated to enmity against the colonists by Lord Dunmore, who failed to come to Lewis' assistance, and this battle has been known in Virginia as the first one of the Revolution.   It is interesting to trace here an association with George Mason's family, through his brother Thomson's eldest son.   On the site of the battle-field has

[1] " Life of John Adams," p. 70, American Statesmen Series.

grown up the village of Point Pleasant, the capital of Mason County, now in West Virginia, the county being named after Stevens Thomson Mason, in 1804. In the summer of 1774 the Fairfax County Committee of Safety had been organized, consisting of twenty-five of the most prominent citizens. These county committees were armed with considerable powers. To them the duty fell of examining the books of merchants to see that no prohibited articles were brought into the colony. And in many cases they raised and equipped the independent companies which were springing up all over Virginia. George Mason, as an active member of the Fairfax Committee, drew up the following plan for forming the independent company of his county, the first, it is believed, on the continent:

"At a meeting of a number of gentlemen and freeholders of Fairfax County in the Colony of Virginia on Wednesday the twenty-first day of September, 1774, George Mason, Esq: in the chair, the following association was formed and entered into.

"In this time of extreme danger with the Indian Enemy in our country, and threatened with the destruction of our civil rights and liberty and all that is dear to British subjects and freemen, we the subscribers, taking into our serious consideration the present alarming situation of all the British colonies upon the continent, as well as our own, being sensible of the expediency of putting the militia of this colony upon a more respectable footing and hoping to excite others by our example, have voluntarily, freely and cordially entered into the following association, which we each of us for ourselves respectively solemnly promise and pledge our honors to each other and to our country to perform. That we will form ourselves into a company not exceeding one hundred men, by the name of the Fairfax Independent Company of volunteers, making choice of our own officers to whom for the sake of good order and regularity, we will pay due submission. That we will meet at such times and places in this county as our said officers (chosen by a majority of the members as soon as fifty have subscribed) shall appoint and direct for the purpose of learning and practising the military exercise and discipline; dress in a regular uniform of blue, turned up with buff, with plain yellow metal buttons, buff waistcoat and breeches and white stockings, and furnished with a good flint lock and bayonet, sling cartouch box and tomahawk. And that we will each of us constantly keep by us a stock of six pounds of gun powder, twenty pounds of lead and fifty gun flints at the least. That we will use our utmost endeavours as well at musters of the said company, as by all other means in our power to make ourselves masters of the military exercise. And that we will always hold ourselves in readiness in case of necessity, hostile invasion or real danger of the commonwealth of which we are members, to defend to the utmost of our power the legal prerogatives of our sovereign King George the 3d and the just right and privileges of our country, our posterity and ourselves upon the principles of the British Constitution. Agreed that all the subscribers to this association do meet on Monday the 17th of October next at eleven o'clock in the forenoon at the Court House in Alexandria." [1]

Washington's diary records that on the 15th of January, 1775, he went to Pohick church, and that Colonel Mason with several other gentlemen came home with him and stayed all night. The following day he went up to Alexandria to a review of the Independent Company and to choose a committee for the county. He was under arms the next day and in the committee in the evening. On this day—the 17th of January—resolutions were passed by the Committee of Safety for arming and organizing the militia of the county.[2] These are understood to have been drafted by Colonel Mason. And the expression that occurs in them, "firmly determined at the hazard of our lives to transmit to our children and posterity those sacred rights to which ourselves were born," so closely resembles the phrase quoted from George Mason's will as to confirm the supposition. The Maryland Convention, which had met on the 8th of December, 1774, had passed resolutions on

[1] Mason Papers.
[2] "American Archives," 4th series, vol. ., p. 1145 ; Appendix viii.

the subject of arming the militia, and the Fairfax Com. mittee state that they "do concur in opinion with the Provincial Committee of the Province of Maryland that a well-regulated militia," etc., and here they quote the exact phrase employed by the Marylanders to signify their ab. horrence of standing armies, and their conviction that the militia is the true defence of a free country. The same formula, with the alteration of a word or two, is repeated in the "Association," which follows, wherein the subscribers enroll themselves into a militia for the county. It is as follows:

"And thoroughly convinced that a well regulated militia composed of the gentlemen, freeholders and other freemen, is the natural strength and only safe and stable security of a free government, and that such militia will relieve our mother country from any expense in our protection and defence, will obviate the pretence of a necessity for taxing us on that account, and render it unnecessary to keep any standing army (ever dangerous to liberty) in this colony."

George Mason, with his vein of sarcastic humor, was the person to appreciate this "exquisite bit of argumentative irony," as Professor Tyler styles it in his biography of Patrick Henry. For Henry uses the phrase also in his resolutions on the subject of the militia, offered in the Convention two months later. The Fairfax County Resolutions were apparently the first of the kind passed in Virginia. And at a meeting in Augusta County in February to elect delegates to the March Convention, in the instructions given them by the County Committee they say:

"We entirely agree in opinion with the gentlemen of Fairfax County, that a well-regulated militia is the natural strength and stable security of a free government, and therefore wish it might be recommended by the Convention to the officers and men of each county in Virginia to make themselves masters of the military exercise, published by order of his Majesty, &c."[1]

[1] 4, American Archives, i., 1254.

The resolutions of Fairfax County for arming the militia were passed on the 17th of January, and on the following day the colony celebrated Queen Charlotte's birthday. The good people of Williamsburg were invited to an elegant ball at the governor's palace, and in compliment to the Old Dominion, Lord Dunmore's youngest daughter was christened *Virginia* on the afternoon of the Queen's birthday.[1] The mimic court at Williamsburg was exerting all its powers to please, but the patriots were not to be turned aside, and the work of preparation went forward. In the following letter, written by Colonel Mason to George Washington the 6th of February, reference is made to a plan "for embodying the people," which he sends to his correspondent:

GUNSTON HALL, Feb. 6, 1775.

DEAR SIR :

My friend Col. Harrison (who is now at your house) promised to spend a day or two with me on his way down. I beg the favor of you to present my compliments to him, and excuse my being under the disagreeable necessity of being from home until the latter end of this week, when if he is not gone down, I shall be very glad to see him here.   Enclosed you have a copy of the plan I drew for embodying the people of this county, in which you 'll be pleased to make such alterations as you think necessary. You will observe I have made it as general as I well could ; this I thought better at first than to descend to particulars of uniform, &c., which perhaps may be more easily done when the companies are made up.

I suppose you have seen the King's speech and the address of both Houses in the last Maryland paper ; from the style in which they speak of the Americans I think they have little hopes of a speedy redress of grievances, but on the contrary we may expect to see coercion and vindictive measures still pursued. It seems as if the King either had not received or was determined to take no notice of the proceedings of the Congress.

I beg my compliments to Mrs Washington and the family at Mount Vernon

and am dear Sir

yr. affec. and obdt. servant

G. M.

[1] *Virginia Gazette*, January 19, 1775.

P. S.—I beg pardon for having almost forgot to say anything in answer to your favor respecting the choice of delegates from this county to attend the Convention at Richmond. It appears to me that the Burgesses for the county are our proper represen-tatives upon this occasion ; and that the best method to remove all doubt or objection, as well as to save trouble, will be for the County Committee to meet and make an entry and declaration of this, as their opinion.

Would it not be proper for the Committee of Correspondence to write to the two Mr. Fitzhughs, Mr. Turberville, and such other gentlemen as live out of this county and have Quarters in it, acquainting them with the orders of the Committee relative to the payment of 3/ for each Tythable, and desiring them to give their overseers, or agents here orders accordingly ?

G. M.[1]

On his return from Maryland, where he had been to visit his mother-in-law, who was ill, Colonel Mason wrote again to Washington ·

GUNSTON HALL, February 17th, 1775.

DEAR SIR :

I returned from Maryland but last night, not being able to leave Mrs. Eilbeck sooner, and don't know how quickly I may be called there again, as I think she is far from being out of danger.

I will if I can be at Alexandria on Monday ; but it is uncertain, as well for the reason above-mentioned, as that I am at this time unwell with a bad cold and a little pain in my breast.

I can't conceive how Mr. Harper could make such a mistake as to buy double the quantity of powder wanted for this county, when he had the order in writing signed by you and me. If there is any ambiguity in the said writing (for I don't now recollect the words) by which Mr. Harper might be led into such a mistake, I think we are in honor bound to take the whole off his hands ; otherwise it does not appear to me that he can reasonably expect it ; though I am exceedingly concerned that any kind of mis-understanding should happen in an affair which must have given Mr. Harper a good deal of trouble, and which I am convinced

---

[1] Washington MSS., State Department.

was undertaken by him merely from public motives, and a desire to oblige the Committee. I remember your mentioning in conversation, to Mr. Harper, an application made to you from Loudon County to procure a quantity of powder for their Committee, upon six months' credit, and telling him if it could be purchased in Philadelphia upon such credit you would see the money paid when it became due; to which he answered that powder was generally a ready-money article there, and at this time in particular he did not imagine it could be got upon credit. I speak from recollection (having had no concern in the affair), but as nearly as I can remember this is the substance of what passed between you and him respecting the Loudon Committee, and may possibly have occasioned the mistake; at least I can account for it in no other way.

I have already paid Messrs. McCrea and Maire half their account. And my half the money due to Mr. Harper for the articles ordered for Fairfax County, is at any minute ready, having kept a sum in gold by me for that purpose, that Mr. Harper should not be disappointed in the payment; but if it will be attended with no inconvenience to him, it will suit me better to make the payment ten days hence than now, because I think in that time I can collect good part of the money from the people, and as the collection will be partly in paper dollars and Pennsylvania money, which, from Mr. Harper's connections to the Northward, may suit him as well, or perhaps better than gold, yet it will not replace the gold with equal convenience to me. I mention this only as matter of mutual convenience, at the same time making a point not to disappoint Mr. Harper; and I must beg the favor of you to communicate this to him, that I may send up the money whenever he wants it, without giving him any trouble on the subject.[1]

I shall send my son George out immediately to make what collection he can, being furnished with a list of Tythables for that purpose. If you incline to do anything of that kind, you shall have a copy of the list, distinguishing those who have paid to him. I think this method will reimburse us sooner, and save commissions and trouble to the sheriff.

[1] This is probably the "Capt. Harper" of Fairfax County, to whom George Mason refers in a letter of July, 1778.

I had gone a good way through the bill for improving the navigation of Potowmack before I went to Maryland, and am happy in finding that I had fallen into many of Mr. Johnston's sentiments, though I was a stranger to them, till I received your letter upon my return last night. I wish it was in my power to spend a day with him on the subject. Some of his remarks are not so intelligible to me as they would be if I had all the queries which he seems to answer. What he mentions of some kind of jealousy least the Virginians should have some advantage, and that there should be some equality between the Maryland and Virginia subscriptions, I can have no idea of. What matter is it whether the majority of the subscribers are Marylanders or Virginians, if their property is put upon an equal footing, and the work is of general advantage to both provinces? Nor can I think his notion of proportioning the tolls to the average profits can well be reduced to practise. A sufficient sum can't be raised by those only who are locally interested ; men who are not will not advance their money upon so great a risk, but with views of great and increasing profit, not to depend upon future alterations. The tolls, to be sure, must be moderate, such as the commodities will bear, with advantage to the makers. It is probable for some years they will yield very little profit to the undertakers, perhaps none ; they must run the risk of this, as well as of the utter failure of the undertaking, and surely if they succeed, they have a just right to the increased profits, though in process of time they may become very great. If I am not misinformed, this is the principle upon which everything of this nature has been successfully executed in other countries. My paper will not permit me to add more at present than that I am,

Dear Sir,

Your affectionate and obedient servant,

G. MASON.[1]

The following letter to Washington, written in March, relates to purchases made for the Fairfax County Committee, and to the bill which Colonel Mason was preparing, at his friend's instance, for the improvement of the Potomac River navigation :

[1] Washington MSS., Department of State.

GUNSTON HALL, March 9th, 1775.

DEAR SIR

I have at last finished the Potomack River Bill, which I now send you, together with some very long remarks thereon, and a letter to Mr. Johnston, into which you 'll be pleased to put a wafer, when you forward the other papers to him.

I also return the Acts of Assembly, and Mr. Johnston's notes, which you sent me. This affair has taken me five times as long as I expected ; and I do assure you I never engaged in anything which puzzled me more ; there were such a number of contingencies to provide for and drawing up laws—a thing so much out of my way. I shall be well pleased if the pains I have bestowed upon the subject prove of any service to so great an undertaking ; but by what I can understand, there will be so strong an opposition from Baltimore and the head of the Bay as will go near to prevent its passage through the Maryland Assembly in any shape it can be offered.

I suppose you have heard of the late purchase made by some North Carolina gentlemen from the Cherokee Indians, of all the country between the Great Conhaway [*sic*] and the Tennessee Rivers.

I think considering this colony has just expended about £100,-000 upon the defence of that country, that this is a pretty bold stroke of the gentlemen. It is suspected some of our Virginia gentlemen are privately concerned in it. I have always expected that the newfangled doctrine lately broached, of the Crown's having no title beyond the Alleghany Mountains till after the purchase at Fort Stanwix, would produce a thousand other absurdities and squabbles. However, if I am not mistaken, the Crown, at that treaty, purchased of the Six Nations all the lands as low as the Tennessee River. So now, I suppose, we must have a formal trial, whether the Six Nations or the Cherokees had the legal right ; but whether this is to be done by ejectment, writ of enquiry, writ of partition or what other process, let those who invented this curious distinction determine. The inattention of our Assembly to so grand an object, as the right of this colony to the Western lands is inexcusable, and the confusion it will introduce endless.

If I knew when you set off for the Convention at Richmond I

would trouble you with two or three Virginia Cavalry Bills, to make my second payment to Mr. Mazzay as I may not perhaps have an opportunity of sending it in April.

We make but a poor hand of collecting ; very few pay, though everybody promises except Mr. Hartshorn, of Alexandria, who flatly refused ; his conscience I suppose would not suffer him to be concerned in paying for the instruments of death. George has been very unwell for some days past ; as soon as he gets well he intends [going] up into the forest.

The family here join in their compliments to Mrs. Washington and the family at Mount Vernon,

> With, Dear Sir,
>
> Your affectionate humble Servant,
>
> G. MASON.[1]

A messenger from " Mount Vernon" arrived that very day at " Gunston Hall," and Colonel Mason wrote a second letter of the same date in reply to his friend. In it he says: " I beg you to inform Mr. Johnston the bill I have drawn is intended only as a ground-work, and that I desire every part of it may be submitted to his correction." He sends Washington, as he tells him, " some cherry-graffs, May-dukes and large black May cherries" for his garden.

The Potomac Company, afterwards merged into the Chesapeake and Ohio Canal Company, of which we hear something at the present day, was projected at least as early as 1762, and was part of the scheme of the Ohio Company for developing the Western lands. At a meeting held in Frederick, Maryland, in May, 1762, a number of prominent gentlemen were elected managers, and Col. George Mercer was one of the two treasurers appointed, the other one being a Marylander. George Mason's Potomac River bill was designed to obtain the necessary legislation on the subject. Thomas Johnson, afterwards Governor of Maryland, and a member in 1774 of the Continental Congress, was the gentleman on the northern side of the Potomac who was at the head of this project in 1774, while Washington and George Mason were its most prominent advocates in Virginia. Washing-

[1] *Ibid.*

ton wrote to Thomas Jefferson as early as 1770 in reply to the latter, and discussed the scheme of opening the inland navigation of the Potomac by private subscription. He looked forward, he said, to seeing "the Potomac a channel of commerce between Great Britain and the immense western territory, a tract of country unfolding to our view." He advocated "a more extensive plan" than one proposed by Thomas Johnson, as a "means of becoming a channel of the extensive trade of a rising empire."[1] The company was formed, consisting of twenty or more gentlemen in Virginia, and an equal number in Maryland, and a meeting was called at Georgetown on the 12th of November, 1774, to appoint from among the whole number of trustees a small and convenient number to act for the whole. Heading the list of the Virginia gentlemen are the names of George Washington, George Mason, Thomson Mason, Bryan Fairfax, Daniel McCarty, and John Carlyle.[2] The work was commenced, but abandoned a year later, as the Maryland Act of Assembly co-operating with Virginia had not been obtained.[3] Ten years later, when the scheme was about to be revived, Washington alludes, in a letter to Jefferson, to these earlier efforts.

"Despairing of any aid from the public," he writes, "I became the principal mover of a bill to empower a number of subscribers to undertake, at their own expense, on conditions which were expressed, the extension of the navigation [of the Potomac] from tide water to Will's Creek, about one hundred and fifty miles.   . The plan, however, was in a tolerably good trim when I set out for Cambridge in 1775, and would have been in an excellent way had it not been for the difficulties met with in the Maryland Assembly.

In this situation I left matters when I took command of the army. The war afterwards called men's attention to different objects, and all the money they could or would raise was applied to other purposes."[4]

[1] Stewart's Report. First session, Nineteenth Congress.
[2] *Virginia Gazette*, November 10, 1774.
[3] *Ibid.*, November 2, 1775.
[4] " Writings of Washington," Sparks, vol. ix., p. 30.

CHAPTER VI.

THE BEGINNING OF THE REVOLUTION.

1775-1776.

The Convention met in Richmond on the 20th of March, 1775, and it was then that Patrick Henry offered his memorable resolutions, "that the colony be immediately put in a state of defence, etc." The battle of Lexington was fought on the 19th of April, and George Mason, in his patriotic enthusiasm, named one of his plantations "Lexington" in honor of the event. Washington's journal records that on the 16th of April he had a number of visitors. General Charles Lee was one of them, and Mr. Harry Lee, Jr., "Light Horse Harry" that was to be. Colonel Mason came in the afternoon, and stayed all night. The next day they went together to Alexandria to a committee meeting and "to a new choice of delegates."

On the 20th of May Colonel Mason wrote to William Lee, who was still in London, notifying him that he had shipped one hundred hogsheads of Virginia, Potomac River, tobacco by the ship *Adventure*. The letter goes on to say:

"I expect the certainty of the exports being stopped here on the tenth of September next, if not much sooner, will raise what tobacco gets to market to an amazing price : indeed was there not this extraordinary cause, I think tobacco must be high, which is my reason for shipping so largely. People in general have not prepared this year for crops of tobacco as usual ; and even those who have will be able to make very little, from the uncommon scarcity of plants, greater than in the noted year

1758, or perhaps than ever was known within the memory of man, and the season now too far advanced to raise more. You may depend upon this information as a certain fact, in all the upper parts of Virginia and Maryland. What is the case in the lower parts, I do not certainly know ; but from the weather I have no doubt but that this scarcity of plants is general through the two colonies." [1]

The year before, in the same month, Jefferson, at " Monticello," had noted in his garden book a severe frost which had killed many of the tobacco plants and was " equally destructive through the whole country." [2] Eleven days after writing this letter to William Lee, George Mason wrote to Richard Henry Lee, then in Congress :

GUNSTON HALL, May 31, 1775.

DEAR SIR :

My son George has a mind to spend some days in Philadelphia, while the Congress is sitting ; and as he has been yet very little in the world, and young fellows are too apt to fall into bad company in a place where they have few acquaintance, I must presume so far on your friendship as to recommend him to your notice and advice, for which I am sure he will be thankful.

We hear nothing from the Congress : I presume their deliberations are (as they ought to be) a profound secret. I hope the procuring arms and ammunition next winter when the ships of war can't cruise upon our coasts, as well as the means of laying in good magazines of provisions, &c., to the northward will be properly attended to.

I could almost wish that we paid the ministry the compliment of stopping our exports to Great Britain and the West Indies at the same time their Restraining Bill takes place, that our operations might have a fair start with theirs, and our measures have the appearance of reprizal. I think you are happy in having Dr. Franklin at the Congress, as I imagine no man better knows the intentions of the ministry, the temper of the nation, and the interest of the minority.

---

[1] MS. Letter.   [2] Randall's " Jefferson," vol. i., p. 76.

The ship you expected from your brother in York River has been arrived about a fortnight. The *Adventure*, I believe, will sail next week. She has been delayed a good deal by the scarcity of craft. My hundred hogsheads (ninety of them in our warehouse) were all ready before the ship came out of Rappahannock, and in order to give her all the dispatch in my power (hearing the captain would not engage sufficient craft) I employed craft myself to carry sixty hogsheads on board. I have wrote by two or three different vessels for insurance at £11 str. p. hhd. ; but if you have an opportunity of writing to your brother from Philadelphia I should be glad to have the order repeated.

I most sincerely wish you health and happiness, and am, dear Sir,

Yr. aff. and obdt. servant,

G. Mason.[1]

By Captain Brown of the *Adventure* George Mason wrote more fully to William Lee, and this second letter has also been preserved. The home of William Lee when in Virginia was at "Greenspring," associated in Virginia history with Sir William Berkeley, whose widow had married Philip Ludwell, ancestor of the Lees. William Lee married his cousin, Hannah Phillippa Ludwell.

VIRGINIA, GUNSTON HALL, June 1st, 1775.

DEAR SIR :

I wrote you the 20th last month, informing you that I should ship you one hundred Hhds. of Tobo. pr. the *Adventure*, Capt. Brown (and sent duplicates pr. different ships) to which I beg leave to refer. As I don't expect the bills of lading will come to my hands before the *Adventure* sails, I have desired the favor of Mr. Edwd. Brown to inclose you one of the bills of lading pr. the ship ; and least any mistake should be made in the bill of lading, or the ship's books, I think it proper to send you an exact list of the said hundred Hhds. Seventy Hhds. thereof marked G.M.—G.^{H}M., G.^{O}M., and G.^{D}M. are my own crops at different Quarters ; the thirty Hhds. marked G.^{D}M. are rent tobacco, but mostly good planter's crops ; they were originally in

[1] Lee Papers, University of Virginia. (*Southern Lit. Messenger*, Oct., 1858.)

the planter's marks ; but I ordered them to be re-marked and numbered, as mentioned in the inclosed list. I hope they will come to an excellent market, and don't doubt your making the most of them ; indeed I should imagine, in the present situation of affairs, tobacco must rise to a price not known before in the present century : but I think it not improbable that the Parliament may stop the export from Great Britain, and prolong the time for payment of the duties, in order to keep a stock for the home consumption. Should you find this likely to happen, I must desire that my tobacco may be sold before the next meeting of Parliament, as such a measure would greatly reduce the price, and I am apprehensive that more than ordinary caution will be necessary in selling to safe hands, as few houses can stand such a shock as the stoppage of the American trade will give. These are suggestions of my own ; I think they are not ill founded, and submit them to your consideration. You may with the greatest certainty rely upon the stoppage of our exports on the 10th of September next, if not sooner ; I am inclined to think they will cease in July, that the operations here may have a fair start with your Fishery and Restraining Bills, which instead of dissolving or weakening the American Associations, will only serve to rivet them by convincing all ranks of people what they have to expect from the present ministry.

The Americans were pretty unanimous before, but the acts of the present session of Parliament, and the blood lately shed at Boston have fixed every wavering mind, and there are no difficulties or hardships which they are not determined to encounter with firmness and perseverance. God only knows the event, and in His hands, confiding in the justice of our cause, we cheerfully trust it ! The Junto before this reaches you, will find how egregiously they have been misinformed and mistaken in the defection they expected in New York, North Carolina, and among the Quakers of Pennsylvania. The New Yorkers no longer hesitate to join with the other colonies in all their measures for obtaining redress ;—the Quakers, to the surprise of everybody, are arming and learning the military discipline ; thirty-two companies of the citizens of Philadelphia appear regularly every morning at sunrise upon the public parade, and as a sample of the defection of North Carolina I send you Governor Martin's speech to his

Assembly and their address. The Provincials have possessed themselves of Ticonderoga and Crown Point, and we have a report here that a deputation of eight Indian chiefs from the Six Nations is arrived at Philadelphia to offer the assistance of their people in the common cause of America, but this wants connrmation.

There is a full meeting of the members of the Congress, but nothing from it has as yet transpired, except their advice to the people of New York, respecting their conduct in case of the arrival of troops there, which no doubt you will have transmitted in the Northern papers.

I beg my compliments to your lady, with whom I formerly had the honour of being acquainted at "Green Spring," and desire to be remembered to your brother, of whose welfare and yours it will always give me pleasure to hear.

I am, dear sir,

Your most obedient servant,

G. MASON.[1]

In a letter of George Mason's, to be given later, written in 1778, there is the following allusion to the Fairfax Independent Company organized by the Fairfax Committee in September, 1774: " My eldest son George engaged early in the American cause, and was chosen ensign in the first Independent Company formed in Virginia, and indeed on the continent. It was commanded by the present General Washington, as captain, and consisted entirely of gentlemen." The Independent Companies were soon to give way to the Minute Regiments, a part of the military establishment of Virginia Colonel Mason was instrumental in organizing while in the July convention of 1775. And George Mason, Jr., then a young man of twenty-two, was appointed in this year a captain of, foot in one of the first Minute Regiments raised in Virginia. The Independent Companies, while they lasted, were warlike enough in intention, as in act also, where opportunity offered. When the powder was removed from Williamsburg in April, 1775, they came eagerly to the

[1] MS. Letter.

rescue, and Hugh Mercer wrote from Fredericksburg to Colonel Washington that he expected to be joined by gentlemen from Fairfax and Prince William. While in Philadelphia attending the first Congress, we are told that "Captain Washington" of the Independent Company of Fairfax made contracts for their equipments, etc.[1] On the 15th of June, 1775, he was appointed commander-in-chief, and five days later Washington wrote a farewell letter to the several Independent Companies of Virginia, which had elected him as their commanding officer, and this letter was sent to the Fairfax Company, to be transmitted by them to the other organizations. The Fairfax Company replied deploring their loss of the "patron, friend, and worthy citizen," while tendering their "hearty congratulations" at his appointment.[2]

At a meeting of the Fairfax Company in Alexandria, previous to Washington's resignation, there was a motion made that the officers should be elected annually, and Colonel Mason prepared a paper to be read in support of the measure. It is a remarkable and interesting document, for in it is to be found an anticipation of the doctrines and phrases which are associated with the great public charters of 1776—the Virginia Bill of Rights, and the Declaration of Independence. Colonel Mason reminds the gentlemen of the company, as a profound politician had wisely observed, "that no institution can be long preserved, but by frequent recurrence to those maxims on which it was formed." And he continues :

"We came equal into this world, and equal shall we go out of it. All men are by nature born equally free and independent. Every society, all government, and every kind of civil compact, therefore, is or ought to be calculated for the general good and safety of the community. Every power, every authority vested in particular men is, or ought to be, ultimately directed to this sole end ; and whenever any power or authority extends fur-

---

[1] "Life and Writings of Washington," Sparks, vol. ii., Appendix xii.
[2] *Ibid.*, vol. iii., p. 4, and note to p. 5.

ther, or is of longer duration than is in its nature necessary for these purposes, it may be called government, but it is in fact oppression.   In all our associations, in all our agreements, let us never lose sight of this fundamental maxim—that all power was originally lodged in and consequently is derived from the people.   We should wear it as a breast-plate and buckle it on as an armour."

The writer alludes to the fact that " this part of the country has the glory of setting so laudable an example," as the formation of the company evinces, where " gentlemen of the first fortune and character among us have become members   have submitted to stand in the ranks as common soldiers, and to pay due obedience to the officers of their own choice."   It was understood that the rotation of officers advocated was not to apply to the captain, to whom is paid the following compliment :

" The exception made in favor of the gentleman, who, by the unanimous voice of the company, now commands it, is a very proper one justly due to his public merit and experience ; it is peculiarly suited to our circumstances, and was dictated, not by compliment, but by conviction." [1]

George Mason made his first appearance in Virginia's revolutionary councils at the July Convention, 1775.   On the 1st of June the General Assembly met in Williamsburg. But the affair of the gunpowder, which had been secretly removed by the governor from the capitol, and was found afterwards stored in a magazine, created such an excitement among the burgesses and the community in general that Dunmore became alarmed and took refuge on board the *Fowey.*   Then followed negotiations between the fugitive governor on the water and the deserted legislature on land, each refusing to go to the other.   The Assembly finally voted that the executive had abdicated his office, and they forthwith dissolved themselves, on the 24th of June, never

[1] Appendix ix.

to meet again under royal rule. The battle of Bunker Hill was fought on the 17th, and the colonies felt themselves committed to revolution. When Washington was made commander-in-chief his place became vacant in the Virginia Convention—a convention more than ever necessary, as on it now devolved the offices of both the defunct legislature and executive,—and George Mason was fixed upon as Washington's successor. Colonel Mason at first hesitated about accepting this nomination. He was ready with his pen always, as has been seen, to serve his country, but his personal attention he thought was needed by his motherless children. On hearing of the proposal to elect him a deputy from Fairfax County, he wrote the following letter declining the honor:

GUNSTON HALL, July 11, 1775.

DEAR SIR :

My friend Mr. Massey sent me yesterday the advertisement for a meeting of the freeholders to-morrow, with a letter from you on the subject ; which was the first notice of the county having any intention of requiring my attending the Convention at Richmond next week as one of its representatives. And though ambition has no longer charms for me I am extremely sensible of the obligation I am under to you and the other gentlemen of Alexandria for your favorable opinion. I have considered the matter with the best judgment I am capable of, and am sincerely concerned that my situation in life will not permit me to accept the appointment.

I entreat you, Sir, to reflect on the duty I owe to a poor little helpless family of orphans to whom I now must act the part of father and mother both, and how incompatible such an office would be with the daily attention they require. This I will not enlarge on. Your own feelings will best explain it ; and I rely on your friendship to excuse me to the gentlemen of the committee and my other friends.

I am dear Sir, &c.,

G. MASON.

To William Ramsay, Esq. ·
    Alexandria.[1]

---

[1] Mason Papers.

The Convention met on Monday, the 17th of July. On the following day it resolved itself into a committee of the whole, to take into consideration the state of the colony, and on Wednesday this committee offered the following resolution : " That a sufficient armed force be immediately raised and embodied, under proper officers, for the defence and protection of this colony." Randall in his biography of Jefferson, referring to the resolution of Henry, in March, and his bold advocacy of defensive preparations, says :

" This unexpected and to the body of the Convention startling proposition produced a most painful effect on the minds of many members. The old moderate leaders, Nicholas, Bland, and Pendleton, the two last members of the late Congress, Harrison, also a member, even Wythe shrunk back from the yawning gulf.
The resolution was supported by its mover and by R. H. Lee, and earnestly pressed by Jefferson, Mason, Page, and by the leaders of what may be termed the movement party." [1]

George Mason was not in the March Convention, but he had answered the call of patriotism, and was now present in July, a leader, as always, in the "movement party." He had early declared his views as to putting the colony in a state of defence, and as a member of the Fairfax Committee, had given a practical demonstration of these opinions ; but on entering the July Convention he opposed all violent measures, exerted himself to prevent the confiscation of the king's quit-rents, and it was not until after the rejection by the king of the second petition of Congress, made on the 8th of July, that he believed in the necessity of declaring independence. Seventeen of the most prominent members of the Convention were appointed a committee to bring in an ordinance pursuant to the resolution for raising troops, and these included Richard Bland, Robert Carter Nicholas, James Mercer, Joseph Jones, George Mason, Thomas Ludwell Lee, and Carter Braxton.[2] Three days

[1] "Life of Jefferson," vol. i., p. 100.
[2] Journal of the Convention.

after the opening of the Convention, George Mason gave notice that on the following Monday he should offer a resolve. This was a non-exportation resolution, a measure which, we have seen, he had much at heart. And accordingly, on Monday, the 24th, the resolve was offered by him, and, after a long debate, carried by a large majority. This we learn through a letter of George Mason's, written on the evening of the same day. The journal simply gives the resolve without naming its author. It was in these words:

"*Resolved*, That no flour, wheat, or other grain, or provisions of any kind, be exported from this colony, to any part of the world, from and after the fifth day of August next, until the Convention or Assembly, or the honorable the Continental Congress, shall order otherwise; that no quantities of the said articles, more than are necessary for the use of the inhabitants, be brought to, collected, or stored in the towns or other places upon or near the navigable waters; that the respective County Committees be directed to take care that this resolve be effectually carried into execution, and that all contracts made for the sale and delivery of any such articles for exportation, between this time and the tenth day of September next, be considered as null and void." [1]

The following letter to Martin Cockburn gives an interesting picture of the busy scene upon which George Mason had now entered. And it will be noticeable that from the first his energy and talent commanded recognition.

RICHMOND, July 24th, 1775.

DEAR SIR :

Having an opportunity pr. Edw'd Blackburn (who promises to drop this at Colchester) I snatch a moment to let you know that I am well, and to desire to be kindly remembered to my dear children, and the family at "Springfield." I have not since I came to this place, except the fast-day and Sunday, had an hour which I could call my own. The committee (of which I am a member) appointed to prepare an ordinance for raising an

[1] *Ibid.*

armed force for the defence and protection of this colony, meet every morning at seven o'clock, sit till the Convention meets, which seldom rises before five in the afternoon, and immediately after dinner and a little refreshment sits again till nine or ten at night. This is hard duty, and yet we have hitherto made but little progress, and I think shall not be able to bring in the ordinance till late next week, if then. This will not be wondered at when the extent and importance of the business before us is reflected on—to raise forces for immediate service—to new-model the whole militia—to render about one-fifth of it fit for the field at the shortest warning—to melt down all the volunteer and independent companies into this great establishment—to provide arms, ammunition, &c.,—and to point out ways and means of raising money, these are difficulties indeed! Besides tempering the powers of a Committee of Safety to superintend the execution. Such are the great outlines of the plans in contemplation. I think I may venture to assert (though nothing is yet fixed on) that in whatever way the troops are raised, or the militia regulated, the staff officers only will be appointed by Convention, and the appointment of all the others devolve upon the county committees. If the colony is parcelled into different districts for raising a battalion in each, I have proposed that the committees of each county in the district appoint deputies of their own members for the purpose; so that every county may have an equal share in the choice of officers for the battalion, which seems to be generally approved.

On Wednesday last I gave notice in Convention, that on Monday I should offer the inclosed resolve; which was accordingly done this day, and after a long debate, carried by a great majority. The Convention will to-morrow appoint a delegate to the Congress in the room of General Washington, when I believe Mr. Wythe will be almost unanimously chosen. As there will be other vacancies, I have been a good deal pressed by some of my friends to serve at the Congress, but shall firmly persist in a refusal, and thereby I hope prevent their making any such proposal in the Convention.

I enclose a letter for my son George (though I suppose he is before this time set off for the Springs) which by some strange mistake came to me from Alexandria per post. We have no news but what is contained in the public papers, which you generally get sooner than we can here.

I am, Dr. Sir, your affectionate Friend and Servant,

G. MASON.[1]

We learn from this letter how laborious were the duties of the committee, of which George Mason was so important a member, and we hear also of the earnest desire of his friends that he should enter Congress. A number of new members were added later to the committee for preparing the military establishment, but it was decided that eleven would be sufficient at any time to proceed to business. In a short time this body reported resolutions recommending companies to be stationed at Pittsburg, then a part of Virginia territory, at Point Pleasant, Fincastle, and other places to protect the inhabitants from the Indians. Various matters occupied the attention of the Convention; the case of Richard Bland, who asked for an investigation of false reports that had been circulated to his injury, and who was fully exonerated; a plan for making saltpetre from trash tobacco; petitions of officers who wanted to take the public monies from the hands of the Royalist Receiver-General; petitions of merchants who considered themselves hardly treated by the non-exportation resolution. On Saturday, the 5th of August, the balloting took place for officers to command the regulars to be enlisted. Patrick Henry was made colonel of the first regiment, Thomas Nelson of the second, and William Woodford of the third regiment.[2] George Mason sat down on the evening of this same Saturday to report the progress of affairs to Mr. Cockburn. He had been unwell, it seems, and had not attended the Convention for several days. On this day, however, he was able to be present, and he was to go out of town to spend Sunday with a friend.

---

[1] "Virginia Hist. Register," vol. ii., p. 21; "Virginia Calendar Papers," vol. i., p. 267.

[2] Journal of the Convention.

RICHMOND, Aug. 25, 1775.

DEAR SIR :

Capt. Grayson informing me that he shall set out on his return home to-morrow, I take the opportunity of writing to you, though I have nothing very agreeable to communicate. We are getting into great confusion here, and I fear running the country to an expence it will not be able to bear—3,000 men are voted as a body of standing troops, to be forthwith raised and formed into three regiments, the first to be commanded by Mr. Patrick Henry, the second by Col. Thos. Nelson, and the third by Mr. Wm. Woodford—a great push was made for Col. Mercer of Fredericksburg to the 1st. Regiment ; but he lost it by a few votes, upon the question between him and Mr. Henry ; though he had a majority upon the ballot.

The expence of the last Indian war will be near £150,000, our share of the expence of the Continental Army £150,000 more, the charge of the troops now raising, and the minute-men with their arms £350,000 ; these added together will make an enormous sum, and there are several charges still behind ; such as the volunteer companies at Williamsburg, the payment of the members of the Convention, &c.—however, nothing is yet absolutely conclusive, and some abridgement may yet perhaps be made ; though at present there is little prospect of it.

As it is proposed that a company of fifty men for the standing army shall be raised in each county, my son George may perhaps have a mind to enter into the service ; in which case, pray tell him that it will be very contrary to my inclination, and that I advise him by all means against it—when the plan for the min-ute-men is completed, if he has a mind to enter into that I shall have no objection ; as I look upon it to be the true, natural and safe defence of this, or any other free country, and as such wish to see it encouraged to the utmost. I should have wrote to him but that it was uncertain whether he was at home, or at the Springs.

I have been very unwell, and unable to attend the Convention for two or three days, but am now getting better and attended again to-day, and I am going out to-morrow to visit a friend in the country. God knows when I shall get home again—remember me kindly to my dear children—the family at "Spring-field" and all friends; and believe me, dear Sir,

Yr. affect. friend and servant,

G. MASON.[1]

Colonel Mason, as it will be seen, was fully alive to the difficulties the Convention had to contend with, and he was fearful that they were undertaking more than the resources of the colony justified, in providing so large a body of troops. It was not until the 9th of August that Patrick Henry, Edmund Pendleton, Benjamin Harrison, and Thomas Jefferson took their seats in the Convention; Richard Henry Lee arriving on the following day. Congress, which had been in session since May, took a month's recess at this time, in order that the Virginia delegation might attend the Convention.[2] Important business was before the Convention on the 10th of August, the appointment of members of Congress in place of Edmund Pendleton, who had resigned on occount of his health, George Washington and Patrick Henry, who had each military offices that incapacitated them for civil service. It has been seen that George Mason's friends had urged him to accept a seat in Congress, and now two thirds of the Convention waited on him to beg him to accept a nomination. But he remained firm in his first resolve, believing that others could serve the country as well, and that his family required his care. Peyton Randolph, Richard Henry Lee, Jefferson, Harrison, Nelson, Bland, and Wythe were appointed for the ensuing year. But Bland, on the day following, in a speech thanking the Convention for the honor paid him, declined serving on account of his advanced age. And then for the third time George Mason was pressed to accept the office, Patrick Henry and Jefferson heading the party who urged it upon him. He was obliged to declare before the Convention his

<hr>

[1] "Virginia Historical Register," vol. ii., p. 21; "Virginia Calendar Papers," vol. i., p. 268.

[2] 4, "American Archives," iii., 1.

reasons for refusing, and this was done with so much feeling as to call tears to the eyes of the president of the Convention, Peyton Randolph. Colonel Mason recommended Francis Lightfoot Lee in his place, and he received the majority of votes, though Carter Braxton was within one of obtaining it. George Mason was on the committee to examine the ballot-box, and he found one ballot for himself, dropped in by some persistent admirer, determined to signify his choice, though throwing away his vote.

This balloting took place on the 15th, and on the 16th of August an important resolve passed the Convention. It was to this effect : that " for the more effectual carrying into execution the several rules and regulations established for the defence and protection of the colony, *a Committee of Safety* be appointed to consist of eleven members, to sit for one year, and not to hold military office after the end of this session." The Convention also on this day ordered that a general test oath be drawn up to be used in the colony, " and that Mr. Parker and Mr. George Mason do prepare and bring in the same." On the following day the balloting took place for the members of the Committee of Safety. Colonel Mason had been reluctant to serve here too, for the same reason that he had declined a seat in Congress. But he was told that his friends would take no refusal. The names of those who composed this distinguished council were Edmund Pendleton, George Mason, John Page, Richard Bland, Thomas Ludwell Lee, Paul Carrington, Dudley Digges, William Cabell, Carter Braxton, James Mercer, and John Tabb. On the ballot for the eleven names on the tickets, Edmund Pendleton received seventy-seven votes, and George Mason seventy-two, the lowest number received being thirty-six. On Saturday, the 19th, Colonel Mason presented the ordinance for establishing a general test. The ordinance for appointing a Committee of Safety passed on Thursday, the 24th, and on Saturday the Convention adjourned.[1] The Tuesday before, George Mason wrote to Martin Cockburn :

[1] Journal of the Convention.

RICHMOND, Aug. 22, 1775.

DEAR SIR :

Col. Blackburn telling me he shall set out for Prince William to-day, I take the opportunity of informing you that I am now pretty well, though I was exceedingly indisposed for several days, some of which I was confined to my bed ; but a little fresh air, good water, and excellent kind and hospitable treatment from a neighboring country gentleman has recover'd me. I have found my apprehensions in being sent to this Convention but too well verified.   Before the choice of delegates for the ensuing Congress, I was personally applied to by more than two-thirds of the members, insisting upon my serving at the Congress, but by assuring them that I could not possibly attend, I prevailed on them not to name me, except about twenty who would take no excuse.   A day or two after, upon Col. Bland's resignation, a strong party was formed, at the head of which were Col. Henry, Mr. Jefferson and Col. Carrington, for sending me to the Congress at all events, laying it down as a rule that I would not refuse if ordered by my country : in consequence of this just before the ballot, I was publicly called upon in Convention and obliged to make a public excuse, and give my reasons for refusal, in doing which I felt myself more distressed than ever I was in my life, especially when I saw tears run down the President's cheeks.   I took occasion at the same time to recommend Col. Francis Lee, who was accordingly chosen in the room of Col. Bland.   But my getting clear of this appointment has availed me little, as I have been since, in spite of everything I could do to the contrary, put upon the Committee of Safety ; which is even more inconvenient and disagreeable to me than going to the Congress. I endeavour'd to excuse myself, and begg'd the Convention would permit me to resign ; but was answered by an universal No.

The 3,000 regular troops (exclusive of the western frontier garrisons) first proposed to be raised are reduced to 1,000, to be formed into two regiments, one of eight, the other of seven companies ; these 15 companies are to be raised in the fifteen western-shore districts, the captains and subaltern officers to be appointed by the committee of the respective district, formed by a deputation of three members from the committee of each county in the district.   The first regiment is commanded by Col. Henry, Lieut.

Col. Christian and Maj'r Eppes ; the second regiment by Col.
Wm. Woodford, Lieut. Col. Charles Scott and Major Spotswood.
A regiment of minute-men of 680 rank and file in each of the
fifteen districts on the western shore, with the same field and
staff officers, chaplain, surgeon, &c., as the regiments of regulars,
and with the same pay when upon duty in the district, or drawn
into actual service—the officers to be appointed by the District
Committees, and commissioned by the Committee of Safety—the
militia officers are all to give up their present commissions, and
be nominated by the respective committees of the counties, the
militia companys to be exercised once a fortnight, except the
three winter months, and general county musters twice a year.
Arms, tents, &c., to be provided for the minute-men at the public
charge. These are the great outlines of our plan of defence,
which I think a good, though very expensive one ; the particulars
would take up too much room for a common letter ; particular
rules are drawn up for the better regulation and government of
the army, to which both the minute-men and militia are subjected,
when drawn out into actual service ; the volunteer companys are
all discharged and melted down in the plan for the regiments of
minute-men—these informations you may rely on, as the ordinance
yesterday received its final fiat.

There are several ordinances under the consideration of the
committee of the whole house and nearly completed, viz.:
one for the raising of money and imposing taxes, one for
furnishing arms and encouraging the making salt-petre, sulphur,
powder and lead, one for appointing a Committee of Safety,
and defining its powers, which are very extensive, one for
regulating the elections of delegates and county committees,
and one for establishing a general test. The Maryland Convention not concurring in the resolve for immediately stopping the export of provision, it became necessary to rescind
ours ; that our ports as well as theirs might be kept open till
the 10th of Sept.—A very sensible petition from the merchants
who are natives of Great Britain has been put into my hands,
and will be presented to-day or to-morrow, praying that some
certain line of conduct may be prescribed to them, and a recommendation to the people from the Convention, respecting
them. As I drew the ordinance for a general test, I have en-

deavoured to make it such as no good man would object to : the merchants here declare themselves well pleased with it. Pray excuse me to Mr. Massey, Mr. McCarty, Mr. Henderson, and all enquiring friends, for not writing to them, and tell them I consider all public news wrote to you as to be communicated to them, and such of my constituents as desire information.

I expect the Convention will arise about the end of this or the beginning of next week. The members of the Committee of Safety (of which I send you a list) meet next Friday ; how long I shall be detained on that business God only knows. My kind regard to my dear family, and to the family at "Spring-field." Conclude me, Dr. Sir,

Yr affect. Friend and Servt.,

G. Mason.

P. S.—Every ordinance goes through all the formalities of a bill in the House of Burgesses, has three readings, &c., before it is passed, and in every respect wears the face of law—Resolves as recommendations being no longer trusted to in matters of importance." [1]

The Convention set forth in a declaration of their body the cause of their meeting, and the necessity of immediately putting the country in a posture of defence.

"A causeless, hasty dissolution drove the representative body to the unhappy dilemma of either sacrificing the most essential interests of their constituents, or of meeting in General Convention to assert and preserve them. Repeated prorogations of our Assembly, when the country was in the greatest distress, rendered a Convention in the month of March last absolutely necessary. The delegates of the people then met in full Convention, the most numerous Assembly that had ever been known in this colony, taking a view of our unhappy situation . . . judged it then our indispensable duty to put the country in a posture of defence. . . . But we again and for all, publicly and solemnly declare, before God and the world, that we do bear faith and true allegiance to his Majesty George III our only lawful and rightful King, that we will so long as may be in our power, defend him and his government. . . . It is our

----

[1] "Virginia Historical Register," vol. ii., p. 21.

fixed and unalterable resolution to disband such force as may be raised in this colony whenever our dangers are removed &c."[1]

With this manifesto the Convention closed its work, and the Committee of Safety took up the reins of government. Its powers as defined by the Convention were as follows: After meeting at a convenient time and place, electing president, vice-president, and clerk, a majority of six or more being present, they might grant commissions to any officer or officers; appoint commissioners, paymasters, commissaries, and contractors; issue their warrants from time to time to the treasurer appointed by Convention to any person for provisions, clothing, tents, etc.; superintend, direct, and appoint stations, marches, and encampments, for the regular forces to be raised; "and if any company of minute-men or militia shall be called out pursuant to the power given the chief commanding officer, or other officers, the said Committee shall and may judge and determine on the necessity and propriety of making such drafts, and give such orders as to discharging or continuing them in service, as to the said Committee shall seem most expedient and necessary." The Committee, moreover, had power in case of necessity to call in assistance from neighboring colonies. All chief commanding officers, as well of regulars as of minute-men and militia, were to pay strict obedience to orders received from the Committee, and in case of neglect were to be reported to the next Convention. The Committee were to keep up a correspondence with the committees of the several counties and corporations, and all their proceedings and transactions were to be fairly entered into a book to be laid before the next Convention. They had power also, and were desired to collect together all arms lately taken away from the public magazine, and all other arms purchased at the public expense.[2]

The Committee of Safty was to meet on Friday, the 25th of August, the day before the adjournment of the Convention, and Colonel Mason looked forward to some detention in Richmond in transacting its affairs. In September, how-

[1] Journal of the Convention. [2] *Ibid.*

ever, he was again at " Gunston Hall," and receiving a visit at this time from Richard Henry Lee, who was on his way back to Congress. The latter wrote to Washington from Philadelphia two days after his arrival, the 26th, giving him news of his "lady" at "Mount Vernon." "Having some business with Colonel Mason," he explains, "I travelled that road."[1] What this business was does not transpire, but it doubtless had some connection with political affairs. We learn, from the following letter of George Mason to Washington, further details of the Convention. It is written less guardedly than the letters meant for Colonel Mason's constituents in Fairfax, and gives us an idea of some of the vexations that beset the eager, earnest natures, such as Mason's, in the new and untried paths before them. And we see that this early legislative body, untrammelled now for the first time, and having sole control of the affairs of the colony, with all its patriotism and its elements of greatness, was not free from the ordinary weaknesses of popular assemblies. The best minds at length took the lead, and stamped their impress on the whole.

GUNSTON HALL, VIRGINIA,
October 14, 1775.

DEAR SIR ·

I wrote to you in July, a little before my being ordered to the Convention, congratulating you upon an appointment which gives so much satisfaction to all America, and afterwards in August, from Richmond ; since which I have to acknowledge your favor of the twentieth August, which nothing but want of health should have prevented my answering sooner, as I shall always think myself honored by your correspondence and friendship. I hinted to you in my last, the parties and factions which prevailed at Richmond. I never was in so disagreeable a situation, and almost despaired of a cause which I saw so ill conducted.—Mere vexation and disgust threw me into such an ill state of health, that before the Convention rose, I was sometimes near fainting in the House. Since my return home, I have had a severe fit of sickness, from which I am now recovering, but am still very weak and low.

[1] "Correspondence of the Revolution," vol. i., p. 51.

During the first part of the Convention, parties ran so high, that we had frequently no other way of preventing improper measures, but by procrastination, urging the previous question, and giving men time to reflect. However, after some weeks the babblers were pretty well silenced, a few weighty members began to take the lead, several wholesome regulations were made, and, if the Convention had continued to sit for a few days longer, I think the public safety would have been as well provided for as our present circumstances permit. The Convention, not thinking this a time to rely upon resolves and recommendations only, and to give obligatory force to their proceedings, adopted the style and form of legislation, changing the word *enact* into *ordain ;* their ordinances were all introduced in the form of bills, were regularly referred to a committee of the whole House, and underwent three readings before they were passed.

I enclose you the ordinance for raising an armed force, for the defence and protection of the colony ; it is a little defaced, by being handled at our District Committee, but it is the only copy I have at present by me. You will find some little inaccuracies in it ; but upon the whole, I hope it will merit your approbation. The minute plan I think is a wise one, and will, in a short time, furnish eight thousand good troops, ready for action, and composed of men in whose hands the sword may be safely trusted. To defray the expense of the provisions made by this ordinance, and to pay the charge of the last year's Indian war, we are now emitting the sum of three hundred and fifty thousand pounds in paper currency. I have great apprehensions, that the large sums in bills of credit, now issuing all over the continent, may have fatal effects in depreciating the value, and therefore opposed any suspension of taxation, and urged the necessity of immediately laying such taxes as the people could bear, to sink the sum emitted as soon as possible ; but was able only to reduce the proposed suspension from three years to one. The land and poll tax (the collection of which is to commence in June, 1777), will sink fifty thousand pounds per year ; and instead of the usual commissions for emitting and receiving, the Treasurer is allowed an annual salary of six hundred and twenty-five pounds.

Our friend, the Treasurer, was the warmest man in the Convention, for immediately raising a standing army of not less than four thousand men, upon constant pay. They stood a considerable time at three thousand, exclusive of the troops upon the western frontiers; but at the last reading (as you will see by the ordinance), were reduced to one thousand and twenty, rank and file; in my opinion, a well-judged reduction, not only from our inability to furnish, at present, such a number with arms and ammunition, but I think it extremely imprudent to exhaust ourselves before we know when we are to be attacked. The part we have to act, at present, seems to require our laying in good magazines, training our people, and having a good number of them ready for action. An ordinance is passed for regulating an annual election of members to the Convention and County Committees; for encouraging the making saltpetre, sulphur, and gunpowder; for establishing a manufactory of arms, under the direction of commissioners; and for appointing a Committee of Safety, consisting of eleven members, for carrying the ordinances of the Convention into execution, directing the stations of the troops, and calling the minute-battalions and drafts from the militia into service, if necessary, &c.

There is also an ordinance establishing articles for the government of the troops, principally taken from those drawn up by the Congress, except that about martial law upon life and death is more cautiously constituted and brought nearer to the principles of the common law.

Many of the principal families are removing from Norfolk, Hampton, York, and Williamsburg, occasioned by the behaviour of Lord Dunmore, and the commanders of the King's ships and tenders upon this station. Whenever your leisure will permit, it will always give me the greatest pleasure to be informed of your welfare, and to hear what is doing on the great American theatre.

I most sincerely wish you health and success equal to the justice of our cause, and am with great respect, dear Sir,

Your affectionate and obedient servant,

GEORGE MASON.

P. S.   I beg the favor of you to remember me kindly to General Lee, and present him my respectful compliments.[1]

---

[1] Washington MSS., Department of State. "Correspondence of the Revolution," vol. i., p. 62.

George Mason speaks in this letter of the alarm occasioned at this time by Lord Dunmore in Lower Virginia. It was expected that he would next appear in the Rappahannock and Potomac rivers, and Colonel Mason, in view of this contingency, moved his family away for safety, and recommended to Mrs. Washington, who was then at "Mount Vernon," that she should leave the neighborhood also. George Mason wrote to General Washington a little later:

" Dunmore has come and gone, and left us untouched except by some alarm. I sent my family many miles back in the country, and advised Mrs. Washington to do likewise as a prudential movement. At first she said ' No ; I will not desert my post ' ; but she finally did so with reluctance, rode only a few miles, and, plucky little woman as she is, stayed away only one night." [1]

Dunmore burned Norfolk in January, and during the summer of 1776 his vessels came up the Potomac as far as Occoquan Falls, in Prince William County, intending, it was said, to lay waste "Gunston Hall" and "Mount Vernon" in the absence of their owners. Lord Dunmore designed to capture Mrs. Washington, it was asserted, had she been at home.[2] The county militia, however, mustered in strong force, and, a heavy storm coming to their aid, his lordship was forced to turn back. Mr. William Brent's house was destroyed by the enemy at this time. His home was near Aquia Creek, and is one of the gentlemen's plantations mentioned in "Smythe's Travels."

On the 1st of December, 1775, the Virginia Convention met again in Richmond, and adjourned later to Williamsburg. George Mason did not attend this Convention, as he was suffering from an attack of the gout. And at his own request his name was dropped from the Committee of Safety. But anxious to do what he could for the cause, he labored, at the instance of the Committee, in preparing for the defence

[1] " Mary and Martha Washington " (J. B. Lossing), p. 137 (extract from an old newspaper).
[2] *Ibid.*, p. 156 ; " Mount Vernon and its Associations."—Lossing.

of the Potomac River.   The following letter on the subject was written to the Maryland Council of Safety :

VIRGINIA, FAIRFAX COUNTY,
Jan. 31st, 1776.

SIR :

Being empowered and directed by the Committee of Safety for this Colony to build two row-gallies, one to carry a 24 and the other an 18 pounder, and provide three armed cutters for the protection of Potomac River, we think it proper to inform your Board that this measure will be carried into execution, with all possible expedition, and that we hope to have your co-operation in adopting some similar plan for the same purpose.   We beg the favor of an answer by the first opportunity, and we are, with the greatest respect, Sir,   Yr most obt. Hble. Serts ,

G. MASON,
JOHN DALTON.

To the Honble. the President
of the Council of Safety for the
Province of Maryland.[1]

The following letter from Colonel Mason to Robert Carter, of " Nomini," relates to the affairs of the Ohio Company, and the survey recently made of their lands, for the expenses of which George Mason had made himself responsible :

GUNSTON HALL, March 12th, 1776.

SIR :

Capt. Hancock Lee and one Mr. Leet are returned from surveying the Ohio Company's 200,000 acres of land, and are now here making out their returns and settling their accounts, in assisting about which I am closely engaged, as I wish to have everything as clear and regular as possible.   They have got it all in one tract, upon a large creek called Licking Creek, which falls into the Ohio river on the southeast side, about 150 miles below the Scioto river, and about 60 miles above the mouth of the Kentucky river, so that it is clear both of Henderson's and the Vandalia Company's claim.   By all accounts it is equal to any land on this continent, being exceedingly rich and level.   The charges of the survey come to about £650 currency, and I have

---

[1] MS. Letter (published in 4, "American Archives," iv., 896).

never received a farthing from the members towards it, except £49 . . 9 . . 9 from Richard Lee, Esq : and £100 sterling from Col. Tayloe (for Mr. Lomax and himself), which with my own quota of £50 sterling makes £199 . . 9 . . 9 sterling. It would be unreasonable that I should advance the remainder, even if I had the money, but the fact is I have it not, and the men are all waiting for their wages, by which I am extremely distressed, having always through life made it a rule to comply punctually with my contracts. On this occasion, upon the credit of the Ohio Company, and the particular promises of several of the members to advance £50 sterling each, I agreed to make myself liable for the charges of this survey, and am now liable to suffer for it.

I ask no pecuniary favor of any man, and desire only justice. I must acknowledge that you were not one of the number who promised to make the said advance, and that you told me, when I last conversed with you on the subject, you believed you should not make any further advances as a member of the Ohio Company, and would rather lose what you had already paid than run any further risk, and it is therefore that I now put it to you as a man of honor, or, what is more intelligible and important, as an honest man, whether you intend to claim any benefit from the survey lately made or not? If you do surely you ought to indemnify me from all but my proportional charge. If you do not, you should let us know it candidly, that your shares may be disposed of for the payment, or sunk in the Company; or if you do not like to be further concerned, and will sell out to me, I will purchase one, or perhaps both your shares. In case you intend to claim your part of this survey, I am convinced you will immediately furnish me with your proportion of the money; and at any rate I flatter myself you will pardon the freedom with which I have expressed myself on the subject, and ascribe it to its true cause, the sincerity, and real regard, with which I am, Sir,

Your most humble servant,

G. MASON.

To the Honorable Robert Carter, Esq :
Westmoreland County.

To the care of }
Richard Lee, Esq.[1] }

---

[1] MS. Letter.

General Washington, in the spring of 1776, was successful over the British at Boston in forcing them to evacuate the city ; this being the first of what by general consent have been considered the three most brilliant events in his military life. He received the congratulations of his friend, Colonel Mason, in a letter from " Gunston Hall," written the 2d of April. George Mason here gives also some account of his own duties as agent of the Committee of Safety. He had turned from law-making and finance to ship-building with the versatility of a vigorous mind, bringing all his accustomed energy of purpose to the task before him. Though in weak health, as he tells his correspondent, this letter shows no trace of the lassitude of which he makes mention, but puts the writer before us alive to the issues of the hour and responsive to its demands.

Virginia, Gunston Hall,
April 2, 1776.

Dear Sir ·

We have just received the welcome news of your having, with so much address and success, dislodged the Ministerial Troops and taken possession of the town of Boston. I congratulate you most heartily upon this glorious and important event— an event which will render General Washington's name immortal in the annals of America, endear his memory to the latest posterity, and entitle him to those thanks which Heaven appointed as the reward of public virtue.

It is the common opinion here that we shall have a visit from General Howe in some of the middle or southern colonies, but it does not seem well-founded. I am very unable to judge of military affairs ; but it appears to me that if General Howe acts the part of a wise man and an experienced officer, he will not venture a sickly, worn-out, disgusted, and disgraced army, in a country where he must meet immediate opposition, and where any misfortune might produce a mutiny or general desertion. I think it much more probable that he will retire to Halifax, give his troops a little time, by ease and refreshment, to recover their spirits, and be in readiness as soon as the season permits, to relieve Quebec ; keeping some ships-of-war cruising off Boston harbour to protect and direct the transports which may arrive. New York, or any of the northern United Provinces are too near Cambridge ; for if he could not maintain the advantageous and strongly fortified post of Boston, what reasonable hope has he of gaining and maintaining a new one, in the face of a superior army ?

You will, perhaps, smile at these speculative and idle suggestions upon a subject which will probably be reduced to a certainty, one way or other, long before this reaches you ; but when I am conversing with you, the many agreeable hours we have spent together recur upon my mind. I fancy myself under your hospitable roof at Mount Vernon, and lay aside reserve. May God grant us a return of those halcyon days, when every man may sit down at his ease under the shade of his own vine and his own fig-tree, and enjoy the sweets of domestic life ! Or, if this is too much, may He be pleased to inspire us with spirit and resolution to bear our present and future sufferings becoming men determined to transmit to our posterity, unimpaired, the blessings we have received from our ancestors.

Colonel Caswell's victory in North Carolina, and the military spirit which it has raised, will be an obstacle to any attempts in that quarter. Maryland and Virginia are at present rather unprepared, but their strength is daily increasing. The late levies have been made with surprising rapidity, and the seven new regiments are already in a manner complete except as to arms, in which they are very deficient ; but arms are coming in, in small quantities, from different parts of the country, and a very considerable manufactory is established at Fredericksburg. Large ventures have been lately made for military stores ; for which purpose we are now loading a ship for Europe, with tobacco at Alexandria. Her cargo is all on float, and I hope to have her under sailing in a few days. Notwithstanding the natural plenty of provisions in this colony, I am very apprehensive of a great scarcity of beef and pork among our troops this summer, occasioned by the people's not expecting a market until the slaughter season was past : I find it extremely difficult to lay in a stock for about three hundred men, in the Marine department of this river.

Ill health, and a certain listlessness inseparable from it, have prevented my writing to you so often as I would otherwise have done; but I trust to your friendship to excuse it. The same cause disabled me from attending the Committee of Safety this winter, and induced me to intreat the Committee to leave me out of it. I continue to correspond constantly with the Board, and I hope am no less usefully employed, thinking it, in such times as these are, every man's duty to contribute his mite to the public service. I have, in conjunction with Mr. Dalton, the charge of providing and equipping armed vessels for the protection of this river. The thing is new to me, but I must endeavor to improve by experience. I am much obliged to the Board for joining Mr. Dalton with me. He is a steady, diligent man, and without such assistance I could not have undertaken it. We are building the row-galleys, which are in considerable forwardness; and have purchased three sloops for cruisers, two of them being only from forty to fifty tons burden, are to mount eight carriage-guns each, three and four pounders; they are not yet fitted up, and we are exceedingly puzzled to get cannon for them. The other, the *American Congress* is a fine stout vessel, of about one hundred and ten tons burden, and has such an easy draft of water as will enable her to run into most of the creeks, or small harbors, if she meets with a vessel of superior force. She mounts fourteen carriage-guns, six and four-pounders, though we have thoughts of mounting two nine-pounders upon her main beam, if we find her able, as we think she is, to bear them; her guns are mounted and to be tried to-morrow. We have twenty barrels of powder, and about a ton of shot ready—more is making; swivels we have not yet been able to procure, but she may make a tolerable shift without, until they can be furnished. We have got some small-arms, and are taking every method to increase them, and hope to be fully supplied in about a week more. Her company of marines is raised and have been for some time exercised to the use of the great guns. Her complement of marines and seamen is to be ninety-six men. We are exerting ourselves to the utmost and hope to have her on her station in less than a fortnight, and that the other vessels will quickly follow her, and be able to protect the inhabitants of this river from the piratical attempts of all the enemy's cutters, tenders, and small craft.

Immediately upon receipt of your former letters, I applied to some of the Maryland Committees, as well as those on this side ; in consequence of which, the several most convenient places on this river were sounded, and thoroughly examined ; but effectual batteries were found, in our present circumstances, impracticable. Mr. Lund Washington tells me he sent you the drafts and soundings taken upon this occasion. A regiment commanded by Colonel Mercer of Fredericksburg, is stationed on this part of the river, and I hope we shall be tolerably safe, unless a push is made here with a large body of men. I think we have some reason to hope the ministry will bungle away another summer, relying partly upon force, and partly upon fraud and negotiation.

The family here join with me in presenting their best compliments to yourself and lady, as well as to Mr. Custis and his. If in any of your affairs here I can render you any acceptable service, I beg you will use that freedom with which I wish you to command dear sir,

Your affectionate and obedient servant,
GEORGE MASON.

To His Excellency General Washington, }
    Head-Quarters at Boston.[1]   }

It is interesting to note, as an instance of George Mason's sagacity, that the " speculations," at which he supposed his military friend would smile, proved, in one point, to be perfectly correct. General Howe did not go to New York, as Washington himself expected he would, but to Halifax, as Mason predicted. In the above letter, Colonel Mason speaks of corresponding constantly with the Committee of Safety. Unfortunately, the letter-book of the Committee has been lost, and none of George Mason's letters are to be found. In the journal of the Committee for February 10th there is this entry : " A letter wrote to Col. George Mason in answer to his of the third." [2]

---

[1] 4, "American Archives," v., 760. "Correspondence of the Revolution," vol. i., p. 178. Washington MSS., Department of State.

[2] MS. Journal, State Library, Richmond.

Washington wrote to George Mason, early in May, giving him a commission to attend to in behalf of young Mr. Custis, his adopted son, who had now attained his majority. He had been married nearly two years, but his property was still in Washington's care.   His sister died, as has .been said, in 1773.   General Washington had been appointed the guardian of his wife's children.

NEW YORK, 10th May, 1776.

DEAR SIR :

The uncertainty of my return, and the justice of surrendering to Mr. Custis the bonds, which I have taken for the moneys raised from his estate and lent out upon interest, as also his moiety of his deceased sister's fortune, consisting altogether of bonds, oblige me to have recourse to a friend to see this matter done, and a proper memorandum of the transaction made. I could think of no one, in whose friendship, care, and abilities I could so much confide, to do Mr. Custis and me this favor, as yourself ; and therefore, I take the liberty of soliciting your aid.

In order that you may be enabled to do this with ease and propriety, I have written to the clerk of the Secretary's office for attested copies of my last settled accounts with the General Court in behalf of Mr. Custis, and the estate of his deceased sister ; with which and the bonds, I have desired him and Mr. Washington to wait upon you for the purpose above mentioned. The amount of the balance due, upon my last settled accounts, to Mr. Custis, I would also have assigned him out of my moiety of his sister's bonds ; and, if there is no weight in what I have said in my letter to Mr. Lund Washington, concerning the rise of exchange, and which, to avoid repetition, as I am a good deal hurried, I have desired him to show you, I wish it may meet with no notice, as I want nothing but what is consistent with the strictest justice, honor, and even generosity ; although I have never charged him or his sister, from the day of my connection with them to this hour, one farthing for all the trouble I have had in managing their estates, nor for any expense they have been to me, notwithstanding some hundreds of pounds would not reimburse the moneys I have actually paid in attending the public meetings in Williamsburg to collect their debts, and transact the several matters appertaining to the respective estates. A variety of occurrences, and my anxiety to put this place as speedily as possible into a posture of defence, will not, at this time, admit of my adding more, than that I am, with unfeigned regard,

Dear Sir, &c.[1]

General Washington also wrote on the same day to Lund Washington, at "Mount Vernon," telling him to take the accounts, and, "with these and the bundle of bonds, which you will find among my papers, I would have Mr. Custis and you repair to Colonel Mason and get him, as a common friend to us both, as a gentleman well acquainted with business, and very capable of drawing up a proper memorandum of the transaction, to deliver him his own bonds, &c.," and he concludes the letter thus: "The many matters which hang heavy upon my hands at present, do not allow me to add more, but oblige me to request as I have not written fully to Colonel Mason on this subject, that you will show him this letter, and if necessary let him have it."

A few notices of George Mason are to be found in the journal of the Committee of Safety for May and June:

"May 29, 1776, a warrant to George Mason, Esq: £3-10-0 for a musquet to 3rd regiment. June 10, George Mason and John Dalton, Esqrs. are requested to view a blanket made at a manufactory lately set up in Pennsylvania, and if they approve thereof, that they contract for the purchase of 2000 upon the best terms they can, to be delivered agreeable to such sample. June 11, Resolved that George Mason, Esq: be authorized to draw on the commissary of provisions here for rations to such seamen as may come to this city engaged for the Potomac River department. June 18, A warrant to George Mason, Esq: pr. use George Mason, Jr. £3-5 for two guns to a detachment of his minute company marched to Hampton."[2]

---

[1] "Writings of Washington," Sparks, vol. iii., p. 383.

[2] MS. Journal, State Library, Richmond.

The great Convention of 1776, the fifth and last of the Virginia colonial Conventions, was to meet on the 6th of May, and there seems to have been no small competition for seats in its councils. Robert Brent wrote to Richard Henry Lee from Aquia on the 28th of April · "In many counties there have been warm contests for seats in our approaching Convention. Many new ones are got in . . . Colonel Mason, with great difficulty returned for Fairfax. Our friend Harry much pushed in Prince William. Will Brent for Stafford in room of Charles Carter."[1] As George Mason had not been in the Convention during the winter or on the Committee of Safety it may have been assumed by the friends of other candidates that his ill-health and known fondness for retirement would prevent him from serving again. But he was now too well known to fail of being brought forward by his many admirers, and he was ready to meet their wishes. "Our friend Harry" of the Brent letter was Colonel Henry Lee of "Leesylvania," the father of the young cavalry officer of twenty-two who was soon afterwards to render the name famous. The Convention met on the appointed day at Williamsburg, but Colonel Mason did not arrive until the 17th. Edmund Pendleton was elected president of the Convention, and in his address to the members soon after he laid before them the unsettled condition of the colony, with almost all the powers of government suspended for nearly two years, and he recapitulated the needs of the people. On the following Friday it was resolved by the Convention to raise thirteen hundred men for the military establishment, and the Committee of Safety was empowered to issue commissions for the several officers required. The Convention, on Wednesday, the 15th, resolved itself into a committee on the state of the colony, and Colonel Archibald Cary reported the famous Resolutions for proposing Independence. These were written by Edmund Pendleton. "Henry and Nelson concerted that the former should speak in favor of a movement for independence, and the

[1] Lee Papers, *Southern Literary Messenger*, new series, vol. vi., No. 3.

latter support him," Edmund Randolph tells us. " This he did," adds our historian, " and Henry stood like a ' pillar of fire ' before the Convention." [1] Meriwether Smith as well as Edmund Pendleton offered resolutions, but those of the latter were accepted. After a preamble setting forth their grievances, these state :

" *Resolved unanimously*, That the delegates appointed to represent this colony in General Congress be instructed to propose to that respectable body to declare the United Colonies free and independent States, absolved from all allegiance to or dependence upon the crown or parliament of Great Britain, and that they give the assent of this colony to such declaration, and to whatever measures may be thought proper and necessary by the Congress for forming foreign alliances and a confederation of the colonies at such a time and in the manner as to them shall seem best :

" Provided that the power of forming government for and the regulations of the internal concerns of each colony be left to the respective colonial legislatures.

" *Resolved unanimously*, That a committee be appointed to prepare a DECLARATION OF RIGHT, and such a plan of government as will be most likely to maintain peace and order in this colony and secure substantial and equal liberty to the people." [2]

Thus the Virginia Convention took the first step which led to the Declaration of Independence on the part of the united colonies. The resolutions have been admired for their condensation, clearness, and vigor, but the preamble was not considered equal to them in style. Great was the rejoicing in Williamsburg over this action of the Convention. There was a military parade in celebration of the event, and the resolutions were read aloud to the troops, in the presence of the members of the Committee of Safety, and the delegates to the Convention, when patriotic toasts were given and the " Continental Union flag " displayed. And at night the town was illuminated. [3]

[1] MS. History of Virginia.   [2] Journal of the Convention.

[3] Moore's " Diary of the Revolution," vol. i., p. 240.

Before the meeting of the Convention the different members had personally or by correspondence discussed the burning question of independence, and the important measure which it involved of forming a new government for Virginia. John Page of "Rosewell," Jefferson's intimate friend, wrote to Richard Henry Lee on the 12th of April: "I think almost every man except the treasurer [Robert Carter Nicholas] is willing to declare for Independency. I would to God you could be here at the next Convention.

If you could I make no doubt you might easily prevail on the Convention to declare for Independency, and to establish a form of government."[1] And that the members were already preparing forms of government to be proposed to the Convention we may readily take for granted. In Congress Richard Henry Lee had talked on the subject with John Adams and others, and it may have been Adams' "Thoughts on Government" which is referred to in the following letter of John Augustine Washington written to Lee April 15th, in which he says:

"That we can no longer do without some fixed form of government is certain. That we have done as well as we have under our present no-form is astonishing, and really not to be accounted for but by Providence. I am happy in hearing from you, that we may expect a well digested form of government to be sent to our next Convention; for true it is that our Convention stands in need of advice, at least in matters of such great importance, and I really fear that this will want more than the last."[2]

On the 10th of May, John Adams introduced in Congress the resolution recommending to the colonies, where they were left without governments sufficient for their needs, to adopt such as they deemed expedient. This resolution passed, and Adams, with Richard Henry Lee and Edward Rutledge, were appointed a committee to prepare a preamble, which was adopted on the 15th of May, the same day that Virginia sent forth her resolutions advocating inde-

[1] Lee Papers, *Southern Literary Messenger*, new series, vol. vi., No. 4.
[2] *Ibid.*

pendence. This preamble denied the royal authority, and looked to the people as the source of the new governments. On Saturday, the 18th of May, there were three letters written to Richard Henry Lee by members of the Conven_tion—Thomas Ludwell Lee, John Augustine Washington, and George Mason, all urging him to join them if possible. Thomas Ludwell Lee sent his brother the Resolutions of the 15th. He says:

" Enclosed you have some printed resolves which passed our Convention to the infinite joy of the people here. The preamble is not to be admired in point of composition, nor has the resolve of Independency that pre-emptory, decided air which I could wish. . . You have also a set of resolves offered by Col. Meriwether Smith, but the first which were proposed the second day by the President—for the debate lasted two days—were pre-ferred. These he had formed from the resolves and preambles of the first day badly put together. Col. Mason came to town yesterday after the arrival of the post ; I showed him your letter, and he thinks with me that your presence here is of the last con-sequence. He designs, I believe, to tell you so by letter to-day.

To form a plan of just and equal government would not perhaps be so very difficult ; but to preserve it from being marred with a thousand impertinences ; from being in the end a jumble of discordant, unintelligible parts, will demand the protecting hand of a master."

John Augustine Washington wrote on the same all-absorbing subject :

" I have the pleasure to enclose you a resolve of our Conven-tion upon the subject of taking up Government, and an instruction to our delegates in Congress to declare the United Colonies free and independent States. It is not so full as some would have wished it, but I hope may answer the purpose. What gave me pleasure was that the resolve was made by a very full house and without a dissenting voice. . . ˜. I hope the great business of forming a well regulated government will go on well, as I think there will be no great difference among our best speakers, Henry, Mason, Mercer, Dandridge, Smith, and I am apt to think the

[1] *Ibid.*, No. 5, p. 325.

President will concur with them in sentiment. The Resolve with regard to Government, &c., was entirely his." [1]

Thus was the work of independence forwarded by the " bolder spirits of Henry, the Lees, Pages, Mason, &c.," of whom Jefferson speaks in his memoirs, with whom he went " at all points." But the men of the moderate party, in the person of Edmund Pendleton, were not behindhand on this occasion, and, now united and unanimous, Virginia initiated the new era in American history.

The following is George Mason's letter to Richard Henry Lee ·

WILLIAMSBURG, May 18, 1776.

DEAR SIR :

After a smart fit of the gout, which detained me at home the first of the session, I have at last reached this place, where, to my great satisfaction, I find the first grand point has been carried *nem. con.*, the opponents being so few that they did not think fit to divide or contradict the general voice. Your brother, Col. T., will enclose you the resolve. The preamble is tedious, rather timid, and in many instances exceptionable, but I hope it may answer the purpose. We are now going upon the most important of all subjects—government ! The committee appointed to pre- pare a plan is, according to custom, overcharged with useless members. You know our Convention. I need not say that it is not mended by the late elections. We shall, in all probability, have a thousand ridiculous and impracticable proposals, and of course a plan formed of hetrogeneous, jarring, and unintelligible ingredients. This can be prevented only by a few men of integ- rity and abilities, whose country's interest lies next their hearts, undertaking this business and defending it ably through every stage of opposition.

I need not tell you how much you will be wanted here on this occasion. I speak with the sincerity of a friend, when I assure you that, in my opinion, your presence cannot, must not be dispensed with. We cannot do without you. Mr. Nelson is now on his way to Philadelphia, and will supply your place in Con- gress, by keeping up the representation of this colony. It will be some time, I presume, before that assembly can be fully pos-

---

[1] *Ibid.*, p. 330.

sessed of the sentiments and instructions of the different provinces, which I hope will afford you time to return.

Pray confer with some of your ablest friends at Congress upon the subject of foreign alliances ; what terms it will be expedient to offer. Nations, like individuals, are governed by their interest. Great Britain will bid against us. Whatever European power takes us by the hand must risk a war with her. We want but two things—a regular supply of military stores, and a naval protection of our trade and coasts. For the first we are able and willing to pay the value, in the produce of our country. For the second we must offer something adequate. To offer what is not worth accepting will be trifling with ourselves. Our exports should not be bound or affected by treaty ; our right to these should be sacredly retained. In our imports perhaps we may make concessions, so far as to give a preference to the manufactures or produce of a particular country. This would indeed have the effect of every other monopoly. We should be furnished with goods of worse quality, and at a higher price than in an open market, but this would only force us earlier into manufactures. It is an important and delicate subject, and requires thorough consideration. I know you will excuse my loose thoughts, which I give you in a hurry, without order but without reserve. I have not time to. copy or correct, having only borrowed half an hour, before I attend the House, which is now meeting. At all events, my dear Sir, let us see you here as soon as possible. All your friends anxiously expect you, and none more than

Your affectionate friend and servant,

G. MASON.

P. S. You who know what business is now before Congress, and in what forwardness, as well as how your colleagues stand affected as to capital points, will be best able to judge whether, at this crisis, you can do most service there or here, and I am sure you will act accordingly.

To Richard Henry Lee, Esquire, of the
   honorable the Continental Congress,
Philadelphia. Per post on public service.[1]

---

[1] MS. Letter. Grigsby quotes from this letter in "History of the Convention of 1776" (note to p. 161). Archives of the Virginia Historical Society.

CHAPTER VII.

1776.

George Mason, detained by sickness from attending the Convention at an earlier day, arrived at Williamsburg on the 17th of May, as has been seen, and took his seat in the Convention on the following morning. The committee to prepare a Declaration of Rights and Constitution, as first named on the 15th of May, consisted of twenty-eight members, among whom were Meriwether Smith, James Mercer, Robert Carter Nicholas, Patrick Henry, Richard Bland, Thomas Ludwell Lee, Dudley Digges, John Blair, John Page, and Edmund Randolph. Madison was added to the committee on the 16th and George Mason on the 18th, each one on the day that he took his seat in the Convention. Colonel Mason was placed on four other committees on the 18th; that of Propositions and Grievances; that of Privileges and Elections; the committee appointed to prepare and bring in an ordinance to encourage woollen, linen, and other manufactories; and the one appointed to prepare and bring in an ordinance to encourage the making of salt, saltpetre, and gunpowder. A letter was received from the Virginia delegates in Congress calling the attention of the Convention to a difficulty which had arisen between some gentlemen who had taken up lands on the Ohio near Pittsburg and the Indians of the vicinity. Of the committee of eighteen appointed to examine into the affair, Patrick Henry, James Mercer, and George Mason were members. On Monday, the

27th of May, Colonel Cary, the chairman of the committee
to prepare a constitution, reported that "the committee had
accordingly prepared a Declaration of Rights, which he
read in his place." It was read a second time at the clerk's
table, and ordered to be referred to a committee of the
whole Convention. The following Wednesday was appointed
as the day when the Convention should take it into consideration, and in the meantime it was to be printed for the perusal
of the members. It came before the Convention, then went
back to the committee, and was again under discussion by
the former on the 3d, 4th, and 5th of June. On the 10th
several amendments were made to it by the Convention, and
on the 12th it passed the Convention on a third reading
nem. con.[1] This paper, it is well known, was drafted by
George Mason.

The same day that this important instrument received the
assent of the Convention, provision was made for supplying
the treasury of the colony, which had now to do its part in
the war for establishing the people in the enjoyment of the
rights just promulgated. The following resolutions passed
the Convention on the 12th of June :

"*Resolved*, That the sum of one hundred thousand pounds, for
the purpose of supplying the regular forces and militia to be employed on the frontiers, and others which may remain on the pay
of the colony, for building vessels, and pay and provisions for
the seamen and marines in the navy, and all other public claims,
ought to be raised by an additional tax of one shilling and three
pence on tithables and of one shilling per hundred acres on land,
payable in the year 1777, and each of the six following years.
Resolved, That Treasury notes to the amount of the said sum of
100,000*l* ought to be issued upon the credit of the said taxes,
redeemable on the first day of January, 1784, and that 70,000*l*
of such notes be issued in dollars, or parts of dollars."

Archibald Cary, Robert Carter Nicholas, George Mason,
and nine other gentlemen were appointed a committee to prepare and bring in an ordinance pursuant to these resolutions.[2]

---

[1] Journal of the Convention.   [2] *Ibid.*

On the 20th of June the Convention appointed delegates to Congress for the coming year, which was in effect renewing the appointment of five of those already in office—Wythe, Nelson, Jefferson, and the two Lees. Two days afterwards, Mr. Digges from the Committee of Safety informed the Convention of their decision as to the disposition of the prisoners lately taken by Captains James and Richard Barron, being two hundred and seventeen Scotch Highland regulars. The non-commissioned officers and cadets they thought should be sent to some secure place on the frontiers, and there kept as prisoners of war ; the seamen should be engaged to serve in a cruiser or galley, if willing, and it would be prudent, they considered, to dispose the privates over the middle counties, one in a family, as prisoners of war yet employed on wages. On the 24th of June, Colonel Cary reported a plan of government for this colony, which was read the first time. The same day, the following important resolutions passed the Assembly, in reference to the claim of Richard Henderson, George Morgan, and others.

" Whereas divers petitions from the inhabitants of the Western Frontiers have been presented to this Convention, complaining of exhorbitant demands on them for lands claimed by persons pretending to derive titles from Indian deeds and purchases, *Resolved*, that all persons actually settled on any of the said lands ought to hold the same without paying any pecuniary or other consideration whatever to any private person or persons, until the said petitions, as well as the validity of the title under such Indian deeds or purchases shall have been considered and determined on by the Legislatures of this country ; and that all persons who are now actually settled on any unlocated or unappropriated lands in Virginia, to which there is no other just claim, shall have the pre-emption or preference in the grants of such lands. *Resolved*, that no purchases of lands within the chartered limits of Virginia shall be made under any pretence whatever, from any Indian tribe or nation without the approbation of the Legislature."

On the 4th of July commissioners were appointed, by a resolution of the Convention to collect and take the evidence on behalf of the government of Virginia against the several persons pretending to claim lands under deeds and purchases from the Indians.[1] Edmund Randolph says of this action of the Convention:

" On the petition of one Richard Henderson and his associates, a great question in the law of nations as applied to America was agitated and decided by the Convention; whether a purchase by individuals, of lands, to which the Indians claimed title by their manner of occupancy was binding upon Virginia, within whose limits they lay. She in terms annulled every such purchase, not confirmed by the government, existing at the time."[2]

On the 26th the plan of government was read a second time and debated upon in the Convention. It was taken up again on the two following days, and several amendments were made and agreed to on the 28th. On the 29th it was read the third time, and passed by a unanimous resolve. This plan of government or Constitution, in its original draft—like the Bill of Rights of which it formed the sequel—was from the pen of George Mason. On this day also the governor was appointed by ballot, Patrick Henry receiving the largest number of votes. A committee was appointed to wait upon the new governor and notify him of his election, and George Mason was made its chairman. He was also named first on a committee to prescribe the oaths of office to be taken by the governor and privy council. Colonel Mason on the 1st of July informed the Convention that the governor had been notified of his appointment, and returned an answer which he presented. A committee was appointed to devise a proper seal for the commonwealth. It was composed of four members: Richard Henry Lee, George Mason, Robert Carter Nicholas, and George Wythe. On the 5th of July, the last day of the Convention, Colonel Mason reported this seal, and George Wythe and John Page were desired to superintend the execution of it.[3]

[1] *Ibid.*   [2] MS. History of Virginia.   [3] Journal of the Convention.

The only letter of George Mason's that is to be found, written at this time, is one to his friend Martin Cockburn, dated the 23d of June, the day before the plan of government was reported to the Convention.   There is nothing in it concerning the important work on which he had been engaged. Doubtless the letter to Mr. Massey, of which Colonel Mason speaks, contained particulars as to his recent labors.   The "Gutridges" (Goodrichs), to whom George Mason makes reference, are thus described by Edmund Randolph:

"Virginia committed but few errors in the selection of men to whom she committed her interests.   But she was not equally fortunate in the repudiation of a father and his three sons, of the name of Goodrich.   They were so original and happy in their genius of ship-building that from the construction of vessels adapted to all the waters of this colony, many cargoes escaped capture and relieved the most urgent wants of the navy and the people.   But upon a doubt, whether upon some occasion they had acted correctly, they were suspected of being unfaithful to the country and forced into the condition of enemies.   Their hostility was not to be appeased.   Their faculties were so applied as to enable them to intercept every vessel which they could discover in the shallowest water and most intricate navigation. It was said that the whole British navy had scarcely made prizes of Virginia ownership to an equal amount with theirs.   Fertile as revolutions generally are in characters equal to every growing necessity, Virginia never repaired the loss which she sustained in these men.   They had explored every vulnerable point and weakness in Virginia, and their hatred kept pace with their knowledge." [1]

Lord Dunmore, who had left Hampton Roads the first of June, was entrenched, at this time, with five hundred men, on Gwynn's Island, in the Chesapeake Bay, opposite Matthews County.

WILLIAMSBURG, June 23d, 1776.

DEAR SIR :

I received your obliging favor yesterday per post, which, not having time to answer then, I take the opportunity of doing to-day per Captain Westcot.   The business you mention shall be

[1] MS. History of Virginia.

attended to so far as Richard Lee, Esq: can inform me ; for neither of the Mr. Steptoe's have been here. Having just wrote a long letter to our friend, Mr. Massey, I must beg leave to refer you to him for what we are doing in Convention. Public news we have none, more than you 'll see in the papers, except that one of that infernal crew, the Gutridge's has just taken a French West India-Man, coming to trade with us, and carried her up to Dunmore's fleet at Guinnis [*sic*] Island ; and Friday arrived here from James River, taken by Captain Barron, two hundred and seventeen Highland soldiers (very likely fellows) of the 42nd. and 71st. Regiments. I only mention this because from Purdie's account one might be puzzled to know whether they were soldiers or emigrants. The cadets, which are only two, will have their parolle, and the common soldiers will be distributed in the middle counties, and permitted to contract for wages with such as will employ them. The Convention have determined to adjourn next Saturday, but I hardly think they will be able to do it so soon. I am rejoiced to hear of my dear children's health, as well as of your family's, to all whom please to remember me kindly. Tell George his recruiting expenses are not allowed, nor any of the Minute officers. I have got a warrant for £3–5–5 for the two guns charged in his account furnished the detachment of his company, which marched with Ensign Cofer. I have just spoken to Captain Lee about the two guns his company carried from Dumfries ; but he says he knows nothing about them, and unless George can make some other proof they will be lost, and no satisfaction received for them, especially as Captain Lee's Company with the rest of the Third Regiment is ordered to march immediately to Carolina. He should also get a certificate from Ensign Cofer for the musket he took of mine from John Tillet's shop ; though I had much rather have the musket returned, for as we have a bayonet for her she would now sell at £5 10s.

As I don't think I can be up in time, George must do the best he can with our harvest, and must be as saving as he can of rum and provisions. Rum now sells here from 10/ to 12/ per gallon. He should have all the scythes and cradles and rakes got in order. Pray excuse haste, and believe me, dear Sir

Your sincerely affectionate   G. M.[1]

[1] Mason Papers.

Of the four important measures which make the Convention of 1776 eminent in the annals of Virginia, and in the history of the American people, three are to be ascribed to George Mason of Gunston, and the fourth, the resolution proposing independence, was passed before Mason took his seat in the Convention. George Mason, then, may be called, with truth, the pen of the revolution in Virginia.

We have two accounts of the Convention of 1776, written by men who were in its councils, both of them belonging to the younger generation of patriots, and both of them narrating their recollections of this eventful period after an interval of many years. Edmund Randolph, in his history of Virginia, and James Madison, in a private letter to one of Colonel Mason's grandsons, give us glimpses into the workings of this important assembly, and as both of them were on the committee charged with the duty of preparing the Bill of Rights and the Constitution, their testimony here should receive careful consideration. And yet, as it will appear, there is reason to doubt the entire trustworthiness of Edmund Randolph's reminiscences, and Madison's memories of this early time are at variance, in an important particular, with a statement of his made a year or two after the Convention met. Edmund Randolph describes the composition of the Convention : ·

" The members who filled the most space in the public eye were Edmund Pendleton, who 'presided, Patrick Henry, who had from some disgust resigned his command of the first Virginia regiment in time to be elected, George Mason, James Mercer, Robert Carter Nicholas, James Madison of Orange, Richard Bland, Thomas Ludwell Lee, Thomas Nelson, George Wythe, and John Blair. These were associated with members whose fortunes and unobtrusive good sense supported the ardor of the more active on the theatre of business." [1]

Then after giving an account of the earlier proceedings he continues :

[1] MS. History of Virginia.

" As soon as the Convention had pronounced the vote of independence, the formation of a constitution or frame of government followed of course. For with the royal authority the existing organs of police and the laws ceased, and the tranquility of society was floating upon the will of popular committees, and the virtue of the people.   Mr. Jefferson who was in Congress urged a youthful friend in the Convention [Edmund Randolph] to oppose a *permanent* constitution, until the people should elect deputies for the special purpose. He denied the power of the body elected (as he conceived them to be agents for the management of the war) to exceed some temporary regimen. The member alluded to communicated the ideas of Mr. Jefferson to some of the leaders in the house, Edmund Pendleton, Patrick Henry, and George Mason. These gentlemen saw no distinction between the conceded power to declare independence, and its necessary consequence, the fencing of society by the institution of government. Nor were they sure, that to be backward in this act of sovereignty might not imply a distrust, whether the rule had been wrested from the king.   A very large committee was nominated to prepare the proper instruments, and many projects of a bill of rights and constitution discovered the ardor for political notice, rather than a ripeness in political wisdom. That proposed by George Mason swallowed up all the rest, by fixing the grounds and plan, which after great discussion and correction, were finally ratified." [1]

Of the three leaders here named, Edmund Pendleton, as the presiding officer, venerable in years and in experience, is put first *pro forma*. But the real headship was divided between Henry and Mason, the one the orator, the other emphatically the writer of the Convention, and the architect and master-builder of the new political structure. Bancroft says George Mason " held most sway over the mind of the Convention."

Edmund Randolph bears witness to the sustaining, illuminating power of Henry's eloquence in the debates on the motion for declaring independence. But in his analysis of

[1] *Ibid.*

the Bill of Rights, Edmund Randolph, overlooking apparently his former assertion that George Mason's draft or "project," as he calls it, "swallowed up all the rest," asserts that two of the articles were to be ascribed to Patrick Henry. "The fifteenth," he says, "recommending an adherence and frequent recurrence to fundamental principles, and the sixteenth on fettering the exercise of religion were proposed by Mr. Henry. The latter coming from a gentleman who was supposed to be a dissenter, caused an appeal to him, whether it was designed as a prelude to an attack on the established church, and he disclaimed such an object."[1] We need not look beyond the life of Patrick Henry himself for a parallel experience to this of George Mason's in having the authorship of papers, on which rest some of his claims to fame, denied him. It is well known that one of the acts of his life on which Patrick Henry looked back with most satisfaction was the fact of having drafted the Resolves of 1765, which, in the words of Jefferson, set the ball of the revolution in motion. Yet Jefferson somewhere says that they were drawn up by George Johnston, and Johnston's descendants have affirmed this also; while Edmund Randolph asserted that they came from the pen of William Fleming. Professor Tyler, the latest biographer of Henry, after examining what he calls a "tissue of rumor, guesswork, and self-contradiction," rightly concludes that the "deliberate statement of Patrick Henry himself that he wrote the five resolutions must close the discussion." Not only has the sole authorship of the Bill of Rights been denied to George Mason, but his claim to having written the first draft of the Constitution has been impugned, on grounds as unsubstantial as those referred to in Henry's case. And over against "guesswork and self-contradiction" we have the "deliberate statement" of George Mason that he wrote the Bill of Rights, and inferentially that he wrote the Constitution, as the two papers are to be considered as one instrument, and they are so denominated by Edmund Randolph, where he classes the two together as "that [project] proposed by George Mason."

[1] *Ibid.*

In the library of the Capitol at Richmond, preserved in a glass case, is the manuscript of the Virginia Bill of Rights which was presented to the State of Virginia, February 15, 1844, by General John Mason, the last surviving son of George Mason of Gunston. General Mason in his letter to the General Assembly on this occasion says of the manuscript :

" It is believed to be the only original draft of that instrument now extant ; none being found in the archives of the common-wealth. The evidences of its authenticity are clear and un-doubted. It came into my possession from the papers of the author soon after his death, more than half a century since. It is throughout in his own handwriting. And its character as the first draft reported to the Convention is declared, as well by the memoranda with his initials prefixed as by the note at the foot of the manuscript. The memoranda describe the paper as the 'Virginia Declaration of Rights in 1776. Copy of first Draught by G. M.' The note at the foot of the manuscript is in these words : 'This Declaration of Rights was the first in America ; it received few alterations or additions in the Virginia Convention (some of them not for the better), and was afterwards closely imitated by the other United States.' " [1]

On the 2d of October, 1778, George Mason wrote to his cousin, Col. George Mercer, then in London, sending him a copy of the Bill of Rights, declaring himself to be the author in these words:

" To show you that I have not been an idle spectator of this great contest, and to amuse you with the sentiments of an old friend upon an important subject, I enclose you a copy of the first draught of the declaration of rights *just as it was drawn and presented by me*, to the Virginia Convention, where it received few alterations, some of them I think not for the better. This was the first thing of the kind upon the continent, and has been closely imitated by all the States." [2]

---

[1] Appendix x.

[2] The draft of the Declaration of Rights sent to Col. George Mercer in 1778 and the letter in which it was enclosed are now in possession of Dr. Thos. Addis Emmet of New York.

And this paper is to be seen now "just as it was drawn and presented" by Colonel Mason. No copy of the Bill of Rights, or of the two articles in question, are to be found among Patrick Henry's papers, nor does Henry anywhere assert his authorship of these two articles, nor was such a claim made for him during his lifetime. There is only the unsupported statement of Edmund Randolph, committed to writing probably thirty years after the events which he recalls; whereas there is the deliberate assertion of George Mason in the confidence of private correspondence only two years and six months from the time of which he speaks that the Declaration of Rights was entirely his own composition, an assertion repeated by him, in substance, in the brief endorsement on the original drafts of this paper now extant. The biographer of Edmund Randolph practically concedes that the latter must have been mistaken in his recollection of the matter.[1]

Corroborative testimony of Mason's authorship of the thirteenth article in the original draft is obtained through the paper drawn up by him for the Fairfax Independent Company in 1775. The first five articles of the Bill of Rights are also to be traced to this paper. In this business of a volunteer company, obscure and local in its nature, we find broad and general principles laid down, and it proved to be, as it were, a study for the great State paper of 1776. One of its postulates was "that no institution can be long preserved, but by frequent recurrence to those maxims on which it was formed." This is the groundwork of the thirteenth article (the fifteenth article, as the Bill of Rights now stands), yet we are asked to believe that George Mason in drafting the Bill of Rights studiously omitted what he had so recently declared of such importance, and that it was supplied by an amendment of Patrick Henry's. The paper, prepared for the conduct of a military organization, would naturally only touch upon civil not upon religious liberty, but in a charter of government the two ideas

[1] "Life of Edmund Randolph," p. 158. By Moncure D. Conway.

would inevitably be found together. And George Mason wrote in the letter from which we have quoted : "We have laid our new government upon a broad foundation, and have endeavored to provide the most effectual securities for the essential rights of human nature, *both in civil and religious liberty.*" The italics are ours. It is not credible that, holding such views, George Mason in his draft of a Bill of Rights should ignore the principle of religious liberty, and in the light of his consistent advocacy of religious freedom, in every stage of his public life from 1776 to 1788, the moral impossibility of his having omitted such an article from his "ground and plan" of a Declaration of Rights is clearly manifest. Mason's paper, it may be affirmed with almost absolute certainty, was prepared by him before he appeared in Convention. The whole subject, very much of it as we find it there, had been thought out, it is apparent, months before and committed to writing. He certainly would not be idle at such a crisis. Nor would it be characteristic of him to present a plan that was in any way crude or incomplete. The principles of his Declaration of Rights were not original with him, of course. They were as old, some of them, as the Roman jurisprudence, and are to be found, more or less developed, in Montesquieu, Algernon Sydney, Locke, and others.

It may be expedient here to examine briefly the history of the Bill of Rights in its passage through the committee and through the Convention to see how the original draft fared in these two ordeals. Among George Mason's papers has been found a copy of the Declaration, the first part of it in the handwriting of Mason and the remainder in the handwriting of Thomas Ludwell Lee. It is interesting as showing the appearance of the paper in one of its stages, as it was passing through the committee, and it indicates the order in which the articles were taken up for consideration. An article relating to *ex post facto* laws was added, and two other amendments were alluded to as likely to be adopted. There are also verbal changes in several of the original articles.[1]

[1] Appendix x.

This is very probably the same draft that Thomas Ludwell Lee sent to his brother, Richard Henry Lee, some time in May, and of which he wrote, on the 1st of June:

" I enclosed you by last post a copy of our declaration of rights nearly as it came through the committee. It has since been reported to the Convention, and we have ever since been stumbling at the threshold. In short, we find such difficulty in laying the foundation stone, that I very much fear for that Temple to Liberty which was proposed to be erected thereon. But laying aside figure, I will tell you plainly that a certain set of aristocrats, for we have such monsters here, finding that their execrable system cannot be reared on such foundations, have to this time kept us at bay on the first line, which declares all men to be born equally free and independent. A number of absurd or unmeaning alterations have been proposed. The words as they stand are approved by a very great majority, yet by a thousand masterly fetches and stratagems the business has been so delayed that the first clause stands yet unassented to by the Convention."[1]

Edmund Randolph says of this discussion that " the declaration in the first article of the Bill of Rights, that all men are by nature equally free and independent, was opposed by Robert Carter Nicholas, as being the forerunner or pretext of civil convulsion. It was answered perhaps with too great an indifference to futurity, and not without inconsistency, that with arms in our hands, asserting the general rights of man, we ought not to be too nice and too much restricted in the declaration of them ; but that slaves, not being constituent members of our society, could never pretend to any benefit from such a maxim."[2] The Bill of Rights consisting of fourteen articles, as reported to the Convention on the 27th of May, contained eighteen, and as finally amended and passed by the Convention on the 12th of June it was reduced to sixteen articles, the one on *ex post facto* laws having been omitted, and the sixth article of the original

[1] Lee Papers. *Southern Literary Messenger*, new series, vol. vi., p. 325.
[2] MS. History of Virginia.

such manner as to they be judged most conducive to the public weal.

4. That no man, or set of men, are entitled to exclusive or separate Emoluments or Privileges from the community, but in consideration of public services; which not being descendible, neither ought the Offices of Magistrate, Legislator or Judge to be hereditary.

5. That the Legislative & Executive powers of the State should be separate & distinct from the Judiciary; and that the Members of the two first may be restrained from Oppression by feeling & participating the burthens of the people, they should, at fixed periods, be reduced to a private Station, return into that Body from which they were originally taken, and the Vacancys be supplied by frequent, certain & regular Elections, in which

Virginia.
Declaration
of Rights
in 1776.

This Declaration of Rights was the first in America; it received some Alterations afterward in the Virginia Convention (some of them not for the better) and was afterwards closely imitated by the other United States.

2 more articles were added & & to & 13 to the 16th & 14th by the & of the Bill — not of the ornamented &

fair obligations towards each other.

draft, which the committee had divided into two, being re-stored to its original unity.[1] The two new articles admitted declared general warrants to be grievous and offensive, and that the people have a right to uniform government. The Convention also inserted a few words into the first article of the original draft, and added something to the fifth. They also restored the fourth article to its original form, which was greatly superior to that proposed by the select committee.

And here in the Convention also an alteration was made in the article on religion. Madison objected to the idea which he thought lay in the word "toleration," and he offered an amendment, given in full by Rives,[2] which, as modified by the committee of the whole, received the sanction of the Convention. It would seem probable that the question of religious liberty, in all its bearings, was discussed by the Convention at this point. And it may have been that Henry offered an amendment also, or, if not, it is likely that he entered with his wonted vehemence into the merits of the subject. Either here or in the select committee, it is proba-ble that his advocacy of the principle of freedom in religion —men remembering the part he had taken in the "Parson's Cause"—may have led to the query from some conservative member as to his designs on the Established Church, as reported by Edmund Randolph. The latter says that an article prohibiting bills of attainder, by whom proposed he does not state, was defeated by Patrick Henry, either in the committee or in the Convention, Henry drawing "a terrify-ing picture of some towering public offender, against whom ordinary laws would be impotent."

In regard to the establishment of religious freedom in Virginia, George Mason's course, as we have said, was both a prominent and consistent one. The first legislation in the Virginia Assembly on this subject may be traced to him, as he was named first on the committee appointed to prepare an act in conformity with the religious section of the Bill of

[1] Appendix x.
[2] " Life of Madison," vol. i., p. 142 (note).
16

Rights, at the meeting of the new House under the Constitution. The second section of this act, undoubtedly drawn up by George Mason, begins with the preamble :

"And whereas there are within this commonwealth great numbers of dissenters from the church established by law who have been heretofore taxed for its support, and it is contrary to the principles of reason and justice that any should be compelled to contribute to the maintenance of a church with which their consciences will not permit them to join, and from which they can derive no benefit : for remedy whereof, and that equal liberty as well religious as civil, may be universally extended to all the good people of this commonwealth, be it enacted, &c."

At this same session a committee of five members was appointed to revise the laws of the commonwealth. These five were Jefferson, Pendleton, Wythe, George Mason and Thomas Ludwell Lee. They met at Annapolis, in January, 1777, and decided on the plan of revision, assigning to each member his part. George Mason afterwards resigned from the committee, but not until the whole scheme was mapped out. In a letter written by Jefferson and Wythe, laid before the June Assembly, 1779, they state :

"In the course of this work we were unfortunately deprived of the assistance of two of our associates appointed by the General Assembly, of the one by death [T. L. Lee], of the other by resignation. As the plan of the work had been settled, and agreeable to that plan it was in considerable degree carried into execution before that loss, we did not exercise the powers given us by the act, of filling up the places by new appointments, being desirous that the plan agreed on by members who were specially appointed by the Assembly, might not be liable to alteration from others who might not equally possess their confidence, it has therefore been executed by the three remaining members." [1]

Among these laws, planned in part by George Mason, was the "Act Establishing Religious Freedom," promulgated in

[1] Hening's "Statutes."

1785. The act suspending the salaries of clergymen, passed in 1776, was renewed each session, until in 1779 all laws providing salaries were finally repealed. The question of a general assessment for the support of religion still remained open. In the act of 1776, reference is made to the " great variety of opinion touching the propriety of a general assessment or voluntary contributions, and as this differ-ence of sentiment cannot now be well accommodated, it is thought prudent to defer this matter to the discussion and determination of a future Assembly." It came up for discus-sion and determination in 1784. Madison at the suggestion of George Mason and George Nicholas, drew up a remon-strance against the assessment, which was extensively circulated and signed throughout the State. Mason had a number of copies printed at his own expense for the purpose of distribution in the several counties. " And," writes Madi-son, " under the influence of the public sentiment thus manifested, the celebrated bill establishing Religious Free-dom [was] enacted into a permanent barrier against any future attempts on the rights of conscience as declared in the great charter prefixed to the Constitution of the State." [1] Madison says the assessment bill was " patronized by the most popular talents in the House." The allusion is to Patrick Henry, and his action is here characterized as an attempt " on the rights of conscience," as declared in what Professor Tyler calls " Henry's article " of the Bill of Rights. [2] And there is a disposition at the present day to class Patrick Henry among the " dissenters," to whom, in the person of this champion, religious freedom in Virginia is said to be chiefly indebted. The disestablishment of the Church in Virginia was the work of its own members, who in laying the foundations of their coun-try's liberty believed they should unselfishly sacrifice the privileges the law had hitherto secured to them, that civil and religious liberty might be found inseparably united.

[1] MS. Letter of Madison, published in Rives' " Life of Madison."
[2] " Life of Patrick Henry," p. 184, American Statesmen Series.

Patrick Henry was one of these patriots, and yet he did not embrace the whole plan of reform in his vision. George Mason saw clearly the course before him, and pursued it unflinchingly to the end; while Henry, on the contrary, nine years after the promulgation of the Bill of Rights, was employing all his oratory and his influence in support of a law taxing the people for religious purposes.

In the Virginia Convention of 1788, George Mason was chairman of the committee to prepare amendments to the Federal Constitution. In all probability, therefore, he fixed the "grounds and plan" here of the Bill of Rights and amendments which were offered in the Convention by Patrick Henry. And among George Mason's papers is a draft of a Bill of Rights and amendments differing in several respects from that adopted by the Convention. The twentieth article of the Bill of Rights in this manuscript is as follows:

"That religion, or the duty which we owe to our Creator, and the manner of discharging it, can be directed only by reason and conviction, not by force and violence, and therefore all men have an equal, natural and unalienable right to the free exercise of religion, according to the dictates of conscience; and that no particular sect or society of Christians ought to be favored or established by law in preference to others."

Thus George Mason, by his acts no less than by his affirmations, sustains the claim made for him, of having in the Convention of 1776 sought to provide "for the essential rights of human nature, both in civil and religious liberty."

In clear, concise language George Mason enunciated in the Virginia Bill of Rights fourteen great principles as the basis of free government. The first declared the natural, inherent right of man to the enjoyment of life and liberty with all the privileges these entailed. In the second the power of rulers and magistrates is traced to its source in the people, to whom they are at all times amenable. There follows thirdly the axiom that the best government is that in which the rights above named are assured ; and the deduction is inevitable that a majority of the community may abolish a government that is inadequate to the purposes for which it was formed. The fourth article declares public services to be the title to public office, and since the former is not descendible, neither should the latter be hereditary. The article that follows enunciates an important principle held in theory by Great Britain, but practically at that time in abey-ance, that is, the separation of the legislative and executive powers from the judicial ; and the concluding clause declares the importance of frequently recurring and regular elections to insure the community from oppression. The sixth article asserts the importance of perfect freedom in the choice of the legislative body ; and in regard to the suffrage, pro-nounces it the right of all men giving evidence of a perma-nent interest in the community, while the concluding clause declares against taxation without the consent of those taxed or their representatives, the same consent being necessary to bind the governed by any law whatever. Continuing this subject, the next article pronounces against the suspension or execution of laws without the consent of the people's representatives. The three articles that follow relate to the rights of a citizen in his relation to the judiciary. In crimi-nal prosecutions he has the four privileges of demanding the nature of his accusation, of being confronted with the accusers and witnesses, of calling for evidence in his favor, and of a speedy trial by an impartial jury of his vicinage. Also, he cannot be found guilty without the jury's unani-mous consent, nor is he compelled to give evidence against himself. And no man's liberty can be taken from him but by the law of the land or the judgment of his peers. The second of these articles pronounces against excessive bail, excessive fines, and cruel or unusual punishments. The last article of this triad declares in favor of the desirability and sacredness of trial by jury in suits respecting property and between man and man. The eleventh article of this Declaration of

Rights holds up the freedom of the press as one of the great bulwarks of liberty. In the twelfth article a well-regulated militia is advocated as the natural and safe defence of a free State ; standing armies are pronounced dangerous in time of peace, and it is declared that the military should be at all times subordinate to the civil power. The thirteenth article relates to the importance of a frequent recurrence to fundamental principles, and a firm adherence to the four civic virtues of justice, moderation, temperance, frugality. The principle of religious liberty is advocated in the fourteenth article as the apex of the pyramid. The two articles that are found in the Bill of Rights as adopted, were not of a fundamental nature. They are inserted in the paper as the tenth and fourteenth articles, so that the two which conclude George Mason's draft appear as the fifteenth and sixteenth in the amended instrument.

A recent writer has noticed that in the extension of the suffrage to " all men having sufficient evidence of permanent common interest with and attachment to the community," provided by the sixth article of the Bill of Rights, George Mason recurred to the theory of the Virginia suffrage law of 1656, that it was " something hard and unagreeable to reason, that any person shall pay taxes, and have no votes in election." [1] The Bill of Rights has been the subject of several critical eulogies by Virginians, of which the first, in point of time, was that contributed by Theodorick Bland in 1819 to the famous revolutionary compilation of Niles.[2] Bland says of it :

" This declaration contains principles more extensive, and much more perspicuously expressed than any then to be found in the supposed analogous instruments of any other age or country. The English magna charta was, strictly speaking, a contract between an assemblage of feudal lords and a king, not a declaration of the rights of man, and the fundamental principles on which

[1] *Virginia Carolorum*, Neill, note to p. 330.
[2] " Principles and Acts of the Revolution," p. 121.

all government should rest. The articles drawn up by the Spanish junta, in the year 1522, under the guidance of the celebrated Padilla, are much more distinct and popular in their provisions than those of the English magna charta. But, although it is admitted that the principles of liberty were ably defended, and better understood at that time in Spain than they were for more than a century after in England, the power of Charles V. proved to be irresistible, the people failed in their attempt to bridle his prerogative, and their liberties were finally crushed. The famous English bill of rights, sanctioned by William and Mary on their ascending the throne, and which, under the name of the petition of rights, appears to have been projected many years before by that profound lawyer, Sir Edward Coke, like magna charta and the articles of the Spanish junta, is a contract with nobility and royalty, a compromise with despotism, in which the voice of the people is heard in a tone of disturbed supplication and prayer. But in this declaration of Mason's man seems to stand erect in all the majesty of his nature, to assert the inalienable rights and equality with which he has been endowed by his Creator, and to declare the fundamental principles by which all rulers should be controlled, and in which all governments should rest. The contrast is striking, the difference prodigious."

Grigsby, in his sketch of George Mason, contrasts the Virginia Bill of Rights with the Petition of Right addressed to Charles I., and the Declaration of Rights on the accession of William and Mary. One of these simply enumerates laws that had been violated, and prays that they may be observed; the other was "wholly historical and retrospective in its scope," while the "Virginia declaration was eminently prospective." Of the latter, this writer says ·

"Some of its expressions may be gleaned from Sydney, from Locke, and from Burgh; but when Mason sat down in his room in the Raleigh Tavern to write that paper, it is probable that no copy of the reply to Sir Robert Filmer, or of the Essay on Government, or of the Political Disquisitions, was within his reach. The diction, the design, the thoughts are all his own. Nor does its beauty and its worth suffer in comparison with similar productions carefully prepared at a later day."

Assuming, however, that George Mason brought his Declaration of Rights with him to Williamsburg, and that he had written it in his library with Magna Charta, etc., and the books above referred to within his reach, a comparison of its text with these sources of inspiration will not diminish its merits as a remarkable and original document. " It is a curious illustration of the supremacy accorded to genius in great conjunctures," writes Grigsby, " that the British Declaration of Right and the Virginia Declaration of Rights were written by men who had recently taken their seats for the first time in deliberative assemblies which were composed of the oldest and ablest statesmen of their respective periods. When Somers drafted the Declaration of Right he had spoken in the House of Commons for the first time only ten days before, and the parliamentary experience of Mason was hardly more extended." But Somers, as he adds, was an able lawyer deeply versed in constitutional learning, " while Mason was a planter, untutored in the schools, whose life . . . had been spent in a thinly settled colony which presented no sphere for ambition." And Grigsby concludes: " The genius of the Virginian appears in bolder relief when contrasted with the genius of his illustrious prototype." [1]   Elsewhere, in regard to the title of this paper of 1776, Grigsby observes :

" It is remarkable that the Virginia Declaration of Rights was always spoken of in debate, even by Mason who drafted it, as the *Bill of Rights*—a name appropriate to the British Bill of Rights, which was first the petition of Right, and was then enacted into a law ; but altogether inapplicable to our Declaration, which had never been a bill, and was superior to all bills. It is true that the Declaration of Rights was read three times in the Convention which adopted it ; but so was the Constitution, which nobody would call a bill." [2]

Comparing the Declaration of Rights with the Declaration of Independence, Grigsby describes the one " as the admira-

[1] " Virginia Convention of 1776," p. 162.
[2] " History of the Virginia Federal Convention," note, p. 260.

ble work of the political philosopher, the other the chaste production of the elegant historian ; and as philosophy is of higher dignity than history, so is the Declaration of Rights superior to the Declaration of Independence." [1] Henry Lee, in his strictures on Jefferson, pays a high tribute to the Bill of Rights and its author, and he singles out the fourth article of the former for special commendation. " Mr. Jefferson," he says, " as a lawgiver was far inferior to a man whom in popular favor and public honors he far outstripped. This man was George Mason. There is more wisdom, more condensation of thought and energy of reasoning in a single clause of the Virginia Bill of Rights from the pen of that truly great man than in all the works of Mr. Jefferson put together. This clause is as follows : ' That no man or set of men is entitled to exclusive or separate emoluments or privileges from the commonwealth but in consideration of public services, which not being descendible neither ought the offices of magistrate, legislator, or judge to be hereditary.' Here is a volume of wit and wisdom for the study of nations embodied in a single sentence and expressed in the plainest language. If a deluge of despotism should sweep over the world and destroy those institutions under which freedom is yet protected, sweeping into oblivion every vestige of their remembrance among men, could this single sentence of Mason's be preserved it would be sufficient to rekindle the flame of liberty and revive the race of freemen." [2]

William C. Rives characterizes the Bill of Rights as " a condensed, logical and luminous summary of the great principles of freedom inherited by us from our British ancestors ; the extracted essence of Magna Charta, the Petition of Right, the Acts of the Long Parliament, and the doctrines of the Revolution of 1688 as expounded by Locke,—distilled and concentrated through the alembic of his [George Mason's] own powerful and discriminating mind. There is nothing more remarkable in the political annals of America than this paper. It has stood the rude test of every vicissitude : and

---

[1] " Virginia Convention of 1776," p. 165.

[2] Lee's " Remarks on Jefferson," p. 127 ; Philadelphia, 1839.

while Virginia has already had three constitutions, the Declaration of Rights of 1776 has stood and yet stands, without the change of a letter, at the head of each one of them however difficult it may be to reconcile with some of its principles the provisions of the later constitutions." [1] The Massachusetts bill of rights and all succeeding instruments of the kind adopted by the different colonies were modelled upon the Virginia charter, and its principles were engrafted in the amendments to the Federal Constitution. Jefferson, in the Declaration of Independence, repeated its cardinal maxims, and adopted many of its phrases. Randall, in his " Life of Jefferson," informs us that the writing-desk on which the latter wrote the Declaration of Independence, in a lodging-house in Philadelphia, has been preserved, and bears an inscription on it in his own handwriting. And it may not be uninteresting to the student of our political history to learn that the table on which George Mason wrote the Bill of Rights is also still in existence. After being carefully cherished for three generations by the family of George Mason's eldest son, it was presented in 1881 to the Virginia Historical Society. [2]

In the absence of any autograph copy of the first draft of the Constitution, George Mason's authorship of it has been denied. And it has been said in support of this assumption that while in his letter to Colonel Mercer he distinctly affirms that he wrote the Bill of Rights, a copy of which he sends his relative, he is silent in regard to his authorship of the Constitution ; and in fact uses the plural pronoun in speaking of it, where he says : " We have laid our new government upon a broad foundation, &c." To this cavil the reply naturally follows that George Mason regarded both papers as parts of one instrument, but the Declaration of Rights as the more important of the two he was at the pains to transcribe for Colonel Mercer's perusal. This new government, which was " to provide the most effectual securities for the essential rights of human nature, both in civil and

---

[1] " Life of Madison," p. 137.   [2] Appendix x.

religious liberty," not only included the charter of rights, and constitution, but the acts of legislation of the first State assemblies. George Mason here speaks in the name of the Convention and the legislative body of the new commonwealth, two years after the government had gone into operation. Many of George Mason's papers are known to have been lost at an early period in a fire which consumed the dwelling-house of one of his sons; and doubtless his draft of a constitution was among these manuscripts. It has been seen that Edmund Randolph, in giving an account of the Convention, says of both the Bill of Rights and the Constitution, that, while many were proposed, George Mason's "swallowed up all the rest." He here uses the singular number, assuming that the two are one instrument. Afterwards he writes of them in the plural number, and says that, "after great discussion and correction, [they] were finally ratified." There was great discussion on the Bill of Rights, but very little "correction"; and the latter word must refer more particularly to the Constitution, which as adopted was somewhat altered and greatly amended, or drawn out into detail. In discussing what he considered the faults of the first Virginia Constitution, Edmund Randolph again corroborates George Mason's authorship of it, in these words: "By a further analysis of the Constitution, a lesson will be taught, that the most expanded mind,—as that of George Mason's was, who sketched the Constitution,—cannot secure itself from oversights and negligences in the tumult of heterogeneous and indistinct ideas of government, circulating in a body, unaccustomed to much abstraction."[1]

While the results of the Convention of 1776 were fresh in the minds of his contemporaries, George Mason's authorship of the Constitution was spoken of, it would seem, as a well established fact. So Madison wrote to Washington, in 1787, referring to one of Mason's objections to the Federal Constitution: "The Constitution of Virginia, drawn up by Col. Mason himself, is absolutely

[1] MS. History of Virginia.

silent on this subject." [1]   It was not until long after Colonel Mason's death that the matter was ever called in question.   In 1825 most of the associates and compeers of George Mason had passed away.   But there were two living, one of them having been in the Convention of 1776, who had successively held the highest office in the gift of the Federal Government: these were Jefferson and Madison.   There was also living a third one of Virginia's revolutionary patriots,—James Monroe, at this time President of the United States.   It was the year before Jefferson's death, when Judge Woodward,[2] in writing the history of this period, perceiving the resemblance between the preamble to the Virginia Constitution and the Declaration of Independence, came to the conclusion that the Constitution was altogether Jefferson's work.   Madison knew this to be incorrect, and he so informed Judge Woodward.   The latter wrote to Jefferson from Washington, enclosing a letter from Madison on the subject, and telling him Monroe's theory :

" President Monroe, who carefully compared the constitution of Virginia with other documents known to have proceeded from your pen, was originally of opinion that my statement was substantially correct,—being under the impression that the draft was first offered by Mr. Mason, at Williamsburg ; yet it was derived from a manuscript furnished by you, from Philadelphia. Since the perusal of the letter of President Madison, President Monroe wavers somewhat from his first statement."

Monroe, who was not in the Convention of 1776, had evidently very indistinct recollections of what he had heard on the subject at the time.   Jefferson replied to Judge Woodward from " Monticello "

" The fact is unquestionable that the Bill of Rights and the Constitution of Virginia were drawn originally by George Mason, one of our really great men, and of the first order of greatness.

[1] " Life and Writings of Washington," vol. ix., p. 547.

[2] A Virginian, judge of the Territory of Florida from 1824 until his death, in 1827.   He had been previously a judge of the Territory of Michigan.

The history of the preamble to the latter was as follows : I was then in Philadelphia, with Congress, and knowing that the Convention in Virginia was engaged in forming a plan of government, I turned my mind to the same subject, and drew a sketch outline of a constitution, with a preamble, which I sent to Mr. Pendleton, President of the Convention, on the mere probability that it might suggest something worth incorporating into that before them. He informed me afterwards, by letter, that he received it on the day on which the committee of the whole had reported to the house the plan they had agreed on, that, that had been so long on hand, so disputed inch by inch, the subject of much altercation and debate, that they were worried with the altercation it had produced, and could not from mere lassitude have been induced to open the instrument again ; but that, being pleased with the preamble of mine, they adopted it in the house, by way of amendment to the report of the committee ; and thus my preamble became tacked on to the work of George Mason."[1]

This Jefferson constitution, in the original draft, has lately come to light, after having been lost apparently for a hundred years, and may be compared with that of George Mason. Jefferson wrote also to Henry Lee, in 1825, or about that time : " That George Mason was the author of the bill of rights, and of the constitution founded on it, the evidence of the day established fully in my mind." Though Jefferson was not in the Convention of 1776, he was associated later with George Mason in the legislation of the new government ; and they were also personal friends, and generally in sympathy on public questions. Madison wrote of the Constitution to Judge Woodward :

" Its origin was with George Mason, who laid before the committee appointed to prepare a plan a very broad outline, which was printed by the committee for consideration, and after being varied on some points and filled up, was reported to the Convention, where a few further alterations gave it the form in which it now stands. The declaration of rights was subsequently [?] from the same hand."

[1] " Jefferson's Works," vol. vii., p. 405.

But two years later Madison writes :

" It is not known with certainty from whom this first plan of government proceeded. There is a faint tradition that Meriwether Smith spoke of it as originating with him. What is remembered by J. M. is that George Mason was the most prominent member in discussing and developing the constitution in its passage through the convention." [1]

In a letter to a grandson of George Mason, written December 29, 1827, Madison repeats this statement. He says of George Mason :

" My first acquaintance with him was in the Convention of Virginia in 1776, which instructed her delegates to propose in Congress a ' Declaration of Independence,' and which formed the ' Declaration of Rights,' and the ' Constitution ' for the State. Being young and inexperienced, I had, of course, but little agency in those proceedings. I retain, however, a perfect impression that he was a leading champion for the Instruction ; that he was the author of the ' Declaration,' as originally drawn, and, with very slight variations, adopted ; and that he was the master-builder of the Constitution, and its main expositor and supporter throughout the discussions which ended in its establishment. How far he may have approved it, in all its features as established, I am not able to say ; and it is the more difficult to make the discovery now, unless the private papers left by him should give the information, as, at that day no debates were taken down, and as the explanatory votes, if such there were, may have occurred in committee of the whole only, and of course, not appear in the journals. I have found, among my papers, a printed copy of the constitution in one of its stages, which, compared with the instrument finally agreed to, shows some of the changes it underwent ; but in no instance, at whose suggestion or by whose votes.

" I have also a printed copy of a sketched constitution which appears to have been the primitive draught on the subject. It is so different, in several respects, from the constitution finally

---

[1] " Writings of Madison," vol. iii., p. 451 ; Rives' " Life of Madison," vol. i., p. 159.

passed, that it may be more than doubted whether it was from the pen of your grandfather. There is a tradition that it was from that of Meriwether Smith ; whose surviving papers, if to be found among his descendants, might throw light on the question. I ought to be less at a loss than I am in speaking of these circumstances, having been myself an added member to the committee. But such has been the lapse of time that, without any notes of what passed, and with the many intervening scenes absorbing my attention, my memory cannot do justice to my wishes. Your grandfather, as the journal shows, was at a later day, added to the Committee, being, doubtless, not present when it was appointed, or he never would have been overlooked." [1]

Madison's memory is seen to be at fault here, in one respect. He says he retained " a perfect impression that he [George Mason] was a leading champion for the Instruction." This, the resolution for declaring independence, as we know, was passed before Mason arrived in the Convention. He was doubtless a "champion" of the measure, but neither Madison nor himself was present when the subject was debated in the Virginia Convention. Rives, in his discussion of the subject, urges a "piece of presumptive evidence" in support of the "faint tradition" that ascribed the Constitution to Meriwether Smith. This consists in the fact that the word "judicative" instead of "judicial" is found in the first draft of the Constitution, and it is also found in the revision of the Bill of Rights by the select committee. This last, Rives assumes, was written by Meriwether Smith, because he was second on the committee, and because a draft of the Bill of Rights in his handwriting was found among his papers. But it seems quite as likely that Thomas Ludwell Lee was the draftsman here as that Meriwether Smith was. However, when Rives wrote that "there is no known instance in which Colonel Mason used the word judicative for judicial," he was not aware, evidently, of the existence of Mason's "Extracts from the Virginia Charters, etc.," written in 1773, in which the word occurs. And in 1765 he

[1] " Life of Madison," p. 160.

wrote of "a court of judicature." George Mason, in the paper of 1773, speaks "of the executive, the legislative, and the judicative powers of the State." And he also has the phrase "our judicial system," showing that he was in the habit of employing both terms.

Col. Meriwether Smith, one of the members representing Essex County in the Convention of 1776, was undoubtedly a man of ability. And like Jefferson, like Richard Henry Lee and others, he had very probably made a draft of a constitution. He had prepared a set of resolves proposing independence, as we know, and a grandson of his, Mr. J. Adams Smith, in 1847 wrote John Tyler the following legend on the subject. It came from Judge John B. Clopton, who recollected "to have seen in Judge Tyler's library his copy of the first volume of Hening's Statutes at large, and there was a MS: note in the hand-writing of Judge Tyler to the resolutions instructing the representatives in Congress from Virginia to propose a declaration of Independence adopted by the Convention of Virginia on the fifteenth of May, 1776, in which Judge Tyler said that Meriwether Smith of the county of Westmoreland was the writer of the resolutions." Mr. J. Adams Smith had also been told twenty years before (which would be in 1827, when Madison wrote of his doubts) by Mr. William F. Pendleton that his "grandfather Meriwether Smith prepared the first written constitution. How he obtained the information, or upon what authority he asserted it, I do not recollect that he informed me."[1] The error of Madison as to the Constitution, and the error of Judge Tyler as to the resolution of independence arose both of them from the fact that a multiplicity of drafts had been offered in the Convention. Smith had his draft of the latter, but Pendleton's was preferred, as also his draft of a bill of rights and constitution, but Mason's was preferred.

Bancroft, referring to the work of the Virginia Convention, says: "In framing the Constitution George Mason had a principal part, aided by the active participation of Richard

[1] MS. letter owned by Lyon G. Tyler, Virginia.

Henry Lee and of George Wythe." [1] If the words " *the*
principal part " were substituted for " *a* principal part " to
describe George Mason's work in framing the Virginia Constitution they would be nearer the truth.   Richard Henry
Lee, from what we know of his views on the subject, was in
essential accord with Mason, and doubtless the two friends
had discussed together the great principles of constitutional
government.   But Lee was not in the Convention, and there
is no evidence that he exercised any controlling influence
over it by correspondence or otherwise.   He was urged to
leave Congress, to aid in the counsels of his State, but did
not do so.   George Wythe, however, came on for the purpose, bringing Jefferson's draft of a constitution with him,
and he wrote to the latter on the 27th of July, giving an
account of the matter, which differs from Jefferson's as
quoted above :

" When I came here the plan of government had been committed to the whole house.   To *those who had the chief hand in
forming it*, the one you put into my hands was shown.   Two or
three parts of this were with little alteration inserted in that."

It is evident that Wythe's " active participation " in
" framing the Constitution " must have been of a very
general and theoretic nature, consisting possibly in suggestions prior to the meeting of the Convention, and again
after the Constitution had passed through the ordeal of the
select committee.   He certainly does not assume for himself
a " chief hand in forming it."   It was at the instance of
Richard Henry Lee that John Adams sketched the draft of
a constitution, when the subject of a change of government
was being discussed by Congress in November, 1775.   And
in January, 1776, John Adams wrote his " Thoughts on Government " in the form of a letter to George Wythe at the
latter's request, and it was published in compliance with the
wish of Richard Henry Lee, to whom it was shown in manuscript.   The pamphlet was sent to various political friends of

[1] " History of the United States," vol. viii., chap. lxviii., p. 434.

17

John Adams, and among others to Patrick Henry, calling forth his letter of the 20th of May, where, in speaking of the magnitude of the work before the Virginia Convention, he wishes for the assistance of the Adamses, John and Samuel, as he had no " coadjutor " equal to the task. This seems not a little singular when we recall the eminent names on the committee in the Virginia Convention. As George Mason had then been but two days in Williamsburg, we must conclude that Henry had either not met him or overlooked the fact of his arrival. The tract of John Adams is not believed to have exercised any influence on the Convention, and it falls short in an important point of the wisdom displayed in George Mason's draft, as it provided for the election of one branch of the legislature, a senate or council to be chosen by the other branch or house, out of its own body or the community at large.

Among Madison's papers was preserved a printed copy of the first draft of the Constitution, the only one that is to be found, and no manuscript copy, as has been said, is believed to be extant. This printed draft was endorsed in the handwriting of Madison as the plan laid before the select committee, " and by them ordered to be printed for the perusal of the members of the House." There is no copy of the Constitution as it was reported to the committee of the whole House, and it is therefore impossible to tell what changes were made by the select committee. As finally passed by the Convention, it was altered in some points, and much expanded, though consisting of the same number of sections, and the articles, which were in the original draft, worded in the form of recommendations, were made into authoritative enactments.[1] It was discussed for three days in the Convention, and reported with amendments, but just what these were cannot now be ascertained.

The Constitution in its original form, after naming the three departments into which the government should be divided, proceeded to define the legislature as consisting

[1] Appendix x.

of two branches which were to meet once a year. The third section described the composition of the "Lower House of Assembly" and the qualifications for the suffrage. The fourth defined the "Upper House of Assembly"; and the fifth related to the right of each House to make its own rules, and extended the right of suffrage. By the sixth section it was declared that all laws should originate in the Lower House, except in the case of money bills. The seventh defined the office of the executive, and the eighth provided for a privy council. The governor and council were given the appointment of militia officers by the ninth section, and the control of the militia under the laws. The tenth provided for the appointment of the several courts by the two Houses of Assembly, to be commissioned by the executive. The following section gave the governor and council the appointment of justices of the peace, and provided for other subordinate officers. The power of impeaching the executive, and other officers of government, by the Lower House, in case of mal-administration, was provided for by the twelfth section. And the thirteenth declared that commissions and writs should run in the name of the commonwealth. A treasurer was provided for by the fourteenth section; and the fifteenth and concluding section stated the manner in which the new government should be introduced. The amendments consisted of an additional clause to the first section, carrying out into more detail its principle of the separation of the three branches of government; the addition of two clauses to the third section; changes in the fifth, seventh, and eighth sections; additional clauses to the ninth section, giving in fuller detail the powers of the executive over the militia; an additional clause to the tenth section; additions to the eleventh and twelfth sections; two amendments to the fourteenth section, and an alteration in the fifteenth section. The change in the third section, in regard to the right of suffrage, merely defined more particularly the qualifications according to the existing law; and the amendments here gave representatives to certain boroughs, and provided for the disfranchisement of others. Edmund Randolph says, in this connection

"It may surprise posterity that, in the midst of the most pointed declamations in the Convention against the inequality of representation in the British House of Commons, it was submitted to in Virginia without a murmur, and even without a proposition to the contrary.   . That the qualification of electors to the General Assembly should be restricted to freeholders, was the natural effect of Virginia having been habituated to it for very many years—more than a century. The members of the Convention were themselves freeholders, and from this circumstance felt a proud attachment to the country in which the ownership of the soil was a certain source of comfort. It is not recollected that a hint was uttered in contravention of this principle. There can be no doubt that, if it had been, it would have soon perished under a discussion." [1]

One of the most noticeable alterations in the Constitution, as sketched by George Mason, is that in the fourth section, relating to the election of the senate. It had been provided that the counties should be divided into twenty-four districts, and each county should choose twelve deputies, or sub-electors, and these deputies in turn were to elect the senate, one from each district. The amendment did away with the sub-electors, making the senate more directly the choice of the people. The provisions in the fifth section for extending the suffrage in two specified cases were not agreed to by the Convention. Here was a "hint" in contravention to the principle of freehold suffrage which evidently "perished under a discussion." George Mason, in attempting to carry out to some extent the suffrage theory of the Bill of Rights, was evidently, as on other occasions, in advance of the majority of his contemporaries. In the seventh section the power of the executive was more fully defined, and further limitations put upon it. Patrick Henry, on the contrary, wished to strengthen the executive, by giving the governor

[1] MS. History of Virginia.

the right of a veto on the acts of the legislature.[1] The alteration in the eighth section had a tendency to weaken still more the executive branch, and strengthen the legis- lative, where the balance of power would have been more strictly observed by the provision of the original draft. The council, which was to consist of eight members, chosen from both Houses, or from the people at large, two of whom were to be removed every three years, their places being supplied by new elections, had, by the plan of George Mason, the power to make this removal by ballot of its own board. As amended, the two members were to be removed by joint ballot of both houses of Assembly. A curious amend- ment to the tenth section was that excluding ministers of the Gospel from seats in the Assembly or council. All per- sons holding lucrative offices were excluded in like manner.

An important amendment was added to the fourteenth section, confirming, on the part of Virginia, the colonies of Maryland, Pennsylvania, and the two Carolinas, in their territories, as defined by their several charters ; excepting, however, the free navigation and use of the two rivers which separated Maryland from Virginia. The western and north- ern boundary of Virginia was declared to be that which was fixed by the charter of 1609, in all other respects ; a boundary defined later by the treaty of peace between Great Britain and France in 1763. No separate government was to be established west of the Alleghanies but by act of the Virginia Legislature, and no purchase of lands to be made from the Indians, but on behalf of the public and by authority of the Assembly. These provisions were taken in part from the Jefferson draft, very probably, and are the clauses to which Wythe refers as inserted, " with little alteration," in the Virginia Constitution. The most notice- able " alteration " was that which reserved to Virginia the free navigation of the rivers Potomac and Pocomoke. And it is very likely that this was due to George Mason's vigilance. His earlier writings show his familiarity with the

[1] *Ibid.*

question of Virginia's charter rights, and his intelligent advocacy of them ; and his work on the Constitution did not stop with the skeleton draft accepted by the committee. He was, as Madison says, prominent in "discussing and developing the constitution in its passage through the Convention."

Jefferson, a few years later, in his "Notes on Virginia," made sweeping strictures on the Constitution, and he asserts in one of his letters that George Mason was willing to see it altered. But there is no evidence of this in anything under Mason's hand that has come down to us. Jefferson maintained that the balance of power between the three departments of government was not duly preserved, the legislature usurping functions that properly belonged to the executive and judiciary, and this opinion is endorsed by a recent writer on the subject.[1] On the other hand, Grigsby writes of the Virginia Constitution :

"It is to the wisdom of Mason we owe the great American principle, that the legislature, the most dangerous of all, should be bound by a rule as stringent as the executive and the judicial [departments]. Even in a republic the legislature might still have been supreme. It is therefore the peculiar honor of Mason that he not only drafted the first regular plan of government of a sovereign state, but circumscribed the different departments by limits which they may not transcend."[2]

It is the opinion of many in Virginia that the changes that have been made in the Constitution of the State since 1776 have not, on the whole, improved it. It was not until 1829 that a new Convention was called to revise it. John Randolph, of Roanoke, was a delegate, and he appeared each morning, it is said, with crape on his hat and sleeves, "in mourning," as he declared, for the old Constitution, as he feared he had come to "witness its death and burial." And he spoke afterwards of the many plans submitted to the

[1] " Johns Hopkins University Studies," third series, " American Constitutions."
[2] Convention of 1776.

Convention, where "every man thought himself a George Mason." [1] Rives wrote in 1859:

" In looking back to the Constitution of 1776 with all the lights which the intermediate experience of eighty years has shed on the science of popular government, we cannot but be struck with the reach of practical wisdom and sagacious statesmanship exhibited in its construction. There cannot be a more striking proof of the real merits and essential wisdom of the Constitution of 1776 than that in an age of change and revolution it firmly maintained its ground, for a period of fifty-four years, against the persevering assaults of a host of critics and theorists, sustained by the authority of some of the highest names in the State ; and, when at last it was superseded by a new experiment, which in its turn has given place to another, that there is hardly now a thinking man of any party in Virginia who would not gladly exchange the modern structure and all its imagined improvements for the ancient Constitution, just as it was, with only a necessary readjustment of the representation to the changes which have taken place in the local distribution of the population." [2]

Virginia's claim to have given to America and to the world the first written constitution of a free State [3] has been strangely denied or suppressed by Northern writers and historians. Bancroft, in his chapter on " The Constitutions of the Several States," says that " Massachusetts which was the first State to conduct a government independent of the king . . assuming that the place of governor was vacant from the 19th July, 1775, recognized the Council as the legal successor to executive power." He then enumerates four other States which formed governments, and makes the extraordinary statement that Virginia was " sixth in the series," though he considerately adds, " first in the completion of her work." [4] The Virginia Convention of July

---

[1] " Howe's Historic Collections."

[2] " Life and Times of Madison," vol. i., pp. 153–158.

[3] The only plausible exception to this statement is the Cromwellian Constitution of 1653 or *Instrument of Government*.

[4] " History of America," vol. ix., ch. xv. See also " Johns Hopkins University Studies," third series. " American Constitutions," etc., etc.

17, 1775, as has been seen, "assuming that the place of governor was vacant," conducted a "government independent of the king," and appointed a Committee of Safety, August 17th, with executive powers for the emergency. Before the other colonies had moved in the matter Virginia declared independence, pronouncing her connection with Great Britain "totally dissolved," on the 29th of June, 1776. New Hampshire and South Carolina, named by Bancroft as forming governments next after Massachusetts, expressly declared them "provisional," and were careful not to renounce their connection with Great Britain. Rhode Island and Connecticut named fourth and fifth by Bancroft, have no pretence whatever to priority over Virginia, the one merely substituting the name of the people for that of the king in its charter, in May, 1776; the other forming its government as late as the 14th of July, 1776. New Hampshire's provisional government, instituted in the winter of 1775–1776, was to last only "during the present unhappy and unnatural contest with Great Britain." In 1784 she framed her regular constitution, with its opening bill of rights. Massachusetts, as Bancroft admits, framed her bill of rights on that of Virginia, and her constitution was not written until 1779.

The adoption of the new seal of the commonwealth was the last act of the Convention of 1776. The design was reported by George Mason, and there is every reason to believe that he was its author. The committee appointed to prepare a seal consisted of Richard Henry Lee, who was, however, not in the Convention, George Mason, Robert Carter Nicholas, and George Wythe. George Wythe and John Page were appointed to superintend the engraving of the seal, which was found not practicable in this country, and the commission was put into the hands of Arthur Lee, then living in Paris. In Girardin's continuation of Burk's "History of Virginia," written under Jefferson's supervision, it is said that Wythe proposed the seal that was adopted by the Convention. But Girardin gives no authority for this statement. And as George Mason was practically the chairman of the committee on the seal, and reported it to the Convention, the conclusion that he designed it is irresistible. He must have penned the words that describe the seal, in that case, and they are remarkable for clearness and precision :

"VIRTUS, the genius of the commonwealth, dressed like an *Amazon*, resting on a spear with one hand, and holding a sword in the other, and treading on TYRANNY, represented by a man prostrate, a crown fallen from his head, a broken chain in his left hand, and a scourge in his right. In the exergon, the word VIRGINIA over the head of Virtus ; and underneath the words *Sic Semper Tyrannis*. On the reverse a group, LIBERTAS, with her wand and *pileus*. On one side of her CERES, with the *cornucopia* in one hand, and an ear of wheat in the other. On the other side ÆTERNITAS, with the globe and phœnix. In the exergon these words : DEUS NOBIS HÆC OTIA FECIT."

Grigsby seems to assume that George Mason designed the Virginia seal[1]; and this is taken for granted by the late Colonel Sherwin McRae in his pamphlet on the history of the seal prepared at the time it was restored by the State of Virginia in 1884. The description of it he regards as "one of the most remarkable specimens of precision in expression to be found in any language, and showing unmistakably that its paternity is the same as that of the celebrated declaration of rights." It is claimed by Colonel McRae, who gave much study to the subject, that no other American State has a seal equal to that of Virginia in classic beauty and appropriateness. And the fact that it was described so carefully at the beginning has been of infinite importance in securing its exact reproduction at the present time. New York having no description of her seal, a new one has been formed recently from the designs of three different seals formerly used by her. The seal of a State, as Colonel McRae declares, "is not a bauble, but an important and necessary element of government; indeed the Convention of 1776 was so impressed with this truth that the great

---

[1] "Virginia Convention of 1776," p. 167.

seal was made a *specific constitutional* provision." And in summing up George Mason's work in the Virginia Convention, the preparation or designing of the State seal is seen to be the third and concluding portion of his notable achievement. "The great seal of Virginia," says the writer above quoted, "is an essential part of George Mason's plan of government. The first is his declaration of rights, then the constitution, and then the great seal—a Corinthian column with its base, shaft, and capital. To Mason belongs the enviable distinction of conceiving and composing the three parts of the plan of government." [1]

[1] Report on the State Seal, House Document, No. xi.; also " New England Historical Register," vol. xxvi.

CHAPTER VIII.

IN THE VIRGINIA ASSEMBLY.

1776–1778.

The American States were now fully embarked on their career of independent political life. The Articles of Confederation, reported in Congress eight days after the Declaration of Independence, were not ratified, however, until 1778, and then only by ten States. But the bond between the colonies, formed in May, 1775, by which they had established a union for their mutual defence, sufficed at this time for all practical purposes. The military outlook in the fall of this memorable year of independence was not an encouraging one. Washington, obliged to evacuate New York, retreated through the Jerseys in the face of the enemy's superior numbers, and repeated disasters marked the record of the patriot army. Considerable alarm was felt throughout the country, an alarm shared by the Virginia Assembly then in session. This, the first republican Assembly of Virginia, met at Williamsburg on the 7th of October. George Mason was one of the members, and, in fact, the legislature was the same body as the Convention of the preceding spring. George Mason did not take his seat immediately, and ten days after the Assembly opened he was writing to the President of Congress as chairman of the Fairfax Committee, enclosing a resolution of the Council of Virginia, in reference to the defences of Alexandria ·

VIRGINIA, FAIRFAX CO., Oct. 17, 1776.

SIR: At the request of the inhabitants of the town of Alexandria, I take the liberty to trouble you with the enclosed order of the Virginia Council, understanding that Messrs. Hughes of Frederick County, Maryland (who are the only persons in this part of the continent to be depended on for cannon,) are under contract with the Congress for all the cannon their works can possibly make in a year, and having no other means of carrying the above-mentioned order of Council into execution, the inhabitants of the said town humbly beg leave through you, Sir, to represent their case to the honorable the Congress, and pray for an order to Messrs. Hughes to furnish them with the cannon wanted, out of those engaged for continental service. They are unacquainted with the terms of Messrs. Hughes contract, but if the price is more than thirty-five pounds, Virginia currency, per ton, the rate our Council have prescribed, they will pay the difference themselves. If the Congress is pleased to indulge them with such an order, the sooner it can be granted the better, as the fortifying the said town will be very advantageous to the trade of great part of Virginia and Maryland, and give considerable encouragement to foreign adventurers, by affording them protection at a good port where they can speedily procure cargoes of country produce.

I beg the favour of an answer as soon as convenience will permit; and am, with much respect, sir, your most obedient, humble servant,

G. MASON,
Chairman of Fairfax County Committee.[1]

While Colonel Mason was thus employed in Fairfax County, in endeavoring to procure cannon for Alexandria, the business of the Assembly was going forward. The attendance of the members, however, not being as full as was desirable, a call of the House was made on the 2d of November, and George Mason among others ordered to be taken into custody by the sergeant-at-arms, as one of the absentees. Three days later he was nominated by the Senate among the five persons to be balloted for as a committee to revise the laws of the commonwealth. On the 11th, as the quaint record states: "The House being informed that Mr. George Mason attended in custody of the

---

[1] 5, "American Archives," ii., 1127.

sergeant-at-arms, and that he had good cause for his absence when the House was called over on the 2nd instant," it was ordered " that he be discharged from custody and admitted to his seat in this House, without paying fees."[1]   He was immediately placed on the committee which had under its consideration the disputed boundary between Virginia and Pennsylvania ; and also on the committee appointed to bring in a bill establishing courts of justice. A petition was soon after laid before the House from a certain William Savage, owner of the "brigantine *Success*," asking redress for the imprisonment in Quantico Creek of all of his sails, seized for the use of the county, by " Foushee Tebbs, gentleman, by order of Col. George Mason "[2]   The inhabitants of Alexandria sent up a petition, about this time, setting forth their defenceless condition and asking for sixteen iron cannon, etc. ; and no doubt Colonel Mason urged their suit with due energy, as it was complied with later.

On the 19th of November important resolutions in regard to religion were passed by the House, and the provision for the support of the established clergy was withdrawn, though the glebe lands, churches, and plate, with all arrears of money and tobacco, were secured to the parishes and their incumbents. George Mason was placed first on the committee of seventeen to whom the work was entrusted of preparing bills in accordance with these resolutions, and, as has been said, drafted the bills. Madison, Jefferson, and Henry were named immediately after him. Many churchmen, like Edmund Pendleton and others, opposed these measures, but the majority were in favor of them. Thus, in the words of Edmund Randolph, did the friends of the church, in the interests of liberty, " cast the establishment at the feet of its enemies." Colonel Mason on the following day was appointed one of a committee of six who were to prepare bills for raising troops, erecting forts, building galleys, and taking other measures for the defence of the commonwealth. Peyton Randolph, President of Congress,

[1] Journal of the Assembly.   [2] *Ibid.*

dying suddenly at this time in Philadelphia, his remains were brought to Williamsburg to be interred, and the Assembly adjourned to attend the funeral on the 26th of November. Other bills which Colonel Mason drew up, either wholly or in part, were those to encourage the making hemp, woollen, linen, and other manufactures; to restrain the operation of the acts for limitation of actions and recording deeds; for the trial of offences committed out of the commonwealth, and to suspend executions for debt. Colonel Mason was also on a committee to prepare a bill for preventing the engrossing of salt, a precious commodity at this time throughout the colony. The bill declaring what shall be treason was soon after under discussion, and a conference on the subject took place between the House and the Senate. Colonel Mason was one of the number appointed by the House to meet the Senate committee, an amendment having been proposed by the Senate to which the House did not agree. On the 17th of December Colonel Mason reported from the committee on the disputed boundary between Virinia and Pennsylvania certain resolutions, of which the first and second were in these words:

" 1. *Resolved*, That it is the mutual interest of the commonwealth of Virginia and Pennsylvania, that the boundaries between them be speedily settled and ascertained, in the most amicable and indisputable manner, by the joint agreement and concurrence of both ; but that this desirable end being unattainable by diffidence or reserve, your committee are concerned to find that the committee of the Pennsylvania Convention have confined themselves to general observations on the cession and release made by the Commonwealth of Virginia, without attempting to show that the temporary boundary proposed was really inconsistent with the same, or offering anything with certainty on the part of Pennsylvania in its stead, until the true limits of their charter could be authentically ascertained and settled.

" 2. *Resolved*, That as the boundaries expressed in the Pennsylvania charter may admit of great doubt, and variety of opinions may arise on the construction, and it is expedient and wise to remove, as much as possible, all cause of future controversy (the great principle upon which the Virginia Convention acted in making the aforesaid cession and release), to quiet the minds of the people who may be affected thereby, and to take from our common enemies an opportunity of fomenting mutual distrust and jealousy, this Commonwealth ought to offer such reasonable terms of accommodation (even if the loss of some territory is incurred thereby) as may be cordially accepted by our sister State, and an end put to all future dispute by a firm and permanent agreement and settlement." [1]

The third resolution defined the boundary line proposed. These resolutions were undoubtedly drafted by Colonel Mason, who showed here the wise and magnanimous spirit evinced later by him in the advocacy of a still more important cession of territory. Saturday, December 21st, was the last day of the session, and the House resolved itself into a committee on the state of America. Resolutions were passed for encouraging the recruiting service, etc.; and it was declared, "that in view of the present imminent danger of America, it is become necessary for the preservation of the State that the usual forms of government should be suspended during a limited time." It was added, however, "that this departure from the constitution of government being in this instance founded only on most evident and urgent necessity ought not hereafter to be drawn into precedent." [2] The Senate amended the resolution by the substitution of the words, "that additional powers be given to the governor and council for a limited time," for the phrase, "that the usual powers of government should be suspended," etc. Colonel Mason carried these resolutions to the Senate, and he was, in all probability, their author. It is said that he declared in the Assembly, in regard to the executive, that "it might be necessary to give unlimited power for a limited time." [3] These resolves, which were to be transmitted to Congress and to the States of Maryland and North Carolina, show how grave the military situation seemed to the

[1] *Ibid.*   [2] *Ibid.*   [3] Tucker's "Jefferson," vol. i., p. 150.

Virginia legislators at this crisis. They gave rise to the story, first told by Jefferson, who had left the Assembly in November, that Virginia designed to appoint a dictator, in the person of the governor, Patrick Henry. But, as Professsor Tyler points out, the resolution was not to give " unlimited " power but " extraordinary " power,[1] and a dictatorship in any serious sense could never have been intended. Certainly George Mason would be the last person to contemplate such a project.

The biographers of Jefferson, having his recollections of the Assembly before them, in which naturally his own part in it is chiefly dwelt on, have uniformly ascribed to him the leading part in its deliberations. In this respect justice has not been done to George Mason. His life never having been written, his papers having been lost and scattered, this is, perhaps, not to be wondered at. This ardent and efficient lawmaker and statesman, with his strenuous personality and his exalted patriotism, whose work and character impressed themselves so forcibly upon his own time, by a strange fatality passed away leaving no provision, apparently, for the establishment of his fame in the eyes of posterity. No recollections, no *Ana* of his are to be found with which to reinforce contemporary record and transmitted tradition. And so it has come to pass that his services in many instances have been wellnigh obscured, and the award that is due him has been given to others. The latest of Jefferson's many biographers, therefore, only more fully accentuates this injustice, when he says of the Assembly of 1776 and its work : " George Mason, George Wythe, and Madison . . . were efficient coadjutors and lieutenants only. Jefferson was the principal and the leader."[2] The word "coadjutor" is Jefferson's, and is used by him in his fine tribute to Mason, where he speaks of him as his colleague in the Assembly from 1776 to 1779, when Jefferson left the legislature to become governor : " I had many occasional and strenuous coadjutors

[1] " Life of Patrick Henry," pp. 197–202.
[2] " Life of Jefferson." Morse. American Statesmen Series.

in debate," he writes, "and one most steadfast, able, and zealous, who was himself a host. This was George Mason, a man of the first order of wisdom among those who acted on the theatre of the Revolution, of expansive mind, pro. found judgment, cogent in argument, learned in the lore of our former constitution, and earnest for the republican change on democratic principles. His elocution was neither flowing nor smooth, but his language was strong, his manner most impressive, and strengthened by a dash of biting cynicism when provocation made it seasonable." [1]

Is it likely that this man of mature years and ripe abilities, who was indeed a host in himself, and so acknowledged to be by those with whom he was associated, had, in the space of six months, sunk from his established leadership in the Virginia Convention, as the architect and builder of the new government, to the position of Jefferson's lieutenant in the Assembly that followed? Jefferson was many years his junior, and certainly not at this time Mason's equal in the experience of political life, or in the essential attributes of true statesmanship. Jefferson's comment in 1825 on the newly published life of Richard Henry Lee, given in a letter to one of this same band of Revolutionary worthies, may be cited here in this connection; "I am not certain whether the friends of George Mason, of Patrick Henry, yourself, and even of General Washington, may not reclaim some of the feathers of the plumage given him, noble as was his proper and original coat." [2] The friends of George Mason would reclaim some of the feathers from the plumage given to Jefferson, and place them where they properly belong.

Tucker gives to Jefferson the whole responsibility and credit of the bill for establishing courts of justice, which he brought in three days after he had taken his seat. At this time George Mason was not in the Assembly, but as soon as he arrived he was placed on the committee which had the bill in hand, and, doubtless, he gave it due attention.

[1] Jefferson's "Works," vol. i., p. 40.   [2] *Ibid.*, vol. vii., p. 422.

18

The laws in relation to landed property, and respecting religion, were the two measures, however, of radical importance, in reference to which it is claimed that Jefferson took the lead.[1] A month before George Mason took his seat in the Assembly, on the 12th of October, Jefferson brought in a bill for the abolishment of entails. And if up to Mason's arrival Jefferson seemed to have taken the initiative in these reforms, as soon as the elder statesman made his appearance he stepped easily to the front. George Mason was, no doubt, the author of the act exempting dissenters from contributing to the support of the established church, an act which Jefferson says, passed only after desperate contests in the committee of the whole house in which Edmund Pendleton and Robert Carter Nicholas led the opposition. Placed on the committee for revising the laws, George Mason's influence was a controlling one here also.

The change made in the Virginia statute of descents, it has been asserted, did not meet with his approval. John Randolph of Roanoke, the brilliant apostle in the succeeding generation of Mason's cardinal political doctrines, who had seen, as he believed, the ill effects on Virginia society of this democratic law of inheritance, once declared: " Well might old George Mason exclaim that the authors of that law never had a son."[2] But it will be seen that George Mason was, in effect, one of "the authors of that law." Jefferson's account of the preliminary work of the committee which met in Fredericksburg January 13, 1777, leaves the matter in no doubt. He says that upon the question whether they should " abolish the whole existing system of laws and prepare a new and complete institute, or preserve the general system and only modify it to the present state of things," Pendleton favored the less conservative course and Lee agreed with him. This, it will be remembered, was Thomas Ludwell Lee. Wythe, George Mason, and Jefferson, however, advocated the more practical plan of simply making suitable

---

[1] " Life of Jefferson," vol. i., p. 92.
[2] Garland's " Life of Randolph," vol. i., p. 19.

alterations in the existing laws. "When we proceeded to the distribution of the work," adds Jefferson, " Mr. Mason excused himself as being no lawyer, he felt himself unqualified for the work, and he resigned soon after." Lee resigned also, for the same reason, and his death occurred a year later. "The other two gentlemen [Pendleton and Wythe] and myself," Jefferson continues, "divided the work among us." The common law was assigned to Jefferson, and he says:

" As the law of Descents and the Criminal Law fell, of course, within my portion, I wished the committee to settle the leading principles of these, as a guide for me in framing them, and with respect to the first, I proposed to abolish the law of primogeniture, and to make real estate descendible in parcenary to the next of kin, as personal property is by the statute of distribution. Mr. Pendleton wished to preserve the right of primogeniture, but seeing at once that that could not prevail, he proposed we should adopt the Hebrew principle, and give a double portion to the elder son. I observed, that if the elder son could eat twice as much, or do double work, it might be a natural evidence of his right to a double portion, but being on a par in his powers and wants, with his brothers, he should be on a par also in the partition of the patrimony, and such was the decision of the other members."

He goes on to speak of other points which were settled, and concludes that then " we repaired to our respective homes for the preparation of the work." [1] The plural pronoun here includes not merely Wythe and Pendleton, but Lee and Mason. And Jefferson and Wythe, in their letter to the Assembly of June, 1779, referring to the later resignation of George Mason and the death of Thomas Ludwell Lee, assert that " the plan of the work had been settled, and agreeable to that plan it was in a considerable degree carried into execution before that loss." [2]

[1] Randolph's " Jefferson," p. 35.
[2] Hening's " Statutes," vol. ix.

Among the few papers of George Mason that yet remain to us, is one drawn up by him at this period, and endorsed by him as the " Plan settled by the committee of Revisors, in Fredericksburg, January, 1777." It opens in the following manner :

" (1.) The common law not to be meddled with, except where alterations are necessary. The statutes to be revised and digested, alterations proper for us to be made ; the diction where obsolete or redundant, to be reformed ; but otherwise to undergo as few changes as possible. The acts of the English Commonwealth to be examined. The statutes to be divided into periods ; the acts of Assembly made on the same subject to be incorporated into them. The laws of the other colonies to be examined, and any good ones to be adopted."

In the margin here is written :

" General rules in drawing. Provisions &c., which would do only what the law would do without them, to be omitted. Bills to be short ; not to include matters of different natures ; not to insert an unnecessary word ; nor omit a useful one. Laws to be made on the spur of the present occasion, and all innovating laws to be limited in their duration."

Then the criminal law is outlined, and after this the law of descents " The lands to which an intestate had title in fee to descend in parcenary, to males and females, in equal portions," and giving the course of descent. The headings in the margin indicate the text that follows. These are : " Dower, Distribution of personal estate, Executions, Debt, Sureties, Land law, New grants and Real actions." The paper concludes thus :

" The first period in the division of the statutes to end with 25th H., 8th. The second to end at the Revolution. The third to come down to the present day. A fourth part to consist of the residuary part of the Virginia laws, not taken up in either of the three first parts ; to which is added the criminal law and land law. The fifth part to be the regulation of property in slaves, and their condition ; and also the examination of the laws of the other colonies."

" Alotment of the parts to each member :

" T. Jefferson to undertake the first part with the law of descents.

" E. Pendleton the second,

" G. Wythe the third,

" G. Mason the fourth ; but if he finds it too much the other gentlemen will take off his hands any part he pleases.

" T. Lee the fifth part." [1]

It is evident from this paper that George Mason had no small share in sketching the plan of revision. And as Jefferson expressly says that, " *agreeable to that plan* it was in a considerable degree carried into execution," before Mason's resignation, we may conclude that the code bears in some places the marks of his workmanship. To George Mason had been allotted the fourth part in the division of labor among the five members; and this included "the residuary part of the Virginia laws, not taken up in either of the three first parts; to which is added the criminal law and land law." Jefferson in his " Notes on Virginia," written in 1781, says of the revision of the laws, that the common law of England was made the basis of the work, that it was necessary to make alterations in that ; and while the British statutes and Virginia Acts of Assembly were retained, they were digested into one hundred and twenty-six new acts, " in which simplicity of style was aimed at, as far as was safe." Among alterations proposed, he mentions, "to establish religious freedom on the broadest bottom." Another object of the revisal was to diffuse knowledge more generally through the mass of the people ; and bills for this purpose were brought forward. It was proposed to lay off every county into small districts of five or six miles square, called hundreds, each to have a school for reading, writing, and arithmetic, the tuition free for the first three years. There were to be twenty grammar schools ; and, lastly, a

[1] Mason Papers.

public library and picture gallery founded. Both religious liberty and the cause of education found a champion in George Mason, as will be manifest in the consideration of his public life. His views on the subject of primogeniture and the law of descents were affirmed in the most practical manner by the provision in his will, drawn up three years before he was called upon to give them expression in the revision of the laws. After providing in turn for each one of his sons, he adds :

" And least the manner in which I have limited and directed the descent of some of my land should occasion any dispute or induce an opinion that I intended to entail them, I hereby declare that it is not my intention to entail any part of my estate upon any of my children, but to give all and each of my sons when they respectively come of age or marry, an absolute fee simple estate in all the lands respectively devised them, and in all such lands also as any of them may happen to take by the death of any of their brothers, the common legal descent of some of my lands being hereinbefore altered only in case any of my sons to whom such lands are respectively devised should die under age and unmarried while their lands remained in the common stock of my estate and had not yet come into their actual possession."

The winter of 1776–77 was brightened at length by the victories of Trenton in December, and Princeton in January, which sent a new impulse through the veins of the disheartened Confederacy. Francis Lightfoot Lee wrote to a friend in Virginia, on the 3d of February, from Baltimore, where Congress was then sitting, having left Philadelphia in alarm when the British crossed the Delaware in December, and he refers to " the change of our affairs, which I hope will something forward the recruiting business." He thinks that " bad management has had a greater share in our bad success than fortune, but is it to be wondered at ; plunged at once into an immense system, without anybody possessed of the knowledge requisite for the proper conducting the different departments which other nations have acquired by the experience of ages; continually pressed by a powerful enemy, so that the present emergency necessarily engrossed all our attention; every necessary for a large army immediately to be procured in a country which had depended for almost everything on foreigners; a number of internal enemies exerting all their faculties to frustrate our endeavours. All things considered, the wonder, I think, is, that we have succeeded so well." He writes of military affairs, that there are "frequent skirmishes, which for the most part are in our favor. Indeed it is pretty certain the enemy's army is mouldering fast with sickness, desertion, and captures, which will prevent their attempting anything of consequence till reinforced, if General W—— can keep enough of the militia together till part of the new army is raised. Our general through the whole campaign has shown himself vastly superior in abilities to the enemy; and I am convinced if he now had 8000 regulars Howe would soon have reason to wish himself at Halifax."[1]

A month later George Mason wrote to Richard Henry Lee, answering a letter from him of the 12th of February, and alluding to some injurious report, that had been circulated affecting his friend's reputation, which Colonel Mason took upon himself to pronounce "an infamous falsehood." This was, in all probability, the beginning of the trouble which lost Lee his seat in Congress, though he was soon after triumphantly vindicated.

GUNSTON HALL, March 4, 1777.

DEAR SIR :

I never heard a word of the report you mention until the day before I received your favor of the twelfth ultimo, when, hearing it accidentally from a second or third hand, I took upon me immediately to contradict it ; and thought I had good authority from the letters I saw, during the sitting of the Assembly, from you and your brother, Col. F. Lee, mentioning the retreat through the Jerseys, to affirm that it was an infamous falsehood. I be-

---

[1] MS. Letter.

lieve it has gained no manner of credit, and don't think it is worth giving you a moment's uneasiness.

The gallies now building I hope will be able to afford sufficient protection to our bay. I am sure there are as many as can possibly be built and manned before the meeting of the Assembly. I should be glad to be informed if the Governor and Council have proposed to the Congress to furnish them out small gallies, in lieu of those they ordered to be built here, for the protection and transportation of their troops over our rivers; and the result.

We have a very extraordinary piece of intelligence (I suppose it is a Tory invention to delay the raising of our army) in Godhart's Baltimore paper of the 25th of February. If there is any truth in it, the British ministry must be hard pushed, and see that a French war is inevitable. Surely Congress will be cautious how they are drawn into a fruitless negotiation, or commit any breach of faith with foreign nations. They best know the powers and instructions given Dr. Franklin. At any rate, let us do nothing to cramp our exports to any part of the world. They are the only means by which we can expect to discharge the enormous debt this war has created. I really think such a publication ought not to have been suffered, and that the author should be inquired after.

I beg to be kindly remembered to your brother, Col. F. Lee, and Mr. Page, and am, dear sir,

Your affectionate friend and servant,

G. MASON.[1]

Colonel Mason wrote to Patrick Henry in April on affairs of the commonwealth:

GUNSTON HALL, April 6, 1777.

SIR :

The express who went from hence last (Mr. Chew), not being yet returned, and therefore not knowing what orders are given about boarding the vessels at Alexandria upon Continental account, I enclose you the three letters brought by the last three vessels, together with one from Mr. Mier to me, mentioning the

---

[1] Lee Papers, University of Virginia. A small part of this letter appeared in the *Southern Literary Messenger,* October, 1858.

state of that business, and the quantity of flour required for the vessels already arrived. The whole towns of Dumfries and Alexandria are under inoculation for the small-pox,—in the latter about six hundred persons, which I fear will prevent the flour waggons coming in.

I should be glad to know how the sail-cloth manufactory goes on ; and whether Mr. Matthews has got any person acquainted with the new machines, introduced a few years ago from Russia, for spinning the thread, which it is said perform the work better and vastly more expeditiously than common wheels. My reason for this inquiry is that I think I can engage a workman, who served an apprenticeship in one of the great sail-cloth manufactories at Hull, and is master of every part of the business, from breaking the hemp to finishing the sail-cloth. He is also acquainted with the use of the clasp-harness and the before-mentioned machines, which by his account are simple and extremely advantageous, and thinks he can instruct a workman to make them. He served his time with a friend of mine in Maryland, who gives him a good character for honesty and diligence ; but knows nothing of his proficiency in his trade further than his being a complete hemp and flax dresser. Upon his coming over here to enter on board a privateer at Alexandria, I stopped him ; and thinking a man so useful to the public ought not to be lost, I prevailed on him, by promising him good wages, and making him hope for some further reward, in case his machines answered, to lay aside his privateering scheme for the present, and keep himself unengaged till I could lay this information before the Council-board.

There are in this county two young Scotch gentlemen, Laughlan McLean and Adam McGlashan, in the list of those ordered by the court to depart the commonwealth. Having engaged their passage in the ship *Allison*, and advanced (as was required) half their passage-money, they imagined their names were, of course, inserted in the list of those who intended to go out in the same ship, and have petitioned for further time. But since they have seen the late proclamation, they are very uneasy least, through any mistake or omission, they may be thought to have neglected the proper requisites, and subject themselves to confinement, which might be fatal to one of them who is in a bad state of health ; and have therefore desired me to apply to your Excellency and the board on their behalf ; and if they are not already included in the indulgence granted to the rest of the ship *Allison's* passengers, to pray the favor of being indulged with such further time as may be necessary until the said ship is ready to sail.   These young men have been my neighbors a considerable time ; and I know their conduct has been so inoffensive and unexceptionable, that, had they called upon some witnesses in this neighborhood of undoubted credit, I think they would have avoided the judgment which hath been passed upon them ; otherwise I should not take the liberty to trouble the board in their favor.

I am, very respectfully, sir,

Your most obedient servant,

G. MASON.

To His Excellency,
    Patrick Henry, Esq.,
       Governor of Virginia.[1]

The spring session of the Assembly opened on the 5th of May.   Thomson Mason was in the House during this session, but George Mason was prevented, by the effects of inoculation, from attending.   On the 22d of May George Mason was elected to represent the State in the general Congress, to fill out the term of Thomas Nelson, who had resigned on account of his health.   Mason received eighty-one votes on the ballot, and Joseph Jones twenty-six.[2]   At the same time the five members for the year beginning on the 11th of the following August were balloted for, which resulted in the election of Benjamin Harrison, George Mason, Joseph Jones, Francis Lightfoot Lee, and John Harvie.   Richard Henry Lee was rejected on each of the five ballots, and as he was already in Congress, it was of course a marked slight, and intentionally inflicted.   George Mason sent in the following letter of resignation, which was received in the House on the 19th of June:

[1] MS. Letter, owned by William Wirt Henry, Esq.
[2] Journal of the Assembly.

GUNSTON HALL, June 14th, 1777.

SIR ·

I hoped to have attended my duty in the House before this time, or I should not so long have delayed writing on the subject with which I now take the liberty to trouble you ; but though I am otherwise thoroughly recovered from the small pox, my arm which has been so much ulcerated where the inoculation was made, still continues so bad, that my being able to attend this session remains doubtful. I must therefore entreat the favor of you sir, to return my thanks to the Assembly for the honor they have been pleased to do me, in appointing me one of their delegates to Congress, and at the same time to inform them that I cannot by any means accept the appointment. My own domestic affairs are so circumstanced as not to admit of my continued absence from home, where a numerous family of children calls for my constant attention ; nor do I think I have a right to vacate my seat in the house of delegates, without the consent of my constituents ; and such of them as I have had the opportunity of consulting are averse to it. Was this not the case, I must acknowledge I have other reasons for declining the appointment ; which to avoid offence, I forbear giving.

I beg you will excuse this trouble, and believe me, with the greatest respect,

Sir, your most obd't Serv't.

G. MASON.

Hon. George Wythe, Esq.,
    Speaker of the House of Delegates. [1] }

On the following day, the 20th of June, Richard Henry Lee took his seat in the Assembly, and called for an inquiry into the charges made against him, with the result of an acquittal, and a vote of thanks from the House, and on the 24th he was elected to Congress in place of George Mason. For reasons not very clearly made out, there was a cabal against Richard Henry Lee at this time. His patriotism had been called in question, and his political rectitude by a certain set inimical to him, but the accusations seem to have been false and frivolous. Colonel Bannister wrote from

---

[1] MS. Letter, State Library, Richmond.

Williamsburg after Lee had made his defence, giving an account of the affair to Theodorick Bland. Bannister, while professing not to be an ally of Richard Henry Lee, pronounced the action of the Assembly in superseding him, in his absence, without a hearing, "a most flagrant act of injustice." After detailing the charges and leaving it to Bland to form his own judgment, Colonel Bannister adds:

" But if they were right in that, what will you say to their consistency and uniformity of opinion, when I tell you, that the very body of men who but a few days before had disgraced, have returned him the thanks of their house? Certainly no defence was ever made with more graceful eloquence, more manly firmness, equalness of temper, serenity, calmness and judgment, than this very accomplished speaker displayed on this occasion, and I am now of opinion he will be re-elected to his former station, instead of Mr. George Mason, who has resigned." [1]

True to his uniformly expressed resolve, not to serve in Congress, George Mason had resigned both the positions to which he had been elected to fill out an unexpired term, and to become one of the delegation for the following year. His preference for private life was sincere and deep-seated; he felt the obligation at this time not to separate himself too far from his motherless children; and he was apparently superior to the ordinary ambition which would covet political honors for their own sake. To serve Virginia in her legislative assemblies seemed to him his highest duty. And only once was he led into a wider field of action, when in 1787 he came forward in a federal council, at a serious crisis, as Virginia's representative. But apart from his general resolves and predilections, George Mason, on this occasion, evidently felt that an injury had been inflicted on his personal friend, Richard Henry Lee, and that in taking the honor it was proposed to confer upon him, he would be superseding Lee. In his life of Jefferson, Randall assumes that had the former been present in the Assembly at the

[1] " The Bland Papers," vol. i., p. 57.

time of the election, the enemies of Lee would not have triumphed. Jefferson had left Williamsburg on the 20th of May, two days before the ballot took place. It seems Lee wrote to Jefferson for the testimony of the latter in his behalf, and it is quite likely he wrote to George Mason and other friends at the same time. But whatever may have been the effect of Jefferson's influence in producing the reaction in favor of Lee, certain it is that George Mason would need no stimulus from Jefferson to urge him to exertion in behalf of Richard Henry Lee, with whom he was much more intimately associated than with Jefferson, and for whose character and abilities he had always the highest regard. Randall writes: " George Mason wore no man's colors, but he generally acted closely with Jefferson. His sympathies were obviously all on Lee's side. Unless Mr. Jefferson's friends had supported Lee on the twenty-fourth of June he could have obtained nothing like such a vote." [1] Jefferson is here again made to pose as leader with his " friends, " lieutenants, and coadjutors, rallying at the word of their chief to the defence of Richard Henry Lee.

Tracing briefly the progress of the war at this time we find in July, 1777, the capture of Ticonderoga by Burgoyne, making a note of discouragement in the summer's record. Two months later, in September, the British fleet under Howe landed in the Chesapeake Bay, despite the defences of which George Mason wrote. The enemy then marched to Philadelphia, and Washington sustained a defeat at the battle of Brandywine. With Philadelphia in the hands of the British and the fugitive Congress at Yorktown, Pennsylvania, the prospect was indeed a gloomy one. But the dark cloud was soon to turn to the Americans its silver lining, and the surrender of Burgoyne at Saratoga in October was felt to be a success amply compensating for the previous disasters.

The Virginia Assembly met in Williamsburg on the 20th of October and both George and Thomson Mason attended its session. It was not, however, until the 14th of No-

[1] "Life of Jefferson," vol. i., p. 210.

vember that the former took his seat. Washington evidently regarded George Mason's presence there as of the utmost importance, and looked to him to take the initiative in certain financial reforms, while the necessary legislation in regard to Virginia's military establishment was also in his hands. In a letter to John Parke Custis, written on the 14th of November, from his camp near Philadelphia, Washington says :

" It is much to be wished that a remedy could be applied to the depreciation of our currency. I know of no person better qualified to do this than Col. Mason, and shall be very happy to hear that he has taken it in hand. Long have I been persuaded of the indispensable necessity of a tax for the purpose of sinking the paper money, and why it has been delayed better politicians than I must account for. What plan Col. Mason may have in contemplation for filling up the Virginia regiments I know not, but certain I am that this is a measure that cannot be dispensed with, nor ought not under any pretext whatsoever. I hope Colonel Mason's health will admit his attendance on the Assembly, and no other plea should be offered, much less received by his constituents. " [1]

Mann Page wrote from " Mansfield" to Richard Henry Lee about two weeks before the date of Washington's letter, and reports, probably having heard it from one of his correspondents in Williamsburg, that " Colonel Mason has not yet gone down ; he is busy, I am told, in preparing a bill for a general assessment and a militia bill. " [2]   On the 14th of November the House was informed that Mr. George Mason was present, and that he had good cause for his absence when the House was called over. He took his seat therefore without paying costs, and was immediately put on the Committees of Privileges and Elections and Propositions and Grievances. The next day he was made Chairman of a committee of six which included Nelson and Jefferson, to whom

[1] " Recollections of Washington," W. P. Custis,   Appendix, p. 546.
[2] " Life of Richard Henry Lee," vol. ii., p. 204.

was referred the petition of a certain Abraham Vanbibber, who had been providing stores from Holland for the States of Virginia and Maryland, and had suffered arrest and im. prisonment through the indiscretion, it was alleged, of a Vir. ginian, Captain Rallo. Thomson Mason was brought in by the sergeant-at-arms ten days later, but it appearing that he was employed in the public service when the House was called he was discharged also without paying any fine. He was put on the committee to report on the state of the several public salt works; and both George and Thomson Mason were added to the committee who were preparing the bill for establishing a court of appeals. Another bill which with Jefferson, Pendleton, and two other members, George Mason was to assist in drawing up, was to prevent forestal. ling, engrossing, and regrating, or buying up goods to sell them again at a higher price. The state of the army chiefly occupying the attention of the House at this time, resolutions were passed to ascertain if any persons had been forestalling the public in the purchase of provisions and other neces. saries for the army, and it was proposed to appoint commis. sioners to seize stores of clothing for the public service, drawing on the treasurer for their value, and charging the United States for those used on Continental service. Com. mittees were formed for both of these purposes, and George Mason was the second person named upon them. It was also determined by the House to raise five thousand volun. teers for six months to reinforce Washington, and one thou. sand tents were to be provided. George Mason, Pendleton, Jefferson, and others, were appointed to bring in the neces. sary bills for these purposes. On the 28th of November it was ordered that a bill be brought in to amend the act for regulating and disciplining the militia, and that Nelson, Jefferson, George Mason, and others were to prepare it. Doubtless this was the bill upon which Colonel Mason was engaged in October.

The same committee were to prepare a bill providing against invasions and insurrections. The bill for raising a number of volunteers to reinforce the army was presented to the House by Colonel Mason on this same day. Some days later the House passed ten more resolutions in regard to the army, for the equipment and regulation of the troops to be raised, and George Mason was also placed on the committee named here to bring in the necessary bills. A committee was appointed to examine the report of the commissioners to whom had been referred the losses sustained by the people of Norfolk, and George Mason was one of their number. He was also placed on the committee to examine into the state of the navy. On the 10th of December the Assembly passed a resolution to empower the governor to order out such part of the militia as might be deemed necessary. They also desired that commissioners be appointed by Congress to repair to Fort Pitt to investigate the disaffection there, and George Mason was named second on a committee to bring in bills for these purposes. On the same day George Mason, Thomas Ludwell Lee, and James Henry were appointed commissioners to meet commissioners to be appointed by the State of Maryland "to consider of the most proper means to adjust and confirm the rights of each, to the use and navigation of and jurisdiction over the Bay of Chesapeake, and the rivers Potomac and Pocomoke."[1] The House, on the 13th of this month, proposed nineteen resolutions in regard to articles to be taxed, in order to provide for the public needs; all of these were agreed to except the tax on dogs. General Nelson, George Mason, with Pendleton, Nicholas, Jefferson, and others formed the committee to bring in the required bills. It would seem that George Mason had been at work also on this measure before coming to the Assembly.

On the 27th of December George Mason and Thomas Jefferson were appointed to prepare a bill "for enabling the public contractors to procure stores of provisions necessary for the ensuing campaign, and for defeating the evil intentions of those who have endeavored to prevent the public therein "[2];

[1] Journal of the Assembly.   [2] *Ibid.*

and this bill was presented to the House by George Mason two days later. A bill to regulate the inoculation for the smallpox within the State of Virginia was given to George Mason and others to prepare. On the 5th of January George Mason, Edmund Pendleton, with other members, were appointed to prepare a bill to prohibit the exportation of beef, pork, and bacon for a limited time. On the same day Colonel Mason was made chairman of a committee for adjusting and settling the titles of claimants to unpatented lands under the former government; and three days later he presented a bill " for establishing a land-office, and for ascertaining the terms and manner of granting waste and unappropriated lands."[1] The bill for regulating inoculation, and the one for adjusting and settling the titles of claimants to unpatented lands were presented to the House by George Mason on the 12th and 14th of January. Two other bills prepared by Colonel Mason about this time were for authorizing the seizure of salt, in the same manner as provisions for the use of the army; and to prevent private persons from issuing bills of credit in the nature of paper money. A proposition of Monsieur Loycante for establishing a corps of artillery in Virginia was referred to a committee consisting of R. H. Lee, Jefferson, George Mason, and others.

The House before closing its session ordered that a copy of the several papers filed in the clerk's office relating to the claim of Richard Henderson and Company and of the Indiana Company be transmitted to George Mason and Thomas Jefferson. And these two cases came up in later sessions, Colonel Mason managing the proceedings for the commonwealth against the unlawful pretensions of the land companies. Shortly before the House adjourned the balloting took place for the five judges of the General Court. Thomson Mason was elected one of these judges. Joseph Jones, John Blair, Thomas Ludwell Lee, and Paul Carrington were the other four. This was the highest criminal court in Virginia, the Supreme Court of Appeals having only civil jurisdiction.

[1] *Ibid.*

In 1830 the number of judges was increased to twenty. The General Court was, however, abolished in 1852. On the 22d of January extraordinary powers were again conferred upon Governor Henry, and two days later the Assembly adjourned. Quit-rents were abolished by the Virginia Assembly at this session, with the one exception of Lord Fairfax's in the Northern Neck. He or his agent was to transmit to the commissioners of the counties in this territory " a rent-roll of all the lands paying quit-rents to the said proprietor in such county and receive from the treasurer twenty shillings for each rent-roll." [1] So George Mason as a landholder in this portion of the Old Dominion was still required to pay quit-rent.

It was during this winter of 1777–8 that Col. George Rogers Clark visited Williamsburg, and in interviews with Governor Henry and the leading men of the Assembly, the famous Illinois campaign was projected. George Mason was an intimate and revered friend of the gallant young soldier, and he was one of the leaders with whom Henry conferred on the subject of Clark's plans. A letter was written by George Wythe, George Mason, and Thomas Jefferson, on the 3d of January, 1778, in which these gentlemen pledged themselves, in case of the success of the expedition, "to exert their influence to obtain from the legislature a bounty of three hundred acres of land for every person in the expedition." [2] The papers of G. R. Clark were, in 1834, in possession of his brother, General William Clark, and they were used by Mann Butler in his history of Kentucky. Copies of some of these papers were given by Butler to the Hon. Lyman C. Draper of Wisconsin, for his contemplated biography of George Rogers Clark. The letter signed by Wythe, Mason, and Jefferson was, however, never seen by Mr. Draper, and he supposes it to have been used as a basis for the act of the Assembly, setting apart 150,000 acres of land opposite Louisville, Kentucky, for Clark's men, and to have been retained in the

---

[1] *Ibid.*   [2] Butler's " History of Kentucky," p. 47 (and foot-note.)

hands of some committeeman who had the matter in charge. Search has been made for it unavailingly among the Force MSS. in the Congressional Library.

On his way home from Williamsburg, Colonel Mason stopped at Thomas Ludwell Lee's, "Bellevue," from which place he wrote to his cousin, James Mercer, appointing a meeting at "Gunston Hall" of these three members of the Ohio Company, to confer upon the measures to be taken to secure their land.

STAFFORD COUNTY, COL. LEE'S,
February 6, 1778.

DEAR SIR :

I fully intended to have taken Fredericksburg on my way from the Assembly and spent an evening with you and my friend Mr. Dick, but was disappointed by the accident of my servant's falling sick on the road, which detained me four or five days at Hubbard's, and obliged me at last, to leave him behind me and hire a servant to this place.

I brought in a bill, this last session, for establishing a land office, and ascertaining the terms and manners of granting waste and unappropriated lands, to create a sinking fund, in aid of the taxes, for discharging the public debt; and another for adjusting and settling the titles of claimers to unpatented land under the former government. They are both put off for the present, but will undoubtedly be taken up, and I hope finally settled in the next session, and as there will only be a short time allowed to the previous claimers to put in their respective claims, and sue out patents, after which they will be barred, it is incumbent upon the members of the Ohio Company to take the proper preparatory steps for making good their title and obtaining a patent for the 200,000 acres actually surveyed, which is all I have any hopes of, and that, I think, is upon such a foundation as that nothing but our own negligence can deprive us of it. It is an object of sufficient importance, I think, to engage our attention, being equal, by all accounts of it, to any land on this continent. There are, however, some very considerable difficulties in putting this business into proper train, which I have not room to explain in a common letter. Your advice and assistance both as a lawyer and a friend, will be much wanted, and I flatter myself if you, Col.

Thomas Lee and myself could spend two or three days together on the subject, we could reduce it to order, and we might then call a meeting of the Company which otherwise would answer no good end. Col. Lee has promised me to come up to my house, in a few days, on this occasion, and will endeavor to make the time convenient to you. I must entreat you to accompany him, and as this is a mere matter of business, and I can say will prove a troublesome one, I shall readily pay on the Company's account, such charge as you think reasonable.

I beg to be kindly remembered to Mrs. Mercer and my young relatives, and am

> Dear Sir,
> Your affectionate kinsman and obedient servant,
> G. MASON.

James Mercer, Esq.[1]

The Mr. Dick mentioned in this letter was John Dick, of Fredericksburg, whose daughter Eleanor, James Mercer had married in 1772.

George Mason was not present at the spring session of the Assembly, which opened on the 4th of May, 1778. And it is possible he was detained by his domestic affairs, or it may have been that he had an attack of the gout. His reputation for zeal and energy, and his evident leadership in the House at this time, receive an amusing confirmation in the following extract from a letter of John Augustine Washington, who wrote from "Bushfield," his estate in Westmoreland, to Richard Henry Lee on the 26th of May: "I have not heard particularly what our Assembly are about; but it is said it will be a short session, unless Col. Mason, who is not yet got down, should carve out more business for them than they have yet thought of. The revision of the Laws, I hear is to be postponed."[2] It would seem that the session was shorter than Colonel Mason had anticipated, and that he did set out for Williamsburg, but found that he was too late, the Assembly having adjourned on the 1st of June. John Parke Custis, who was in the House at this time as a

---

[1] MS. Letter. [2] Lee Papers, *Southern Literary Messenger*, vol. vi., No. 5.

delegate from Fairfax, refers to Colonel Mason in a letter he writes to Washington from " Mount Vernon," June 17th. Young Custis, after sending his correspondent the titles of the acts passed, at the session just closed, adds:

" Our delegation to Congress, I am sorry to say, is not so good as I could wish or as we might have had, if the act for preventing members of Congress sitting in the Assembly had been repealed. A bill for that purpose was brought in and shared the same fate with the other [a bill for regulating trade.] I have often wished my colleague had been present ; we might have prevented this evil. He is most inexcusable in staying away. He got as far as Colonel Blackburn's and heard the house had broken up. If that act had been repealed, our delegation would have been very respectable."

The British commissioners came to America in June, 1778, on their fruitless errand of negotiation, and on the 28th of this month the battle of Monmouth was fought. The arrival of the French fleet stimulated afresh the hopes of the Americans, and we find in George Mason's letters written a little later to Richard Henry Lee, how cheering the prospect seemed at this time to ardent patriots. Let us hope the claret that was expected from France arrived safely, in which Colonel Mason was to drink his toasts to the French allies and the blundering British ministry. Lord Chatham indeed was dead, the " wise and good man "—dead at an hour fortunate for himself and for America, just as he was about to give his name and influence against the cause of which he had so long been the champion.

July 21st, 1778, GUNSTON HALL.

DEAR SIR :

I am much obliged to you for the last papers, and the agreeable news they contain. American prospects brighten every day ; nothing I think, but the speedy arrival of a strong British squadron can save the enemy's fleet and army at New York ; indeed as to their fleet I trust the blow is already struck. We are apt to

---

[1] " Recollections of Washington," Appendix, p. 549.

wish for peace, I confess I am, although I am clearly of opinion that war is the present interest of these United States. The Union is yet incomplete, and will be so until the inhabitants of all the territory from Cape Breton to the Mississippi are included in it. While Great Britain possesses Canada and West Florida, she will continually be setting the Indians upon us, and while she holds the harbors of Augustine and Halifax, especially the latter, we shall not be able to protect our trade or coasts from her depredations ; at least for many years to come. The possession of these two places would save us more than half a million a year, and we should then quickly have a fleet sufficient for the common protection of our own coasts ; for without some strongholds in America, or naval magazines in our neighborhood, Great Britain could seldom or never keep a squadron here. If she loses her army now in America, or is obliged to withdraw it, one of which I think must happen, this important object will probably be obtained in the course of another campaign. If the British ministry act consistently and in character, they will not recognise our independence until this business is completed, and until our prejudices against Great Britain are more firmly rooted, and we become better reconciled to foreign manners and manufactures. It will require no great length of time to accomplish this, and then the wisdom of British councils will seize the auspicious moment and acknowledge our independence.

Lord Chatham's death does not seem to be mentioned in the papers with certainty ; but from the infirm condition in which he appeared in the House of Lords in April, the account is more than probable. One cannot help being concerned at the death of a wise and good man ; yet it is certainly a favorable event to America. There was nothing I dreaded so much as his taking the helm, and nothing I more heartily wish than the continuance of the present ministry. After his most Christian Majesty, and happiness and prosperity to the French nation, my next toast shall be, "Long life and continuance in office to the present British ministry," in the first bottle of good claret I get and I expect some by the first ships from France.

If tickets in the second class of the lottery are put into the hands of the sellers in the former, I can very conveniently furnish myself here. I presume the sellers must be furnished with lists of the twenty-dollar prizes in the first class, to enable them to make proper discounts to the purchasers in the second.

Your tobacco is sold at 60/, the highest price which has been given here ; the money shall be transmitted, by the first safe hand, to Mrs. Lee of Bellevieu, as you desired.

A very worthy friend of mine in this county, Capt. Harper, had a partial and unjust judgment (as he thinks) lately given by a Court of Admiralty in North Carolina, against a vessel of his, taken by Goodrich in Currabuck Inlet, and recovered by his own captain's hands, for salvage, in favor of some militia companies. And what was worse, instead of unlading the vessel, or securing her in a place of safety, after they had taken her out of the possession of Harper's captain, they only took out some hogsheads of molasses and sacks of salt, and suffered her to remain in the same spot, with the greatest part of her cargo on board, until Goodrich returned from New York (whither he had carried some other prizes), and cut the vessel out from her moorings. So that Capt. Harper sustains a loss of the vessel and the whole cargo, to the amount of several thousand pounds, and is totally at a loss how to proceed, not knowing what mode Congress have prescribed for redress in such cases. You will oblige me exceedingly in informing me whether any Court of Vice-admiralty is established for the trial of appeals from the Courts of Admiralty in the different States, and where it sits ; if there is yet no such court whether Congress, in the meantime, takes cognizance of such matters ; in short, what will be the proper steps for Capt. Harper to take to come at justice.

I beg my compliments to your colleagues, particularly to your brother Col. F. Lee, and my friend Mr. Thos. Adams, and am, dear Sir,

Your sincerely affectionate friend and servant,

G. MASON.[1]

GUNSTON HALL, Aug. 24th, 1778.

DEAR SIR ·

We have had such various and vague accounts of our affairs to the northward and of the movements of the French fleet, that I am extremely anxious to know with certainty what is doing. Is our army drawn near to King's Bridge ? Are the enemy's out-

---

[1] Lee Papers, University of Virginia. (Published, in part, in the *Southern Literary Messenger*, Oct., 1858.)

posts abandoned ? Is New York effectually besieged ? Are, or can the enemy be prevented from foraging upon Long Lsland and Staten Island ? Is the Cork fleet of victuallers arrived at New York ; or was the report a piece of artifice ? or has any such fleet actually sailed ? Has Lord Howe's fleet left Sandy Hook and gone to Rhode Island, or were the English ships which appeared there a fleet lately from Great Britain, and what has been the consequence of their meeting with Count D'Estaing's squadron ? Are the French land forces landed upon Rhode Island, to act in concert with Gen. Sullivan, or are they thought to be able to Burgoyne the British troops there ? I am almost ashamed of having asked you so many questions. I think they are nearly equal to the string with which old Col. Cary once harassed Dr. Francis upon his coming on shore at Hampton. If Lord Howe, with his fleet, has really left New York, the British army must be in the most desperate circumstances, and his intention must be to draw off the attention of the French squadron until the troops can embark, and run down to the southward, where they can get provisions, for I hardly think they can have provisions for a long voyage.

The money received for your tobacco is sent down to Mrs. Lee at " Belleview," as you desired. I wish the tobacco had not been sold so soon, as the price is risen 15/ per hundred since.

If the Congress or any of your friends should have occasion to purchase a quantity of tobacco in this part of the country, I would beg leave to recommend my friend and neighbor, Mr. Martin Cockburn. He was regularly bred to business in a very capital house in London, and I know no man whose attachment to the American cause, or whose integrity, diligence and punctuality can be more thoroughly confided in. I am not fond of giving recommendations, but I am so well acquainted with Mr. Cockburn that I know I can recommend him with safety. God bless you, my dear sir, and believe me

Your affectionate friend and servant,

G. MASON.[1]

Col. George Mercer, who had gone to London as the Ohio Company's agent in 1763, returned to Virginia in the

---

[1] *Ibid.*

unfortunate character of stamp agent in 1765, but was soon back again in England, where he remained until some time in 1767, when he revisited his native land, bringing with him an English bride. This lady died in Richmond the following year, and Colonel Mercer soon after returned to London. His correspondence with George Mason, after an interruption of several years, was renewed in 1778. In reply to a letter of Colonel Mercer's, George Mason wrote to his cousin, giving some account of himself and his public work, dating his retrospect from the death of his wife in 1773.

"VIRGINIA, GUNSTON HALL, Oct. 2d, 1778.
" MY DEAR SIR :

"It gave me great pleasure upon receipt of your favor of the 23d of April by Mr. Digges, to hear that you are alive and well in a country where you can spend your time agreeably, not having heard a word from you or of you for two years before.

"I am much obliged by the friendly concern you take in my domestic affairs, and in your kind inquiry after my family ; great alterations have happened in it. About four years ago I had the misfortune to lose my wife ; to you who knew her and the happy manner in which we lived, I will not attempt to describe my feelings. I was scarce able to bear the first shock, a depression of my spirits and a settled melancholy followed, from which I never expect or desire to recover. I determined to spend the remainder of my days in privacy and retirement with my children, from whose society alone I could expect comfort. Some of these are now grown up to men and women, and I have the satisfaction to see them free from vices, good-natured, obliging and dutiful. They all still live with me and remain single except my daughter Sally, who is lately married to my neighbor Mr. McCarty's son. My eldest daughter Nancy (who is blessed with her mother's amiable disposition) is mistress of my family, and manages my little domestic matters with a degree of prudence far above her years. My eldest son George engaged early in the American cause and was chosen ensign of the first Independent Company formed in Virginia, or indeed on the continent ; it was commanded by the present General Washington as captain, and consisted entirely of gentlemen. In the year 1775 he was appointed a captain of foot in one of the first Minute Regiments raised here, but was soon obliged to quit the service by a violent rheumatic disorder, which has followed him ever since, and I believe will force him to try the climate of France or Italy. My other sons have not yet finished their education ; as soon as they do, if the war continues, they seem strongly inclined to take an active part.

"In the summer of '75 I was, much against my inclination dragged out of my retirement by the people of my county, and sent a delegate to the General Convention at Richmond, where I was appointed a member of the first Committee of Safety, and have since at different times been chosen a member of the Privy Council and of the American Congress, but have constantly declined acting in any other public character than that of an independent representative of the people in the House of Delegates, where I still remain from a consciousness of being able to do my country more service there than in any other department ; and have ever since devoted most of my time to public business to the no small neglect and injury of my private fortune ; but if I can only live to see the American Union firmly fixed and free government well established in our western world, and can leave to my children but a crust of bread and liberty, I shall die satisfied, and say with the Psalmist, 'Lord now lettest thou thy servant depart in peace.'

" To show you that I have not been an idle spectator of this great contest, and to amuse you with the sentiments of an old friend upon an important subject, I inclose you a copy of the first draught of the Declaration of Rights just as it was drawn by me and presented to the Virginia Convention, where it received few alterations, some of them, I think, not for the better. This was the first thing of the kind upon the continent, and has been closely imitated by all the other States. There is a remarkable sameness in all the forms of government throughout the American Union, except in the States of South Carolina and Pennsylvania ; the first having three branches of legislature, and the last only one. All the other States have two. This difference has given general disgust, and it is probable an alteration will soon take place to assimilate these to the constitutions of the other States. We have laid our new government upon a broad foundation, and have endeavored to provide the most effectual securities for the essential rights of human nature, both in civil and religious liberty.   The people become every day more and more attached to it, and I trust that neither the power of Great Britain, nor the power of Hell will be able to prevail against it.   There was never an idler or a falser notion than that which the British ministry have imposed upon the nation, that this great Revolution has been the work of a faction, of a junto of ambitious men, against the sense of the people of America.   On the contrary, nothing has been done without the approbation of the people, who have indeed outrun their leaders, so that no capital measure hath been adopted until they called loudly for it.   To any one who knows mankind there needs no greater proof than the cordial manner in which they have co-operated, and the patience and perseverance with which they have struggled under their sufferings, which have been greater than you at a distance can conceive, or I describe.

"Equally false is the assertion that independence was originally designed here.   Things have gone such lengths that it is a matter of moonshine to us whether independence was at first intended or not, and therefore we may now be believed.   The truth is, we have been forced into it as the only means of self-preservation, to guard our country and posterity from the greatest of all evils, such another infernal government (if it deserves the name of government) as the Provinces groaned under in the latter ages of the Roman Commonwealth.   To talk of replacing us in the situation of 1763, as we first asked, is to the last degree absurd and impossible.   They obstinately refused it while it was in their power, and now that it is out of their power they offer it.   Can they raise our cities out of their ashes?   Can they replace in ease and affluence the thousands of families whom they have ruined?   Can they restore the husband to the widow, the child to the parent, or the father to the orphan?   In a word, can they reanimate the dead?   Our country has been made a scene of desolation and blood.   Enormities and cruelties have been committed here which not only disgrace the British name, but dishonor the human-kind.   We can never again trust a people who have thus served us ; human nature revolts at the idea.   The die is cast, the rubicon is passed, and a reconciliation with Great Britain upon the terms of returning to her government is impossible. No man was more warmly attached to the Hanover family and the Whig interest of England than I was ; and few men had stronger prejudices in favor of that form of government under which I was born and bred, or a greater aversion to changing it. It was ever my opinion, that no good man would wish to try so dangerous an experiment upon any speculative notions whatsoever, without an absolute necessity. The ancient poets, in their elegant manner of expression, have made a kind of being of necessity, and tell us that the gods themselves are obliged to yield to her.

"When I was first a member of the Convention I exerted myself to prevent a confiscation of the King's Quit Rents, and although I was for putting the country immediately into a state of defence, and preparing for the worst, yet as long as we had any well-founded hopes of reconciliation, I opposed to the utmost of my power all violent measures, and such as might shut the door to it. But when reconciliation became a lost hope, when unconditional submission or effectual resistance were the only alternatives left us, when the last dutiful and humble petition from Congress received no other answer than declaring us rebels and out of the King's protection, I from that moment looked forward to a revolution and independence as the only means of salvation ; and will risk the last penny of my fortune, and the last drop of my blood, upon the issue. For to imagine that we could resist the efforts of Great Britain still professing ourselves her subjects, or support a defensive war against a powerful nation, without the reins of government in the hands of America (whatever our pretended friends in Great Britain may say of it), is too childish and futile an idea to enter into the head of any man of sense. I am not singular in my opinions : these are the sentiments of more than nine tenths of the best men in America.

"God has been pleased to bless our endeavors in a just cause with remarkable success. To us upon the spot who have seen step by step the progress of this great contest, who know the defenceless state of America in the beginning, and the numberless difficulties we have had to struggle with, taking a retrospective view of what is passed, we seem to have been treading upon enchanted ground. The case is now altered, American prospects brighten and appearances are strongly in our favor. The British ministry must and will acknowledge us independent States, but (judging the future by the past) if they act consistently, they will delay this until mutual injuries and resentments are further aggravated, until our growing prejudices against Great Britain are more firmly rooted, and until we become better reconciled to foreign manufactures and foreign manners. It will not require many years to accomplish this, and then the wisdom of British councils will seize the auspicious moment to recognize the independence of America.

"The present plan of the British ministry seems to be to corrupt and bribe the Congress ; but in this, as they have in everything else, they will be disappointed ; not that I imagine that there are no rotten members in so numerous a body of men. Among the twelve apostles there was a Judas—but they are too much in the power of the Assemblies of their respective States, and so thoroughly amenable to the people, that no man among them, who values his own life, dares to tamper ; and upon this rock the safety of America is founded.

"I have thus given you a long and faithful, and I fear you will think a tedious account of the political state of affairs here ; my opportunities of knowing them are equal to most men's, and the natural anxiety you must have to be well informed of the situation of your native country, at so important a crisis, will apologize for the trouble.

"We have had 200,000 acres of land laid off, marked and bounded in one survey for the Ohio [Company]." [1]

---

[1] An incomplete copy of this letter is preserved in the Mason family, and among the Lee Papers, Harvard University, is a copy with several paragraphs in addition, though the conclusion and signature are wanting. The letter was first published in Niles' "Principles and Acts of the Revolution," from the Mason draft.

CHAPTER IX.

VIRGINIA AND THE LAND COMPANIES.

1778–1779.

Through this letter to Colonel Mercer, of 1778, we look in upon the family circle at "Gunston Hall," and see the grave statesman surrounded by his sons and daughters, some of them now grown to manhood and womanhood, and the eldest daughter, who so resembled her mother in character, presiding over her widowed father's house. The first marriage in the family had just taken place. The second daughter, Sarah, then about twenty, married Daniel McCarty, Jr., the son of Col. Daniel McCarty, of "Mount Airy," in Fairfax County. The young couple settled at "Cedar Grove," in the same neighborhood. Of this sister, her brother, John Mason, used to say in after years, that he never remembered to have heard her speak a cross word. A lovely portrait of her is preserved by her descendants, taken in her widowhood, when about forty, with the delicate features and auburn hair inherited from her mother, framed in a close-fitting widow's cap. It will be seen from Colonel Mason's account of his political career, that he had been elected more than once to the Council, but had refused this place, as well as a seat in the Continental Congress, desiring only to be "an independent representative of the people in the House of Delegates." The Virginia planter, obliged to send abroad for many of the household stuffs required in his family, and now cut off from Great Britain, and, by the progress of the war, finding it difficult to communicate with France, was in some perplexity on this score, in 1778, as will be seen by the following letters from Colonel Mason to Richard Harrison, merchant in Martinique :

VIRGINIA, GUNSTON HALL,
October 24th, 1778.

DEAR SIR :

I sent you by Capt. John Sanford of the sloop *Flying-Fish*, last voyage, a few silver dollars, to discharge the little balance you was so kind to advance for me, in the goods purchased and sent me by him from Martinique ; but he informed me, upon his return, that not meeting with any safe opportunity of sending the money from St. Eustatia he had brought it back again. I therefore desired him to carry it out again, this last voyage, and if he did not find you at St. Eustatia (as he told me he expected) to endeavour to give it a conveyance from thence to you to Martinique.

I am uneasy at not having heard anything respecting the goods you ordered for me last year from France, and must beg you will let me know whether you have any, and what late advices concerning them. As hostilities are now commenced between France and England, and they seem to be making very free with each others' ships, they will be probably in as great danger in a French bottom, coming to the West Indies, as to this continent. Will it not therefore be better, if they are not yet shipped for Martinique, to direct your correspondent to ship them immediately to Virginia, in the first good vessel, and consign them to me ? In which case I would have a proper insurance made on them in France, and in case of loss, the goods reshipped as before and again insured. However, I submit this to you, not doubting but you will do therein for the best ; and remain, dear Sir,

Your most obedient servant,

G. MASON.

To Richard Harrison, Esq :
Merchant in Martinique.

Capt. Johns,
of the *Dolphin.*[1]

---

[1] MS. Letter.

Richard Harrison had returned to Virginia when George Mason wrote again.

GUNSTON HALL, November 9, 1778.

DEAR SIR ·

I have your favor of the 5th inst. and heartily congratulate you on your safe return to your native country and friends.

I set off to-morrow morning for the Assembly. I expect mv stay in Williamsburg will be pretty long, during which, if anything should occur in which I can serve you there it will give me pleasure.

I hardly know what steps will be best to take with respect to Mr. Lemozin. It really looks as if he preferred keeping the money in his hands to sending out the goods ordered. I shall be a considerable loser by his negligence, even if he now sends the goods, as the hostilities between the French and English make the risk much greater, and consequently the insurance higher, whereas if he had sent them out at first, they would have come with very little charge to Martinique, and almost the only risk would have been from thence hither. As the bills and invoice were remitted in your name, I can't with propriety, write to him, or give orders on the subject, and must therefore beg the favor of you to do it, by different opportunities, desiring him to send the goods immediately, by the first good vessel to Virginia, if they are not already shipped to Martinique, reminding him to insure, and in case of loss to reship the same articles and insure again. It will be most convenient to have them sent to Potomac, but as an opportunity for that purpose may not speedily offer, if they are sent to James or York river, I would have them addressed to the care of Col. William Aylett at Williamsburg ; if to Rappahannock, to the care of Col. Thos. Jett, merchant near Leeds Tavern. I think it may not be amiss to mention to Mr. Lemozin his very extraordinary delay in this business, and the inconvenience and loss incurred by it, and to let him know that if the order is not speedily executed, the money will be drawn out of his hands, and put into those of some other merchants who will be more punctual. Or if you have any other correspondent at this place, whom you think safe, I believe it might be well to desire the favor of him to make inquiry about it, or to send him a draft on Mr. Lemozin for the money, in case the goods are not bought when it arrives, for I presume if they are not by that time they never will by that gentleman.

Upon the whole, I leave it entirely to you, sir, to take such measures therein as you judge best, and am, dear sir,

Your most obedient servant,

GEORGE MASON.

Richard Harrison, Esq ·
Alexandria.[1]

The Assembly met on the 5th of October, and Colonel Mason was not in his place. The House was called over two days later, and both George and Thomson Mason were among the missing members who were ordered to be taken into custody by the sergeant-at-arms. Thomson Mason arrived in the sergeant's custody on the 23d, and was obliged to pay fees; but it was not until the 19th of November that Colonel Mason "attended, in custody of the sergeant-at-arms, and was discharged, paying fees."[2] In the meantime Thomson Mason had been placed on the more prominent committees, and was employed on the business of the important memorials presented to the House. He was made chairman of the committee who were appointed to search the public records for papers on the subject of the claim of Richard Henderson & Company. The case was heard at the bar of the House, and it was decided that all purchases made from the Indians, of lands within the chartered boundaries of Virginia should be considered void, and the purchase of Henderson & Company was of this nature; but that in consideration of the expense they had incurred in quieting the Indians and making settlements, some compensation should be made them. Thomson Mason was then made chairman of the committee appointed to decide what compensation was equitable.[3] No doubt Colonel Mason was corresponding with his brother at this time, and felt it less obligatory to hasten his own arrival in the

---

[1] MS. Letter. [2] Journal of the Assembly. [3] *Ibid.*

20

Assembly, as Thomson Mason was present and could attend to this business for him.

On the 4th of November Colonel Wood of the 8th Virginia regiment presented a memorial, setting forth the sufferings of the soldiers. A committee of five was appointed to confer with Colonel Wood on this subject. Thomson Mason was on this committee, and a bill was brought in for supplying the deficiency of the Virginia troops in the Continental service. A letter from Colonel Wood to General Washington, dated the 12th of November, enables us to look in upon the Virginia Assembly at this time. But the soldier's view of the military situation was by no means that of the more sanguine legislators, it would appear. And the slow methods of the law-makers were not to the taste of the impatient warrior.

"WILLIAMSBURG, 12th November, 1778.

"SIR·

"I have been here near three weeks without being able, as yet, to get a final determination on any part of the business I came to transact. On my arrival, I discovered that the whole legislative body were highly pleased, with a thorough persuasion, that the war was at an end, that the British troops were embarking, and that there was not the most distant probability they would again return to the continent. On Gov. Henry's laying your Excellency's letter before the House, I was happy to find it effectually roused them from their lethargy. They immediately appointed Mr. Mason, Mr. Page, Mr. Nelson, and Mr. Parker a committee to confer with me on the state of the troops belonging to the Virginia line. . . . A great part of the present session has been taken up in considering the grants made by the Cherokees to Henderson and Company, which they have at last declared totally void. I shall continue here till the bill for recruiting the regiments passes, and other matters respecting the army are considered, which I am afraid will not be long before Christmas, if I am to judge from their manner of doing business. . . ." [1]

[1] "Correspondence of the American Revolution," Sparks, vol. ii., p. 229.

Colonel Clark had been successful in his expedition, and with Virginia troops had conquered for his State the large domain in the Northwest, already hers by charter right, now to be known as the county of Illinois. And on the 19th of November, the day George Mason arrived in the Assembly, the letters and papers of Colonel Clark were read and referred to a committee composed of Thomson Mason, George Mason, and others, who accordingly prepared a bill "for establishing a county to include the inhabitants of this commonwealth, on the western side of the Ohio River, and for the better government of those inhabitants."[1] The next day a petition of the Ohio Company was brought before the House asking that those members living in Maryland and Virginia receive land patents as soon as a land-office is established, "each in his own name, for his due share or proportion of two hundred thousand acres of said grant." This was the land surveyed for the company to which Colonel Mason makes reference in the letter to George Mercer. And doubtless George Mason presented the petition. He was placed this day on five committees—that of Privileges and Elections, Propositions and Grievances, the Committee on Trade, that for appointing commissioners to ascertain the claims to unpatented lands, and the committee for settling a compensation for Richard Henderson and Company. On the 21st a memorial was presented to the House by George Mason and ordered to be read at a future day. A resolution of thanks to Colonel Clark was passed by the House on the 23d, acknowledging the country's indebtedness to this officer, who "with a body of Virginia militia has reduced the British posts in the western parts of this commonwealth, on the river Mississippi and its branches." Colonel Mason was put on two other committees at this time, charged with preparing bills providing against invasions and insurrections, and to ascertain the mode of impressing wagons and horses. George Mason's memorial was read on this day, "setting forth that he hath a claim to a consider-

[1] Journal of the Assembly.

able quantity of land upon the western waters, due to him upon charter importation rights, which hath been recognized by the Governor and Council during the British government, as legal and valid : that conscious of the uprightness of his conduct and soundness of his title, he has proceeded to locate and survey the lands which he thus claims, in the most legal and authentic manner ; and praying that his title and locations and surveys may be confirmed." [1]

Jefferson made his appearance in the Assembly on the last day of November, and on this day the bill for establishing the county of Illinois was brought in by Thomson Mason, chairman of the committee charged to prepare it. A bill amending the act to establish a board of auditors was committed to Jefferson, George Mason, and several others. And both George and Thomson Mason were united with Jefferson, Tyler, and one other member, in preparing a bill for establishing a court of appeals. The memorial of the Indiana Company, and their claim to certain lands purchased of the Indians at Fort Stanwix in 1768, was deferred for consideration to the May session. Colonel Mason, on the 12th of December, gave in the report of the committee to whom the disputed boundary question between Virginia and Pennsylvania had been referred. It was resolved that the southern boundary offered by the Pennsylvania Assembly was inadmissible, and that unless the whole offer made by Virginia was accepted no part of it would be considered binding. And it was proposed that commissioners from each State should meet and fix the boundaries.

On the 15th George Mason presented a bill to prohibit the distillation of spirits from corn, wheat, rye, and other grain, for a limited period. And he was at this time appointed, with one other member of the Assembly, to bring in a bill for the more general diffusion of knowledge. The action of the Assembly, the year before, for establishing schools in Virginia was one of the public measures for which Tucker gives Jefferson the chief credit. But in all probability

[1] *Ibid.*

George Mason had quite as much to do with it; and the bill on the subject passed at this session was his work. Colonel Mason was also on the committee to whom a memorial from William and Mary College had been referred, asking for aid to carry on their work of education. Letters from the governor, from the president of Congress, and the Virginia delegates were received on the 15th, and referred to a select committee of which George Mason was chairman. Jefferson and Thomson Mason were named immediately after him on the committee. Colonel Mason reported, the next day, from this committee the following resolutions:

" That all persons exporting grain or other victual contrary to the act of Assembly laying an embargo for a certain time, ought to be rendered incapable of carrying on any trade or commerce within the commonwealth of Virginia ; and that the master of any vessel building within the State of Virginia, or coming into it, shall give bond with sufficient security, to the naval officer of the district, that he will not, during the stay of the vessel, load or take on board any articles other than shall be necessary for sustenance of the crew for her voyage ; that persons who purchase grain or other victual, other than for the consumption of their families, or for manufacture, ought to be declared by law engrossers ; and that persons who illegally take upon themselves the character of public agents or contractors, should be punished."

And in accordance with these resolutions, George Mason, on the 18th, presented a bill for the more effectual execution of the act, laying an embargo for a limited time. The following day Colonel Mason brought in a bill explaining the act to enable the officers of the Virginia line, and to encourage the soldiers of the same, to continue in continental service. A resolution to raise a regiment of six hundred men to guard British prisoners, and for other purposes, was carried to the Senate for confirmation by Thomson Mason. And resolutions to instruct the board of commissioners to make such alterations in the arrangements of the navy, and to direct such fortifications and batteries on Chesapeake Bay as might be deemed necessary for the protection of trade, were carried to the Senate by George Mason.[1] And a message from the House to the Senate was delivered by Colonel Mason on the 19th, which was to this effect :

" That they have agreed to a resolution, that a certain tract of country, to be bounded by the Green River, and a southeast course from the head thereof to the Cumberland mountains, with the said mountains to the Carolina line, with the Carolina line to the Cherokee or Tennessee River, with the said river to the Ohio River, and with the Ohio to the said Green River, ought to be reserved for supplying the officers and soldiers in the Virginia line, with the respective proportions of land, which have been or may be assigned to them by the General Assembly, saving and reserving the land granted to Richard Henderson and Company, and their legal rights to such persons as have heretofore actually located lands and settled thereon, within the bounds aforesaid." [2]

This tract of land embraced a large portion of the State of Kentucky. The Virginia Assembly adjourned on this day, the 19th of December, getting through their work before Christmas, contrary to Colonel Wood's forebodings. It will be seen that this had been a busy session for Colonel Mason, and that he and his brother Thomson had been foremost in all its legislation.

One of the most important acts of the Assembly at this time was to provide for the government of the domain recently secured to Virginia by Colonel Clark. And it is an interesting circumstance to record in connection with George Mason, that the most valuable contemporary information as to this brilliant expedition of Clark's is to be found in a letter addressed by him to his friend and patron at " Gunston Hall." The letter of George Rogers Clark to Governor Jefferson from Kaskaskias, written in April, 1779,

[1] *Ibid.*   [2] Journal of the Senate.

gives an official account of his exploits, which is not nearly so full as the recital he makes Colonel Mason.[1] From this letter to George Mason, presented by him to the Kentucky Historical Society, we learn of the almost paternal relation which Mason seemed to hold to the impetuous and gallant young soldier, and of the warm regard and esteem that subsisted between the two friends. Unfortunately no letter of Mason to Clark has been preserved, and of the latter's letters to Colonel Mason there is but the one memorial remaining of what was doubtless a not infrequent correspondence. Colonel Clark, whom John Randolph, of Roanoke, calls the American Hannibal, and whose expedition across the drowned lands of the Wabash he compares to the African general's passage of the Thrasimene marsh, gives in simple and graphic detail the story of his arduous achievements. He wrote from Louisville on the 19th of November, 1779, and prefaces his recital with the following respectful and affectionate apology for former negligence :

" My Dear Sir : Continue to favor me with your valuable lessons ; continue your reprimands as though I was your son ; when suspicious think not that promotion or conferred honor will occasion any unnecessary pride in me ; you have infused too many of your valuable precepts in me to be guilty of the like, or to show any indifference to those that ought to be dear to me. It is with pleasure that I obey in transmitting to you a short sketch of my enterprise and proceeding in the Illinois, as near as I can recollect, or gather from memorandums." [2]

We follow the writer, then, in his narration of the journey into the wilderness, to these remote posts, and see his firm yet conciliating treatment of the citizens in the old French

[1] A letter written to Patrick Henry, then Governor of Virginia, by Colonel Clark, on the 24th of February, 1779, the day of Governor Hamilton's surrender, captured by the British and lost sight of for more than a century, is in the Haldimand Collection, British Museum, and a copy of it is at Ottawa, Canada.

[2] Clark's " Campaign in the Illinois," Cincinnati, 1869.

towns, and his bold and skilful policy with the Indians.   Of the latter he writes :

" It may appear otherwise to you, but I always thought we took wrong methods of treating with Indians, and strove as soon as possible to make myself acquainted with the French and Spanish mode, which must be preferable to ours, otherwise they could not possibly have such great influence among them ; when acquainted with it, it exactly coincided with my own idea, and I resolved to follow that same rule as near as circumstances would permit."

After the capture of Kaskaskias, on the Mississippi, Clark, leaving the town in charge of some of his men, went on to La Prairie du Rocher (*Lapraraderush*, Clark spells it).

"The ladies and gentlemen immediately assembled at a ball for our entertainment ; we spent the forepart of the night very agreeably, but about 12 o'clk. there was a very sudden change, by an express arriving informing us that Gov. Hamilton [military governor of Detroit] was within three miles."

Great was the confusion that followed ; but Colonel Clark, while promptly making his arrangements to return to the fort, was resolved, with true soldierly nonchalance, to enjoy the passing hour.   " I thanked them," he says, " for the care they had of my person, and told them it was the fate of war, that a good soldier never ought to be afraid of his life where there was a probability of his doing service by venturing of it, which was my case.   That I hoped that they would not let the news spoil our diversion sooner than was necessary, and that we would divert ourselves until our horses was ready, forced them to dance, and endeavored to appear as unconcerned as if no such thing was in agitation.   This conduct inspired the young men in such a manner that many of them was getting their horses to share fate with me." Clark, though, fully felt the gravity of the situation, as he tells his correspondent.   However, Governor Hamilton did not come.   Yet, a little later, the young commander adds : " Our situation still appeared desperate, it was at this moment I would have bound myself seven years a slave to have had five hundred troops." Captain McCarty and his men were sent for from the little French village where they had been stationed, and then followed the difficult and distressing march from Kaskaskias to Vincennes. The low lands were flooded, the soldiers had nothing to eat, and their sufferings from hunger and exposure were terrible. Colonel Clark says of this episode:

"If I was sensible that you would let no person see this relation, I would give you a detail of our sufferings for four days in crossing these waters, and the manner it was done, as I am sure that you would credit it; but it is too incredible for any person to believe except those that are well acquainted with me as you are, or had experienced something similar to it. I hope you will excuse me until I have the pleasure of seeing you personally."

Safely on dry ground again, they lay for some time in a grove of trees to dry their clothes by the sun's heat. "A thousand ideas flushed in my head at this moment," writes Clark, and he tells of his plans, and the dangers and contingencies that seemed imminent. But his daring and energy were soon to be crowned with success, and Governor Hamilton, completely taken by surprise, became an easy prey.

"In a few hours I found my prize sure, certain of taking every man that I could have wished for, being the whole of those that incited the Indians to war; all my past sufferings vanished; never was a man more happy."

Colonel Clark tells a touching story of an old French gentleman, one of the volunteers that had joined him, who had a son who was in the employment of Hamilton, and at the head of a party of Indians. The American commander had ordered the leader of the Indians to be put to death. He was painted as an Indian warrior, and his father, not knowing who it was, in his zeal stood over the prisoner with drawn sword to prevent his escape. The poor youth, as the executioner's tomahawk was raised to strike him down, cried to heaven for aid in his extremity. The French officer recognized his child's voice, and of course the execution was stayed, and the intercession of the father saved the young man's life. Colonel Clark concludes his letter thus: "I shall not for the future leave it in your power to accuse me for a neglect of friendship, but shall continue to transmit to you whatever I think worth your notice" And he then adds in a postscript :

" As for the description of the Illinois country, which you seem so anxious for, you may expect to have by the ensuing fall, as I expect by that period to be able to give you a more general idea of it. The different nations of Indians, their traditions, numbers, &c., you may expect in my next." [1]

It can easily be imagined with what pleasure this recital of interesting and heroic adventure was read aloud to the family circle at "Gunston." Colonel Clark had probably been a frequent visitor there, and was regarded with pride and affection by the head of the house, who advised and counselled his young friend evidently as if he were a son. George Rogers Clark was at this time about twenty-five. He was a native of Albemarle County, but had been for several years a resident of Kentucky. Already distinguished in the border warfare as well as in the civil affairs of his new home, and identified in later life with its fortunes, he is claimed as one of the founders of this commonwealth. Kentucky, however, was at this time a Virginia county, and it was as a Virginian and at the head of two or three thousand Virginia troops that Colonel Clark conquered for his State the new county of Illinois, from which five commonwealths were to emerge later.

Colonel Mason wrote to General Washington on the 8th of March, 1779, asking for letters of introduction for his eldest son, George, who was about to sail to Europe for his health. And Washington replied promptly to his friend's request.

[1] *Ibid.*

Virginia, Gunston Hall,
Dear General :   March 8, 1779.

I shall make no other apology for my long silence, than can. didly telling you the cause of it. Sensible of the constant and great load of public business upon your hands, and knowing how little time you had to spare, I thought it was wrong to intrude upon it, by a correspondence of mere private friendship, or the communication of matters of little importance. This and this only, is the reason I have not wrote to you frequently, for I can truly say there is not a man in the world who more cordially wishes you every blessing, has a higher sense of the important services you have rendered our common country, or who feels more satisfaction in being informed of your prosperity and welfare. And if anything should occur in your affairs here, in which I can be of any manner of service, you can't confer a greater obligation on me than giving me the occasion.

I have at this time, sir, a particular favor to beg of you. My son George, who has been long afflicted with an obstinate rheumatic complaint, for which he has used the Berkley and Augusta Springs in vain, has determined to try the effect of some of the southern climates of Europe, for a year or two, and intends to go out in a vessel which will sail soon from Alexandria. Whether he will fix his residence in France, Spain, or Italy, must depend upon the advice of the physicians in Paris ; but most probably it will be at Montpelier, or somewhere in the south of France. And as I have no acquaintance, and he will be an utter stranger in France, you will oblige me exceedingly by giving him letters of introduction, as the son of a friend of yours, to the Marquis de la Fayette and Doctor Franklin, at Paris, whose notice will be a great satisfaction and advantage to him.

I have also another affair to trouble you with. There is one, Mr. Smith, from Loudon County, who entered as a lieutenant in the regiment of riflemen first raised by Mr. Stinson, and afterwards commanded by Col. Rawlins. He was taken prisoner at Fort Washington, and has remained in the enemy's hands ever since, under very harsh treatment. His wife, who is said to be a worthy woman, and has a number of small children, is exceedingly distressed by her husband's long captivity. She has heard from him lately, and upon his telling her that he had no prospect of being exchanged soon, she is apprehensive that by some mistake, he has been overlooked in the course of the cartel, and not had his due turn, and has therefore applied to me to ask the favor of you to cause an enquiry to be made concerning him, and direct his being exchanged as soon as it can regularly be done.

I beg you will pardon this trouble, and believe me, with the greatest sincerity, dear sir,

Your most affectionate & obdt. servant,

G. Mason.[1]

CAMP AT MIDDLEBROOK,
March 27, 1779.

Dear Sir :

By some interruption of the last week's mail, your favor of the 8th did not reach my hands till last night. Under cover of this, Mr. Mason (if he should not have sailed,) to whom I heartily wish a perfect restoration of health, will receive two letters : one of them to the Marquis de la Fayette, and the other to Doctor Franklin, in furnishing which I am happy, as I wish for instances in which I can testify the sincerity of my regard for you.

Our commissary of prisoners hath been invariably and pointedly instructed to exchange those officers first, who were first captivated, as far as rank will apply, and I have every reason to believe he has obeyed the order, as I have refused a great many applications for irregular exchanges in consequence, and I did it because I would not depart from my principle, and thereby incur the charge of partiality. It sometimes happens, that officers later in captivity than others, have been exchanged before them, but it is in cases where the ranks of the enemy's officers in our possession do not apply to the latter. There is a prospect now, I think, of a general exchange taking place, which will be very pleasing to the parties and their connexions, and will be a means of relieving much distress to individuals, though it may not, circumstanced as we are at this time, be advantageous to us considered in a national and political point of view. Partial exchanges have, for some time past, been discontinued by the enemy.

Though it is not in my power to devote much time to private correspondences, owing to the multiplicity of public letters (and

---

[1] Washington MSS., Department of State.

other business) I have to read, write, and transact, yet I can with great truth assure you, that it would afford me very singular pleasure to be favored, at all times, with your sentiments in a leisure hour, upon public matters of general concernment, as well as those which more immediately respect your own State (if proper conveyances would render prudent a free communication). I am particularly desirous of it at this time, because I view things very differently, I fear, from what people in general do, who seem to think that the contest is at an end, and to make money, and to get places, the only thing now remaining to do. I have seen without despondency, (even for a moment,) the hours which America has styled her gloomy ones—but I have beheld no day since the commencement of hostilities, that I have thought her liberties in such imminent danger as at the present. Friends and foes seem now to combine to pull down the goodly fabric we have hitherto been raising at the expense of so much time, blood, and treasure, and unless the bodies politic will exert themselves to bring things back to first principles, correct abuses, and punish our internal foes, inevitable ruin must follow. Indeed we seem to be verging so fast to destruction, that I am filled with sensations to which I have been a stranger, till within these three months. Our enemy behold with exultation and joy, how effectually we labor for their benefit, and from being in a state of absolute despair and on the point of evacuating America, are now on tiptoe. Nothing, therefore, in my judgment, can save us, but a total reformation in our conduct, or some decisive turn to affairs in Europe. The former, alas! to our shame be it spoken! is less likely to happen than the latter, as it is now consistent with the views of the speculators—various tribes of money makers—and stockjobbers of all denominations, to continue the war for their own private emolument, without considering that their avarice and thirst for gain must plunge everything (including themselves) in one common ruin.

Were I to indulge my present feelings and give a loose to that freedom of expression which my unreserved friendship for you would prompt me to, I should say a great deal on this subject. But letters are liable to so many accidents, and the sentiments of men in office sought after by the enemy with so much avidity, and besides conveying useful knowledge (if they get into their hands) for the superstructure of their plans, are often perverted to the worst of purposes, that I shall be somewhat reserved, notwithstanding this letter goes by private hand to Mount Vernon.   I cannot refrain lamenting, however, in the most poignant terms, the fatal policy too prevalent in most of the States, of employing their ablest men at home in posts of honor or profit, till the great national interests are fixed upon a solid basis.   To me it appears no unjust simile to compare the affairs of this great continent to the mechanism of a clock, each State representing some one or the other of the smaller parts of it, which they are endeavoring to put in fine order, without considering how useless and unavailing their labor, unless the great wheel or spring which is to set the whole in motion, is also well attended to and kept in good order.   I allude to no particular State, nor do I mean to cast reflections upon any one of them— nor ought I, it may be said, to do so upon their representatives ; but as it is a fact too notorious to be concealed, that C—— is rent by party—that much business of a trifling nature and personal concernment withdraws their attention from matters of great national moment at this critical period—when it is also known that idleness and dissipation takes place of close attention and application, no man who wishes well to the liberties of his country, and desires to see its rights established, can avoid crying out :   Where are our men of abilities ?   Why do they not come forth to save their country ?   Let this voice, my dear sir, call upon you, Jefferson, and others.   Do not, from a mistaken opinion, that we are about to sit down under our own vine and our own fig tree—let our hitherto noble struggle end in ignominy. Believe me when I tell you there is danger of it.   I have pretty good reasons for thinking, that [the] administration a little while ago had resolved to give the matter up, and negotiate a peace with us upon almost any terms ; but I shall be much mistaken if they do not now, from the present state of our currency, dissentions, and other circumstances, push matters to the utmost extremity.   Nothing, I am sure, will prevent it, but the interposition of Spain and their disappointed hopes from Russia.

I thank you most cordially, for your kind offer of rendering me service.   I shall without reserve, as heretofore, call upon you whenever circumstances occur that may require it, being with the sincerest regard, dear sir, your most obedient and affectionate humble servant,

GO. WASHINGTON.

George Mason, Esq., Gunston Hall.[1]

The preceding letter of Washington's presents a gloomy picture of American affairs as seen through the eyes of the anxious commander-in-chief. Since the battle of Monmouth the previous June, there had been no important engagement. The army was in winter quarters in New Jersey. Washington had spent five weeks in Philadelphia, in consultation with Congress, and a defensive campaign had been resolved upon. The party dissensions in Congress had impressed Washington most unfavorably, and he urged it upon George Mason that it was his duty, as it was that of the patriots in general, to come to the aid of the Confederation in their Congress rather than to remain in the State legislature. Washington had written in a similar strain to Benjamin Harrison the previous December, using the image which appears in the letter to Colonel Mason, comparing the political system to the mechanism of a clock. And this favorite figure is repeated in a letter to Archibald Cary some years later. " I cannot help asking," writes Washington to Harrison, "where are Mason, Wythe, Jefferson, Nicholas, Pendleton, Nelson, and another I could name?"[2] Congress was about to lose another eminent Virginian. Richard Henry Lee sent in his resignation at the May session of the Assembly, confessing his disgust in a letter to Jefferson, having been persecuted, as he declared, "by the united voice of toryism, speculation, faction, envy, malice, and all uncharitableness." He hopes that he will not be blamed for this step, but he thinks he is powerless alone to do any service. "It would content me, indeed," he adds, "to sacrifice every consideration to the public good, that

---

[1] " Virginia Historical Register," vol. v., p. 96.   Bancroft's " History of the Constitution," vol. i., Appendix, 281.

[2] " Life and Writings of Washington," Sparks, vol. vi., p. 150.

would result from such persons as yourself, Mr. Wythe, Mr. Mason, and some others being in Congress; I would struggle with persevering ardor through every difficulty in conjunction with such associates." [1]

The following letter from Colonel Mason to Richard Henry Lee, thanking him for letters of introduction to be used by his son, George Mason, Jr., in France, is full of interest.

GUNSTON HALL, April 12, 1779.

DEAR SIR :

I am much obliged to you for the letters you sent my son George. He sailed last week for Cadiz, in a fine sloop, mounting eight carriage and ten swivel guns. His present plan is to go from Cadiz up the Straits, in some neutral bottom with a Mediterranean pass, to Toulon or Marseilles, and as he will probably not go to Nantes (at least for some considerable time) he will forward your letter to your son, post paid from Cadiz ; unless some vessel is going from thence to that part of France. When I wrote to you this sloop was intended for Holland, but her destination was changed.

I observe, by a late publication, Congress expects Great Britain will carry into execution her threats of a predatory vindictive war. I have no objection to the Fast they have recommended ; these solemnities, if properly observed, and not too often repeated, have a good effect upon the minds of the people ; and if ever there was a national cause in which the Supreme Being could be safely and confidently appealed to, ours is one ; but at the same time, no necessary measure on our part should be omitted. I can not but think it would have good effects if a manifesto was published upon the occasion, and a particular recommendation to the different States of the Union to cause exact accounts and valuations to be made of all the private property which the British forces shall wantonly destroy, or the devastations they may make contrary to the practice and custom of civilized nations ; that compensation may be demanded, whenever a negotiation shall take place, and if refused, that the damage may be levied upon Great Britain by duties upon what-

---

[1] "Life of R. H. Lee," by Richard H. Lee, vol. ii., p. 45.

ever trade she may at any time hereafter carry on with the United States.—Being warned that her mischief must one day fall upon her own head, may be a means of restraining her, and at any rate it is a piece of justice due to the sufferers.

I see the Maryland Declaration upon the subject of confederation, and their modest claim to part of the back lands, after skulking in the dark for several months, has at last made its appearance : it has confirmed me in an opinion I have long had, that the secret and true cause of the great opposition to Virginia's title to her chartered territory was the great Indian purchase between the Obache and the Illinois Rivers, made in the year 1773 or 1774, in which Governor Johnston and several of the leading men in Maryland are concerned with Lord Dunmore, Governor Tryon, and many other noblemen and gentlemen of Great Britain. Do you observe the care Governor Johnston (for I dare say the Declaration is his manufacture) has taken to save this Indian purchase. In the explanatory articles which the Maryland Assembly require before they will accede to the Confederation, after reserving the back lands as a common stock to the United States, is the following exception : "not granted to, surveyed for, or *purchased by* individuals at the commencement of the present war." Were Congress to declare that every purchase of lands heretofore made, or hereafter to be made of any Indian nation, except by public authority and upon public account should be void, it would, in my opinion, be more effectual, upon this subject, than all the argument in the world. Had the British ministry employed a Mansfield or a Wedderburne to have managed the matter they could not more effectually have pleaded the cause of Great Britain than this Declaration has. In the year 1744 when the Canada Bill was passed by the British Parliament, the bounds of that province were extended so as to include the whole country between the Ohio and the Mississippi Rivers ; this being before the rupture between Great Britain and her colonies, the Parliament's authority to pass such a bill cannot be impeached upon any other ground than the right of some of the old colonies to that country by their charters. Aware of this and to prevent giving too great an alarm, a clause of exception was inserted, saving to any of the colonies the territory within their respective charters ; but the

21

Declaration, denying the right of any of the States by their charters, if it proves anything, proves that all that country is part of the British province of Canada ; and unless the United States conquer Canada by force of arms, what claim have we upon it, or what arguments could we urge in a negotiation with Great Britain, for curtailing the bounds of Canada, as settled by the Canada Bill, but that the country they included was part of the chartered territory of the other colonies, at the time the said bill passed, and the consequences of suffering the bounds of Canada to remain, in that extended manner, surrounding great part of the United States, are too obvious to mention.

We have no news, except that report says things are going badly to the southward, but of the state [of affairs] I presume Congress has authentic accounts. It is highly probable that the enemy's view is to trail our main army by a long and painful march to the Southern part of the United States ; but I think we had better risk anything that can happen there than make such an experiment. I sincerely wish you health and happiness, and am,

Dear sir,

Your affectionate friend and servant,

G. MASON.[1]

The plan Colonel Mason proposes for retaliatory measures on the enemy, he elaborated later in a letter to be submitted to Congress. His shrewd observations on the articles of the Maryland Assembly, and the consequences that could be drawn from their stipulations, merit special attention. The Articles of Confederation were finally signed in this year by Maryland, the last State to accede to them.

The Virginia Assembly met on the 3d of May, 1779, and both George and Thomson Mason were delegates. The latter was elected from Elizabeth City County ; and having after his election changed his residence, he sent in his resignation, but the House would not accept it.[2] At the follow-

---

[1] Mason Papers.

[2] William C. Rives, in a letter to one of Thomson Mason's descendants, refers to this action of the Assembly as "a most emphatic homage to the value of his public services, such an one as was rendered afterwards in the case of Mr. Jefferson."

ing session, Thomson Mason still finding it inconvenient to attend the Assembly, resorted to the expedient of accepting nominally the appointment of coroner, by which means his seat in the House was vacated. The first mention of George Mason in the journal of the Assembly occurs on the 17th of May, when he was made chairman of a committee to prepare a bill " for ascertaining the losses and requiring retribution to the citizens of this commonwealth for depre-dations of the enemy on private property." [1] He was also added to the committees to prepare a bill for establishing a land-office, and to prepare one for the better regulation and disciplining of the militia. Two days later Colonel Mason, Jefferson, and others were appointed a committee to bring in a bill for settling the rate of exchange and mode of judgments on foreign debts, which bill was presented to the House by Colonel Mason on the 15th of June. On the 31st of May, the Speaker laid before the House a letter from the Virginia delegates in Congress, enclosing certain proceedings of the Assembly of Maryland respecting the Confederation, which papers were read and referred to a committee con-sisting of Jefferson, George Mason, and three others.

The ballot for governor was taken on the 1st of June, and Jefferson was elected in the place of Patrick Henry. George Mason was one of a committee of three appointed to notify the new governor of the vote of the Assembly. Colonel Mason was on this day added to the Committee of Propositions and Grievances. The memorial of Penet, Wendall, & Co. was presented to the House on the 2d. setting forth that having agreed with Congress for estab-lishing a manufactory of artillery and small-arms in some one of the States of Virginia, Maryland, Pennsylvania, and Jersey, they have determined on this State, and asking cer-tain advantages may be afforded them by the legislature upon terms and conditions therein expressed. The com-mittee of fourteen to whom the memorial was referred included Colonel Mason, Patrick Henry, Tyler, General

[1] Journal of the Assembly.

Nelson, and other prominent members of the House. On the 4th of June the House went into Committee of the Whole on the state of the Commonwealth, and resolutions were passed respecting aliens, citizenship, and the sale of confiscated property. The committee appointed to bring in the bills for these purposes consisted of Charles Carter, George Mason, Patrick Henry, and five others. Jefferson takes the credit of this measure. He says:

"Early in the session of May, 1779, I prepared and obtained leave to bring in a bill declaring who should be deemed citizens, asserting the natural right of expatriation, and prescribing the mode of exercising it. This, when I withdrew from the House on the 1st of June following, I left in the hands of George Mason, and it was passed on the 26th of that month."[1]

On the 8th and 9th of June, the House discussed the claim of the Indiana Company, and the following resolutions were passed, and were carried to the Senate by George Mason:

"*Resolved*, that the Commonwealth of Virginia hath the exclusive right of a pre-emption, from the Indians, of all lands within the limits of its own chartered territory, as declared by the act and constitution of government in 1776, that no person or persons whatsoever have, or ever had, a right to purchase any lands within the same from any Indian nation except only persons duly authorized to make such purchases on the public account, formerly for the use and benefit of the colony, and lately of the Commonwealth ; and that such exclusive right of pre-emption will and ought to be maintained by this Commonwealth to the utmost of its power.

"*Resolved*, that every purchase of lands heretofore made by the King of Great Britain from any Indian nation or nations within the before-mentioned limits doth and ought to enure for ever to and for the use and benefit of this Commonwealth, and to and for no other purpose whatsoever.

"*Resolved therefore*, that the deed from the Six United Nations of Indians, bearing date on the third day of November, 1768, for

[1] Jefferson's "Works," vol. i., p. 40.

certain lands between the Alleghany Mountains and the river Ohio, above the mouth of the little Kanawha Creek, to and for the use and benefit of a certain William Trent, gentleman, in his own right, and as attorney for sundry persons in the said deed named, as well as all other deeds which have been or shall be made by any Indian or Indians, or by any Indian nation or nations, for lands within the limits of the charter and territory of Virginia as aforesaid, to or for the use or benefit of any private person or persons shall be and the same are hereby declared utterly void, and of no effect." [1]

This is all that appears in the journal in regard to the case of the Indiana Company. It was managed, on the part of the Assembly, by Colonel Mason, who, in a letter written in the latter years of his life, gives his recollections of the matter. In the November session, 1791, Morgan's claim was brought forward, and a final effort made by the company to overturn the Virginia settlement, and George Mason wrote to a member of the House in response to a request for information on the subject ·

" I have searched all my papers endeavoring to find my former argument in the Assembly, when I was appointed to collect the evidence and manage this business on behalf of the commonwealth, which (if I could have found it) would have given the fullest information, but I imagine I must have lent it to some member of the Assembly, who has never returned it ; and conceiving the matter, after so full an investigation and positive determination as it then had, forever at an end, I was the less careful in preserving my notes and papers. Several depositions were then produced, and some witnesses examined at the bar of the House, proving the mysterious and clandestine conduct of Sir William Johnston (the King's agent) at the treaty at Fort Stanwix, when the Indiana Company obtained their deed from the Indians. The council books were also produced, in which were many entries, previous to the Indiana Company's purchase, for lands much further to the westward. The Indiana Company's deed from the Indians was set aside, and a declaratory

[1] Journal of the Assembly.

act passed upon the subject, as well as my memory serves me, in the May session of 1779, principally upon the following points :

"First, the purchase of the same lands from the Six Nations of Indians, at the Treaty of Lancaster, in the year 1740, for the use of Virginia, and paid for with our money. The book containing the records of this treaty and the deed of purchase was then produced, but I have understood has been since destroyed, as well as all the other Indian treaties, made here under the King's government, with the books and papers of the council and of the Committee of Safety, when General Arnold's troops burned the foundry at Westham in which they had been placed upon the enemy's marching towards Richmond.

"Second, because the Six Nations, who originally claimed the lands by conquest, had lost their title (even if they had not sold them at the treaty of Lancaster) by the same means by which they first gained it—conquest—their tributaries and tenants, the Shawnese and Delewares, with a mixture of the Six Nations, having been expelled and driven over the Ohio (from whence they never returned), and the lands on this side the Ohio conquered in the war, which happened a little before the Indiana Company's purchase.

"Third, independent of the above reasons, the deed to the Indiana Company, by the law of Virginia ought to have been recorded (like all other deeds) either in the county where the land lay, as in Augusta, which was the then frontier county of Virginia, or in the general court. That for the want of this, the deed, if there had been no other objection, was void as to all subsequent purchasers, and that the settlers upon the land under Virginia titles, of which there were a great many before the deed was recorded in Augusta, were, in the equitable construction of the law, to be considered as purchasers.

"Fourth, because the consideration of the deed was a compensation to the Indian traders for the losses they had suffered, and it was thought they had no more right to require compensation than a merchant who had his ship taken by an enemy's privateer, or any other sufferer in the common calamities of war.

"Fifth, because the traders to whom the Indian deed was named, being everyone of them citizens of Pennsylvania, from which this trade with the Indians was carried on, if they had been entitled to compensation at all, ought to have had such compensation out of the lands within the chartered territory of Pennsylvania, for whose benefit the trade had been carried on, by her own citizens, and not out of the lands of Virginia ; and this appeared in the strongest, or if I may be allowed the expression, more barefaced point of view, as Pennsylvania had, at that same treaty of Fort Stanwix, made a large purchase from the Indians of land within her own charter. I presume the legislature cannot regularly give any decision in favor of the Indiana Company without repealing the before mentioned declaratory act, and the consequences of such a repeal may extend much farther and produce effects which may not at first be foreseen. Among other things it would certainly open a door to the revival of Col. Henderson's and Company's claim to Kentucky, nor can any man tell where it would end." [1]

It is interesting to compare George Mason's account with the report of his argument made by one of the company whose claims he opposed. He was appointed, we are here told, with another gentleman who did not act, " to manage the interests of the Commonwealth of Virginia, upon this occasion, and the substantial parts of his chief arguments (as taken in writing by a gentleman who attended the House, William Trent, Esq., Member of the House of Assembly of New Jersey) were as follows: Col. Mason insisted greatly upon political expediency. . . . Col. Mason also insisted that the Commonwealth of Virginia had the right of pre-emption of all lands within its chartered boundaries. Col. Mason next insisted that the King had a right only to purchase as a trustee for the use of the State of Virginia, and the sale to the proprietors of Indiana was bad, as it was made to foreigners. . . . It was urged likewise by Col. Mason that the Treaty of Lancaster confirmed by that of Loggs Town, transferred to the King the lands for the use of the State of Virginia . It was further insisted upon by Col. Mason that if the House of Delegates gave up the Treaty of Lancaster they would furnish the neighboring

[1] Mason Papers.

States with the best arguments for a share in our back lands, therefore it is expedient that this treaty should be supported as the interests of the State are concerned in it ; and the only way to prevent other States from claiming the back lands would be to insist thoroughly on the right of pre-emption. Col. Mason next insisted that countenancing the grant to the proprietors of Indiana would exclude a fund which might be secured to the State by the sale. . . Col. Mason concluded his arguments against the proprietors of Indiana, by saying : ' If we have in this case deviated from the rules of strict distributive justice, the *salus populi* to which I have so often referred in this House, has been the incitement, and it has been expedient for the good of the Commonwealth.' He then moved the House to come to certain resolutions, and June the 17th, 1779, the Legislature of Virginia passed a law respecting the right of pre-emption, and therein declared the title of the proprietors of Indiana to be utterly void and of no effect." [1]

The periods in the text indicate the space taken up by the counter arguments of the pamphleteer. And as the report of George Mason's argument is that of one interested in refuting it, the notes are neither as fair nor as full as they might have been. Especially is the conclusion attributed to Colonel Mason to be taken with suspicion.

In his preface to the fifth volume of the " Virginia Calendar Papers," Mr. Sherwin McRae refers to the deposition of Patrick Henry given in the Henderson case at Williamsburg, June 4, 1777,[2] as affording a striking picture of the great power for mischief of these companies. And he ascribes to Henry's course in the first Virginia Convention, and in the first Continental Congress in opposition to the land companies, an overwhelming influence on the leading men of the State : " The public virtue which George Mason saw in his

---

[1] "Plain Facts, A Vindication of the Grant of the Six Nations to the Proprietors of Indiana against the Decision of the Legislature of Virginia." Phila., 1781. An anonymous tract, attributed by some writers to Benjamin Franklin.
[2] " Virginia Calendar Papers," vol. i.

first conversation with Mr. Henry was Virginia's shield," writes the editor of the "Calendar Papers." With at least equal propriety this eulogy might be applied to George Mason, the chosen champion in the Legislature of Virginia of her rights in this matter. Throughout his public career he steadfastly opposed the pretensions of the land com_ panies, and to his exertions their overthrow was finally due.

Other work of George Mason's in the Assembly at this time was a bill for discouraging extensive credits and repeal- ing the act prescribing the method of proving book debts. He was also one of a committee of three to bring in a bill constituting the court of appeals, and for giving salaries to certain officers of government. The petition of John Bal- lendine in regard to the navigation of the James was referred to a committee of ten, of which Colonel Mason was chairman. He was also appointed to prepare a bill " declar- ing and asserting the rights of the commonwealth concerning purchasing land from the Indian natives." On the day before the closing one of the session, June 25th, Colonel Mason reported from the committee to whom the memorial of Penet & Co. had been referred, accepting their proposal, giving them an interest in the canal, foundry, and other works belonging to the public on James River. They were to have also three thousand acres of land and a place proper for a furnace, together with a coal mine, and were to examine plans on both sides of the James River for these works, other than Mr. Ballendine's. They expected to be reimbursed for their expenditure by a speedy importation of arms and military stores, and contracted for an annual supply of cannon and small-arms after the completion of their works. George Mason also reported on the petition of John Ballendine, desiring that the government appoint proper persons to adjust matters between the Common- wealth and Mr. Ballendine, and cause the contracts entered upon to be carried into speedy execution.[1]

[1] Journal of the Assembly.

Richard Henry Lee wrote to Colonel Mason on the 9th of June, and Mason replied on the 19th. Lee enters at length into a discussion of the corruptions of the time. He had resigned his seat in Congress, as has been said, much dissatisfied with its course, and he was prepared to take as pessimistic a view of public affairs as that expressed by the commander-in-chief. The measures he urges upon the Virginia Assembly, through his friend, were carried out, in great part, no doubt, through the latter's exertions.

CHANTILLY, June 9th, 1779.

DEAR SIR :

I am much obliged to you for your favor of the 4th, but greatly concerned for your state of health. The force of party and the power of fortune it seems to me, are leagued to distress if not to ruin America. There never was a time when the fullest exertion of ability and integrity was more necessary to rescue us from impending ills. The inundation of money appears to have overflowed virtue, and I fear will bury the liberty of America in the same grave. Believe me, Sir, it is not from improper despondence that I think in this manner. Look around you, do you anywhere see wisdom and integrity, and industry prevail either in council or execution ? The demon of avarice, extortion, and fortune-making seizes all ranks. And now, to get into office is another thing for getting into wealth on public funds and to the public injury. I well know that much of this will in all countries take place in time of war, but in America, unfortunately at this time, nothing else is attended to. And such is the state of things, so unequally is this mass of money distributed, that I assure you my apprehensions are great that this heavy tax will come with crushing weight on great numbers of honest, industrious men, whilst a number of others who have amassed thousands by illicit means will not feel the burthen. I hope some method will be fallen on to make the tax touch the speculators, monopolists, and those people concerned in staff departments of commissary, quartermaster, &c., &c. who have acquired vast wealth on very pernicious principles. In choosing the executive officers of government, integrity, ability, and industry must be attended to, or we are inevitably ruined. The millions we issue are with such profusion wasted, that they produce only heavy taxes without good to the community. This I apprehend arises from want of wisdom, diligence, or integrity somewhere. In truth there is so little attention paid to the expenditure of the public money, and the public accounts are so irregularly settled, or rather not settled at all, that it affords opportunities and gives temptation to men not truly moral to venture on bad practises in hopes of impunity. To me it appears of indispensable necessity that instructions be given to your delegates in Congress in terms peremtory and express that they move Congress, and never cease to urge it, that the most immediate and effectual settlement be made of all public accounts, calling to strict account all those who have been entrusted with public money, admitting not of evasive and dilatory pleas. That they have ready to lay before the Assembly, at its next meeting their proceedings herein, and if it is not done, the reasons why. I mean this latter part, in order to prevent those kind of put offs and go byes which I have seen so very often practised.

There is another point on which I think instructions greatly necessary, because I apprehend abuse has already taken place to considerable extent, and may, if not prevented, go much further. It is to prevent the practise of delegates from any State, and more particularly one delegate from any State, from obtaining from Congress money on the credit of the State he or they come from without the orders of that particular State. In time, when death or bankruptcy shall have removed delegates or incapacitated them, these grants may be refused by the States, or some of them, and public discord and confusion be the result. This practise began originally upon the necessity members were under of getting money due to them for wages to support their necessary expenses, and so far as that, strictly confined there, nothing ill would have resulted. But I have reason to think it has been carried much further. Your treasurer should be ordered to remit the wages of the delegates in due season, and the practise of taking money from the Continental treasury without express order be totally inhibited. If necessity compelled, why, then, there was no resisting the measure, but it does seem strange, that when the quantity of money in circulation has almost stopped its currency and introduced universal corruption of manners, which hath obliged the laying of a most weighty tax, that our Assembly should order a million of pounds to be emitted. I greatly fear the effect of this, as well in reality, as from the operation it will have on the apprehensions of men in the other States!

It is, I think, to be feared, that the enemy's late success in this State will encourage other visits, and behooves us both in the deliberative and executive departments, to be as well prepared in every respect as possible to prevent the like success on their part and injury on ours. The first thing is to remove temptation by never suffering stores of any kind to be collected in considerable quantities near where troops may be landed from vessels protected by ships of war. Where the enemy want provisions and wish to destroy our means of defence, surely magazines of provisions and of warlike stores ought to be places the most secure. It appears to me that expensive fortifications are not the thing. Mere batteries to protect vessels against small sea force is all of this kind that can for the present be attempted with propriety and success. Extreme mismanagement has, I suppose, alienated our minds from our true, just and natural defence by vessels of war. I think it may be demonstrated that eight gallies on our part and six on that of Maryland, well-manned, fitted and commanded, carrying thirty-two and twenty-four pounders, and constructed as were the Congress gallies built at Philadelphia, would with ease baffle the attempts of such a force as came here last. This is a kind of movable battery which proceeding with the enemy would disappoint them, whilst forts on land will be avoided when the foe is weak and always fall when they are strong. And these forts, under the idea of strength delude men to make collections which they otherwise would not, and which tempt an enemy to come for plunder where they would not otherwise visit.

On the subject of public accounts and public expenses, Dr. Lee in a late letter to Congress : " Indeed there has been hitherto such licentiousness suffered in the conduct of our affairs, that these gentlemen [meaning Ross, Williams, &c., &c., &c.] seem to think it both an affront and injustice to be called upon for a clear and unequivocal account of the expenditure of the public money. It seems clear to me that if all the millions expended are thus accounted for, the *burthens* and *poverty* of the *public* will increase

with the *opulence* of *individuals,* and soon become intolerable."
This is a melancholy truth.   Squire Lee will show you a copy of
a letter to this very Ross, whom Braxton writes so prettily about,
from the commissioners by which you may judge how he is going
on.   This man has had more than 400,000 livres of France ad.
vanced him by Deane, besides remittances from America.   He is
one of the commercial league on public funds.

As this is a safe opportunity, I enclose you the State papers
you desired me to get, and at your leisure be pleased to let me
have a copy as I have not had time to take one.   I rejoice greatly
at the news from South Carolina.   God grant it may be true.   If
this should force the enemy to reason and to peace, would you
give up the navigation of Mississippi and our domestic fishery on
the banks of Newfoundland?   The former almost infinitely
depreciating our back country and the latter totally destroying
us as a maritime power.   That is taking the name of indepen.
dence without the means of supporting it.   If you have any news
and time to write it I pray you to do so, and excuse this long
trespass on your patience and your business.

I am most affectionately yours,

RICHARD HENRY LEE.[1]

WILLIAMSBURG June 19th, 1779.

DEAR SIR :

Col. Layota coming to pay you a visit at Chantilly, gives me an
opportunity of informing you not of the news but of the dearth
of news at this place.   All our pleasing accounts from Charles
Town, I fear are vanished into nothing, at least nothing that can
be depended on.

The great business of the legislature goes on heavily, the members inattentive, tired and restless to get away.   In this situation
of things, you will know what sort of investigation the most important subjects are likely to have, and that reason and sound
argument will have little avail.   The Indiana Company's title,
after two or three days' debate, and every effort within and without doors, to support it, is rejected : and an act passed, in the
most explicit terms, firmly asserting the Commonwealth's exclusive right of pre-emption from the Indians, within our own

---

[1] Mason Papers.

territory, declaring that all deeds or cessions heretofore made to the Crown shall inure to the use and benefit of the Commonwealth, and that all deeds which have been or shall be made by the Indians, for the separate use or benefit of any person or persons whatever, are void and of no effect.

The Land Office bill, upon very proper principles, and a bill for settling the titles of claimers under the former government, have passed the House of Delegates, and are now before the Senate. What alterations they may undergo I know not, but some to the latter bill, made yesterday in the committee by the Senate, at the instance of their Speaker, are very absurd and unjust ; they are to be reported to-morrow, and as the old bruiser will then have his mouth shut in the chair, perhaps they may be set right. My charter rights I believe will be established, and my location preserved to me, upon resurveying the same lands, that is upon putting a considerable sum of money out of my pocket into the county surveyor's, for the State will not gain a copper by it. Our friend B——n and some others did everything they could to invalidate them.

The Ohio Company were not permitted a special investigation of their claim, obliged to submit to the description in a general bill, and thus in fact denied a hearing, and yet every attempt that art or cunning could suggest, made to introduce particular words to exclude them. I have spared no trouble, nor omitted anything in my power to procure them justice ; the only chance now left, is to get their claim referred to the Court of Appeals, and to preserve to them the right of their location, by resurveying the same lands, if their claim shall be established upon a hearing before the said court, and in this I have still hopes of succeeding : two days more will determine it.

The principal bills still before our House are upon the subjects of the militia invasion, or insurrection ; raising troops for the immediate defence of the Commonwealth ; settling the real and personal estates of British subjects and lodging the proceeds in the public treasury, subject to the further order of the General Assembly ; naturalization ; ascertaining the damage done by the enemy on private property that compensation may in due time be demanded, or levied by exclusive duties on the British trade with us at anytime hereafter ; on the mode of proving book debts and discouraging extensive credits ; and on the more effectual manner of supplying our troops with the articles necessary for their comfortable accommodation, and preventing embezzlement. Most of these bills now stand committed. Whether the House will have patience to go through them all is uncertain ; I fear not, many members declaring that they will stay no longer than next Saturday, at all events, and some that they will go away sooner. We should not have had a House now, but for a little piece of generalship. I got our friend Mr. Page to undertake procuring an order that the clerk should grant no certificate to any member for his wages until the Assembly should have adjourned, unless upon leave of absence. Some of the fellows threatened, and kicked, and struggled, but could not loosen the knot. We are endeavoring to digest a scheme for laying a tax on specific commodities, which I think will have more effect in preventing the further depreciation of our money, than anything we have done or can do besides.

We have had Mr. Pinet [Penet] and Co.'s memorial several days before a select committee, the members of which seem well inclined to encourage so important an undertaking ; if this can properly be said of men who are too indolent to attend to anything. The committee have met, or rather failed to meet, at my lodgings every morning and evening for this fortnight. Ballendine has got possession of the key to the navigation of James River, and is acting exactly the part of the dog in the manger. I am very uneasy about it, and fearful nothing decisive will be done, and the gentlemen left in doubt and disgust. I have got pretty well over my late fit of the gout, but remain in a very indifferent state of health, to which vexation has not a little contributed.

I had almost forgot to inform you of our new election of members to Congress ; it is indeed a disagreeable subject, for in my opinion (except our late governor who I hardly think will serve and Gabriel Jones) we never had so bad one. I enclose you a list of them, and I think you will hardly blame me for taking care in time to keep out of such company.

I beg to be kindly remembered to our friend Parker, and am with my compliments to your lady and family, dear Sir,

Your affectionate friend and servant,

G. MASON.[1]

---

[1] Lee Papers, University of Virginia. Published in part in *Southern Literary Messenger*, October, 1858.

The device of Colonel Mason to keep the members in their seats recalls a somewhat similar incident related of Samuel Adams. In the Provincial Congress of Massachusetts, 1774, when the vigorous measures of Adams alarmed the timid and time-serving, some of them pleaded sickness as an excuse to leave, and in order to stop these desertions, Samuel Adams proposed that on their return to their constituents they should inform the latter that they were no longer represented, so that other members could be elected. This suggestion had the desired effect.[1]

Colonel Mason speaks his mind freely to his friend in the above letter, and it is evident that he had much to struggle against in the Assembly in carrying out his purposes. To the Speaker of the Senate, Col. Archibald Cary, he gives a pugilistic title, which doubtless "Old Iron" would have taken as a compliment. "B——n" is evidently meant for Carter Braxton. And there is a passage in Edmund Randolph's history, which, it seems not unlikely, has reference to Colonel Mason and the opposition of Braxton to his claim, with the triumph of the former over his adversary. No names are mentioned, but it is of this session of the Assembly and the passage of the laws establishing a land-office that Randolph is writing, and he tells of " a member of the Assembly who was honorably interested in charter importation rights," and of the scheme of another member to thwart him :

" The other, sensible that a direct attack upon them [the charter-rights] would be too gross, assaulted the surveys, by which they had been located upon particular rich lands, for some mistake in form. Upon which a vote was obtained declaring them to be void. Elated by this victory, and poorly versed in the subject, this hunter after formal defects, did not see the force of a small amendment in a part of the bill, remote from the clause which had been defeated. Thus justice was protected by dexterity   thus an impotency of character cheats itself with a momentary flash of triumph, and teaches us not to confide in a legislator who does not view the whole ground and persevere to the last, as the same consequences might have followed in a better cause."[2]

[1] Welles' " Life of Samuel Adams," vol. ii., p. 252.   [2] MS. History of Virginia.

CHAPTER X.

THE CESSION OF WESTERN TERRITORY.

1779–1780.

During the summer of 1779 two military achievements at the North cheered the hearts of patriots throughout the country. These were the successful expedition of Wayne against Stony Point on the Hudson in July, and the capture of Paulus Hook (Jersey City) by "Light-Horse Harry" Lee in August. At the South the British were overrunning Georgia and South Carolina, and when the Virginia Assembly met in October, it was shortly after the failure of the siege of Savannah then held by the enemy.

George Mason had written Richard Henry Lee while in the May Assembly of a scheme he and his associates were "endeavoring to digest," which was for "laying a tax on specific commodities," and he looked forward to its good effects in preventing the further depreciation of the Virginia currency. He seems to have taken the matter in hand during the summer, and when the Assembly met again in October he had the bill ready to bring forward. John Parke Custis, then a delegate from Fairfax County, wrote to Washington, October 26th, from "Mount Vernon," making this reference to the subject

"Our neighbor, Colonel Mason, is preparing a remedy against the depreciation of our money, which I think will do him great credit. He is preparing a bill for a general assessment on all property, by which he will draw in £5,000,000 per annum. His valuation of property is very low, which will render his plan very

agreeable to the people. He has, likewise, a plan for recruiting
our army, which I think a very good one ; but I am fearful they
will not succeed, by his not attending the Assembly which met
last Monday. He proposed to set off this day ; but as it is
a rainy day he will be disappointed. I wish he may set off when
the weather will permit ; his attendance in Assembly is of the
greatest importance to this State, as it was never so badly represented as at present." ˙

The Assembly met on Monday, October 4, 1779, and
John Parke Custis must have written his letter on or before
the 11th, the Monday after, as he says the Assembly met
"last Monday." The date of his letter is therefore incor-
rectly given as the "26th October." George Mason took
his seat in the House on Friday the 15th, and probably
contemplated leaving home on the previous Monday, but
was detained by bad weather. The committee was at this
time named for bringing in the important bill "concerning religion," and George Mason and Patrick Henry were
among its sixteen members. On the 16th a writ was
issued for the election of a new delegate from Elizabeth
City County in the room of Thomson Mason, "who
hath accepted a coroner's commission."[2] Colonel Mason
was placed upon several committees, and a number of
bills were brought in by him in rapid succession. On the
18th he presented one for providing a great seal for the
commonwealth, and directing the lesser seal of the commonwealth to be affixed to all grants for lands, and to commissions civil and military. The seal was to be the same as
directed in the Convention of 1776, "save only that the
motto on the reverse be changed to the word *Perseverando*."[3]
George Mason presented also, on this same day, a bill for
discouraging extensive credits, and prescribing the method
of proving book debts. He was placed, at the same time,
on committees to bring in a bill for regulating ordinaries

[1] " Recollections of Washington," G. P. Custis, Appendix, p. 563.
[2] Journal of the Assembly.
[3] Hening's " Statutes," vol. x.

and restraint of tippling-houses, and a bill to establish cross-posts.

General Nelson, on the following day, reported from the Committee of Propositions and Grievances, of which George Mason was also a member, a certain "grievance" of Dr. William Savage, whose brig was lying in Quantico Creek in the summer of 1776, when its sails were seized and taken possession of for the use of the Potomac navy, by order of George Mason and John Dalton, acting for the Committee of Safety. The act for the annual appointment of delegates to Congress was to be amended, and Henry, Nelson, Mason, and others were of the number to prepare the bill. A charge brought against some of the sheriffs of the counties for breach of trust, and misapplying the money received in taxes, lending it to private individuals to lay out in the land-office, was to be investigated, and Colonel Mason was chairman of the committee appointed for this purpose. A bill for regulating the importation of salt, and laying an embargo thereon for a limited time, was entrusted to a committee of three—Page, Mason, and Baker. The committee for preparing a bill to establish courts of assize consisted of John Taylor, George Mason, and ten others, among whom was Patrick Henry. And Colonel Mason was one of a committee of nine who were to amend the act establishing the Board of War. On the 23d he was made chairman of a committee of six, who were to bring in a bill for marking and opening a road over the Cumberland Mountains into the county of Kentucky, and this bill was presented by Colonel Mason four days later. He was placed on a committee, on the 26th, to bring in a bill for appointing commissioners to ascertain the value of lands throughout this State. And about the same time he was appointed on a committee to prepare a circular-letter to the several counties of the State on the subject of taxation.

On the 1st of November the House went into a Committee of the Whole on the state of the commonwealth, and passed the following important resolution: "That all attempts to possess lands within this State, without the countenance of law, are violent infringements of the rights of this commonwealth, and should be prevented by prompt exertion."[1] George Mason was one of a committee of five to whom was assigned the duty of preparing a bill in conformity to this resolve. A motion to bring in a bill suspending the operation of the act for removing the seat of government to Richmond, passed in the negative. George Mason voted in favor of the motion, which would seem to show that he preferred the old capital to the new one. This was the last Assembly held in Williamsburg. A bill for encouraging the importation of salt was consigned to a committee of three, of whom George Mason was one. The bill for the better regulation and discipline of the militia was put off until the May session, a procrastinating measure against which Colonel Mason recorded his vote. On the 8th of November, the bill concerning claims to certain waste or unappropriated lands, which had been before the committee of the whole House, was referred, together with a memorial of the commissioners for settling and adjusting the titles of claimers to unpatented lands in the counties of Yohoghania, Monongalia, and Ohio, to a committee of six, on which Colonel Mason was the member named after the chairman, John Taylor. George Mason was appointed, on the following day, chairman of a committee to bring in a bill for regulating and collecting certain officers' fees, and for other purposes; and a bill concerning tobacco fees. The House on the 10th appointed by ballot a Committee of Ways and Means, of which Colonel Mason was made chairman.

On the 13th, in Committee of the Whole House on the state of the commonwealth, the following resolution was passed:

"That a remonstrance be drawn up to the Honorable, the American Congress firmly asserting the rights of this Commonwealth to its own territory, complaining of their having received petitions from certain persons styling themselves the Indiana and

[1] Journal of the Assembly.

Vandalia Companies, upon claims which not only interfere with the laws and internal policy, but tend to subvert the government of this commonwealth, and introduce general confusion ; and expressly excepting and protesting against the jurisdiction of Congress therein, as unwarranted by the fundamental principles of the Confederation."

Munford, Mason, and Henry were appointed a committee to prepare the remonstrance. On the 10th of December George Mason reported from the committee appointed to prepare a Remonstrance to Congress on the subject of the Indiana and Vandalia claims and the proceedings of Congress thereon. The Remonstrance was read and agreed to, and Colonel Mason carried it to the Senate for their concurrence.[1] It bears date December 14th, when it was forwarded to Congress.

Remonstrance to Congress.

" December 14, 1779.

" The General Assembly of Virginia ever attentive to the recommendations of Congress and desirous to give the great council of the United States every satisfaction in their power, consistent with the rights and constitution of their own commonwealth, have enacted a law to prevent present settlements on the northwest side of the Ohio river, and will on all occasions endeavor to manifest their attachment to the common interest of America, and their earnest wishes to remove every cause of jealousy and promote that mutual confidence and harmony between the different States so essential to their true interest and safety.

" Strongly impressed with these sentiments, the General Assembly of Virginia cannot avoid expressing their surprise and concern, upon the information that Congress had received and countenanced petitions from certain persons styling themselves the Vandalia and Indiana Companies, asserting claims to lands in defiance of the civil authority, jurisdiction and laws of this commonwealth, and offering to erect a separate government within the territory thereof. Should Congress assume a jurisdiction, and arrogate to themselves a right of adjudication, not only unwar-

[1] *Ibid.*

ranted by, but expressly contrary to the fundamental principles of the Confederation ; superseding or controlling the internal policy, civil regulations, and municipal laws of this, or any other State, it would be a violation of public faith, introduce a most dangerous precedent which might hereafter be urged to deprive of territory or subvert the sovereignty and government of any one or more of the United States, and establish in Congress a power which in process of time must degenerate into an intolerable despotism.

" It is notorious that the Vandalia and Indiana Companies are not the only claimers of large tracts of land under titles repugnant to our laws ; that several men of great influence in some of the neighboring States are concerned in partnerships with the Earl of Dunmore and other subjects of the British King, who under purchases from the Indians, claim extensive tracts of country between the Ohio and Mississippi rivers ; and that propositions have been made to Congress evidently calculated to secure and guaranty such purchases ; so that under colour of creating a common fund, had those propositions been adopted, the public would have been duped by the arts of individuals, and great part of the value of the unappropriated lands converted to private purposes.

" Congress have lately described and ascertained the boundaries of these United States, as an ultimatum in their terms of peace. The United States hold no territory but in right of some one individual State in the Union : the territory of each State from time immemorial, hath been fixed and determined by their respective charters, there being no other rule or criterion to judge by ; should these in any instance (when there is no disputed territory between particular States) be abridged without the consent of the States affected by it, general confusion must ensue ; each State would be subjected in its turn to the encroachments of the others, and a field opened for future wars and bloodshed ; nor can any arguments be fairly urged to prove that any particular tract of country within the limits claimed by Congress on behalf of the United States, is not part of the chartered territory of some one of them, but must militate with equal force against the right of the United States in general ; and tend to prove such tract of country (if north-west of the Ohio river) part of the British province of Canada.

"When Virginia acceded to the articles of confederation, her rights of sovereignty and jurisdiction within her own territory were reserved and secured to her, and cannot now be infringed or altered without her consent. She could have no latent views of extending that territory; because it had long before been expressly and clearly defined in the act which formed her new government. The General Assembly of Virginia have heretofore offered Congress to furnish lands out of their territory on the north-west of the Ohio river, without purchase money, to the troops on continental establishment of such of the Confederated States as had not unappropriated lands for that purpose, in conjunction with the other States holding unappropriated lands and in such proportion as should be adjusted and settled by Congress; which offer when accepted they will most cheerfully make good to the same extent, with the provision made by law for their own troops, if Congress shall think fit to allow the like quantities of land to the other troops on continental establishment. But although the General Assembly of Virginia would make great sacrifices to the common interest of America, (as they have already done on the subject of representation,) and will be ready to listen to any just and reasonable propositions for removing the *ostensible* causes of delay to the complete ratification of the Confederation, they find themselves impelled by the duties which they owe to their constituents, to their posterity, to their country, and to the United States in general, to remonstrate and protest; and they do hereby, in the name and on behalf of the Commonwealth of Virginia, expressly protest against any jurisdiction or right of adjudication in Congress, upon the petitions of the Vandalia or Indiana. Companies, or on any other matter or thing subversive of the internal policy, civil government, or sovereignty of this or any other of the United American States, or unwarranted by the articles of the Confederation." [1]

There is no doubt that Colonel Mason was the author of this valuable paper, reported by him to the Assembly. He would naturally be selected as the fittest person to prepare it, as his management of the cases of the Henderson and

[1] Hening's "Statutes," vol. x., p. 537.

Indiana Companies, for the Commonwealth of Virginia, had made him familiar with the whole controversy. And the Remonstrance bears internal evidence that it proceeded from the same pen that drew up other papers and letters on the subject, bearing George Mason's signature. A tribute is paid to the Remonstrance by Hinsdale, who in his valuable work on the northwestern territory, makes a full acknowledgment of Virginia's title. Referring to the several land claims of Virginia, Connecticut, and New York, he says :

" Particular attention should be drawn to the bearing of the question with which we are dealing on the national boundaries. *Virginia states the point with great force in her remonstrance ;* and it is perfectly clear in the light of the facts already presented, that a denial of the western titles on the grounds that the western lands belonged to the Crown, tended to subvert the very foundation on which Congress instructed its foreign representatives to stand while contending with England, France and Spain for a westward extension to the Mississippi." [1]

Colonel Mason's views in regard to disestablishment may be traced in his action during this session on the several bills relating to religion brought forward. While in favor of religious liberty, and desirous that the Anglican Church should stand on the same footing as other denominations, he wished to secure to the Church her property, and believed in no system of ecclesiastical spoliation. He was made chairman of two committees of three : the one to bring in a bill for repealing the act of Assembly which provided for the payment of the salaries heretofore given to the clergy of the Church of England (repeated at every session), and the other to prepare a bill for saving and securing the property of the Church, heretofore by law established. Colonel Mason was also at this time appointed one of a committee to prepare a bill concerning orphans and legatees. He made a report from the committee appointed to inquire into

---

[1] Hinsdale's " Old Northwest," p. 215.

the conduct of the delinquent sheriffs; and on the same day, November 17th, reported from the Committee of Ways and Means in regard to the bill to amend the act concerning escheats and forfeitures from British subjects. On the following day George Mason was appointed to prepare a bill for ascertaining the loss and requiring retribution for the depredations of the enemy on private property, which bill he presented the same day. On the 27th he presented the bill to prevent the misapplication of the money collected for taxes by the sheriffs, and a bill for settling the rate of exchange and mode of judgments on foreign debts. He also reported from the Committee of Ways and Means certain economical regulations in relation to widows of soldiers who had died in the service of the United States or of Virginia.

On the 29th of November the House in Committee of the Whole came to the following resolution: "That the civil and military establishments of the Illinois ought to be augmented and supported, and that the Governor be empowered to procure a credit in New Orleans for that purpose; and that this House will make good and provide proper funds for the fulfilling any engagements that he, with the advice of the Council, may enter into, to answer that desirable end."[1] This was referred to a committee of six, of which General Nelson was named chairman, and George Mason was second on the list of members. On the following day fifteen resolutions were passed by the House, in relation to the troops, the navy, and other matters of importance, and two committees were appointed to prepare the bills required, Colonel Mason being placed on both of them. On the 10th of December the Remonstrance to Congress was reported, as has been said; and on the 11th, Colonel Mason from the Committee of Ways and Means reported several resolutions in reference to the requisitions of Congress, which were referred to the Committee of the Whole House on the state of the commonwealth. Resolutions in regard to taxes and

[1] Journal of the Assembly.

duties passed by the House were referred to the Committee of Ways and Means to be shaped into bills. Colonel Mason, from this committee, reported on the 16th certain resolutions reached by them, concerning the supplies necessary for the State expenditure. The following day he presented a bill for raising a supply of money for the service of the United States. [1] The preamble states:

" Whereas the Continental Congress, impelled by the exigencies of a war, the object of which is civil liberty, have demanded supplies from the United States, adequate to the annual expenditure, whereby the ruinous expedient of future emissions of paper money will be avoided ; and since this State is bound by its own interest, and by the faith of freemen, so often, and so solemnly pledged, to support the glorious cause with their lives and their fortunes ; since taxation alone can obviate that embarrassment in finance, which is now the last hope of the enemy ; and since one of two alternatives, between which no friend to his country can hesitate, is unavoidable ; either to support the common cause by taxation, or after having lavished so much blood and treasure, to submit to an humiliating, inglorious and disadvantageous peace ; in order, therefore, to comply with the said requisitions, supported by justice and warranted by necessity, be it enacted, &c." [2]

The additional duties were a poll tax, a tax on slaves, on carriages, on merchandise, and on liquors, foreign and domestic.

Other bills prepared by George Mason at this time were two in relation to finance ; a bill providing a farther supply for the exigencies of government, and one for establishing a fund to borrow money for the service of the United States and for other purposes. This act appropriated five eighths of a tax in tobacco as a fund for borrowing £5,000,000 upon interest, the other three eighths of the amount of taxes to be collected by this act were to be reserved for purchasing military stores, etc. [3] Colonel Mason also brought in a bill

---

[1] *Ibid.*   [2] Hening's " Statutes," vol. x.   [3] *Ibid.*

to confirm the titles of purchasers of escheated and forfeited estates. On the 21st he was made chairman of a committee of five to prepare a bill in relation to the treasurer, allowing him one eighth per cent. on all monies brought into the treasury on any subsequent loans in consequence of the sales of British property, etc. Friday, Christmas Eve, was the last day of the session. The House in committee on the state of the commonwealth came to several resolutions, attesting their realization of the gravity of the military situation at this time. They provided for calling out the militia, for the defence of York, and for measures to be taken in case of invasion. These resolutions were carried to the Senate by George Mason.

The following resolve of the House recalls the passage on this subject in the letter from Richard Henry Lee to Colonel Mason, and was evidently penned by the latter, who carried it to the Senate:

" That it be an instruction to the Virginia delegates in Congress to use their endeavors to procure a settlement of public accounts since the commencement of the present war, stating the expenditure of each year under distinct heads ; that they give the strongest assurances to Congress of the cheerfulness with which Virginia will bear her share of the burthen of the present war, until it shall please the Supreme Disposer of events to grant us peace upon safe and honorable terms ; and that although the General Assembly hath made provisions for complying with the demands of Congress to the utmost extent of their requisitions, yet they cannot help observing with very great concern, that no account of expenditures, or of the application of the public money, has ever yet been laid before them ; and also that Congress be informed they do insist upon it as their right and of justice due to the Commonwealth, that an account and estimate of future requisitions for the service of the United States, distinguished under their proper heads, ought to be annually transmitted to the General Assembly."

The Assembly before adjourning gave expression to their views as to the encroachments of Congress on the rights of the States.   They transmitted to the Virginia delegation a resolution setting forth their alarm at the assumption of power lately exercised by Congress in resolutions respecting the price of provisions, etc.   They admitted the right of Congress to recommend measures to the States, but they contended that the States alone could judge of their utility and expediency, either approving or rejecting them.   And Virginia could not submit to the declaration which would make any State *answerable* for not agreeing to the recommendations of Congress, as this " would establish a dangerous precedent against the authority of the legislature and the sovereignty of the separate States." [1]

Turning aside from Colonel Mason's public to his private life, an important event marks its records in the spring of 1780.   This was his second marriage.   The following are the marriage articles :

" Articles of Agreement indented, made, concluded and agreed upon this   day of April, Anno Domini, one thousand seven hundred and eighty, between George Mason of Gunston Hall in the Commonwealth of Virginia, Esquire of the one part, and Sarah Brent of the town of Dumfries in the commonwealth aforesaid of the other part.

" Whereas a marriage, by God's permission, is shortly to be had and solemnized between the said George Mason and Sarah Brent, they the said parties, in consideration thereof, do mutually covenant, promise, and agree in manner and form following, videlicet :

" *Imprimis*, that immediately upon the said indented marriage taking effect, the possession and use of all and every of the slaves belonging to the said Sarah Brent shall be vested in the said George Mason and be held by him during the coverture ; and in case there is no issue of the said marriage, living at the time of its dissolution by the death of either of the said parties, then the said slaves and their increase shall return to the said Sarah Brent, and the absolute property thereof be vested in her and her heirs, or such person or persons as she shall devise the same to by her last will and testament.

[1] Journal of the Assembly.

"*Item.*—That in case the said Sarah Brent shall survive the said George Mason, and there shall be no issue of the said marriage living at the time of his death ; in that case the said Sarah Brent shall be put into possession of 400 acres of the said George Mason's land in Dogue Neck in Virginia, and hold the same during her natural life, in lieu and in full satisfaction of her dower and legal share of and in the said George Mason's estate real and personal. But in case the said Sarah Brent shall survive the said George Mason, and there shall be issue of the said marriage living at the time of his death, then the above agreement and every part thereof shall be utterly void to all intents and purposes as if the same had never been made ; and in that case the said slaves and their increase shall be considered as part of the said George Mason's estate and the absolute property thereof be vested in him and his heirs ; and the said Sarah Brent shall be entitled, as his widow, to her dower and legal share of and in the said George Mason's estate both real and personal, anything herein contained to the contrary notwithstanding. In witness whereof the said George Mason and Sarah Brent have hereunto set their hands and seals the day and year above written." [1]

In the Gunston family Bible there is this notice of the marriage in Colonel Mason's handwriting :

" George Mason of Gunston Hall in Fairfax County, Virginia, aged about fifty-four years, and his second wife Sarah Brent, daughter of George Brent, Esq., of Woodstock, in the county of Stafford, aged about fifty years, were married on Tuesday, the eleventh day of April, in the year 1780, by the Rev. Mr. James Scott, Rector of Dettingden parish in the county of Prince William in Virginia."

The name of Brent, it will be remembered, has early associations with the Mason family, in connection with the border warfare that preceded Bacon's Rebellion. Sarah Brent, the second wife of George Mason of Gunston, a lady of amiable and domestic character, was fourth in descent from Col. George Brent, the friend and neighbor of Col.

[1] Mason Papers.

George Mason, the ex-cavalier. Robert Brent, a brother of Mrs. Mason, married into the Carroll family of Maryland, and his son, George Brent, a captain in the Revolution, represented Stafford County in the Virginia Assembly. One of Mrs. Mason's sisters married James Douglas, a relative of the Duke of Douglas, and spent her latter years in Scotland with her husband's family. Another sister, Jane Brent, married Richard Graham, who like James Douglas was one of the Scotch merchants settled in Dumfries. And a son of Jane Graham married the widow of George Mason of "Lexington," Colonel Mason's eldest son.[1]

The General Assembly met at Richmond on the 9th of May, 1780. Richard Henry Lee was in the House at this time, and he and George Mason were conspicuous in their support of the measure proposed by Congress, to call in all the old State and Continental bills and re-issue notes at the rate of one dollar for forty of the old money. Patrick Henry took the lead in opposition to this plan of Congress. Colonel Mason was tardy in his attendance at this session, and it is not until the 22d of May that his name appears in the journal of the House. On this day it was ordered that the Committee of Ways and Means, appointed on the 19th and consisting of nine members, among whom were General Nelson, Richard Henry Lee, and Patrick Henry, should be increased by the addition of one other member, to be appointed by ballot. The new member elected was George Mason. On the same day Colonel Mason was added to the committee to prepare a bill " for the more general diffusion of knowledge."

A committee of three, consisting of Mason, Henry, and Tazewell, was appointed on the 23d to prepare a bill for repealing part of the act for sequestering British property, enabling those indebted to British subjects to pay off such debts, and directing the proceedings in suits where such subjects are parties, which bill, prepared by Colonel Mason, passed the same day. On the 24th of May a motion was

[1] MS. Book of the Brent Family.

made, by Colonel Mason it would seem, that an address be sent to the Virginia delegates in Congress. This address, which after a third reading was agreed to *nemine contra. dicente*, and carried by George Mason to the Senate for its concurrence, set forth the alarming condition of affairs in South Carolina, and the danger of North Carolina, the evident design of the enemy in this campaign appearing to be the conquest of the Southern States. The General Assembly, as the address asserted, was making every exertion to raise and send forward a body of militia, "but conscious that such aid alone will not only be ineffectual, but too slow in its operation ; and considering the present general attack by the Indians on their western, and the prospect of an immediate invasion on their eastern frontier, in repelling which a great part of their militia will necessarily be employed ; they think it their duty to call the attention of Congress to this important object, and earnestly to conjure them without delay, to adopt the most effectual means of defending and maintaining the Southern States, which the General Assembly of Virginia apprehend cannot be effected, but by a farther speedy and powerful reinforcement of Continental troops, and a supply of arms for the North Carolina militia, to whom the government of Virginia hath already furnished all it is able to spare." [1]

Virginia was then truly, in size and importance, the empire State of the American Confederacy. But much of her territory was scantily peopled, and the war had crippled her resources. On her western borders she had to guard against the Indian foe, who were in alliance with the British, and on the east she was wellnigh defenceless against the British fleets in her navigable waters. And now the States south of her were invaded, making her situation one of still greater peril.

Turning again to the journal of the House, we find Colonel Mason appointed on the committee to amend the act for reviving several public warehouses for the inspection

[1] Journal of the Assembly.

of tobacco. He also prepared a bill to enable the sheriff of the county in which the General Court may sit to summon a grand jury. On the 1st of June the House, in Committee of the Whole on the state of the commonwealth, came to several resolutions for meeting the public emergencies. Information had reached them from Congress of authentic intelligence that a powerful land and naval force was expected in North America to act with the Continental troops against the common enemy. But the exhausted state of the Continental treasury prevented Congress from acting with sufficient vigor in directing the movements of the army. A supply of money was required from Virginia of over a million dollars for replenishing the treasury. The House proposed, among the extra means to raise this sum, that subscriptions be requested from members of the Assembly and from gentlemen in the country and towns adjacent, and advances of money and tobacco. Colonel Mason carried these resolutions to the Senate, and it is more than likely therefore that they were drafted by him. Five days later Colonel Mason made the following report from the Committee of Ways and Means. In order to provide provisions and arms necessary for the militia and troops " in the present alarming and critical situation of the war with a powerful enemy," they proposed that commissioners be appointed in all the counties eastward of the Alleghany Mountains, to examine into the state and quantity of provisions in possession of every person and family, and after allowing them what was necessary for their support, to seize the surplus for the public use, giving certificates to the owners to be paid by the public at their real value at the time the same shall have been delivered. This resolution passed the House and the Committee of Ways and Means was instructed to prepare the necessary bill.

The House at this time took action in regard to the plan of Congress, proposed in March, for reviving public credit. Nearly two hundred millions of dollars had been issued, none of which had been redeemed, and forty paper dollars were now worth only one in specie. The House in Committee of the Whole resolved : " That ample and certain funds ought to be established for sinking the quota of the continental debt due from this State in ten years " ; an amendment passed substituting fifteen for ten years. But a second amendment was defeated. This was, to strike out from the word " that " to the end of the resolution, and to insert, " the act of Congress of the 18th March last ought to be adopted, that this Commonwealth will take upon itself its due proportion of the one hundred and eighty millions of dollars issued by Congress, and recommended to be speedily called in by taxes or otherwise ; and that the General Assembly will redeem or call in the same, and also establish certain funds for the redemption of this Commonwealth's due proportion of the new money to be issued in lieu thereof, in the manner and time proposed by Congress, as far as the circumstances of this Commonwealth will admit." The vote was fifty-nine to twenty-five against this amendment, George Mason and Richard Henry Lee voting for it and Patrick Henry against it. Another amendment proposed shared the same fate. This was, to add to the end of the resolution as amended by the substitution of fifteen for ten years, the following :

"But there having been so general and great depreciation in the said paper money issued by Congress, that for many months past it hath, by common consent, been circulated, paid and received at rates not exceeding one-fortieth part of the value of gold and silver, whereby the public debt hath been nominally increased to such an enormous sum as renders it impracticable to discharge the same at the value expressed in the bills ; and it is unreasonable and unjust that the good people of this Commonwealth, or of the other United States, should be burthened with grievous and oppressive taxes, to appreciate the said money to so much higher value than the present money holders have received it for, *Resolved*, that in the payment of the taxes for the redemption thereof, one Spanish silver dollar ought to be received for forty of the said paper dollars, and other silver and gold coins in the

23

same proportion ; and that so much of this Commonwealth's quota of the said paper money as shall remain outstanding at the end of the said fifteen years ought to be discharged in gold or silver coin at the same rate." [1]

The vote as recorded here also shows George Mason and Richard Henry Lee on the side of the amendment. It is very probable that George Mason drafted both of these resolutions that were intended to carry out the measure advocated by Congress. And it is known that Colonel Mason strove earnestly to influence the Assembly in its favor. But he and his allies saw themselves temporarily defeated, through the opposition of Patrick Henry. And for two weeks the subject was dropped, to be taken up again and brought to a different issue. The House passed resolutions, that certain funds ought to be established for furnishing to the Continent the quota of this State, for the support of the war for the current year, and that a specific tax ought to be laid for the use of the Continent, in full proportion to the abilities of the people, and the Committee of Ways and Means was ordered to prepare the bills. On the 8th of June Colonel Mason reported from the above committee a bill for procuring an immediate supply of provisions and other necessaries for the use of the army. Important resolutions were passed by the House on the following day, investing the governor and council with full powers to call forth the force and resources of the State against the enemy ; providing that one million of pounds be emitted for the present purposes of the war; and that certain funds ought to be established, at the next session of the Assembly, and applied to the redemption of the money to be emitted for the present purposes of the war in fifteen years.

On the 22d of June, two weeks after the defeat of the measure sustaining the action of Congress, the House in Committee of the Whole passed the following resolution : "That this Commonwealth will concur with a majority of

[1] *Ibid.*

the United States, in adopting and carrying into execution the resolves of Congress of the 18th of March last, as far as the circumstances of the people, and the present situation of public affairs will admit." George Mason was made chairman of the committee of eleven to whom was consigned the preparation of the required bill. The vote on this occasion stood fifty-two to thirty-four.[1] By patience and perseverance Mason and Lee had gained their object, and the Assembly reversed its former decision. Edmund Randolph says of this contest over the resolves of Congress :

"George Mason and Richard Henry Lee advocated them as being the only expedient remaining for the restoration of public credit. Patrick Henry poured forth all his eloquence in opposition ; but proposed nothing in their place. He disseminated, however, the jealousy which has since been denominated anti-federal, and stated some precise objections to the plan as being incompetent upon its own principles. For a time this scheme of Congress was negatived. Omnipotent as Henry was while present and exerting himself in the Assembly, he had one defect in his politics. He was apt to be contented with some *general* vote of success, but his genius did not lead him into detail. For a debate on grand, general principles he was never surpassed here, but more laborious men who seized occasions of modifying propositions, which they had lost on a vote, or of renewing them at more fortunate seasons, often accomplished their purpose, after he had retired from the session. In this instance, the perseverance of Mason and Lee, introduced in Henry's absence the same resolutions, and they were carried into a law."[2]

Mr. Lyon G. Tyler in his sketch of Judge Tyler adopts the same view, as to the change effected on this occasion in the vote of the House, ascribing it chiefly to the fact that Patrick Henry was not present when the subject was again brought up.[3] It would seem, however, more reasonable to

[1] *Ibid.* [2] MS. History of Virginia.
[3] "Letters and Times of the Tylers," vol. i., p. 74.

suppose that in the fortnight's interval the sentiment of the House had reached a conclusion which was recommended to the judgment of the whole country, and had been supported in the Assembly by the arguments and oratory of two of its leading members.

On the 30th Colonel Mason presented the bill for calling in and redeeming the money now in circulation, and for emitting and funding new bills of credit, according to the resolutions of Congress of the 18th of March last.[1] The preamble is as follows:

"Whereas the just and necessary war into which the United States have been driven, obliged Congress to emit bills of credit before the several States were sufficiently organized to enforce the collection of taxes, or funds could be established to support the credit of such bills; by which means the bills so emitted soon exceeded the sum necessary for a circulating medium, and consequently depreciated so as to create an alarming redundancy of money, whereby it is become necessary to reduce the quantity of such bills; to call in and destroy the excessive mass of money now in circulation; and to utter other bills, on funds which shall ensure the redemption thereof. And whereas the certain consequences of not calling in and redeeming the money now in circulation in the depreciated value at which it hath been generally received, would be to encrease the national debt thirty-nine times greater than it really is, and consequently subject the good people of this Commonwealth to many years of grievous and unnecessary taxation. And since Congress by their resolutions of the 18th March last have called upon the several States to make proper provision for the purposes aforesaid, be it therefore enacted, &c."[2]

The House at this session agreed to the boundary between Virginia and Pennsylvania, as arranged at Baltimore by commissioners from the States in August, 1779. Another subject having reference to a neighboring State claimed the attention of the Assembly at this time. On the 4th of July a motion was made that the House agree to the

[1] Journal of the Assembly.　　　　[2] Hening's "Statutes," vol. x.

following resolutions. And as Colonel Mason was made chairman of the committee of six to whom the resolutions were referred, it is probable that he was the mover of them :

" The General Assembly of Virginia, having at a former session, proposed to the neighboring Commonwealth of North Carolina to pass mutual laws, for securing real property to the owners, whether claimed by title of record or actual settlement, who on running the late boundary line might be found not to be in the State they settled under, and wishing to establish a principle for abolishing all local distinctions between States in one Union whose citizenship is or ought to be reciprocal, have observed with great pleasure that the legislature of North Carolina have in part closed with their proposition by passing a law October, 1779, for the purpose of establishing titles by actual settlement. But by a subsequent law, the operation of the first act is suspended until their next session ; in order to do justice between patentees under this government and mere actual settlers claiming the same land ; as it is doubtful whether the said patentees are in the said first law provided for ; as a speedy decision of the matter would quiet the minds of men immediately interested therein, which it is hoped the Assembly of North Carolina will give at their next session ; and that they may have all necessary information on the subject.

" *Resolved*, That it be represented to the Assembly of North Carolina that there were under the regal government several modes of gaining a title to lands, none of which became complete except by the obtaining a patent written on parchment and signed by the Governor for the time being ; that a claim to unappropriated lands was only supportable between the time of entry, and the time of obtaining such patent, after which the title of the patentee became indefeasible, unless by another patent of prior date ; that no title by settlement was recognized under said former government, such title being first established by a resolution of Convention, May 24, 1776 ; which declared that all persons settled on any unlocated or unappropriated lands to which there was none other just claim, should have the pre-emption or preference in the grant of such lands, but that this resolution could never have retrospect so as to defeat prior patentees ; and thus prove so injurious to fair purchasers ; neither can lands before patented come within the description of unlocated or unappropriated. This Assembly find themselves, therefore, impelled by every motive of law and justice warmly to solicit the Assembly of North Carolina to establish the several titles to lands under their former proposition, and must also inform the said Assembly that patentees and purchasers under them have a right, by the laws of this State, to a preference to all other claims ; and that a deprivation of this right would involve several fair and bona fide purchasers in unmerited loss, since they could never have foreseen that which was thought to be impossible, to-wit : that a title under an express patent might be defeated. They will further observe, also, that a certificate from the register of the Land Office, is the legal mode of fixing the authenticity of patents. The Assembly of Virginia again profess their willingness, on being informed of the ultimate determination of the Assembly of North Carolina, to meet them on the most liberal ground, and to do everything on their part that right may take place therein."

The House then resolved that the treasurer be required to forbear receiving money for the purchase of any waste or unappropriated lands, except upon certificate of settlement or pre-emption rights until the further orders of the General Assembly therein ; and George Mason carried this resolution to the Senate.

On the 6th of July it was ordered that the Committee of Ways and Means to whom the petitions of the merchants had been referred be discharged from the duty of preparing bills upon them, and this work was assigned to a committee of three—Richard Henry Lee, George Mason, and one other member. Colonel Mason, four days later, presented a bill for giving further powers to the governor and council ; and at the same time he was made chairman of a committee of eleven, who were to prepare a bill "for emitting and funding a sum of money for supplying the present urgent necessities of this Commonwealth." The motion to consider a bill " to revise and amend the several tender laws which have been passed in this Commonwealth " was defeated, and it was put off until the October session, George Mason and Richard Henry Lee voting against this motion for delay. On the 11th the House in Committee of the Whole made several amendments to the bill for giving further powers to the governor and council; and when a motion was made and lost that the clause enforcing martial law in case of invasion be struck out, Mason and Lee both voted in the negative. Resolutions of the House that the delegates of Virginia in Congress be desired to transmit quarterly accounts, were carried to the Senate by Colonel Mason, and at the close of the session he presented the bill for emitting and funding a sum of money for supplying the present urgent necessities of the common-wealth, and a bill amending the act for raising a supply of money for the use of the United States and for other purposes.[1]

It will be seen that Colonel Mason took a very prominent part in the work of this session, and might indeed be called its leading spirit. And we learn from a letter of his to Joseph Jones, then in Congress, written shortly after the Assembly closed, that George Mason's exertions and influence helped to bring to a conclusion the settlement of the boundary question between Virginia and Pennsylvania, which had been long in dispute. Colonel Mason believed that his own State was giving up some of her just rights, but his desire to heal dissensions and strengthen the union led him to counsel acceptance of the agreement notwithstanding. The same liberal temper was manifested in his attitude on the subject of the cession of the Northwestern Territory. Joseph Jones, a prominent member of Virginia's delegation in Congress, had written to George Mason to ascertain his views on this matter, and in Colonel Mason's reply he gives what is believed to be the first fully digested plan of the cession, as it was subsequently carried out. The manuscript was found among the Bland papers, and is signed simply by the writer's initials. In a letter to Madison, however, Colonel Mason alludes to this communication, so there can be no doubt as to its authorship.

[1] Journal of the Assembly.

July 27th, 1780.

The agreement of the commissioners from the two States, for settling the dispute of territory between Virginia and Pennsylvania, by fixing the line commonly called Mason and Dixon's line as the southern boundary of Pennsylvania, and from the termination of five degrees, of west longitude, on the said line, to be computed from the Delaware river, extending a meridian line for the western boundary of Pennsylvania, has been at last ratified by our Assembly, on condition that the titles of individuals within the disputed territory should be confirmed according to their priority, whichever State they were acquired under ; that the inhabitants shall remain free from taxes until December next, and shall not be chargeable with arrears. Justice demanded the first of these, to which I think there can be no objection on the part of Pennsylvania, unless suggested by the private views of some great landmongers ; and good policy, I hope, will induce her to assent to the whole, to conciliate the affections of her new citizens, without which she will find herself involved in a very disagreeable business with these people.

I think it the duty of a staunch whig, and friend to his country, to do everything in his power to remove any cause of ill will or disagreement with a sister State ; and therefore (though I clearly saw from the proceedings that our commissioners had been overmatched by those of Pennsylvania) I labored the ratification of the agreement, as heartily as I ever did any subject in my life. There was so strong an opposition that we were able to carry it only by a small majority ; for this reason, and from my attachment to the common cause of America, I sincerely wish the dispute may now be closed, and not remitted again to our Assembly. You will observe from a clause in the resolve that we have not been influenced by pecuniary motives, in the annexed conditions.

If you will cast your eye upon the late maps, you will perceive that the five degrees of longitude from the Delaware, will extend Mason and Dixon's line within twenty or thirty miles, perhaps less, of the Ohio ; and that between the meridian line or western boundary of Pennsylvania and the river there will remain a long narrow slip of land, so detached from Virginia as to be of little value to her, unless she retains her territory on the north-west of the Ohio.

Nothing has been moved in our Assembly respecting our western territory since the remonstrance to Congress, nor do I think there will be shortly, unless there are some propositions from Congress on the subject ; but I am sure the most judicious men in our legislature, and the firm friends to American independence, are well disposed for the sake of cementing our union, and accelerating the completion of the Confederation, to make great cessions to the United States, and wish for such reasonable propositions from Congress as they can unite in supporting. You will observe a hint in the Remonstrance to this purpose ; it was intended to bring on offers from Congress, and there can't be a fitter time than the present, upon our having settled our dispute with Pennsylvania. I dare not presume to give my opinion upon this subject, farther than as an individual member ; but, from the best judgment I am able to make, (and I have taken some pains to inform myself,) I think if Congress would offer the guaranty of the United States, for our remaining territory, this commonwealth will agree to Mason and Dixon's line, from the intersection of the meridian, drawn from the fountain of the main north branch of [the] Potomac, to the Ohio river, as the northern boundary of Virginia, saving to the people north of the said line, on the long slip of land between the western boundary of Pennsylvania and the said Ohio river, their titles previously founded under our laws ; and will also agree to fix the north-west bank of the Ohio river, from thence to the North Carolina line, in latitude 36° 30' as the western boundary of Virginia ; granting to the inhabitants of the United States the full and free use of the navigation of the said river ; but if the North Carolina line shall be found to be south of the confluence of the Ohio and Mississippi, (which at present is uncertain,) then, and in that case, the western boundary of Virginia to be extended from the mouth of the Ohio down the Mississippi river, to the intersection of the said North Carolina line, ceding and relinquishing to the United States the right and title of Virginia, both in the soil and sovereignty of the country, northward and westward of the said boundaries, upon the following conditions :

1st. That the territory so ceded shall be laid out and formed into not less than two separate and distinct states or governments. The time and manner of doing it to be at the discretion of Congress.

2dly.   That Virginia shall be allowed and fully reimbursed by the United States her expenses in reducing the British posts at the Kaskaskias and St. Vincents [Vincennes], the expense of maintaining garrisons, and supporting civil government there, since the reduction of the said posts, and in general all the charge she has incurred on account of the country on the north side of the Ohio river, since the declaration of American independence.

3dly.   That the French and Canadian inhabitants and other settlers at the Kaskaskias, St. Vincents and the neighboring villages, who have professed themselves citizens of Virginia, shall have their possessions and titles confirmed to them, and shall be protected in the enjoyment of their rights and liberty ; for which purpose troops shall be stationed there, at the charge of the United States, to protect them from the incroachments of the British forces at De Troit, or elsewhere, unless the events of war shall render it impracticable.

4thly.   As Col. George Rogers Clarke planned and executed the secret expedition by which the British posts were reduced, and was promised, if the enterprise succeeded, a liberal gratuity in lands in that country, for the officers and soldiers who first marched thither with him ; that a quantity of land not exceeding one hundred and fifty thousand acres, be allowed and granted to the said officers and soldiers, to be laid off in one tract, the length of which not to exceed two-thirds of the breadth, in such place on the north-west side of the Ohio, as the majority of the officers shall choose, and to be afterwards divided among the said officers and soldiers, in due proportions according to the laws of Virginia.

5thly.   That the said Col. George Rogers Clarke shall be permitted to hold, and shall have confirmed and granted to him, in fee simple for ever, without purchase money other than a nominal legal consideration, a certain tract of land, of seven miles and a half square, at the great falls of the Ohio, binding upon the river, upon the north-west side thereof, which hath been given him by the Wabache Indians for his services, and as a testimony of their friendship to him, and of their attachment to the commonwealth of Virginia and the cause of America.

6thly.   In case the quantity of good lands on the south-east side the Ohio, upon the waters of Cumberland river, and between the Green river and the Tennessee river, which have been reserved

by law for the Virginia troops upon Continental establishment
and upon their own State establishment, should (from the North
Carolina line bearing in further upon the Cumberland lands than
was expected) prove insufficient for their legal bounties ; that the
deficiency shall be made up to the said troops, in good lands on
the north-west side of the Ohio river, (within the territory to be
ceded to the United States as aforesaid,) in such proportions as
have been engaged to them by the laws of Virginia.

7thly. That all the lands within the territory so ceded to the
United States, and not reserved for, or appropriated to any of
the herein-before-mentioned purposes, or disposed of in bounties
to the officers and soldiers of the American army shall be considered as a common fund for the use and benefit of such of the
united American States as have become, or shall become members of the Confederation, or federal alliance of the said States
(Virginia inclusive) according to their usual respective proportions in the general charge and expenditure, and shall be faithfully and "*bona fide*" disposed of for that purpose, and for no
other use or purpose whatsoever ; and therefore that all purchases
and deeds from any Indian or Indians, or from any Indian
nation or nations, for any lands within any part of the said
territory, which have been or shall be made for the use or benefit
of any private person or persons whatsoever shall be deemed and
declared absolutely void and of no effect, in the same manner as
if the said territory had still remained subject to and part of the
Commonwealth of Virginia.

By the charter of 1609, Virginia is to extend from the cape or
point of land called Cape or Point Comfort, all along the sea-
coast to the northward two hundred miles, and from thence *west
and north-west* into the land, &c.   Giving this the most confined
construction—that is, *a due west course* into the land, &c., the
northern boundary of Virginia would pass through the western
boundary of Pennsylvania, and strike the Mississippi between
the 41st and 42d degrees of latitude.   According to the late
agreement the southern boundary of Pennsylvania, viz., Mason
and Dixon's line (as well as I can recollect, for I have not now
the papers by me) is in latitude 39° 45' 18", and her western
boundary a meridian line drawn from the termination of five
degrees of longitude, computed from the Delaware ; consequently

Virginia would cede to the United States, west of Pennsylvania and north of latitude 39° 45′ 18″, a tract of land in length from north to south not less than eighty or ninety miles, and in breadth from east to west, the whole distance between the western boundary of Pennsylvania and the Mississippi river, probably not less than three or four hundred miles ; besides the extensive country between the Ohio and Mississippi, lying south of latitude 39° 45′ 18″. In the whole a territory of more than fifty millions of acres, larger than all the territory remaining to Virginia between the Atlantic Ocean and the Ohio river, and between the States of Pennsylvania, Maryland, and North Carolina ; and from its levelness and fertility of soil, capable of sustaining more than double its number of inhabitants. Taking the subject in this point of view (which is not an exaggerated one) I trust Virginia will be considered as acting upon a large and liberal scale, and sacrificing her own local interests to the general cause of America ; and that the before-mentioned conditions are so moderate and reasonable that they can hardly be objected to by any real friend of American independence ; yet, lest they should be thought by any unnecessary or capricious, I will beg leave to offer some reasons in their support.

The first condition is so evidently proper that little need be said on it. The power of one State owning such an extensive and fertile territory, whose situation is naturally, and whose commercial interest and connexions may in process of time, become so different from the others might be dangerous to the American union.

The 2d and 3d, justice as well as policy require. Virginia has indeed a right to expect much more, particularly the charges of an expedition over the Ohio in the year 1774, which, though carried on by Lord Dunmore under the former government, has been paid for by the present, and the money emitted for that purpose is still in circulation, and is to be redeemed by the taxes imposed by our last session of Assembly.

The French and Canadian inhabitants have received no titles from Virginia, further than a declaration that they should have their private property confirmed to them and be protected in the enjoyment of all their just rights as citizens.—I understand they possess only small portions of land contiguous to their respective

villages, which they cultivate ; and to which, perhaps, they have
no other legal title than the possession, under the encouragement
or acquiescence of the former government.

These people have great interest with the neighboring Indians
and also with the French and Canadian inhabitants about Fort
De Troit ; they raise provisions sufficient to support strong garrisons, at the Kaskaskias and St. Vincents, are well affected to
the United States, and may, if properly encouraged, be very useful to them, as their strength is by no means inconsiderable.

4th and 5th. The Commonwealth of Virginia hath yet given
no titles to any lands on the north-west side of the Ohio ; but the
public faith stands pledged to Colonel Clarke and his officers and
men (in all about one hundred and eighty), who reduced the
British posts of Kaskaskias and St. Vincents, for a liberal reward
in the lands they conquered. This handful of men has performed more than two or three thousand men and two general
officers, on the two expeditions against that country, ordered by
Congress, at the expense of several millions ; and their success
has been of great importance to the United States ; by fixing
garrisons behind the Indian towns and deterring them from
sending their warriors far from home, and by drawing from the
British to the American interest several tribes of Indians ; the
frontiers of the middle-states have been more effectually protected than they would have been by ten times the number of
troops stationed upon the Ohio ; and by putting Virginia in
possession of these posts, they have not only taken them out of
the hands of the British, but have prevented the Spaniards from
possessing themselves of them ; which, but for that circumstance,
they would most undoubtedly have done last year in their expedition up the Mississippi, when they took possession of every
other British post upon that river ; in which case that country
would have been lost to the United States and left to be disputed
between Spain and Great Britain, upon a treaty of peace. The
possession of these posts has prevented Spain from meddling
with the country on this side the Mississippi, above the mouth
of the Ohio, and will afford a strong argument in favor of our
claim upon a treaty with Great Britain. It leads also to the
reduction of the British garrison at Fort De Troit ; the situation
of St. Vincents rendering it by far the most convenient place

from whence to carry on an expedition for that purpose.   Colonel Clarke's enterprising genius, his great interest with the back inhabitants, his influence with the western Indians, and his knowledge of the country, qualify him better than any man in America for conducting such an expedition.   When these things are properly considered, I make no doubt that Congress will cheerfully agree to the conditions in favor of Colonel Clarke and his regiment.

6th.   When the law passed for opening a land office, a large tract of country, on the south-east side the Ohio, between the said river and the great mountains, and between the Green river, the North Carolina line, and the Tennessee river, was reserved for the Virginia troops, on Continental and State establishment; which was then thought amply sufficient for the purpose; the finest body of this reserved land being upon the waters of the Cumberland river and the North Carolina line being extended lately by the authority of the .   States, and bearing on much farther upon the Cumberland lands than was expected, it is feared there may not remain a sufficient quantity of good lands for the said troops ; this may not, perhaps, be the case, but lest it should, it is incumbent upon Virginia, at all events before she make a cession of so large a part of her territory, to reserve the certain means of fulfilling her engagements to her own troops, both upon Continental and State establishment ; the latter are but few, most of the troops raised for the local defence of the State having been from time to time added to the Continental establishment.

7th.   Without some such stipulation as this, there is reason to apprehend much abuse in this business.   It is notorious that several gentlemen of great influence in the neighboring States were, and still are, concerned in partnership with Lord Dunmore, some other of the late American governors, and several of the British nobility and gentry, in a purchase for a mere trifle, about the year 1773, from the Indians, of a large tract of country, containing by their own computation between twenty and thirty millions of acres, on the north-west side the Ohio ; that there is another company claiming in the same manner an extensive tract adjoining the other ; and if fame speaks truth, these two companies, since the declaration of American independence, have united their interests; which they have spared no pains to strengthen, by disposing of shares to members of Congress, &c. Any man who reads with attention the Maryland Declaration will perceive that Assembly has been so far imposed upon, as to insert a clause evidently calculated to secure and guaranty these purchases; by which means, under the popular pretence of establishing a common fund, the public would be duped by the arts of individuals, and the most valuable part of the territory to be ceded by Virginia, would be applied to private purposes. However just and necessary, therefore, this condition may be, private interest will probably suggest many objections to it; but I am pretty confident Virginia will ever consider it as a "*sine qua non.*"

I have given you the trouble of a tedious epistle; but the importance of the subject and your own request have brought it on you, and render an apology unnecessary. I am certain there will be a strong opposition here to the cession of such an extensive territory. As I think I have some weight in our Assembly, and more upon this than any other subject, I earnestly wish Congress may take up the consideration, and transmit reasonable proposals to our next session, that I may have an opportunity of giving them my aid; being anxious to do this last piece of service to the American Union, before I quit the Assembly, which I am determined to do at the end of the next session. I am, &c.,

G. M.

N. B.—Mr. Jones was desired to communicate the contents of this letter to his colleagues in the delegation.[1]

Madison was one of these colleagues, and to him Colonel Mason wrote a few days later:

GUNSTON HALL, August 2d, 1780.

DEAR SIR:

By late letters from Europe I understand a treaty of alliance will soon be concluded between his Catholic Majesty and the United States, upon which it is presumed Congress will find it necessary to appoint a consul in Spain, for the superintendence and protection of our trade. Should this be the case, I beg

---

[1] Bland Papers, Charles Campbell, vol. ii., Appendix (D).

leave to recommend Mr. Richard Harrison as a very proper person for the office. This gentleman is a native of Maryland, but about the beginning of the present troubles, removed to the island of Martinique, where he resided about two years, learned the French language, and transacted a good deal of business for Virginia and some other of the United States in a manner that gave general satisfaction. He is now settled at Cadiz, but when I heard from him last was in Madrid, and I am authorized to say will undertake the office, if he is appointed to it, presuming that Congress will think Cadiz the most proper place for the residence of an American consul. I have always been cautious in giving recommendations for public offices ; but my knowledge of Mr. Harrison's diligence, integrity and commercial knowledge, from a personal acquaintance with him, convinces me he will discharge such an office with reputation to himself and advantage to the commercial interest of America.

I have written a long letter to Mr. Jones (who desired my sentiments) upon the subject of our back lands ; not doubting the harmony and confidence subsisting between him and his colleagues in the delegation, I have desired him to communicate the contents, and must beg leave to recommend the subject to your particular attention

Our Assembly considered Mr. Griffen's appointment to the office of a judge in the new Court of Admiralty established by Congress not only as vacating his seat in Congress, but rendering him ineligible, during his continuance in office, and therefore elected Colonel Theo. Bland to succeed him, who had accepted the appointment, and will soon attend Congress.

I am, dear Sir,

Your most obedient servant.

G. MASON.[1]

The progress of the war in the South was most discouraging to the Americans at this time. Charleston had fallen into the enemy's hands the 12th of May, 1780, and General Gates, the hero of Saratoga, exchanging his northern laurels for southern willows, as he had been forewarned might be the case, on the 16th of August was defeated at Camden.

---

[1] Madison MSS., Department of State.

General Washington wrote to George Mason in October, introducing General Greene, the newly appointed commander of the Southern Department :

HEAD QUARTERS, PASSAIC FALLS,
October 22d, 1780.

DEAR SIR ·

In consequence of a resolve of Congress, directing an inquiry into the conduct of Major-General Gates, and authorizing me to appoint some other officer in his place during this inquiry, I have made choice of Major-General Greene, who will, I expect, have the honor of presenting you with this letter.

I shall, without scruple introduce this gentleman to you as a man of ability, bravery and coolness. He has a comprehensive knowledge of our affairs, and is a man of fortitude and resources. I have not the smallest doubt, therefore, of his employing all the means which may be put in his hands to the best advantage, nor of his assisting in pointing out the most likely ones to answer the purposes of his command. With this character I take the liberty of recommending him to your civilities and support; for I have no doubt, from the embarrassed situation of Southern affairs, of his standing much in need of the latter from every gentleman of influence in the Assemblies of those States.

As General Greene can give you the most perfect information in detail of our present distresses and future prospects, I shall content myself with the aggregate account of them ; and, with respect to the first, they are so great and complicated, that it is scarcely within the powers of description to give an adequate idea of them. With regard to the second, unless there is a material change both in our civil and military policy, it will be in vain to contend much longer.

We are without money, and have been so for a long time, without provision and forage, except what is taken by impress ; without clothing, and shortly shall be (in a manner) without men. In a word, we have lived upon expedients till we can live no longer ; and it may truly be said, that the history of this war is a history of false hopes and temporary devices, instead of system—and economy, which results from it.

If we mean to continue our struggles (and it is to be hoped we shall not relinquish our claims), we must do it upon an entire

24

new plan. We must have a permanent force, not a force that is constantly fluctuating, and sliding from under us as a pedestal of ice would leave a statue on a summer's day, involving us in expense that baffles all calculation, an expense which no funds are equal to. We must at the same time contrive ways and means to aid our taxes by loans, and put our finances upon a more certain and stable footing than they are at present. Our civil government must likewise undergo a reform ; ample powers must be lodged in Congress as the head of the Federal Union, adequate to all the purposes of war. Unless these things are done, our efforts will be in vain, and only serve to accumulate expense, add to our perplexities, and dissatisfy the people, without a prospect of obtaining the prize in view. But these sentiments do not appear well in a hasty letter, without digestion or order. I have not time to give them otherwise, and shall only assure you that they are well meant, however crude they may appear. With sincere affection,

I am, dear Sir,

Your most obedient servant,

GEORGE WASHINGTON.[1]

General Greene went to Richmond, where the Assembly was in session, stopping on his way at " Mount Vernon," and very probably visiting " Gunston Hall." He wrote to Washington from Richmond, that his letters had been of singular service, and expressed his thanks for their warm recommendations. General Henry Lee wrote to George Mason from the Southern Department in November, offering a position in his command to William Mason, at this time a captain in the Continental service. Colonel Mason replied as follows ·

GUNSTON HALL, DECEMBER 13, 1780.

DEAR SIR :

I received your favor of the 30th November, and have the warmest sense of your very friendly offer to my son William, whose inclination I well know would strongly incline him to accept it, in which I would most cheerfully indulge him if I had

---

[1] Lee's " Memoirs of the War in the Southern Department," p. 210 note. New York, 1869.

any thought of continuing him in the military line, as in that case it would give me great satisfaction to place him under the direction of a gentleman who has rendered such important services to our country, and in whose friendship I could so thoroughly confide. But I have ever intended him for civil and private life ; his lot must be that of a farmer and country gentleman, and at this time there is a particular domestic circumstance which will require his return as soon as his present time of service expires. Permit me, sir, to return you my thanks for the very friendly part you have acted, and to assure you that I am with the greatest esteem and regard,

Your most obedient servant,

G. MASON.[1]

[1] *Ibid.*, p. 30.

APPENDIX.

I.

In the name of God, Amen, I, George Mason, Senr., of the county of Stafford in the colony of Virginia, being sick and weak in body, but perfect and sound memory, praised be God for it, do make and ordain this my will, revoking and making null and void all former will or wills by me heretofore made and this only to be my last Will and Testament.

I give and bequeath my soul to Almighty God that gave it me, hoping that through the meritorious Death and Passion of our Saviour and Redeemer Jesus Christ, to receive absolution and remission for all my sins, and my body to the Earth to be decently buried according to the Discretion of my Executors hereafter named.

Imprimis, I give and bequeath unto my son, French Mason, all the land which I bought of Martin Scarlet and Thomas James, to him and his heirs forever. Item, I give unto my son French Mason, Primo, Scanderback, Peter, Sarah, Nicholas, and Jenny, six negro slaves which he is now already possest with, to him and his heirs forever. Item, I give and bequeath unto my son Nicholson Mason, all the land which I bought of Edward Rockwood, in Maryland, to him and his heirs forever. Item, I give and bequeath unto my son, Nicholson Mason, Charles, Moal, Billy, Nanny, Lucy, Nelly, and Digg, seven slaves, to him and his heirs forever. Item, I give and bequeath unto my son Francis Mason, all the land that I bought of Madame Brent, Rawleigh Travers, and William Lambeth, to him and his heirs forever. Item, I give and bequeath unto my son Francis Mason

Bryant Foley, to him and his heirs forever. Item, I give and bequeath unto my son Francis Mason, Harry, Walker, and Jacob, three negro slaves, to him and his heirs forever. Item, I give and bequeath unto my son, Thomas Mason, all the land which I bought of Alexander Waugh, to him and his heirs forever. Item, I give and bequeath unto my son, Thomas Mason, all the land which I bought of William Moss in Maryland, and all the land I bought of Michael Valandigham in Stafford County, to him and his heirs forever. I give and bequeath unto my son, Thomas Mason, Bess and Mudaley, two negro slaves, to him and his heirs forever. I give and bequeath unto my daughter, Elizabeth Mason, one negro man called Tom, to her and her heirs forever, and one feather bed, bolster, rug, pair blankets, and two pair sheets. Item, I give and bequeath unto my daughter, Simpher Rosa Mason, one negro slave called Valentine, to her and her heirs forever, and one feather bed, bolster, rug, blankets, and two pair sheets. Item, I give and bequeath unto my daughters, Elizabeth and Simpher Rosa Mason, all that land which I hold in partnership with James Hereford, being nine hundred and nine acres by computation, be the same more or less, equally to be divided to them and their heirs forever. Item, I give and bequeath unto my daughter, Catherine Mason, all the land where Thomas Brookes now lives and the rest of the land at the head of Potomack Creek, which my brother-in-law, Joseph Waugh, did grant and convey unto me, unto her and her heirs forever. Item, I give and bequeath unto my daughter Catherine Mason, one mulatto girl called Sarah, to her and her heirs forever, and one feather bed, bolster, rug, pair blankets, and two pair sheets. Item, I give and bequeath unto my son George Mason, two silver candlesticks, snuffers, and snuff dish belonging to the same, forever. Item, I give and bequeath all the rest of my silver plate to be equally divided between my dear and loving wife, Sarah Mason, and my son Nicholson Mason, to be and to remain to their heirs forever. Item, I give and bequeath unto my daughter Sarah Mason, one feather bed, bolster, rugg, pair blankets and two pair sheets forever. Item, I give and bequeath unto my dear and loving wife, and my son Nicholson Mason all the rest of my household stuff, beds, furniture, pots, pans, pewter either Iron or Wooden ware, be it of what nature soever equally to be divided between them two, and my sons Thomas and Francis Mason, each of them to have, share and share alike of the said household furniture aforesaid. Item, I give and bequeath unto my dear and loving wife Sarah Mason, all my stock, both Cattle and Hoggs. Item, I give and bequeath all of my Tobacco money and goods to be equally divided between my Dear and Loving wife and my son Nicholson Mason, my Family being first cloathed. Item, I give unto my son-in-law William Darrall, five hundred pounds of Tobacco which shall be paid unto him after my decease. Item, I give and bequeath unto my son-in-law George Fitzhugh, Five hundred pounds of Tobacco to be paid him after my decease. I give and bequeath unto John Heedman two hundred acres of land which lies in Cockpit Point, unto him and his heirs forever, and all my wearing apparell. Item, I do constitute, ordain and appoint my Loving sons George Mason and Nicholson Mason, Ex'rs of this, my last Will and Testament, to see all things duly performed according to the true intent and meaning of this my will.

In witness whereof I have hereunto set my hand and seal this 29th day of June, 1715.

GEORGE MASON.

Signed, sealed and delivered in the presence of us.

JAMES HEREFORD (Signed).
HUGH × FARRALL (Signed).
MARY × LEWIS (Signed).
H. PARRY.

At a court held for Stafford County the 14th day of November, Anno Domini, 1716, the last will and testament of George Mason, gent., deceased, was presented unto court by George Mason, who made oath thereto (Nicholson Mason having departed this life before the said will was proved), and being prov'd by the oath of Henry Parry, one of the witnesses thereto, is admitted to record, and on the motion of the said George Mason, and his performing what is usual in such cases, certificate is granted him for obtaining a probate thereof in due form, and the will ordered to be recorded, and is recorded.

Per THOS. FITZHUGH, Cl. Cur.

[1] Extracted from the "Book of Landed Possessions of John Mercer of Marlboro,'" the property of Prof. James Mercer Garnett.

MASON WILLS.

There were on record at Stafford Court House in 1845 two wills, of which the following memoranda remain ·

The last will and testament of George Mason, of Acquia, Stafford County, dated October 18, 1710, and recorded May 11, 1711, leaving his wife Margaret his sole executrix and the following children his heirs : George, William, Lyman, Mary Ann.

2.

The last will and testament of George Mason, of Stafford County in the colony of Virginia, dated June 19 and recorded September 14, 1715, leaving, after a few legacies to his sisters Margaret Bennett and Ann French Mason, his whole estate to his wife Mary Mason and his sole executrix. There are no children mentioned in the will.

Whether one or both of these gentlemen were of the same family as George Mason of Gunston it is now impossible to determine. It has been asserted in one of the family MSS. that George Mason of Gunston was the fifth of his line, and not the fourth, and that his grandfather married a Miss French. Legal documents seem to demonstrate that there were but three in the direct line, counting the founder of the family, before George Mason of '76· Mary Fowke was without doubt his grandmother, and his great-grandmother was probably a Miss French—a name well known and prominent in the colony.

MASON—FOWKE—MASON.

Col. Enoch Mason of "Clover Hill," Stafford County, descended, it seems probable, from the same stock originally as Col. George Mason, intermarried with the Fowkes and became allied, therefore, to Col. George Mason's descendants. Sarah, the daughter of Gerard and Elizabeth Dinwiddie Fowke, married Wiley Roy. Their daughter Lucy married Col.

Enoch Mason. There were ten children of this marriage, of whom one only survives, Dr. Gerard Fowke Mason of Charles. town, West Virginia. The descendants of Col. Enoch Mason are numerous, and socially prominent in Virginia and other States. Elizabeth Dinwiddie Fowke was a first cousin of George Mason of Gunston.

MASON—FITZHUGH.

Col. William Fitzhugh, son of George and Mary Mason Fitzhugh, married first Mrs. Martha Turberville, *née* Lee, a daughter of Richard Lee and niece of Col. Thomas Lee of "Stratford." By this marriage he had one son, George Lee Mason Fitzhugh. Colonel Fitzhugh married secondly Mrs. Ann Rousby, *née* Frisby, of "Rousby Hall," Calvert County, Maryland, and the children of this marriage were Peregrine, William, and John Fitzhugh. Peregrine and William were both officers in the Revolutionary War, and the former served on General Washington's personal staff. All of these sons left descendants. Col. William Fitzhugh, at an early period of his life, entered the British army and served with Admiral Vernon in his attack on Carthagena. In that expedition he was the friend and companion of Lawrence Washington, as he was afterwards equally intimate with General Washington. He resigned his commission as captain in Gooch's regiment of foot in June, 1776, and distinguished himself in the civil service of Maryland during the Revolution, serving in the Convention which framed the Constitution, and in the Legislature of the State. He was also at one time a member of the Council. As a member of the Committee of Vigilance of Calvert County he was active in organizing a force for the protection of its shores from the predatory boat excursions of the enemy. But during his absence from his home in 1780 and in 1781, the enemy landed there and burned the buildings and furniture, and carried off forty-two of his slaves. Contiguous to "Rousby Hall," the plantation on which he lived, was the farm of "Millmount," where Colonel Fitzhugh had established a mill or manufactory for making ship-bread for the supply of vessels trading in the Chesapeake.

II.

SCHEME FOR REPLEVYING GOODS UNDER DISTRESS FOR RENT.
GEORGE MASON, DECEMBER 23, 1765.

The policy of encouraging the importation of free people and discouraging that of slaves has never been duly considered in this colony, or we should not at this day see one half of our best lands in most parts of the country remain unsettled and the other cultivated with slaves ; not to mention the ill effect such a practice has upon the morals and manners of our people.   One of the first signs of the decay and perhaps the primary cause of the destruction of the most flourishing government that ever existed was the introduction of great numbers of slaves, an evil very pathetically described by the Roman historians.   But it is not the present intention to expose our weakness by examining this subject too freely.   That the custom of leasing lands is more beneficial to the community than that of settling them with slaves is a maxim that will hardly be denied in any free country. Though it may not be attended with so much immediate profit to the landholder, in proportion as it is useful to the public, the invitations from the Legislature to pursue it should be stronger. No means seem so natural as securing the payment of rents in an easy and effective manner.   The little trouble and risk attending this species of property may be considered as an equivalent to the greater profit arising from the labor of slaves, or any other precarious and troublesome estate.

The common law (independent of any statute) gives the landlord a right to distrain upon anything on his land for the rent due ; that is, it puts the remedy into his own hands.   But as so unlimited a power was liable to be abused, it was found necessary to punish the abuse of it by penal statutes, made *in terrorem*, to preserve justice and prevent the oppression which the poor might otherwise suffer from the rich ; not to destroy the landlord's right, which still remained unimpeached, and has not only been exercised in this colony from its first settlement, but has obtained in our mother-country from time immemorial.   Uninterrupted and long experience carry with them a conviction of general utility.

The fluctuating state of our trade, the uncertainty of our markets, and the scarcity of money frequently render it imprac-ticable for the debtor to raise money out of his effects to dis-charge a sudden and perhaps unexpected judgment, and have introduced a law giving the debtor a right to replevy his goods under execution by bond with security (approved by the creditor) to pay the debt and costs with interest in three months; which bonds are returnable to the clerk's office whence the execution issued, to remain in the nature of judgments, and final executions may be obtained upon them when due by a motion to the court with ten days' notice to the parties. The Legislature considering distresses for rents in the same light with executions for common debts, has thought fit to extend the same indulgence to them, though it would not be hard to show that the cases are by no means similar, and that the reasons which are just in the former do not hold good in the latter. By comparing the laws there also appears such an inconsistency in that relating to replevin bonds for rent as may render the method prescribed difficult, if not impracticable; there being no previous record (as in the case of executions), the bonds do not seem properly returnable to the clerk's office, nor is that matter clearly expressed or pro-vided for in the act. This has not hitherto been productive of much inconvenience, though contrary to the course and spirit of the common law, the landlord may thereby be brought into a court of judicature before he can get the effect of a just and legal distress, but in our present circumstances it will occasion mani-fest injustice. If the officer making a distress, upon being offered security, refuses to take a bond for want of stamped paper, the goods of the tenant must be immediately exposed to sale and he deprived of the indulgence intended by the Act of Assembly. If the officer takes a replevin bond as usual, the landlord will lose his rent, the tenant then having it in his power to keep him out of it as long as he pleases; for in the present confusion and cessation of judicial proceedings, the landlord will not have an opportunity of applying to court for an execution when the bond becomes payable; or, if he does, the clerk will not venture to issue one. In either case there is such a hardship as calls for the interposition of the Legislature.

These inconveniencies, it is conceived, may be obviated if the tenant, instead of replevying his goods by bond, had a right to supersede the distress for three months by application to a single magistrate, who should be empowered and required, upon the tenant producing, under the hand of the person making distress, a certificate of the rent distrained for and costs, to take from the principal and good securities a conditional confession of judgment, in the following or some such form.

"Virginia, . . . County S. S.—You, A. B., C. D. and E. F. of the said county do confess judgment unto G. H. of the county of   for the sum of   due unto the said G. H. for rent, for which distress has been made upon the goods of the said A. B. and also for the sum of   . .   the costs of the said distress: which said sums of   . .   and   . . costs with legal interest from the date hereof to be levyed of your or either of your body's goods or chattels for the life of the said G. H. in case the said A. B. shall not pay and satisfy to the said G. H. the said sums of   . .   and   .   costs with interest thereon as aforesaid within three months at furthest from the date hereof. Taken and acknowledged the   day of . . . before me, one of his majesty's justices of the peace for the said county of   Given under my hand the day and year aforesaid.
"To T. K., Sheriff or Constable
(as the case is)."

Which confession of judgment should restore to the tenant his goods, and be returned by the officer to the landlord, who at the end of the three months (giving the parties ten days' notice) should be entitled to an execution thereon, to be awarded by a single magistrate also.

This method will protect the tenant from oppression by confirming the indulgence the Act of Assembly formerly gave him, at the same time that it secures the landlord in the payment of his rent. And it can hardly be objected to as giving a single magistrate a new and dangerous jurisdiction, when it is considered that the application to a court on replevin bonds for rent was mere matter of form, in which the court could exercise no judicial power, and that an execution might as safely be awarded by a magistrate out of court in the case of rents, where (as has been before observed) there was no original record or jurisdiction in the court but by the common law the sole power vested in the landlord, who, should the proposed alteration take place, will be as liable to be punished for the abuse of it as he was before. If the form of the judgment recommended is objected to as subjecting the body to execution in a case where the goods only were originally liable, let it be considered that it is at the tenant's own request the nature of his debt is changed ; that when the landlord sues for rent, he may upon a judgment order a fi : fa : or a ca : sa : at his own option, and that he may do the same thing in the case of replevin bonds.

If some such alteration as is here proposed should be thought necessary, any little errors or deficiencies in this scheme may be easily corrected in drawing up the law.[1]

A draft of the " Address of the House of Burgesses to Governor Fauquier in 1765," in the handwriting of George Mason, has come to light recently among the Washington manuscripts in the State Department. It has been supposed hitherto that Richard Henry Lee was the author of this address, as it is found among his papers. It is possible that both Mason and Lee made copies from an original, of which the authorship is unknown. The paper, however, in its close reasoning and concise expression, is very much in George Mason's style. It is published in the *Southern Literary Messenger*, February, 1860.

III.

TO THE COMMITTEE OF MERCHANTS IN LONDON.

VIRGINIA, POTOMACK RIVER,
June 6th, 1766.

GENTLEMEN :

There is a letter of yours dated the 20th of February last, lately printed in the public papers here, which, though addressed to a particular set of men, seems intended for the colonies in general ; and, being upon a very interesting subject, I shall, without further

---

[1] Manuscripts in Department of State.

preface or apology, exercise the right of a freeman in making such remarks upon it as I think proper.

The epithets of parent and child have been so long applied to Great Britain and her colonies, that individuals have adopted them, and we rarely see anything from your side of the water free from the authoritative style of a master to a schoolboy

" We have with infinite difficulty and fatigue got you excused this one time ; pray be a good boy for the future, do what your papa and mama bid you, and hasten to return them your most grateful acknowledgements for condescending to let you keep what is your own ; and then all your acquaintance will love you, and praise you, and give you pretty things ; and if you should at any time hereafter happen to transgress, your friends will all beg for you, and be security for your good behaviour ; but if you are a naughty boy, and turn obstinate, and don't mind what your papa and mama say to you, but presume to think their commands (let them be what they will) unjust or unreasonable, or even seem to ascribe their present indulgence to any other motive than excess of moderation and tenderness, and pretend to judge for yourselves, when you are not arrived at the years of discretion, or capable of distinguishing between good and evil ; then everybody will hate you, and say you are a graceless and undutiful child ; your parents and masters will be obliged to whip you severely, and your friends will be ashamed to say anything in your excuse : nay, they will be blamed for your faults. See your work—see what you have brought the child to. If he had been well scourged at first for opposing our absolute will and pleasure, and daring to think he had any such thing as property of his own, he would not have had the impudence to repeat the crime."

" My dear child, we have laid the alternative fairly before you, you can't hesitate in the choice, and we doubt not you will observe such a conduct as your friends recommend."

Is not this a little ridiculous, when applied to three millions of as loyal and useful subjects as any in the British dominions, who have been only contending for their birth-right, and have now only gained, or rather kept, what could not, with common justice, or even policy, be denied them ? But setting aside the manner, let me seriously consider the substance and subject of your letter.

Can the honor of parliament be maintained by persisting in a measure evidently wrong ? Is it any reflection upon the honor of parliament to show itself wiser this year than the last, to have profited by experience, and to correct the errors which time and indubitable evidence have pointed out ?

If the Declaratory Act, or Vote of Right, has asserted any un-just, oppressive, or unconstitutional principles, to become "waste paper" would be the most innocent use that could be made of it; by the copies we have seen here, the legislative authority of Great Britain is fully and positively asserted in all cases whatso-ever. But a just and necessary distinction between legislation and taxation hath been made by the greatest and wisest men in the nation ; so that if the right to the latter had been disclaimed, it would not have impeached or weakened the vote of right ; on the contrary, it would have strengthened it, for nothing (except hanging the author of the Stamp Act) would have contributed more to restore that confidence which a weak or corrupt ministry had so greatly impaired.

We do not deny the supreme authority of Great Britain over her colonies ; but it is a power which a wise legislature will exer-cise with extreme tenderness and caution, and carefully avoid the least imputation or suspicion of partiality. Would to God that this always had been, that it always may be the case ! To make an odious distinction between us and our fellow-subjects residing in Great Britain, by depriving us of the ancient trial, by a jury of our equals, and substituting in its place an arbitrary civil-law court—to put it in the power of every sycophant and informer ("the most mischievous, wicked, abandoned and prof-ligate race," says an eminent writer upon British politics, "that ever God permitted to plague mankind ") to drag a freeman a thousand miles from his own country (whereby he may be de-prived of the benefit of evidence) to defend his property before a judge, who, from the nature of his office, is a creature of the ministry, liable to be displaced at their pleasure, whose interest it is to encourage informers, as his income may in a great meas-ure depend upon his condemnations, and to give such a judge a power of excluding the most innocent man, thus treated, from any remedy (even the recovery of his costs) by only certifying that *in his opinion* there was a *probable* cause of complaint ; and thus to make the property of the subject, in a matter which may reduce him from opulence to indigence, depend upon a word before unknown in the language and style of laws ! Are these among the instances that call for our expression of "filial gratitude to our parent-country"? These things did not altogether depend upon the stamp act, and therefore are not repealed with it.

Can the foundations of the state be sapped and the body of the people remain unaffected ? Are the inhabitants of Great Britain absolutely certain that, in the ministry or parliament of a future day, such incroachments will not be urged as precedents against themselves? Is the indulgence of Great Britain manifested by prohibiting her colonies from exporting to foreign countries such commodities as she does not want, and from importing such as she does not produce or manufacture, and therefore cannot furnish but upon extravagant terms? One of your own writers (I think it is Bishop Burnet) relates a remarkable piece of tyranny of the priesthood in Italy : "They make it an article of religion," says he, "for the people to mix water with their wine in the press, by which it is soured ; so that the laity cannot drink a drop of good wine, unless they buy it from the convents, at whatever price the clergy think fit to set upon it." I forbear to make the application.

Let our fellow-subjects in Great Britain reflect that we are descended from the same stock with themselves, nurtured in the same principles of freedom ; which we have both sucked in with our mother's milk ; that in crossing the Atlantic Ocean, we have only changed our climate, not our minds, our natures and dispositions remain unaltered ; that we are still the same people with them in every respect ; only not yet debauched by wealth, luxury, venality and corruption ; and then they will be able to judge how the late regulations have been relished in America.

You need not, gentlemen, be afraid of our "breaking out into intemperate strains of triumph and exaltation " ; there is yet no cause that our joy should exceed the bounds of moderation.

If we are ever so unfortunate [as] to be made slaves, which God avert ! what matter is it to us whether our chains are forged in London or at Constantinople ? Whether the oppression comes from a British parliament or a Turkish divan ?

You tell us that " our task-masters will probably be restored."

Do you mean the stamp officers, or the stamp ministry? If the first, the treatment they have already found here will hardly make them fond of returning. If the latter, we despise them too much to fear them. They have sufficiently exposed their own ignorance, malice and impotence. The cloven foot has been too plainly seen to be again concealed ; they have rendered themselves as obnoxious to Great Britain as to America.

If the late ministerial party could have influenced the legisla-ture to have made so cruel and dangerous an experiment as at-tempting to enforce the stamp-act by military power, would the nation have engaged heartily in such an execrable cause ? Would there have been no difficulty in raising and transporting a body of troops sufficient to occupy a country of more than two thousand miles in extent ? Would they have had no dangers to encounter in the woods and wilds of America ? Three millions of people driven to desperation are not an object of contempt. America, however weak in herself, adds greatly to the strength of Great Britain ; which would be diminished in proportion by her loss ; with prudent management she might become an im-penetrable bulwark to the British Nation, and almost enable it to stand before the stroke of time.

Say there was not a possibility of failing in the project, what then would have been the consequence ? Could you have destroyed us without ruining yourselves ? The trade of Great Britain is carried on and supported principally by credit. If the American [*Query.* London ?] merchant has an hundred thousand pounds due to him in the colonies, he must owe near as much to his woolen-draper, his linen-draper, his grocer, &c., and these again are indebted to the manufacturer, and so on ; there is no determinate end to this commercial chain ; break but one link of it and the whole is destroyed. Make a bankrupt of the mer-chant by stopping his remittances from America, and you strike at the credit of every man who has connections with him ; there is no knowing where the contagion would stop. You would overturn one another like a set of ninepins. The value of your lands and produce would fall, your manufacturers would starve for want of employment, your funds might fail, your public credit sink, and let but the bubble once burst, where is the man who could undertake to blow it up again ?

These evils are for the present removed. Praised be Almighty God! Blessed be our most gracious sovereign! Thanks to the present mild and prudent temper of parliament. Thanks to the wise and honest conduct of the present administration. Thanks to the unwearied diligence of our friends, the British merchants and manufacturers; thanks to that happy circumstance of their private interest being so interwoven with ours that they could not be separated. Thanks to the spirited and disinterested conduct of our own merchants in the northern colonies, who deserve to have their names handed down with reverence and gratitude to posterity. Thanks to the unanimity of the colonies themselves. And many thanks to our generous and able benefactor, Mr. Pitt, who has always stood forth a champion in the cause of liberty and his country. No thanks to Mr. Grenville and his party, who, without his genius or abilities, has dared to act the part that Pericles did, when he engaged his country in the Peloponnesian War, which, after a long and dreadful scene of blood, ended in the ruin of all Greece, and fitted it for the Macedonian yoke.

Some bungler in politics will soon, perhaps, be framing schemes for restraining our manufactures—vain attempt. Our land is cheap and fresh; we have more of it than we are able to employ; while we can live in ease and plenty upon our farms, tillage and not arts will engage our attention. If, by opening the channels of trade, you afford us a ready market for the produce of our lands, and an opportunity of purchasing cheap the conveniences of life, all our superfluous gain will sink into your pockets, in return for British manufactures. If the trade of this continent with the French and Spaniards, in their sugar islands, had not been restrained, Great Britain would soon have undersold them, with their own produce, in every market of the world. Until you lay us under a necessity of shifting for ourselves, you need not be afraid of the manufactures of America. The ancient poets, in their elegant manner of expression, have made a kind of being of necessity, and tell us that the gods themselves are obliged to yield to her.

It is by invitations and indulgence, not by compulsion, that the market for British manufactures is to be kept up and increased in America: without the first you will find the latter as ineffectual, as destructive of the end it aims at, as persecution in

25

matters of religion ; which serves not to extinguish but to confirm the heresy. There is a passion natural to the mind of man, especially a free man, which renders him impatient of restraint. Do you, does any sensible man think that three or four millions of people, not naturally defective in genius, or in courage, who have tasted the sweets of liberty, in a country that doubles its inhabitants every twenty years, in a country abounding in such variety of soil and climate, capable of producing, not only the necessaries, but the conveniences and delicacies of life, will long submit to oppression ; if unhappily for yourselves oppression should be offered them ?   Such another experiment as the stamp-act would produce a general revolt in America.

Do you think that all your rival powers in Europe would sit still and see you crush your once flourishing and thriving colonies, unconcerned spectators of such a quarrel ?   Recollect what happened in the Low Countries a century or two ago. Call to mind the cause of the revolt. Call to mind, too, the part that England herself then acted. The same causes will generally produce the same effects ; and it requires no great degree of penetration to foretell that what has happened may happen again.   God forbid there should be occasion, and grant that the union, liberty and mutual happiness of Great Britain and her colonies may continue uninterrupted to the latest ages !

America has always acknowledged her dependence upon Great Britain. It is her interest, it is her inclination to depend upon Great Britain. We readily own that these colonies were first settled, not at the expence but under the protection of the English government ; which protection it has continued to afford them ; and we own, too, that protection and allegiance are reciprocal duties.   If it is asked at whose expence they were settled, the answer is obvious—at the expence of the private adventurers, our ancestors ; the fruit of whose toil and danger we now enjoy. We claim nothing but the liberty and privileges of Englishmen, in the same degree, as if we had still continued among our brethren in Great Britain ; these rights have not been forfeited by any act of ours ; we cannot be deprived of them, without our consent, but by violence and injustice ; we have received them from our ancestors, and, with God's leave, we will transmit them, unimpaired, to our posterity.   Can those who have hitherto acted

as our friends, endeavour now, insidiously to draw from us concessions destructive to what we hold far dearer than life ?

> " If I could find example
> Of thousands that by bare submission had
> Preserv'd their freedom, I 'd not do 't ; but since
> Nor brass, nor stone, nor parchment bears not one ·
> Let cowardice itself forswear it."

Our laws, our language, our principles of government, our
intermarriages, and other connections, our constant intercourse,
and above all our interest, are so many bands which hold us to
Great Britain, not to be broken but by tyranny and oppression.
Strange that among the late ministry there should not be found
a man of common sense and common honesty, to improve and
strengthen these natural ties by a mild and just government,
instead of weakening and almost dissolving them by partiality
and injustice !   But I will not open the wounds which have been
so lately bound up, and which still require a skilful and a gentle
hand to heal them.

These are the sentiments of a man who spends most of his
time in retirement, and has seldom meddled in public affairs,
who enjoys a moderate but independent fortune, and, content
with the blessings of a private station, equally disregards the
smiles and frowns of the great ; who, though not born within the
verge of the British Isle, is an Englishman in his principles, a
zealous assertor of the Act of Settlement, firmly attached to the
present royal family upon the throne, unalienably affected to his
Majesty's sacred person and government, in the defence of which
he would shed the last drop of his blood ; who looks upon
Jacobitism as the most absurd infatuation, the wildest chimera
that ever entered into the head of man ; who adores the wisdom
and happiness of the British Constitution ; and if he had his
election now to make, would prefer it to any that does or ever
did exist.   I am not singular in this my political creed ; these
are the general principles of his Majesty's subjects in America ;
they are the principles of more than nine-tenths of the people
who have been so basely misrepresented to you, and whom you
would lately have treated as rebels and outlaws, a people to
whom you can never grant too much, because you can hardly

give them anything which will not redound to the benefit of the giver.

If any person should think it worth his while to animadvert upon what I have written, I shall make no reply. I have neither ability nor inclination to turn author. If the maxims I have asserted and the reflections I have made are in themselves just, they will need no vindication ; if they are erroneous, I shall esteem it a favour to have my errors pointed out, and will, in modest silence, kiss the rod that corrects me.

I am, Gentlemen, your most obedient servant,

A VIRGINIA PLANTER.[1]

IV

ASSOCIATION AT WILLIAMSBURG—1769.

We, his Majesty's most dutiful subjects, the late representatives of all the freeholders of the colony of Virginia, avowing our inviolable and unshaken fidelity and loyalty to our most gracious sovereign, our affection for all our fellow-subjects of Great Britain, protesting against every act or thing which may have the most distant tendency to interrupt or in anywise disturb his Majesty's peace and the good order of his government in this colony, which we are resolved at the risk of our lives and fortunes to maintain and defend ; but at the same time being deeply affected with the grievances and distresses with which his Majesty's American subjects are oppressed, and dreading the evils which threaten the ruin of ourselves and our posterity by reducing us from a free and happy people to a wretched and miserable state of slavery, and having taken into our most serious consideration the present state of the trade of this colony, and of the American commerce in general, observe with anxiety that the debt due to Great Britain for goods imported from thence is very great, and that the means of paying this debt, in the present situation of affairs, are likely to become more and more precarious ; that the difficulties under which we now labour are owing to the restrictions, prohibitions, and ill advised regulations in

---

[1] Copy of a letter transmitted to the printer of the *Public Ledger* in London, June, 1766.

several late acts of parliament of Great Britain, in particular the late unconstitutional act imposing duties on tea, paper, glass, etc., for the sole purpose of raising a revenue in America, is injurious to property and destructive to liberty, hath a necessary tendency to prevent the payment of the debt due from this colony to Great Britain, and is of consequence ruinous to trade; that notwithstanding the many earnest applications already made, there is little reason to expect a redress of these grievances : Therefore, in justice to ourselves and our posterity, as well as to the traders of Great Britain concerned in the American commerce, we, the subscribers, have voluntarily and unanimously entered into the following resolutions, in hopes that our example will induce the good people of this colony to be frugal in the use and consumption of British manufactures, and that the merchants and manufacturers of Great Britain may, from motives of interest, friendship, and justice, be engaged to exert themselves to obtain for us a redress of those grievances under which the trade and inhabitants of America at present labor. We do therefore most earnestly recommend this our association to the serious attention of all gentlemen merchants, traders, and other inhabitants of this colony, in hopes that they will very readily and cordially accede thereto.

First, It is unanimously agreed on and resolved, this 18th day of May, 1769, that the subscribers, as well by their own example as all other legal ways and means in their power, will promote and encourage industry and frugality, and discourage all manner of luxury and extravagance.

Secondly, That they will not at any time hereafter, directly or indirectly, import, or cause to be imported, any manner of goods, merchandise or manufactures, which are, or shall hereafter be taxed by act of parliament for the purpose of raising a revenue in America (except paper not exceeding eight shillings sterling per ream, and except such articles only as orders have been already sent for), nor purchase any such after the first day of September next, of any person whatsoever, but that they will always consider such taxation in every respect as an absolute prohibition, and in all future orders direct their correspondents to ship them no goods whatever taxed as aforesaid, except as is above excepted.

Thirdly, That the subscribers will not hereafter, directly or indirectly, import, or cause to be imported, from Great Britain, or any part of Europe (except such articles of the produce or manufacture of Ireland as may be immediately and legally brought from thence, and except also such goods as orders have been already sent for), any of the goods hereinafter enumerated, viz., spirits, wine, cider, perry, beer, ale, malt, barley, pease, beef, pork, fish, butter, cheese, tallow, candles, oil, fruit, sugar, pickles, confectionary, pewter, hoes, axes, watches, clocks, tables, chairs, looking-glasses, carriages, joiner's and cabinet work of all sorts, upholstery of all sorts, trinkets and jewelry, plate and gold, and silver-smith work of all sorts, ribband and millinery of all sorts, lace of all sorts, India goods of all sorts (except spices), silks of all sorts (except sewing silk), cambric, lawn, muslin, gauze (except bolting-cloths), calico or cotton stuff of more than two shillings per yard, woolens, worsted stuffs of all sorts of more than one shilling and sixpence per yard, broadcloths of all kinds at more than eight shillings per yard, narrow cloths of all kinds at more than three shillings per yard, hats, stockings (plaid and Irish hose excepted), shoes and boots, saddles, and all manufactures of leather and skins of all kinds, until the late acts of parliament imposing duties on tea, paper, glass, etc., for the purpose of raising a revenue in America are repealed ; and that they will not, after the first of September next, purchase any of the above enumerated goods, of any person whatsoever, unless the above mentioned acts of parliament are repealed.

Fourthly, That in all orders which any of the subscribers may hereafter send to Great Britain, they shall and will expressly direct their correspondents not to ship them any of the before-enumerated goods until the before mentioned acts of parliament are repealed ; and if any goods are shipped to them, contrary to the tenor of this agreement, they will refuse to take the same, or make themselves chargeable therewith.

Fifthly, That they will not import any slaves, or purchase any imported, after the first day of November next, until the said acts are repealed.

Sixthly, That they will not import any wines of any kind whatever, or purchase the same from any person whatever, after the first day of September next, except such wines as are already ordered, until the acts of parliament imposing duties thereon are repealed.

Seventhly, For the better preservation of the breed of sheep, that they will not kill, or suffer to be killed, any lambs that shall be yeaned before the first day of May, in any year, nor dispose of such to any butcher, or other person whom they may have reason to suspect intends to kill the same.

Eighthly and lastly, That these resolves shall be binding on all and each of the subscribers, who do hereby each and every person for himself, upon his word and honor, agree that he will strictly and firmly adhere to and abide by every article in this agreement, from the time of his signing the same, for and during the continuance of .the before mentioned acts of parliament, or until a general meeting of the subscribers, after one month's public notice, shall determine otherwise, the second article of this agreement still and forever continuing in full power and force.

Peyton Randolph, Robert Carter Nicholas, Richard Bland, Archibald Cary, Richard Henry Lee, Charles Carter, George Washington, Carter Braxton, Severn Eyre, Richard Randolph, Patrick Henry, junr., Peter Johnston, Henry Lee, Nathaniel Terry, Thomas Whiting, Thomas Jefferson, Thomas Nelson, junr., James Walker, John Alexander, Champion Travis, George Ball, Thomas Harrison, Thomas Claiborne, John Blair, junr., *Thomson Mason*, &c., &c., &c.[1]

NON-IMPORTATION RESOLUTIONS.

Article of George Mason's left out by the Burgesses.

Sixth Resolve.

If the measures already entered into should prove ineffectual, and our grievances and oppressions should notwithstanding be continued, then, and in that case, the subscribers will put a stop to their exports to Europe of tar, pitch, turpentine, timber, lumber, and skins and furs of all sorts, and will endeavor to find some other employment for their slaves and other hands than cultivating tobacco, which they will entirely leave off making, and will enter into such regulations as may be necessary with regard to the rents and other tobacco debts.

[1] Burk's " History of Virginia," vol. iii., p. 345, note.

Corrections Made in Letter to Washington, April 23d.

Among the enumerated goods, after the articles oil and fruit, is added *sugar.* After millinery of all sorts is added, *lace of all sorts.* After the article of gauze is added *(except boulting-cloaths).*

In the fifth Resolve the word *slaves* in the second line is struck out, and the word hereafter is added between the word *any* and the word *imported.* At the end of the sixth Resolve, after tobacco-debts, are added the words, *due to them.*

N. B.—The reason of making this last alteration is that at a time when the government endeavored to call everything seditious, it might be urged that the subscribers took upon them a sort of legislative authority, in declaring they would make regulations relative to tobacco debts ; now they have an undoubted right to make what regulations they please in debts due to themselves as the option will still remain in the debtor.

(To George Washington, Esq : from G. Mason.)

V.

EXTRACTS FROM THE VIRGINIA CHARTERS, WITH SOME REMARKS ON THEM MADE IN THE YEAR 1773.

In 1676 K. Ch. 2nd gave a Charter "To the Colony of Virginia" confirming the antient importation right of 50 acres for every person imported into the Colony. This seems to acknowledge and confirm the Company's right to the charter to be in the Colony after the dissolution of the former.

See Sect. 4th of the 3rd Charter of James 1st, by which harbors, fisheries, &c : &c : &c : are granted to the Company, which being of a public nature must plainly inure to the people of the Colony, after the dissolution of the Company if this dissolution had been legal.—*Sed quære.*

Anno 1606, April 10.—Charter or Letters Patent first granted by King James the First to the two companys commonly called the London Company and the Plymouth Company for two several Colonies to be made in Virginia, and other parts and Territories of America along the Sea Coasts between 34 Degrees and 45 Degrees of North Latitude.

Sect. IV.—Vizt : To Sir Thomas Gates, Sir George Somers, and others called the First or London Company to begin to settle and plant the first Colony any where upon the said Coast of Virginia or America, between 34 Degrees and 41 Degrees of North Latitude ; and granting them all the country &c from the said first seat of their settlement or plantation for the space of fifty English Miles all along the said Coast, towards the West and South West as the Coast lieth ; and for the like space of fifty miles all along the said coast, towards the East and North East, or towards the North, as the coast lieth : with all the Islands within one hundred miles directly over against the said sea-coast ; and also all the country from the said fifty miles every way on the Sea Coast, directly into the Main Land, for the space of one hundred English Miles, and that none other of His Majesty's subjects shall plant or inhabit behind, or on the back side of them towards the Main Land without the express Licence or Consent of the Council of that Colony thereunto in writing first had and obtained.

Sect. V.—And to Sir Thomas Hanham, Raleigh Gilbert and others called the second or Plymouth Company to begin to settle and plant the second colony anywhere upon the coast of Virginia and America between 38 Degrees and 45 Degrees of North Latitude, and granting them all the country &c from the said first seat of their colony or plantation for the like space of fifty miles all along the said coast towards the West and Southwest, or towards the South, as the coast lieth, and for the like space of fifty miles all along the said coast towards the East and North East, or towards the North, as the coast lieth, with all the islands within one hundred miles directly over against the said sea coast ; and also all the country from the said fifty miles every way on the sea-coast, directly into the mainland, for the space of one hundred miles ; and that none other of His Majesty's subjects shall plant or inhabit behind, or on the back side of them towards the Main Land, without the express licence of the council of that colony in writing thereunto had and obtained.

Sect. VI.—Provided that the plantation or habitation of such of the said Colonies as shall last plant themselves as aforesaid, shall not be made within one hundred miles of the other of them that first began to make their Plantation as aforesaid.—

Sect. VII.—Granting and ordaining that each of said Colonies shall have a Council which shall govern and direct all matters and causes, which shall arise or happen within the same several Colonies &c : with many privileges and immunities ; among others :—

Sect. XV.—That all and every the persons being his Majesty's subjects which shall dwell and inhabit within any or every of the said Colonies or Plantations, and every of their children which shall happen to be born within the limits and precincts of the said several Colonies and Plantations, shall have and enjoy all Liberties, Franchises and Immunities to all Intents and purposes, as if they had been abiding and born within the realm of England or any other of His Majesty's Dominions.

Sect. XVIII.—And finally that His Majesty, his Heirs and Successors, upon petition for that purpose, shall and will by Letters Patent, under the Great Seal of England, give and grant to such persons their heirs and assigns as the respective Councils for the said two Colonies, or the most part of them, shall for that purpose nominate and assign, all the Lands, Tenements, and Hereditaments which shall be within the precincts limited for the said two Colonies respectively, as aforesaid, to be holden of His Majesty, his Heirs and Successors as of their Manor of Greenwich in the county of Kent, in free and common socage only, and not in capite. With a clause declaring the full and perfect efficacy of such letters patent, so to be granted as aforesaid.[1]

Sect. VI. Anno 1609, May 23.—The Company for the said first or Southern Colony (to this day called the Colony and Dominion

---

[1] In consequence of this charter the first or Southern Colony, which still retains the name of Virginia, was undertaken and begun by several persons in and about London (Dec. 19, 1606) who fitted out two or three ships under the command of Capt. Christopher Newport, which sailed from England to America (April 26, 1607). The first land they discovered on this coast was the southern point or cape of Chesapeake Bay ; which they called Cape Henry (the name it still retains) ; here they first landed and after spending some days in examining the country and looking for a proper place for their settlement, they fixed upon a peninsula (May 13) about forty miles up Powhatan River (since called James River) and on the north side of it, which they called James Town, in compliment to the King, the name it has ever since retained. At this place the seat of Government remained for a great many years, and from this beginning proceeded the Colony of Virginia.

of Virginia) having been joined by a great number of the nobility and principal gentry in England, a second and more extensive Charter was granted them by King James the first, incorporating them by the name of the Treasurer and Company of the Adventurers and Planters of the City of London for the first Colony in Virginia : reciting, confirming, explaining and enlarging the former Charter by granting them all those lands, Countries, and Territories situate, lying and being in that part of America called Virginia, from the point of land called Cape or Point Comfort all along the Sea Coast to the northward, two hundred miles, and from the said point of Cape Comfort all along the sea-coast to the southward, two hundred miles, and all that space or circuit of Land, lying from the sea-coast of the precinct aforesaid, up into the land, throughout from sea to sea, west and north-west, and also all the Islands lying within one hundred Miles along the Coasts of both seas of the precinct aforesaid ; with all the Soils, Grounds, &c. forever ; To be holden of his Majesty, his Heirs and his Successors, as of their Manor of East Green-wich ; in free and common socage, and not in capite.

SECT. VII.—Nevertheless charging, commanding, warranting and authorising the said Treasurer and Company to convey assign and set over such particular portions of Lands, Tenements, and Hereditaments unto such His Majesty's subjects naturally born, or Denizens, or others, as well Adventurers as Planters, as by the said Company shall be nominated, appointed and allowed ; wherein respect to be had as well of the Adventure, as to the special service, Hazard, Exploit, or Merit of any person so to be recompensed, advanced, or rewarded.[2]

[2] Pursuant to the above last recited clause, Sec. VII., the said Company in the year 1616 (Sir George Yeardly being then their Governor in Virginia) ordained and ordered that 50 acres of land should be assigned and granted to every person removing himself into the said Colony from Great Britain or Ireland ; and to every person who should import others, 50 acres for every person so imported. This was the first Rise of the ancient custom of granting lands upon Importation Rights, which is now no less than 158 years old. It appears to have been interwoven with the Constitution of the Colony from its first settlement, and constantly practised afterwards. In the year 1621 two remarkable instances occur. 50,000 acres were granted to one Captn. Newce, for the importation of 1,000 persons and sixty *young maids,* being brought over by private adventurers to make wives for the planters,

Sect. VIII.—Appointing and ordaining that the said Company shall have a perpetual Council residing in England, which Council shall have a seal for the better government, and administration of the said plantation, besides the legal seal of the Company or Corporation.

Sects. IX. and X.—Nominating the particular members of the said Council, and also the Treasurer for the time being.

Sect. XI.—And granting and declaring that the said Council or Treasurer, or any of them, shall from thenceforth be nominated, chosen, continued, displaced, changed, altered, and supplied, as Death or other several occasions shall require, out of the Company of the said Adventurers, by the voice of the greater number of the said Company and Adventurers, in their Assembly for that purpose. Provided always that every Counsellor so newly elected, shall be presented to the Lord Chancellor of England, or to the Lord High Treasurer of England, or to the Lord Chamberlain of the Household of His Majesty, His Heirs and Successors for the time being, to take his Oath of a Counsellor to His Majesty, his Heirs and Successors for the said Company of Adventurers and Colony in Virginia.

Sect. XIII.—Giving and granting for His Majesty, his Heirs and Successors, full power and authority to the said Council, as well at the present time, as hereafter from time to time, to nomi-

---

50 acres of land for each was granted to the persons who imported them. After the Government was taken into the hands of the Crown, upon the dissolution of the Virginia Company, the same Right and Custom was always continued, as appears from the old patents and records in the Secretary's office. In the year 1662 an Act of Assembly was made prescribing the manner of proving such Importation rights to lands, by obtaining certificates thereof to entitle the Claimers to surveys and patents. And in the year 1676 the said custom and right was solemnly confirmed and continued, according to the ancient usage and practice, by charter from King Charles the Second, to the Colony of Virginia, under the great seal of England, which charter was recognised by Act of Assembly in the year 1677 prescribing the form of patents for the future, in which form is recited the continuance and confirmation of the said ancient right and privilege ; which hath been enjoyed by the subjects of this Colony ever since, and great quantities of land from time to time granted accordingly. So that Mr. Stith, in his History of Virginia (which is chiefly extracted from ancient records), mentioning this right and custom, had good reason for his remark, " That this is the ancient, legal, and a most indisputable method of granting lands in Virginia."

nate, make, constitute, ordain and confirm, by such name or names, stile or stiles, as to them shall seem good, and likewise to revoke, discharge, change and alter as well all and singular Governors, officers and ministers, which already have been made, as also which shall be by them thought fit and needful to be made or used, for the Government of the said Colony and Plantation.

SECT. XIV.—And also to make, ordain and establish all manners of Orders, Laws, Directions, Instructions, Forms, and Ceremonies of Government and Magistracy, fit and necessary for and concerning the Government of the said Colony and Plantation, and the same to abrogate, revoke, and change, not only within the precincts of said Colony, but also upon the seas in going and coming to and from the said Colony, as they in their good discretion shall think to be fitted for the good of the Adventurers and Inhabitants there.

SECT. XXII.—Declaring also for his Majesty, his Heirs and Successors, that all and every the persons, being the subjects of his Majesty, his Heirs and Successors, which shall go and inhabit within the said Colony and Plantation, and every of their children and posterity which shall happen to be born within any of the limits thereof, shall have and enjoy all Liberties, Franchises, and Immunities of free Denizens and natural subjects within any of their other Dominions, to all Intents and Purposes as if they had been abiding and born within the Realm of England, or any other of the Dominions of his Majesty, his Heirs and Successors.[3]

---

[3] There can be no doubt but this and every clause relating to the people and inhabitants in general (not to the particular property of the Company) under the Faith of which our Ancestors left their native land, and adventured to settle an unknown country, operates and inures to the benefit of their posterity forever, notwithstanding the dissolution of the Virginia Company, had such dissolution been ever so legal. But a new doctrine has been lately broached by the writers against America. "That the charters granted to the Colonies were originally illegal, as containing powers and rights which the Crown, being only one branch of the Legislature, could not grant, and having never been confirmed by Act of Parliament, that they are of course void and of no effect." The first assertion happens to be false ; and if it was true, the consequences deduced from it are erroneous. When America was discovered, the sending abroad colonies had been unknown in Europe from the times of the ancient Greeks and

Sect. XXIII.—Giving and granting also unto the said Treas_urer and Company, and their Successors, and to such Governors, Officers and Ministers, as shall be by the aforesaid Council constituted and appointed, according to the nature and limits of their Offices, and places, respectively, that they may from time to time, for ever hereafter, within the said precincts of Virginia, or in the way by sea thither, and from thence, have full and absolute power and authority to correct, punish, pardon, govern, and rule all such the subjects of his Majesty, his Heirs and Successors, as shall from time to time adventure themselves in any voyage thither, or that shall at any time hereafter inhabit in the precincts and territories of the said Colony as aforesaid, according to such Orders, Ordinances, Constitutions, Directions, and Instructions, as shall by the said Colony, as aforesaid, be established. So

---

Romans (for the irruptions of the Goths and other barbarous nations can't be regarded in that light). To the people of Great Britain the scene then opening was entirely new; and altho' the people removing from thence, to settle Colonies in America, under the auspices and protection and for the benefit of Great Britain, would by the laws of Nature and Nations, have carried with them the Constitution of the Country they came from, and consequently been entitled to all its advantages, yet not caring to trust altogether to general principles applied to a new subject, and anxious to secure to themselves and their posterity, by every means in their power, the rights and privileges of their beloved laws and Constitution, they entered into a solemn compact with the Crown for that purpose. Under the faith of these compacts, at their own private expense and Hazard, amidst a thousand Difficulties and Dangers, our Ancestors explored and settled a New World : their posterity have enjoyed these rights and privileges from time Immemorial ; and have thereby (even if the Charters had been originally defective) acquired a legal Title. It ought to wear well ; for it has been dearly earned. King, Lords, and Commons compose the British Legislature, but the Constitution has lodged the Executive power in the Crown. The Disposition of foreign or newly-acquired Territory hath ever belonged to the Executive. This power has been constantly exercised by our Kings in numberless instances. At the conclusion of the last war, Martinico, Guadaloupe, &c. (tho' acquired at the National Expense), were disposed of by the Crown, and however the policy may have been censured, the King's right was never disputed. If the Crown can make an absolute and unlimited alienation to Foreigners ; a fortiori can it make a modulated Grant to Subjects. The American Charters, therefore, are legal ab origine. Equally false and absurd is the Idea of Great Britain's Right to govern these Colonies as conquered Provinces, for we are the Descendants, not of the Conquered, but of the Conquerors.

always as the said Statutes, Ordinances, and Proceedings, as near as conveniently may be agreeable to the Laws, Statutes, Government, and Policy of the Realm of England.

SECT. XXVI.—Declaring his Majesty's Royal will and pleasure that in all questions and doubts that shall arise upon any difficulty of construction or interpretation of any thing contained either in this or in former letters patent, the same shall be taken and interpreted in the most beneficial manner for the said Treasurer and Company, and their successors, and every member thereof. And concluding with the following clause :

SECT. XXIX.—Any Act, Statute, Ordinance, Provision, Proclamation or Restraint to the contrary hereof, had, made, ordained, or provided, or any other Thing, clause, or matter whatsoever, in any wise, notwithstanding.

Anno 1612, Sect. I.—A third charter was granted by King James the first to the same Virginia Company, reciting and confirming their former charters, and setting forth that the said Company had petitioned for an enlargement of their former letters patent ; II. as well for a more ample extent of their Limits and Territories into the seas adjoining to, and III. upon the Coast of Virginia, as also for some other matters and Articles concerning the better Government of the said Company and Colony ; in which point the former letters patent do not extend so far as Time and Experience hath found to be needful and convenient.

SECT. IV.—Giving, granting and confirming unto the said Treasurer and Company and to their Heirs and Successors forever, all and singular, those Islands whatsoever situate, lying and being in any part of the Ocean or Seas bordering upon the Coast of the said first Colony of Virginia, and being within three hundred leagues of any of the parts heretofore granted to the said Treasurer and Company in the former letters patent, and being within or between the one and fortieth and thirtieth degrees of Northern Latitude, together with all and singular the soils, lands, Grounds, Havens, ports, Rivers, Waters, Fishings, Mines, and Minerals &c and all and singular other Commodities, Jurisdictions, Royalties, privileges, Franchises, and preheminences, both within the said Tract of land upon the Main, and also within the said Islands and Seas, adjoining, whatsoever and thereunto or thereabouts, both by sea and Land, being or situate, —To be holden as of the Manor of East Greenwich &c.[4]

SECT. VII.—Ordaining and granting that the said Company, once every week, or oftener, at their pleasure, might hold a Court and Assembly, for the better order and government of the said plantation ; to consist of the Treasurer or his Deputy, and at least five of the Council and fifteen other Members of the Company, which should be a sufficient court for the ordering and dispatching all such casual and particular Occurrences and Matters of less consequence and weight, as shall from time to time happen, concerning the said plantation.

SECT. VIII.—But that for the ordering and disposing of matters and affairs of great weight and importance, and such as concern the Publick weal, particularly the manner of Government from time to time, to be used, the ordering and disposing of the lands, and the settling and establishing of a Trade, there should be held upon four different certain Days (therein named) one great and general Assembly ; which four Assemblies to be called and stiled the four Great and General Courts of the Council and Company of Adventurers for Virginia, and shall have full power and authority, from time to time and at all times hereafter, to elect and chuse discreet persons to be of the said

[4] This clause Sect. IV. of this Charter, respecting the ports, rivers, waters, and Fishings, and a clause of the same nature in Sect. VI. of the second Charter (not particularly suited in these Extracts), being of a publick nature in which the people and Inhabitants were interested, as well as the Company, it is presumed could not be destroyed or avoided by the Dissolution of the Virginia Company, and may avail us if the proprietor of Maryland should ever disturb the peace or possession of any of the people of this Colony, by an attempt to exercise the Rights he pretends to claim on the South side of the Potomack River of which he hath never been in possession ; for upon an attentive examination of the Virginia Charters, perhaps it may appear that the said proprietor hath little title, except length of possession, to many of the powers he holds. How far these Charters can be urged against the claim he is now setting up to that tract of country between the great North and South Branches of Potomack River, the Inhabitants of which have been long settled there as a part of this Colony, under the Faith of its Laws, and are represented in our Legislature, and who, if the said proprietor's claim was to be established (besides the risque of their present titles to the Lands) would be forced from under the immediate protection of the crown, and subjected to a proprietary government ; whereby their Lives and Fortunes migh be at the mercy, not of their Sovereign, but of a fellow Subject, may soon become a question of Importance.

Council of the said Colony, and to nominate and appoint such officers as they shall think fit and requisite for the Government, managing, ordering, and dispatching the affairs of the said Company, and shall likewise have full power and authority to ordain and make such Laws and Ordinances for the good and welfare of the said plantation, as to them from time to time shall be thought requisite and meet ; so always as the same be not contrary to the Laws and Statutes of the Realm of England.

SECT. XVI. to SECT. XIX.—Giving and granting to the said Treasurer and Company full power and Authority, Liberty, and Licence to erect, and publish, open and hold, one or more Lottery or Lotteries within the City of London, or within any other City or town in England, with divers orders for the Regulation and Encouragement of such Lottery or Lotteries.

SECT. XX.—Declaring that in all questions and Doubts, that shall arise upon any Difficulty of Construction or Interpretation, of anything contained in these or any other of the former Letters Patent, the same shall be taken and interpreted in most ample and beneficial manner for the said Treasurer and Company and their Successors and every member thereof.

SECT. XXI.—And lastly ratifying and confirming unto the said Treasurer and Company, and their Successors forever all and all manner of privileges, Franchises, Liberties, Immunities, Profits and commodities, whatsoever granted unto them in any of the former letters patent, and not in these presents revoked, altered, changed, or abridged, any Statute, Act, Ordinance, provision, proclamation, or Restraint, to the contrary thereof &c. notwithstanding.[5]

Anno 1621, July 24th.—The Treasurer, Council, & Company in England passed and established an Ordinance under the Common Seal of the said Company, for settling the Constitution and Form of Government in Virginia.[6]

[5] The principal Design of this third Charter, besides making some new regulations in the Government of the Company and Colony, and empowering them to raise money by Lotteries in England, seems to be to grant to the said Company the Islands of Bermudas, otherwise called Somer-Islands, which the said Virginia Company, within a few years, sold to Sir George Somers and others, called the Somer-Island Company ; which was afterwards dissolved, much about the same time and in the same manner with the Virginia Company.

[6] This Ordinance was brought over the October following by Sir Francis Wyatt (who succeeded Sir George Yeardly in the Government here), and is

Sect. I.—Declaring their motives and Authority for the same, and ordaining and declaring, that from II. thenceforward there should be two supreme Councils in Virginia for the better government of the said Colony. The one of which Councils, to be called the Council of State (whose office shall chiefly be, assisting with their care, advice and circumspection, to the Governor), shall be nominated, placed and displaced, from time to time, by them the said Treasurer, Council, and Company and their successors—nominating for the present, the members of the said Council of State, viz.:—Sir Francis Wyatt, the then Governor, and nineteen other gentlemen therein named ; earnestly praying and desiring, and strictly charging and commanding the said Counsellors and Council to bend their Care and Endeavours to assist the Governor ; first and principally, in the advancement of the Honour and Service of God, and the enlargement of his Kingdom amongst the Heathen people ; and next in erecting the said Colony in due obedience to His Majesty, and all lawful Authority, from His Majesty's directions ; and lastly in maintaining the people in Justice and Christian Conversation amongst themselves, and in strength and ability to withstand their enemies. And this Council to be always, or for the most part to be residing about or near the Governor.[7]

generally presumed to have been the original plan and first Draught of our Constitution, from which the Assembly of Virginia took its rise ; but it was in fact rather a confirmation of that form of Government which the people here, in Imitation of their Mother Country, had before adopted ; for it appears from ancient records, that two years before this, viz.:—in June, 1619, Sir George Yeardly held an assembly of the representatives of the people. Counties were not yet laid off ; but the several Townships. settlements, or Hundreds elected their representatives, from whence the said Assembly was first called the House of Burgesses, a name proper to the Representatives of Burroughs or Towns (but conveying a diminution and inadequate idea of an Assembly representing the whole body of the people), which custom hath very improperly continued to this day, altho' all our Representatives, four members only excepted, have for a great length of time been chosen by the shires or counties.

[7] The powers by this clause vested in the members of the first Virginia Council belong properly to a Council of State. But to what an alarming and enormous Height hath the Jurisdiction of their successors increased ? In whose hands are lodged the Executive, the Legislature, and the Judicative powers of the State, and consequently the Life, Liberty, and property of the subject ? That this hath not yet produced much Evil or Opposition is candidly acknowledged, because the Council has generally been composed of men whose character,

SECT. IV.—The other Council more generally to be called by the Governor once Yearly, and no oftener, but for very extraordinary and important occasions, shall consist for the present, of the said Council of State, and of two Burgesses out of every town, Hundred, or other particular plantation, to be respectively chosen by the Inhabitants ; which Council shall be called the

Interest, and Connections here, have restrained them within the bonds of Moderation.   Because the Emoluments of the office are not a sufficient Temptation to Mercenary Strangers to solicit the appointment.   And because Luxury, venality, and a general corruption of manners have not yet thoroughly taken root among us.   But when it is considered that this Board is entirely dependant upon the Crown ; that the authority of its members is not hereditary, and if it was that it could descend but to one of their children ; that no man's Rank or Fortune, how great soever, can exempt him from the common course of human affairs ; and that their own posterity must quickly be distributed among the different classes of mankind, and blended with the mass of the people, there cannot be a more striking proof of the prevalence of the lust of power in the mind of man than that these gentlemen should be tenacious of Jurisdiction as unsafe and dangerous to their own Families as to the Community.   Not only mean and sordid but extremely shortsighted and foolish is that species of self-interest which in political questions opposeth itself to the publick good ; for a little cool reflection must convince a wise man that he can no other way so effectually consult the permanent Interest of his own Family and posterity as by securing the just rights and privileges of that society to which they belong.   But it is easier to describe a Disease in the Body politic, than to point out a proper Physician.   Perhaps the lenient hand of a wise and patriotic Prince—perhaps some noble and public-spirited Governor, who would then indeed deserve a statue.   Perhaps the Constitution may by degrees work itself clear by its own innate strength, the virtue and Resolution of the Community—as hath often been the case in our Mother Country.   This last is the natural Remedy ; if not counteracted by that slow poison, which is daily contaminating the minds and morals of our people. Every Gentleman here is a petty tyrant.   Practised in Arts of Despotism and Cruelty, we become callous to the Dictates of humanity and all the finer feelings of the Soul.   Taught to regard a part of our species in the most abject and contemptible Degree below us ; we lose that idea of the dignity of Man, which the Hand of Providence has implanted in us for great and wise purposes. Habituated from our infancy to trample upon the rights of human nature, every generous, every liberal sentiment, if not extinguished, is enfeebled in our minds. And in such an infernal school are to be educated our future Legislators and Rulers.   The laws of Impartial Providence may even by such means as these, avenge upon our posterity the injury done a set of wretches whom our injustice hath debased almost to a level with the Brute Creation.   These Remarks may be thought foreign to the design of the annexed Extracts.   They were extorted by a kind of irresistible perhaps an enthusiastic Impulse, and the Author of them, conscious of his own good intentions, cares not whom they please or offend.

General Assembly, wherein (as also in the said Council of State) all matters shall be decided, determined, and ordered by the greater part of the voices then present, reserving to the Governor always a negative voice. And this General Assembly shall have full power to treat, consult, and conclude, as well of all emergent occasions, concerning the publick weal of the said Colony, and every part thereof, as also to make, ordain, and enact such general Laws and orders for the Behalf of the said Colony, and the good government thereof, as shall from time to time appear necessary or requisite.[8]

[8] It is plain from this clause that the Gentlemen of the Council were originally no more than so many constant members of the Assembly, without being elected by the people ; that they sat with the Governor in the same House, and had a common Vote in all matters with the Representatives of the people ; that a negative was lodged in the Governor alone ; and that the House thus constituted was called the General Assembly ; the stile yet retained in all our legislative proceedings, tho' great alterations have been since made in the original Constitution :—In this situation the Council continued long after the Virginia Company was dissolved, and the Government of the Colony was vested in the crown. In those early times, when the number of the people's representatives was small, the influence of the Council in the General Assembly was very considerable ; at first, indeed, they made a majority ; but in process of Time, as the country became more inhabited, Counties were laid off, and the number of our Representatives greatly increased, the vote of the members of the Council was in a manner sunk in such a numerous Assembly ; and the democratical part of our Constitution had no other check than the Governor's negative. This might be productive of inconvenience, to remedy which the Gentlemen of the Council, of their own mere motion, thought proper to walk up stairs ; and formed in imitation of the English House of Peers a separate and distinct Branch of the Legislature. That such a separate Branch, such an intermediate Power between the people and the Crown is really necessary, no candid man, well-informed in the principles of the British Constitution, and acquainted with the tumultuary nature of Publick Assemblies, will deny ; but he may, with great propriety urge, that the members of this Intermediate Branch of the Legislature, should have no precarious tenure, that it should at least be for life, and whether their Authority was hereditary or not, that they should be equally independent of the Crown and of the people ; and that neither the Administration nor the common Judicative powers of the State can be safely lodged in their hands.

As some amendments in our judicial proceedings have lately been proposed, it may not be amiss to mark here a Capital Error in the Constitution of our Supreme Courts. When any man thinks himself injured by a Court of Law, or a Decree of Chancery, the British Constitution hath given him an appeal ; this is an inherent right in the subject, of which he can't be deprived, without being robbed of a valuable part of his Birth-Right, and the most effectual means that

SECT. V.—Whereas in all other things requiring the said General Assembly, as well as the said Council of State to imitate and follow the policy of the form of Government, Laws, Customs, and manner of Trial, and other administration of Justice, used in the Realm of England, as near as may be, even as the said Treasurer and Company themselves by his Majesty's letters patent are required.

SECT. VI.—Provided that no Law or Ordinance made in the said General Assembly shall be, or continue in force and validity, unless the same shall be solemnly ratified and confirmed in a General Quarter Court of the said Company in England, and so ratified, be returned to them under the said Company's seal. It being their intent to afford the like measure, also unto the said Colony, that after the Government of the said Colony shall once have been well framed, and settled accordingly; which is to be done by the said Treasurer and Company, as by Authority derived from his Majesty, and the same shall have been by them so declared, no orders of Court afterwards, shall bind the said Colony unless they be ratified in like manner in the General Assemblys.[9]

human wisdom could devise to secure the property of individuals. A court of Appeals, therefore, or that Court which is the Dernier Resort, should be so constituted as that no suit could originate there, for otherwise, when the subject is aggrieved, he is left without redress. This useful distinction seems hitherto to have been totally neglected in this Colony.

[9] This ordinance or Charter for settling a form of Government in Virginia, was made by the Treasurer, Council and Company in England by virtue of the powers vested in them for that purpose by the 14th and 23rd Sections of King James second Charter and the 8th section of his third Charter to the said Company; and being made while the said powers were in full force and efficacy, and the authority of the Company unquestionable, there can be little doubt of its Validity; and that it gave the people of Virginia as good a title to chuse their own Representatives to enact laws, as if it had been made and granted by the King himself; but this does not now seem to be a subject much worth our Enquiry; for if this Ordinance was annihilated, our Rights as British subjects, and particularly that invaluable one of chusing our own Representatives in a Virginia Parliament which we have uniformly enjoyed and exercised for more than One hundred and fifty years, could be shaken only by Violence and Injustice aided by our own Folly, or by Force of Arms. Some parties and Factions having arisen in the Virginia Company, and several disputes having happened with the King and his Ministry, King James the first, by proclamation dated July 24th, 1624, forbid and suppressed the Courts of the said Company at their usual

1676, Oct. 10.—Charter under the great seal of England, granted by King Charles the Second to the Colony of Virginia, Declaring and granting for his Majesty, his heirs and Successors, that all the subjects of his Majesty, his Heirs, and Successors from time to time, inhabiting within the Colony and Plantation of Virginia shall have their immediate Dependence upon the

place of meeting in the City of London, and soon after the Lords of his Majesty's privy Council appointed a new Governor of the said Company, which being expressly contrary to their Charters, they refused to acquiesce in such appointment, and thus rejecting the officers nominated by the British Ministry, and forbid to act under their own, their Courts and Meetings were discontinued and their Business and Proceedings stopped, for though there had been a Quo Warranto brought in the King's Bench, and the process served upon several of the members, who entered their defence ; the same was never brought to any Decision or Hearing ; but the Company, chagrined with the Discouragements and opposition received from the King and Ministry, disgusted with the Schisms and Factions in their own body, and wearied with so great and constant Expence, after some faint struggles submitted, and quietly gave up, or rather forbore any further Exercise of their Rights, and the Government of the Colony was taken into the King's Hands. An Event (however illegally and arbitrarily brought about) very happy for the people of Virginia ; who were thereby taken from under a proprietary Government, and placed under the immediate Government and Protection of the British Crown.

The bounds of the Colony (as well as the form of Government) remained unaltered until King Charles the First, in the Year 1632, by Charter to Cecilius Calvert, Lord Baron of Baltimore, established the proprietary and province of Maryland. That Country being then uninhabited, the importance of it little known or attended to, and the Scene of Confusion introduced by the Civil war in England, prevented the people of Virginia making any opposition. In the succeeding Reign (with equal inattention in the Virginians) the provinces of Pennsylvania and Carolina were erected, the Southern part of the first and the Northern part of the latter being within the ancient limits of Virginia. The Dutch and Swedes having possessed themselves of the Country on the Sea-Coast, between New England and Maryland, King Charles the Second, in the year 1664, granted all the country so usurped to his Brother, the Duke of York, and an English Fleet having reduced the Dutch and Swedish settlements, the Duke of York parcelled out that Country to under proprietors, one of whom was William Penn, the Son of Admiral Penn All these Proprietors, except William Penn, afterwards sold or surrendered their Charters to the Crown. Mr. Penn retained his part, and had it increased and confirmed to him in consideration of a debt due from the King to his Father, and from thence arose the Province of Pennsylvania.

There being few or no settlements on the Southern parts of this Coast, a Grant was made, in the year 1663, by King Charles the Second to several of

Crown of England under the Rule and Government of such Governor or Governors as his Majesty, His Heirs or Successors. shall from time to time appoint in that Behalf : and of or upon no other person or persons whatsoever.[10]

That the Governor for the time being shall be resident in that Country, except his Majesty, his Heirs or Successors shall at any time command his attendance in England or elsewhere, in which

his Courtiers, viz.—the Earl of Clarendon, the Duke of Albemarle, the Lord Craven, the Lord Berkeley, the Lord Ashly Cooper, Sir George Carteret, and Sir William Colleton ; for the Country called Carolina, the greatest part of which (the Earl of Granville only retaining his ancestor's, Sir Geo. Carteret's part) was sold by the Heirs of these Proprietors to the Crown, and out of it were formed the provinces of North Carolina South Carolina and Georgia. And by these means have the Ancient and Original Boundaries been contracted, and the Colony and Dominion of Virginia reduced to its present Limits. In the year 1669 a grant was made by King Charles the second to Henry, Earl of St. Albans, John, Lord Berkeley, Sir William Moreton, and John Tretheway, Esqr., of all that tract of Land or Territory lying between the Rappahannock and Potomack Rivers, commonly called the Northern Neck (now in possession of the right honourable the Lord Fairfax), and altho' there was a promise that the same should not infringe or prejudice any contract or Grant whatsoever before made or granted by the Governor and Council of Virginia, and that the said Patentees, their Heirs and Assigns, and all the Inhabitants of the said tract of Land or Territory should be in all things subject and obedient to such Laws and Constitutions, as were, or should be made by the Governor, Council, and Assembly of Virginia ; yet some Royalties and considerable powers being thereby Vested in the said Patentees, it roused the attention of the General Assembly, who, apprehensive that the people might be injured or oppressed by men of such powerful interest, in the year 1674 passed an Act of Address and Supplication asserting the Rights and Privileges granted to this Colony by his Majesty's Ancestors, representing the Dangers and ill-consequences of such Grants to Lords and others, and praying that his Majesty would be graciously pleased to revoke the said Grant, and for securing them from fears in time to come of being removed from His Majesty's immediate protection, to confirm their Liberties, Privileges, Immunities, Rights and Properties, as aforesaid by His Majesty's Royal Charter. Certain Gentlemen were appointed to present this Act, which procured the last Charter ever granted to this Colony, viz.—that from King Charles the Second, bearing date the 10th Day of October, in the 28th year of his Reign, An. Dom., 1676, as on the other side.

[10] This first clause expressly operates against the Establishment of any new Government or Proprietary in any part of Virginia. For the King is as much bound by the Act of his Predecessors as any Private Subject holding an Estate from his Ancestor is bound by the Act of such Ancestor. And accordingly, this Charter effectually put a stop to all further applications of that nature.

case a Deputy shall be chosen, to continue during the absence of such Governor in manner as hath been formerly used, unless his Majesty, his Heirs or Successors shall think fit to nominate such Deputy. And if any Governor shall happen to die, then another Governor shall and may be chosen, as hath been formerly used, to continue until his Majesty, his Heirs, or Successors shall appoint a new Governor.[11]

Confirming and establishing all lands possessed by the several and respective planters and inhabitants of Virginia to them and their heirs forever, where the property of any particular man's interest in any lands there, shall not be altered or prejudiced by Reason thereof.

Declaring and granting that there shall be assigned out of the Lands not already appropriated for each of such of the subjects of his Majesty, his Heirs and Successors, as shall from time to time go to dwell in the said Plantation, fifty acres of Land, as according as hath been used and allowed since the first Plantation, to be held of his Majesty, his Heirs and Successors, as of their Manor of East Greenwich in their County of Kent, in free and common socage.[12]

And that all Lands possessed by any subject inhabiting in Virginia, which is escheated, or shall escheat to his Majesty, his Heirs and Successors, shall and may be enjoyed, by such Inhabitant, or Possessor his Heirs and Assigns forever, paying two pounds of

[11] The Rule established by his present Majesty, requiring the Governor to reside here, is exactly conformable to this clause of the Charter, and considering how fully it is expressed, especially when construed in the manner required by the last clause (which applies to every part of the charter) it is strange that it remained so long unattended to.

[12] By this clause the old custom, first introduced about sixty years before by the Virginia Company, of granting lands for the Importation of people, which had been constantly continued and exercised after the Dissolution of the said Company, is clearly and authentically confirmed and established, according to the ancient usage and practice, and being thereby made a part of the Constitution of Virginia, cannot be avoided or invalidated by any proclamation, Instruction, or other Act of Government (vid. Notes 2nd and 10th). This and the following Clause, granting all Escheat Lands to the Possessor upon a fixed moderate Composition, are certainly Articles of great Importance ; and will be still more so if by any new Regulation of Government, the Quit Rent of the Crown Lands here should hereafter be raised, as all lands coming under the description of either of those clauses would be exempt from such new Regulation.

Tobacco, Composition for every Acre, which is the rate set by his Majesty's Governor according to his Majesty's Instruction to him in that Behalf.

And that the Governor and Council of Virginia, for the time being, and in the absence of the Governor, the Deputy Governor and Council, or any five or more of them, whereof the Governor or his deputy to be always one, shall and thereby have full power and authority to hear and determine all Treasons, Murders, Felonies and other offences committed or done, or to be committed or done within the said Government, so as they proceed therein, as near as may be, to the Laws and Statutes of the Kingdom of England.[13]

And lastly of his Royal Goodness, graciously to continue to favour the subjects of his Majesty, his Heirs and Successors, which then did, or thereafter should inhabit in the said Country of Virginia, and to give the more liberal and ample Encouragement to plantations there, declaring his Royal Will and Pleasure, to be that every Clause, Article and Sentence in these his said letters Patent[14] contained, shall be from time to time, forever there-

[13] This clause investing the Governor and Council with full power and authority to hear and determine all Treasons and other offences committed within Government, expounded (as required by the last clause) in the most beneficial and available sense, for the advantage of his Majesty's subjects here, is very inconsistent with the extraordinary measure lately adopted by the British Ministry,—a plan so contrary to the first principles of Liberty and Justice, as would much better become the Divan at Constantinople, than the Cabinet at London.

[14] By this charter the Subjects of Virginia are forever to remain under the immediate protection of the British Crown, and be subject only to its Government here. The Governor is to reside in this country. The titles of their lands are confirmed to the inhabitants. Any vacant Lands are from time to time to be granted for the Importation of people into the Colony according to antient custom ; and all the Lands which shall at any time escheat, are confirmed to the Possessors upon certain moderate terms.

The Governor and Council have full power and authority to try all Treasons and other offences committed here, and the Design of the Charter is declared to be to continue to favour the subjects which then did, or afterward should inhabit the said Country of Virginia, and for the more liberal and ample Encouragement to plantations there, (that is, to encourage the increase and extension of the settlements there) every part of the charter is to be construed and take effect in the most advantageous and available sense for the Benefit of the subjects of the said Country of Virginia. The country of Virginia is only mentioned at large and in general Terms in this charter, and not described or ascertained by

after, as often as any Ambiguity, Doubt or Question shall or may
happen to arise thereupon, expounded, construed, deemed and

any particular limits or boundaries. It can't be confined to the country then
settled, which would be totally inconsistent with the Design of giving encouragement " to Plantations there" and would exclude more than nine-tenths of the
present Inhabitants. It can't mean the Country at that time purchased from or
ceded by the Indians, for this would also exclude the greatest part of the
present Inhabitants. Nor can posterior purchases of Lands from the Indians
be used as arguments against the extent of this charter, without impeaching the
Crown's Right to those Lands at the time of making the Charter. A Doctrine
of a dangerous nature, and diametrically opposite to the claims of Great Britain
in her Negotiations and Treaties with other Nations as well as the Reasons for
which the King entered into the late war, one of which was the Incroachments
made by the French upon the Territory of Virginia. If such purchases could
operate against the extent of the Virginia Charter, they would have operated
against the grant of the Northern Neck ; far the greater part of which was
possessed by the Indians, when the said grant was made, and not purchased
from them for many years after. So late as Queen Anne's Reign the Blue
Ridge of Mountains separated the possessions of the British Subjects here, from
those of the Indians. Yet in the last reign, the King and Council gave Lord
Fairfax a Judgment for the lands to the Fountain Head of Potomack River,
near fourscore miles beyond the Blue Ridge. As our settlements were extended,
and the wild game destroyed, the Indians have been found to remove further for
the convenience of Hunting. As they retired purchase after purchase hath been
made of them, and temporary Lines or Boundaries from time to time accordingly settled between them, and the English Inhabitants here. It is not above
fifty years since the people of Virginia settled beyond the Blue Ridge ; it is near
thirty years since they first began to settle on the West side of the Alleghany
or Appalachian Mountains and at this time there are several thousand Families settled to the Westward of the said Mountains on the Branches and
Waters of the Ohio River. When the Colony of Virginia was settled, the
Lands first purchased of the Indians were only upon and near the Mouths
and larger parts of the Rivers, then to the Falls of the said Rivers, then to
the Blue Ridge of Mountains ; afterwards to the Alleghany Mountains ; and
lately to the River Ohio. Many of these purchases have been made since
the Charter of Charles the Second. If the said Charter was not affected
by the former purchases from the Indians neither is it by the last, nor can
it be by any purchase made hereafter. For (not to mention the liberal and
beneficial manner of Construction which we have a right to) the plain, natural, and obvious meaning of the charter is, to grant and confirm certain
Rights, Privileges, and Immunities to all his Majesty's subjects who then
did or ever should inhabit that tract of country in America usually called
Virginia, according to the Descriptions and Boundaries of the original Charters,
not before otherwise appropriated or disposed of by His Majesty's Ancestors. In
this situation hath it remained from the time of this last charter, and in this
manner hath Virginia been constantly laid down ever since in all the English

taken to be meant and intended, and shall inure and take effect in the most beneficial and available sense, to all intents and pur-

Maps, as well those published by publick authority, as others, to wit, Bounded on the North by Maryland and Pennsylvania, on the East by the Atlantic Ocean, on the South by Carolina, and on the West by the great South Sea or by the Western Limits of the British Dominions, which was never clearly ascertained until the last Treaty of Peace in the year 1763, fixed them by a line drawn along the middle of the River Mississippi. Several Acts of the British Crown and Government, as well as many laws of this Colony (which receiving the Royal Assent are also Acts of the British Crown and Government) have from time to time corresponded with and confirmed these Bounds of Virginia. It will be sufficient to mention a few instances, as there are none which contradict them. In the fourth year of the Reign of Queen Anne, An. Dom. 1705, an act of Assembly was made here, empowering the Governor for the time being, with the consent of the Council, by Charter or Grant, under the seal of the Colony to grant to any such person or persons, their heirs, executors, administrators, or Assigns, as should at his or their own charge, make discovery of any Town or Nation of Indians situate, or inhabiting to the Westward of, or between the Appalatian Mountains, the sole liberty and Right of trading to and with all and every such Town or Towns, Nation or Nations of Indians so discovered as aforesaid for the space of fourteen Years, then next ensuing, with such clauses or articles of Restraint or Prohibition, of all other persons from the said Trade and under such Penalties and Forfeitures as shall be thought convenient. In an additional Instruction from his late Majesty King George the Second to Sir William Gooch, Bart., Lieut. Governor and Commander in Chief of the Colony and Dominion of Virginia, or to the Commander in Chief of the said Colony for the time being, Given at the Court of St. James the 16th Day of March 1748/9 in the 22nd Year of his Reign reciting a petition which had been presented to his Majesty by the Ohio Company ; the said Governor is directed and required forthwith to make the Petitioners and their Associates a Grant or Grants of two hundred thousand Acres of Land betwixt Romanetto's and Buffaloe Creek on the South Side of the River Alleghany, otherwise Ohio and betwixt the two Creeks and the Yellow Creek, on the North Side of the said River or in such other parts of the West of the Alleghany Mountains as shall be adjudged most proper by the said Petitioners, for making settlements thereon, within His Majesty's Colony of Virginia.

In the year 1753 an Act of Assembly was made here, '' For further encouraging persons to settle on the Waters of the Mississippi,'' Declaring that it would be a means of cultivating a better correspondence with the neighbouring Indians, if a further encouragement were given to Persons who have settled or shall settle upon the waters of the Mississippi, in the County of Augusta (which was then the frontier county and quite across this Colony), and that a considerable number of persons as well his Majesty's natural born subjects, as foreign Protestants were willing to come to this Colony with their Families and Effects, and settle upon Lands near the said waters, in case they can have encouragement for so doing ; that settling that part of the country will add to the strength and security

poses for the Profit and advantage of the subjects of his Majesty, his Heirs and Successors of Virginia aforesaid, as well against his

of the Colony in general and be a means of augmenting his Majesty's Revenue of Quit Rents. And enacting, "That all persons being Protestants who have already settled or shall hereafter settle and reside upon any Lands situate to the Westward of the Ridge of Mountains that divides the Rivers Roanoke, James and Potomack from the Mississippi in the County of Augusta, shall be and are exempted and discharged from the payment of all publick, County and Parish Levies, for the term of fifteen years next following."

And in the year 1754 another Act of Assembly was made here "For the Encouragement and Protection of the Settlers upon the waters of the Mississippi," Declaring that many of his Majesty's faithful subjects had been encouraged by the Acts of the General Assembly heretofore made, to settle and inhabit on his Lands in this Colony on and near the Waters of the River Mississippi ; and that it hath been represented to the General Assembly that the subjects of the French King, and by their instigation the Indians in alliance with them, had encroached on His Majesty's said Lands, murdered some of his subjects and taken others captive and spoiled them of their Goods and effects ; impowering the Treasurer of this Colony to borrow a sum of money upon interest, nominating certain Directors, (members of both Houses of Assembly) and impowering them from time to time with the Consent and approbation of the Governor or Commander in Chief for the time being, to direct and appoint how the said money shall be applied towards protecting and defending his Majesty's subjects, who then were settled or hereafter should settle on the waters of the River Mississippi, And laying sundry duties and Taxes on the inhabitants of this Colony for raising a Fund to repay the Money to be so borrowed. And for the same purposes were several hundred thousand Pounds granted by the General Assembly, and levied upon the people of Virginia, during the course of the late war. And soon after the conclusion of the war, to wit in the year . . . it being thought expedient in order to conciliate the minds of the Indians then but lately withdrawn from the French interest, to extend a temporary line or Boundary between the Inhabitants of this Colony and the Southern Indians, across the Alleghany Mountains to the Ohio River ; the sum of . . . was granted by the General Assembly and levied upon the people of Virginia . . . charge thereof upon a formal requisition made by the crown for that purpose.

These quotations and examples are sufficient to show in what sense the Charter of King Charles the Second respecting, the Bounds of this Colony, hath been always understood ; and to demonstrate that the country to the westward of the Alleghany Mountains on both sides the Ohio River, is part of Virginia. And consequently that no new Government or Proprietary can legally be established there—Nor hath any attempt of that sort ever been made from the time of the said charter until the late extraordinary application of Mr. Walpole and his associates, to the Crown to grant them a Proprietary charter and create a new Government between the Alleghany Mountains and the River Ohio, (in direct violation of the Virginia Charters,) which would not only have taken away great part of the territory of this Colony, but would have removed from under the

Majesty, his Heirs, and Successors, as against all and every other person and persons whatsoever, any Law, Statute, Custom, or Usuage, to the Contrary thereof in anywise, notwithstanding.

immediate protection of the Crown and the Government of Virginia, several thousand inhabitants, settled there under the faith of the said Charters, as well as many subsequent acts of Government and the Encouragement of Publick Laws. It would also have greatly injured the only regular Seminary of Learning in Virginia, by reducing one of the principal Branches of its Revenue, the profits arising from a grant of the Office of Surveyor General of Virginia, made by their Majesties King William and Queen Mary to the President and Professors of William and Mary College, and have introduced a precedent of a very alarming and dangerous nature to the Liberties, Rights and Privileges of His Majesty's subjects of this Colony. To this illegal and injurious attempt several Gentlemen in Virginia, the Ohio Company were made in some measure accessory, without their knowledge and very contrary to their Inclination ; but at their first General Meeting after having received notice of it ; they unanimously declared their Disapprobation of the measure, and their absolute Refusal of having any concern in it ; which Regulation they not only entered in their own Books and communicated to the members of their Company in England ; but for their Justification to posterity sent a copy thereof to the Governor and Council to be entered, if they thought fit, on their Journals. This project of Mr. Walpole's was fabricated by the same fertile . . . who first suggested it to the Earl of —— to apply to the Crown for a grant of the Islands in Delaware Bay ; which probably would have taken effect, to the ruin of many reputable Families, if his Lordship, after a Day's debate before the Lords of the Council, had not had grace enough to be ashamed of it, and drop his pretensions. And tho' the scheme for a new Government on the Ohio, for the present seems to be rejected or suspended, yet considering how favourably it was entertained by some of the publick Boards in England, it may be proper for the General Assembly of Virginia, at this time to assert our Rights by a Dutiful Remonstrance and Petition to the Crown.

Which is humbly submitted to their Consideration.

N. B.—The first charter for Carolina, the orders to the Commissioners for running a Dividing Line between North Carolina and Virginia, with their proceedings and report thereon, the Articles of the Peace of Utrecht and Aix la Chapelle, with the proceedings of the Commissioners of the two Nations, respecting the boundaries of the English and French Colonies, the Royal Instructions from time to time to the Governors of Virginia, the several orders of the Council relative to the Back Lands, the Judgment of the King and Council upon the Patent Fee in Governor Dinwiddie's time, and several other Publick Documents may throw much light upon this interesting subject.[1]

[1] A draft of the above in George Mason's handwriting was preserved by Richard Henry Lee, and was formerly to be found at the University of Virginia, among the Lee Papers. A copy was made from it in 1842 for Genl. John Mason, from which this is transcribed. The original draft is now missing.

VI.

Copy of the petition presented to the Governor and Council, June, 1774, by George Mason, praying entries, or warrants, for lands due for the importation of people, according to the Royal Charter.

TO HIS EXCELLENCY THE GOVERNOR AND THE HONORABLE THE COUNCIL OF VIRGINIA.

The memorial and petition of George Mason of the county of Fairfax Humbly Sheweth :

That in the charter granted by King James the first to the Virginia Company in the year 1609 is among others a clause declaring "That it is his royal will and pleasure, and charging, commanding, warranting and authorising the treasurer and the said Company and their successor, to convey, assign and set over, such particular portions of lands, tenements and hereditaments, unto such his Majesty's loving subjects, naturally born, denizens or others, as well adventurers as planters, as by the said Company shall be nominated, appointed and allowed, wherein respect to be had as well of the proportion of the adventure, as of the special service, hazard, exploit, or merit of any person, so to be recompenced, advanced, or rewarded," pursuant to which, within a few years after, fifty acres of land were ordered to be assigned and granted to every person importing himself into this colony ; and to every person who should import others, fifty acres for each person so imported. This, as your Memorialist conceives was the original, or first rise of the ancient custom of granting lands in Virginia, upon Importation-Rights, which is now more than an hundred and fifty years old, and appears to have been interwoven with the constitution of the colony from its first settlement. That the same was constantly practised during the said Company's government here, and after the government was taken into the hands of the crown, upon the dissolution of the Virginia Company, the same custom and Rights was always allowed and continued, as appears by the patents and records in the Secretary's office ; the titles to great part of the lands in this colony being founded upon importation rights ; and the constant style of the old patents is, "the said lands being due by and for the transportation, or by and for the importation of   . persons into this colony." That in the year 1662, an act of General Assembly was made prescribing the manner of proving rights to lands due for the importation of servants and obtaining certificates thereon, to entitle the importers to surveys and patents, and giving such proofs and certificates the preference to actual surveys without them, and in the same year, another Act of Assembly was made, reciting that the former laws concerning deserted lands, reserved to the first taken-up, his rights to take up land in another place, and enacting that for the future, in case of deserted lands, the rights as well as the lands shall be forfeited, and the grantee made incapable of using any of them afterwards. From which law it is clear that Importation-Rights are always good, until they have been applied to patents for land, and the said land forfeited by want of seating and planting. That in the year 1676, the said custom and right to lands was solemnly confirmed and continued by charter and letters patent from King Charles the Second to the Colony of Virginia, under the great seal of England "*as according as hath been used and allowed from the first plantation*" ; to be held of his Majesty, his heirs and successors, as of their manor of East Greenwich in their "county of Kent, in free and common soccage," and declaring "That all and every clause, article and sentence, in the said letters patent contained, shall be from time to time for ever hereafter, as often as any ambiguity, doubt or question shall or may happen to arise thereupon, expounded, construed, deemed and taken to be meant and intended, and shall enure and take effect, in the *most beneficial and available sense*, to all intents and purposes, for *the profits and advantages of the subjects of Virginia,* as well against *his Majesty, his heirs and successors*, as against all and every other person or persons whatsoever," which charter was recognised by an Act of Assembly in the year 1677, prescribing a particular form *of all patents* for the future, in which form is recited "That his Majesty had been graciously pleased, by his said letters patent, to continue and confirm the ancient right and privilege of granting fifty acres of land *for every person imported* into his Majesty's colony of Virginia," and it appears from the patent Record Books, that all lands in this colony, except escheat lands, were granted upon Importation-Rights only ; until in or about the year 1710, when Treasury-Rights, or paying a certain consideration in money to the crown for lands were first introduced here, but that the same never affected lands claimed under the royal charter, for the ancient rights to lands due for the importation of people still continued upon the same footing as before, and hath ever been held sacred and inviolable and subject to no new charge or imposition whatever, and great quantities of land, from time to time granted accordingly. That from the earliest times of this colony there hath been allowed to the Secretary, and the clerks of counties by law, a certain fee for certificates of rights to land ; and upon the last regulation of the Fee Bill in Virginia, within these few years, the legislature allowed to the county court clerks " for proving rights for land, produced at one time, belonging to one person, and certificates thereof, a fee of thirteen pounds of tobacco," and to the Secretary "for recording a certificate of rights, fifteen pounds of tobacco," and by an Act of Assembly made in the year 1710, when Treasury-Rights were first introduced, it was (among other things) enacted, " That upon the passing of any patent for land thereafter, the Secretary of this Colony and Dominion for the time being, should cause such patent to be duly entered upon the Records of his office, together with the certificate of rights *either by importation* or by money paid the receiver-general of this colony," which your Memorialist is well informed hath continued to be the practice ever since ; and that these two modes of granting lands, since the year 1710, as before mentioned have never in the least interfered with each other, as the crown could only alter the terms, or fix a new price upon the lands, to which there was no legal right. So that Mr. Stith, in his History of Virginia (which is chiefly extracted from records), mentioning the custom of granting lands for the importation of people, had good reason for his remark that " this is the ancient, legal, and a most indubitable method of granting lands in Virginia." And your Memorialist, with all due submission, begs leave to observe, that the King being as much bound by the act of his royal predecessors, as any private subject, holding an estate from his ancestors is bound by the act of that ancestor ; and the before mentioned ancient right to any vacant or ungranted lands in this colony, having been solemnly continued and confirmed by the said charter from King Charles the Second, in manner hereinbefore mentioned, the same was thereby made part of the law and constitution of this country, and hath remained so ever since ; and therefore cannot be avoided, injured, invalidated, or in any manner affected, by any proclamation, instruction, or other act of government, nor subject to any new charge, expence, burden, or imposition whatsoever. For which reasons, your Memorialist most humbly conceives that any instruction or late regulations, respecting the ungranted lands in this colony, from our present most gracious sovereign, ever observant of the laws, and attentive to the just rights of his people, were never meant, or intended to affect lands due as aforesaid, under the royal charter. That your petitioner confiding in and upon the faith of the before mentioned royal charter, laws and custom, hath been at great trouble and expence, and hath laid out considerable sums of money, in purchasing from the importers legal certificates of rights to large quantities of land, due for the importation of people from Great Britain and Ireland into this colony, and prays that he may be admitted to entries for the said lands, upon the western waters, in the county of Fincastle, upon his producing the usual certificates and assignments ; or that his Excellency the governor will be pleased to grant your petitioner his warrants for surveying the same, whichever his Excellency and this honorable board shall judge most proper. And your petitioner will ever pray.

G. MASON.[1]

VII.

FAIRFAX COUNTY RESOLUTIONS.

At a General Meeting of the Freeholders and other Inhabitants of the County of Fairfax, at the Court House, in the town of Alexandria, on Monday, the 18th day of July, 1774.

George Washington, Esq :, Chairman, and Robert Harrison, Gentleman, Clerk :

1. *Resolved*, That this Colony and Dominion of Virginia cannot be considered as a conquered country, and, if it was, that the present inhabitants are not of the conquered, but of the con-

---

[1] Manuscripts, Department of State.

querors. That the same was not settled at the national expense of England, but at the private expense of the adventurers, our ancestors, by solemn compact with, and under the auspices and protection of, the British Crown, upon which we are, in every respect as dependent as the people of Great Britain, and in the same manner subject to all his Majesty's just, legal and constitutional prerogatives; that our ancestors, when they left their native land, and settled in America, brought with them, even if the same had not been confirmed by Charters, the civil constitution and form of Government of the country they came from, and were by the laws of nature and nations entitled to all its privileges, immunities, and advantages, which have descended to us, their posterity, and ought of right to be as fully enjoyed as if we had still continued within the realm of England.

2. *Resolved*, That the most important and valuable part of the British Constitution, upon which its very existence depends, is, the fundamental principle of the people's being governed by no laws to which they have not given their consent by Representatives freely chosen by themselves, who are affected by the laws they enact equally with their constituents, to whom they are accountable, and whose burthens they share, in which consists the safety and happiness of the community; for if this part of the Constitution was taken away, or materially altered, the government must degenerate either into an absolute and despotic monarchy, or a tyrannical aristocracy, and the freedom of the people be annihilated.

3. *Resolved*, Therefore, as the inhabitants of the American colonies are not, and from their situation, cannot be represented in the British Parliament, that the Legislative power can, of right, be exercised only by our Provincial Assemblies, or Parliaments, subject to the assent or negative of the British Crown, to be declared within some proper limited time; but as it was thought just and reasonable that the people of Great Britain should reap advantages from the colonies adequate to the protection they afforded them, the British Parliament have claimed and exercised the power of regulating our trade and commerce, so as to restrain our importing from foreign countries such articles as they could furnish us with of their own growth and manufacture, or exporting to foreign countries such articles and portions of our produce

as Great Britain stood in need of, for her own consumption or manufacture. Such a power directed with wisdom and moderation seems necessary for the general good of that great body politic of which we are a part, although in some degree repugnant to the principles of the Constitution. Under this idea, our ancestors submitted to it, the experience of more than a century during the government of his Majesty's royal predecessors hath proved its utility, and the reciprocal benefits flowing from it produced mutual uninterrupted harmony and good will between the inhabitants of Great Britain and her colonies who during that long period always considered themselves as one and the same people ; and though such a power is capable of abuse, and in some instances hath been stretched beyond the original design and institution, yet to avoid strife and contention with our fellow-subjects, and strongly impressed with the experience of mutual benefits, we always cheerfully acquiesced in it while the entire regulation of our internal policy, and giving and granting our own money, were preserved to our own Provincial Legislatures.

4. *Resolved,* That it is the duty of these Colonies, on all emergencies, to contribute in proportion to their abilities, situation, and circumstances, to the necessary charge of supporting and defending the British Empire of which they are a part ; that while we are treated upon an equal footing with our fellow-subjects, the motives of self-interest and preservation will be a sufficient obligation, as was evident through the course of the last war ; and that no argument can be fairly applied to the British Parliament's taxing us, upon a presumption that we should refuse a just and reasonable contribution, but will equally operate in justification of the Executive Power taxing the people of England, upon a supposition of their Representatives refusing to grant the necessary supplies.

5. *Resolved,* That the claim, lately assumed and exercised by the British Parliament, of making all such laws as they think fit, to govern the people of these colonies, and to extort from us our money without our consent, is not only diametrically contrary to the first principles of the Constitution, and the original compacts by which we are dependent upon the British Crown and government ; but is totally incompatible with the privileges of a free

people and the natural rights of mankind, will render our own legislatures merely nominal and nugatory, and is calculated to reduce us from a state of freedom and happiness to slavery and misery.

6. *Resolved*, That taxation and representation are in their nature inseparable ; that the right of withholding, or of giving and granting their own money, is the only effectual security to a free people against the encroachments of despotism and tyranny ; and that whenever they yield the one, they must quickly fall a prey to the other.

7. *Resolved*, That the powers over the people of America now claimed by the British House of Commons, in whose election we have no share, on whose determinations we can have no influ-' ence, whose information must be always defective and false, who in many instances may have a separate, and in some an opposite interest to ours, and who are removed from those impressions of tenderness and compassion arising from personal intercourse and connexions, which soften the rigors of the most despotic govern-ments, must, if continued, establish the most grievous and intol-erable species of tyranny and oppression, that ever was inflicted upon mankind.

8. *Resolved*, That it is our greatest wish and inclination, as well as interest, to continue our connexion with, and dependence upon, the British government ; but though we are its subjects, we will use every means, which Heaven hath given us, to prevent our becoming its slaves.

9. *Resolved*, That there is a premeditated design and system, formed and pursued by the British ministry, to introduce an arbitrary government into his Majesty's American dominions ; to which end they are artfully prejudicing our sovereign, and in-flaming the minds of our fellow-subjects in Great Britain, by propagating the most malevolent falsehoods, particularly that there is an intention in the American colonies to set up for inde-pendent States ; endeavouring at the same time, by various acts of violence and oppression, by sudden and repeated dissolutions of our Assemblies, whenever they presume to examine the ille-gality of ministerial mandates, or deliberate on the violated rights of their constituents, and by breaking in upon the American charters, to reduce us to a state of desperation, and dissolve the

original compacts by which our ancestors bound themselves and their posterity to remain dependent upon the British crown; which measures unless effectually counteracted, will end in the ruin both of Great Britain and her colonies.

10. *Resolved*, That the several acts of Parliament for raising a revenue upon the people of America without their consent, the creating new and dangerous jurisdictions here, the taking away our trials by jury, the ordering persons, upon criminal accusations, to be tried in another country than that in which the fact is charged to have been committed, the act inflicting ministerial vengeance upon the town of Boston, and the two bills lately brought into Parliament for abrogating the charter of the province of Massachusetts Bay, and for the protection and encouragement of murderers in the said province, are part of the above mentioned iniquitous system. That the inhabitants of the town of Boston are now suffering in the common cause of all British America, and are justly entitled to its support and assistance; and therefore that a subscription ought immediately to be opened, and proper persons appointed in every county of this colony to purchase provisions, and consign them to some gentleman of character in Boston, to be distributed. among the poorer sort of people there.

11. *Resolved*, That we will cordially join with our friends and brethren of this and the other colonies, in such measures as shall be judged most effectual for procuring redress of our grievances, and that upon obtaining such redress, if the destruction of the tea at Boston be regarded as an invasion of private property, we shall be willing to contribute towards paying the East India Company the value; but as we consider the said Company as the tools and instruments of oppression in the hands of government, and the cause of our present distress, it is the opinion of this meeting, that the people of these colonies should forbear all further dealings with them, by refusing to purchase their merchandise, until that peace, safety, and good order, which they have disturbed be perfectly restored. And that all tea now in this colony, or which shall be imported into it shipped before the 1st day of Septemper next, should be deposited in some store-house to be appointed by the respective committees of each county, until a sufficient sum of money be raised by subscription

to reimburse the owners the value, and then to be publicly burned and destroyed ; and if the same is not paid for and destroyed as aforesaid, that it remain in the custody of the said committees, at the risk of the owners, until the act of Parliament imposing a duty upon tea, for raising a revenue in America, be repealed ; and immediately afterwards be delivered unto the several proprietors thereof, their agents, or attorneys.

12. *Resolved*, That nothing will so much contribute to defeat the pernicious designs of the common enemies of Great Britain and her colonies, as a firm union of the latter, who ought to regard every act of violence or oppression inflicted upon any one of them, as aimed at all ; and to effect this desirable purpose, that a Congress should be appointed, to consist of deputies from all the colonies, to concert a general and uniform plan for the defence and preservation of our common rights, and continuing the connexion and dependence of the said colonies upon Great Britain, under a just, lenient, permanent, and constitutional form of government.

13. *Resolved*, That our most sincere and cordial thanks be given to the patrons and friends of liberty in Great Britain, for their spirited and patriotic conduct, in support of our constitutional rights and privileges, and their generous efforts to prevent the distress and calamity of America.

14. *Resolved*, That every little jarring interest and dispute, which has ever happened between these colonies, should be buried in eternal oblivion ; that all manner of luxury and extravagance ought immediately to be laid aside, as totally inconsistent with the threatening and gloomy prospect before us ; that it is the indispensable duty of all the gentlemen and men of fortune to set examples of temperance, fortitude, frugality, and industry, and give every encouragement in their power, particularly by subscriptions and premiums, to the improvement of arts and manufactures in America ; that great care and attention should be had to the cultivation of flax, cotton, and other materials for manufactures ; and we recommend it to such of the inhabitants, as have large stocks of sheep, to sell to their neighbors at a moderate price, as the most certain means of speedily increasing our breed of sheep, and quantity of wool.

15. *Resolved*, That until American grievances be redressed, by

restoration of our just rights and privileges, no goods or merchandise whatsoever ought to be imported into this colony, which shall be shipped from Great Britain or Ireland after the 1st day of September next, except linens not exceeding fifteen pence per yard, coarse woolen cloth, not exceeding two shillings sterling per yard, nails, wire and wire cards, needles and pins, paper, saltpetre, and medicines, which may be imported until the 1st day of September, 1775 ; and if any goods or merchandise, other than these hereby excepted, should be shipped from Great Britain, after the time aforesaid, to this colony, that the same immediately upon their arrival, should either be sent back again, by the owners, their agents or attorneys, or stored and deposited in some warehouse, to be appointed by the committee for each respective county, and there kept at the risk and charge of the owners, to be delivered to them, when a free importation of goods hither shall again take place. And that the merchants and venders of goods and merchandise within this colony ought not to take advantage of our present distress, but continue to sell the goods and merchandise which they now have, or which may be shipped to them before the 1st day of September next, at the same rates and prices they have been accustomed to do, within one year last past ; and if any person shall sell such goods on any other terms than above expressed, that no inhabitant of this colony should at any time, forever thereafter, deal with him, his agent, factor, or storekeepers for any commodity whatsoever.

16. *Resolved*, That it is the opinion of this meeting, that the merchants and venders of goods and merchandise within this colony should take an oath, not to sell or dispose of any goods or merchandise whatsoever, which may be shipped from Great Britain after the 1st day of September next as aforesaid, except the articles before excepted, and that they will, upon receipt of such prohibited goods, either send the same back again by the first opportunity, or deliver them to the committees in the respective counties, to be deposited in some warehouse, at the risk and charge of the owners, until they, their agents, or factors, be permitted to take them away by the said committees ; the names of those who refuse to take such oath to be advertised by the respective committees in the counties wherein they reside. And to the end that the inhabitants of this colony may know what merchants

and venders of goods and merchandise have taken such oath, that the respective committees should grant a certificate thereof to every such person who shall take the same.

17. *Resolved,* That it is the opinion of this meeting, that during our present difficulties and distress, no slaves ought to be im. ported into any of the British colonies on this continent ; and we take this opportunity of declaring our most earnest wishes to see an entire stop forever put to such a wicked, cruel, and unnatural trade.

18. *Resolved,* That no kind of lumber should be exported from this colony to the West Indies, until America be restored to her constitutional rights and liberties, if the other colonies will accede to a like resolution ; and that it be recommended to the general Congress to appoint as early a day as possible for stopping such export.

19. *Resolved,* That it is the opinion of this meeting, if American grievances be not redressed before the 1st day of November, 1775, that all exports of produce from the several colonies to Great Britain should cease ; and to carry the said resolution more effectually into execution, that we will not plant or cultivate any tobacco, after the crop now growing; provided the same measure shall be adopted by the other colonies on this continent, as well those who have heretofore made tobacco, as those who have not. And it is our opinion also, if the Congress of deputies from the several colonies shall adopt the measure of non-exportation to Great Britain, as the people will be thereby disabled from paying their debts, that no judgments should be rendered by the courts in the said colonies for any debt, after information of the said measure's being determined upon.

20. *Resolved,* That it is the opinion of this meeting that a solemn covenant and association should be entered into by the inhabitants of all the colonies upon oath, that they will not, after the times which shall be respectively agreed on at the general Congress, export any manner of lumber to the West Indies, nor any of their produce to Great Britain, or sell or dispose of the same to any person who shall not have entered into the said covenant and association ; and also that they will not import or receive any goods or merchandise which shall be shipped from Great Britain after the 1st day of September next, other than the before

enumerated articles, nor buy or purchase any goods except as before excepted, of any person whatsoever, who shall not have taken the oath herein before recommended to be taken by the merchants and venders of goods ; nor buy or purchase any slaves hereafter imported into any part of this continent, until a free exportation and importation be again resolved on by a majority of the representatives or deputies of the colonies. And that the respective committees of the counties, in each colony, so soon as the covenant and association becomes general, publish by advertisements in their several counties, a list of the names of those (if any such there be) who will not accede thereto ; that such traitors to their country may be publicly known and detested.

21. *Resolved,* That it is the opinion of this meeting that this and the other associating colonies should break off all trade, intercourse, and dealings, with that colony, province, or town, which shall decline or refuse to agree to the plan, which shall be adopted by the general Congress.

22. *Resolved,* That should the town of Boston be forced to submit to the late cruel and oppressive measures of government, that we shall not hold the same to be binding upon us, but will, notwithstanding, religiously maintain and inviolably adhere to such measures as shall be concerted by the general Congress, for the preservation of our lives, liberties, and fortunes.

23. *Resolved,* That it be recommended to the deputies of the general Congress, to draw up and transmit an humble and dutiful petition and remonstrance to his Majesty, asserting with decent firmness our just and constitutional rights and privileges ; lamenting the fatal necessity of being compelled to enter into measures disgusting to his Majesty and his Parliament, or injurious to our fellow-subjects in Great Britain ; declaring, in the strongest terms, our duty and affection to his Majesty's person, family, and government, and our desire to continue our dependence upon Great Britain ; and most humbly conjuring and beseeching his Majesty not to reduce his faithful subjects of America to a state of desperation, and to reflect, that from our sovereign there can be but one appeal. And it is the opinion of this meeting, that after such petition and remonstrance shall have been presented to his Majesty, the same should be printed in the public papers, in all the principal towns in Great Britain.

24. *Resolved,* That George Washington and George Broad-water, lately elected our representatives to serve in the General Assembly, be appointed to attend the Convention at Williams-burg on the 1st day of August next, and present these Resolves, as the sense of the people of this county, upon the measures proper to be taken in the present alarming and dangerous situation of America.[1]

25. *Resolved,* That George Washington, Esqr., John West, George Mason, William Ramsay, William Rumney, George Gilpin, Rob. Hanson Harrison, John Carlyle, Robt. Adam, John Dalton, Philip Alexander, James Kirk, William Brown, Charles Broadwater William Payne, Martin Cockburn, Lee Massey, William Hartshorne, Thos. Triplet, Charles Alexander, Thomas Pollard, Townshend Dade, Jr., Edward Payne, Henry Gunnell, and Thomas Lewis, be a committee for this county ; that they or a majority of them, on any emergency, have power to call a general meeting, and to concert and adopt such meas-ures as may be thought most expedient and necessary.

26. *Resolved,* That a copy of these proceedings be transmitted to the printers at Williamsburg to be published.

ROBT. HARRISON, *Clerk.*[2]

VIII.

FAIRFAX COUNTY COMMITTEE.

Extracts from the Proceedings of the Committee of Fairfax County, on the 17th of January, 1775.

George Washington, Esquire, Chairman.
Robert H. Harrison, Clerk.

Resolved, That the defenceless state of this county renders it indispensably necessary that a quantity of ammunition should be

---

[1] The draft of the Resolutions in the handwriting of George Mason, and found among the Washington papers, (see Sparks, vol. ii., Appendix,) ends here with the 24th Resolution. A copy preserved in the State Library, Rich-mond, has two additional ones, appointing the Fairfax Co. Committee, whose names are there given.

[2] From a MS. draft in the Capitol at Richmond.

immediately provided ; and as the same will be for the common benefit, protection, and defence of the inhabitants thereof, it is but just and reasonable that the expenses incurred in procuring the same should be defrayed by a general and equal contribution. It is therefore recommended that the sum of three shillings per poll, for the purpose aforesaid, be paid by and for every tithable person in this County, to the Sheriff or such other collector as may be appointed, who is to render the same to this Committee, with a list of the names of such persons as shall refuse to pay the same, if any such there be.

Resolved, That this Committee do concur in opinion with the Provincial Committee of the Province of Maryland, that a well regulated militia, composed of gentlemen, freeholders, and other freemen, is the natural strength and only stable security of a free government, and that such militia will relieve our mother country from any expense in our protection and defence, will obviate the pretence of a necessity for taxing us on that account, and render it unnecessary to keep Standing Armies among us—ever dangerous to liberty ; and therefore it is recommended to such of the inhabitants of this County as are from 16 to 50 years of age, to form themselves into companies of 68 men ; to choose a captain, 2 lieutenants, an ensign, 4 sergeants, 4 corporals, and 1 drummer, for each company ; that they provide themselves with good firelocks, and use their utmost endeavours to make themselves masters of the Military Exercise, published by order of his Majesty in 1764, and recommended by the Provincial Congress of the Mass. Bay, on the 29th of Oct. last.

Fairfax Co., Va., Association.—Threatened with the destruction of our ancient laws and liberty, and the loss of all that is dear to British subjects and freemen, justly alarmed with the prospect of impending ruin,—firmly determined, at the hazard of our lives, to transmit to our children and posterity those sacred rights to which ourselves were born ; and thoroughly convinced that a well regulated militia, composed of the gentlemen, freeholders, and other freemen, is the natural strength and only safe and stable security of a free government, and that such militia will relieve our mother country from any expense in our protection and defence, will obviate the pretence of a necessity for taxing us on that account, and render it unnecessary to keep any standing army (ever dangerous to liberty) in this Colony, we the subscribers, inhabitants of Fairfax County, have freely and voluntarily agreed, and hereby do agree and solemnly promise, to enroll and embody ourselves into a militia for this county, intended to consist of all the able-bodied freemen from eighteen to fifty years of age, under officers of their own choice, and for that purpose to form ourselves into distinct companies of sixty-eight men each, and so soon as the said companies or any of them in convenient neighborhoods and districts are completed, to choose from among our friends and acquaintance, upon whose justice, humanity, and bravery we can rely, a captain, two lieutenants, an ensign, and four sergeants, for each company, every captain respectively to appoint four corporals and a drummer for his company, which election of officers is to be annual in any company, if the majority of the company think fit ; and whenever a sufficient number of companies shall be made up, all the said companies are to be formed into a regiment, under the command of a colonel, lieutenant colonel, and major, to be chosen by the captains, lieutenants, and ensigns of the said companies ; which election of field officers is to be annual also, if a majority of the officers think fit.   And such of us as have, or can procure rifle-guns, and understand the use 'of them, will be ready to form a company of marksmen or light-infantry for the said regiment, choosing our own officers as aforesaid, and distinguishing our dress, when we are upon duty, from that of the other companies, by painted hunting-shirts and Indian boots, or caps, as shall be found most convenient ; which regulation and establishment is to be preserved and continued until a regular and proper militia law for the defence of the country, shall be enacted by the legislature of this colony.   And we do each of us for ourselves respectively, promise and engage to keep a good firelock, in proper order, and to furnish ourselves as soon as possible with, and always keep by us, one pound of gunpowder, four pounds of lead, one dozen gun-flints, and a pair of bullet moulds, with a cartouch-box, or powder-horn, and bag for balls.   That we will use our best endeavors to perfect ourselves in the military exercise and discipline, and therefore will pay due obedience to our officers, and regularly attend such private and general musters as they shall appoint.   And that we will always hold ourselves in readiness, in case of necessity, hostile invasion, or real danger, to defend and preserve to the utmost of our power, our religion, the laws of our country, and the just rights and privileges of our fellow-subjects, our posterity, and ourselves, upon the principles of the English Constitution.[1]

IX.

FAIRFAX INDEPENDENT COMPANY.

A moment's reflection upon the principles on which this company was first instituted, and the purposes for which it was formed, will evince the propriety of the gentleman's motion; for it has been wisely observed by the deepest politician who ever put pen to paper, that no institution can be long preserved, but by frequent recurrence to those maxims on which it was formed.

This company is essentially different from a common collection of mercenary soldiers. It was formed upon the liberal sentiments of public good, for the great and useful purposes of defending our country, and preserving those inestimable rights which we inherit from our ancestors; it was intended in these times of extreme danger, when we are threatened with the ruin of that constitution under which we were born, and the destruction of all that is dear to us, to rouse the attention of the public, to introduce the use of arms and discipline, to infuse a martial spirit of emulation, and to provide a fund of officers; that in case of absolute necessity, the people might be the better enabled to act in defence of their invaded liberty. Upon this generous and public-spirited plan, gentlemen of the first fortune and character among us have become members of the Fairfax Independent Company, have submitted to stand in the ranks as common soldiers, and to pay due obedience to the officers of their own choice. This part of the country has the glory of setting so laudable an example: let us not tarnish it by any little dirty views of party, of mean self-interest or of low ambition.

We came equals into this world, and equals shall we go out of it. All men are by nature born equally free and independent.

---

[1] American Archives, fourth series, vol. i., 1145.

To protect the weaker from the injuries and insults of the stronger were societies first formed ; when men entered into compacts to give up some of their natural rights, that by union and mutual assistance they might secure the rest ; but they gave up no more than the nature of the thing required. Every society, all government, and every kind of civil compact therefore, is or ought to be, calculated for the general good and safety of the community. Every power, every authority vested in particular men is, or ought to be, ultimately directed to this sole end ; and whenever any power or authority whatever extends further, or is of longer duration than is in its nature necessary for these purposes, it may be called government, but it is in fact oppression.

Upon these natural just and simple positions were civil laws and obligations framed, and from this source do even the most arbitrary and despotic powers this day upon earth derive their origin. Strange indeed that such superstructures should be raised upon such a foundation ! But when we reflect upon the insidious arts of wicked and designing men, the various and plausible pretences for continuing and increasing authority, the incautious nature of the many, and the inordinate lust of power in the few, we shall no longer be surprised that free-born man hath been enslaved, and that those very means which were contrived for his preservation have been perverted to his ruin ; or, to borrow a metaphor from Holy Writ, that the kid hath been seethed in his mother's milk.

To prevent these fatal effects, and to restore mankind to its native rights hath been the study of some of the best men that this world ever produced ; and the most effectual means that human wisdom hath ever been able to devise, is frequently appealing to the body of the people, to those constituent members from whom authority originated, for their approbation or dissent. Whenever this is neglected or evaded, or the free voice of the people is suppressed or corrupted ; or whenever any military establishment or authority is not, by some certain mode of rotation, dissolved into and blended with that mass from which it was taken, inevitable destruction to the state follows.

> " Then down the precipice of time it goes,
>   And sinks in moments, which in ages rose."

The history of all nations who have had liberty and lost it, puts these facts beyond doubt. We have great cause to fear that this crisis is approaching in our mother country. Her constitution has strong symptoms of decay. It is our duty by every means in our power to prevent the like here.

If it be objected to the intended regulation that there may be inconvenience in changing officers who, by having served as such, have acquired a superior degree of military knowledge, the example and experience of the most warlike and victorious people that ever existed is directly against such a suggestion.

While the Roman Commonwealth preserved its vigour, new consuls were annually elected, new levies made, and new officers appointed ; a general was often recalled from the head of a victorious army, in the midst of a dangerous and important war, and a successor sent to finish the expedition which he had begun. A long and almost constant series of success proved the wisdom and utility of measures which carried victory through the world, and at the same time secured the public safety and liberty at home ; for by these means the people had always an inexhaustible fund of experienced officers, upon every emergency, untainted with the dangerous impressions which continued command naturally makes. But when by degrees these essential maxims of the state were undermined, and pretences were found to continue commanders beyond the stated times, their army no longer considered themselves the soldiers of the Republic, but as the troops of Marius or of Sylla, of Pompey or of Cæsar, of Marc Antony or of Octavius. The dissolution of that once glorious and happy commonwealth was the natural consequence, and has afforded a useful lesson to succeeding generations.

It has been lately observed by a learned and reverend writer, that North America is the only great nursery of freemen now left upon the face of the earth. Let us cherish the sacred deposit. Let us strive to merit this greatest encomium that ever was bestowed upon any country. In all our associations ; in all our agreements let us never lose sight of this fundamental maxim— that all power was originally lodged in, and consequently is derived from, the people. We should wear it as a breastplate, and buckle it on as our armour.

The application of these general principles to the subject before us is too obvious to need a minute illustration. By investing our officers with a power for life, or for an unlimited time, we are acting diametrically contrary to the principles of that liberty for which we profess to contend, and establishing a precedent which may prove fatal. By the purport of the proposed regulation every objection is obviated, every inconvenience removed ; and the design of the institution strictly adhered to. It is calculated to prevent the abuse of authority, and the insolence of office on the one hand, and create a proper spirit of emulation on the other ; and by an annual rotation, will in a few years breed a number of officers. The proposed interval of a year will defeat undue influence or cabals ; and the capacity of being rechosen afterwards, opens a door to the return of officers of approved merit, and will always be a means of excluding unworthy men, whom an absolute rotation would of necessity introduce. The exception made in favor of the gentleman who by the unanimous voice of the company now commands it, is a very proper one, justly due to his public merit and experience ; it is peculiarly suited to our circumstances, and was dictated, not by compliment, but conviction.

In a company thus constituted, no young man will think himself degraded by doing duty in the ranks, which he may in his turn command, or has commanded. For these reasons I very cordially give my assent to the gentleman's motion, and hope it will have the unanimous approbation of this company. If any of the members continue to think that the choice of the officers ought to be confined to this town, they can introduce it by way of amendment to the motion, and the merits of the proposition may be freely discussed.[1]

X.

ORIGINAL DRAFT OF THE DECLARATION OF RIGHTS—GEORGE MASON.

A Declaration of Rights made by the Representatives of the good people of Virginia, assembled in full and free convention, which rights do pertain to them and their posterity, as the basis and foundation of government.

[1] Mason Papers, MS. copy.

1. That all men are created equally free and independent, and have certain inherent natural rights, of which they cannot, by any compact, deprive or divest their posterity ; among which are the enjoyment of life and liberty, with the means of acquiring and possessing property, and pursuing and obtaining happiness and safety.

2. That all power is by God and Nature vested in, and consequently derived from, the people ; that magistrates are their trustees and servants, and at all times amenable to them.

3. That government is, or ought to be, instituted for the common benefit, protection, and security of the people, nation, or community. Of all the various modes and forms of government, that is best which is capable of producing the greatest degree of happiness and safety, and is most effectually secured against the danger of mal-administration ; and that whenever any government shall be found inadequate or contrary to these purposes, a majority of the community hath an indubitable, unalienable, and indefeasible right to reform, alter, or abolish it, in such manner as shall be judged most conducive to the public weal.

4. That no man, or set of men, are entitled to exclusive or separate emoluments or privileges from the community, but in consideration of public services ; which not being descendible, neither ought the offices of magistrate, legislator, or judge to be hereditary.

5. That the legislative and executive powers of the State should be separate and distinct from the judicial ; and that the members of the two first may be restrained from oppression by feeling and participating the burthens of the people, they should, at fixed periods, be reduced to a private station, and return into that body from which they were originally taken, and the vacancies be supplied by frequent, certain, and regular elections.

6. That elections of members to serve as representatives of the people in the legislature ought to be free, and that all men, having sufficient evidence of permanent, common interest with and attachment to the community, have the right of suffrage, and cannot be taxed, or deprived of their property for public uses, without their own consent, or that of their representatives so elected, nor bound by any law to which they have not, in like manner, assented for the common good.

7. That all power of suspending laws, or the execution of laws, by any authority, without consent of the representatives of the people, is injurious to their rights, and ought not to be exercised.

8. That in all capital or criminal prosecutions, a man hath a right to demand the cause and nature of his accusation, to be confronted with the accusers and witnesses, to call for evidence in his favor, and to a speedy trial by an impartial jury of his vicinage, without whose unanimous consent he cannot be found guilty, nor can he be compelled to give evidence against himself; and that no man be deprived of his liberty, except by the law of the land or the judgment of his peers.

9. That excessive bail ought not to be required, nor excessive fines imposed, nor cruel and unusual punishments inflicted.

10. That in controversies respecting property, and in suits between man and man, the ancient trial by jury is preferable to any other, and to be held sacred.

11. That the freedom of the press is one of the great bulwarks of liberty, and can never be restrained but by despotic governments.

12. That a well regulated militia, composed of the body of the people, trained to arms, is the proper, natural, and safe defence of a free State; that standing armies in time of peace should be avoided, as dangerous to liberty; and that in all cases, the military should be under strict subordination to, and governed by, the civil power.

13. That no free government, or the blessing of liberty, can be preserved to any people but by a firm adherence to justice, moderation, temperance, frugality, and virtue, and by frequent recurrence to fundamental principles.

14. That religion, or the duty which we owe to our Creator, and the manner of discharging it, can be directed only by reason and conviction, not by force or violence; and, therefore, that all men should enjoy the fullest toleration in the exercise of religion, according to the dictates of conscience, unpunished and unrestrained by the magistrate, unless, under color of religion, any man disturb the peace, the happiness, or the safety of society. And that it is the mutual duty of all to practise Christian forbearance, love, and charity towards each other.

(Two more articles were added, viz., the 10th and 14th in the adopted bill—not of fundamental nature.)

This Declaration of Rights was the first in America ; it received few alterations or additions in the Virginia Convention (some of them not for the better), and was afterwards closely imitated by the other United States.

[This paper in all its parts is in the handwriting of George Mason—a memorandum is prefixed : " Virginia Declaration of Rights in 1776. Copy of first Draught by G. M." The note at the foot is also in George Mason's hand.]

VIRGINIA DECLARATION OF RIGHTS—ORIGINAL, IN THE HAND-
WRITING OF GEORGE MASON AND THOMAS L. LEE AND SO
ENDORSED BY T. L. LEE.

A Declaration of Rights, made by the Representatives of the good people of Virginia, assembled in full Convention ; and recommended to posterity as the basis and foundation of their government.

That all men are born equally free and independent and have certain inherent natural rights, of which they cannot, by any compact, deprive or divest their posterity ; among which are the enjoyment of life and liberty, with the means of acquiring and possessing property, and pursuing and obtaining happiness and safety.

That power is, by God and nature, vested in, and consequently derived from the people ; that magistrates are their trustees and servants, and at all times amenable to them.

That government is, or ought to be instituted for the common benefit and security of the people, nation, or community. Of all the various modes and forms of government that is best, which is capable of producing the greatest degree of happiness and safety, and is most effectually secured against the danger of male-administration. And that whenever any government shall be found inadequate, or contrary to these purposes, a majority of the community hath an indubitable, inalienable and indefeasible right to reform, alter or abolish it, in such manner as shall be judged most conducive to the public weal.

That no man, or set of men are entitled to exclusive or separate emoluments or privileges from the community, but in consideration of public services ; which not being descendible, or heredi-tary, the idea of a man born a magistrate, a legislator, or a judge is unnatural and absurd.

That the legislative and executive powers of the State should be separate and distinct from the judicative ; and that the members of the two first may be restrained from oppression, by feeling and participating the burthens they may lay upon the people, they should, at fixed periods, be reduced to a private station, and returned, by frequent, certain, and regular elections, into that body from which they were taken.

That no part of a man's property can be taken from him, or applied to public uses, without the consent of himself, or his legal representatives ; nor are the people bound by any laws, but such as they have, in like manner, assented to, for their common good.

That in all capital or criminal prosecutions, a man hath a right to demand the cause and nature of the accusation, to be confronted with the accusers or witnesses, to call for evidence in his favour, and to a speedy trial by a jury of his vicinage, without whose unanimous consent he cannot be found guilty ; nor can he be compelled to give evidence against himself. And that no man, except in times of actual invasion or insurrection, can be imprisoned upon suspicion of crimes against the State, unsupported by legal evidence.

That no free government or the blessing of liberty can be preserved to any people, but by a strict adherence to justice, moderation, temperance, frugality, and virtue ; and by frequent recurrence to fundamental principles.

That religion or the duty which we owe to our divine and omnipotent Creator, and the manner of discharging it, can be governed only by reason and conviction, not by force or violence ; and therefore that all men should enjoy the fullest toleration in the exercise of religion, according to the dictates of conscience, unpunished and unrestrained by the magistrate, unless under color of religion, any man disturb the peace, the happiness, or safety of society, or of individuals. And that it is the mutual duty of all, to practise Christian tolerance, love and charity towards each other.

That in all controversies respecting property, and in suits between man and man, the ancient trial by jury is preferable to any other, and ought to be held sacred.

[T. L. Lee begins here.]

That the freedom of the press, being the great bulwark of liberty, can never be restrained but in a despotic government.

That laws having a retrospect to crimes, and punishing offences committed before the existence of such laws, are generally dangerous, and ought to be avoided.

N. B. It is proposed to make some alteration in this last article when reported to the house. Perhaps somewhat like the following :

That all laws having a retrospect to crimes and punishing offences committed before the existence of such laws are dangerous, and ought to be avoided, except in cases of great and evident necessity, when the safety of the State absolutely requires them.

This is thought to state with more precision the doctrine respecting ex post facto laws and to signify to posterity that it is considered not so much a law of right, as the great law of necessity, which by a well known maxim is allowed to supersede all human institutions.

Another is agreed to in Committee condemning the use of general warrants ; and one other to prevent the suspension of laws, or the execution of them.

The above clauses, with some small alterations, and the addition of one or two more, have already been agreed to in the Committee appointed to prepare a declaration of rights ; when this business is finished in the house, the Committee will proceed to the ordinance of government.

T. L. LEE.

DECLARATION OF RIGHTS AS FINALLY ADOPTED.

A Declaration of Rights made by the representatives of the good people of Virginia, assembled in full and free Convention ; which rights do pertain to them, and their posterity, as the basis and foundation of government.

I. That all men are by nature equally free and independent, and have certain inherent rights, of which, when they enter into a state of society, they cannot, by any compact, deprive or divest their posterity ; namely, the enjoyment of life and liberty, with the means of acquiring and possessing property, and pursuing and obtaining happiness and safety.

II. That all power is vested in, and consequently derived from the people ; that Magistrates are their trustees and servants, and at all times amenable to them.

III. That government is or ought to be, instituted for the common benefit, protection, and security of the people, nation, or community ; of all the various modes and forms of government, that is best, which is capable of producing the greatest degree of happiness and safety, and is most effectually secured against the danger of mal-administration ; and that when any government shall be found inadequate or contrary to these purposes, a majority of the community hath an indubitable, unalienable, and indefeasible right, to reform, alter, or abolish it, in such manner as shall be judged most conducive to the public weal.

IV. That no man, or set of men, are entitled to exclusive or separate emoluments or privileges from the community, but in consideration of public services ; which not being descendible, neither ought the offices of Magistrate, Legislator, or Judge to be hereditary.

V. That the Legislative and Executive powers of the State should be separate and distinct from the Judiciary ; and that the members of the two first may be restrained from oppression, by feeling and participating the burthens of the people, they should, at fixed periods, be reduced to a private station, return into that body from which they were originally taken, and the vacancies be supplied by frequent, certain, and regular elections, in which all, or any part of the former members, to be again eligible, or ineligible, as the laws shall direct.

VI. That elections of members to serve as representatives of the people, in Assembly, ought to be free ; and that all men having sufficient evidence of permanent common interest with and attachment to, the community, have the right of suffrage, and cannot be taxed or deprived of their property for public uses without their own consent, or that of their representatives so elected, nor bound by any law to which they have not, in like manner, assented for the public good.

VII. That all power of suspending laws, or the execution of laws, by any authority without consent of the representatives of the people, is injurious to their rights and ought not to be exercised.

VIII. That in all capital or criminal prosecutions a man hath a right to demand the cause and nature of his accusation, to be confronted with the accusers and witnesses, to call for evidence in his favor, and to a speedy trial by an impartial jury of his vicinage, without whose unanimous consent he cannot be found guilty, nor can he be compelled to give evidence against himself ; that no man be deprived of his liberty except by the law of the land, or the judgment of his peers.

IX. That excessive bail ought not to be required, nor excessive fines imposed, nor cruel and unusual punishments inflicted.

X. That general warrants, whereby an officer or messenger may be commanded to search suspected places without evidence of a fact committed, or to seize any person or persons not named, or whose offence is not particularly described and supported by evidence, are grievous and oppressive, and ought not to be granted.

XI. That in controversies respecting property, and in suits between man and man, the ancient trial by jury is preferable to any other and ought to be held sacred.

XII. That the freedom of the press is one of the great bulwarks of liberty, and can never be restrained but by despotic governments.

XIII. That a well regulated militia, composed of the body of the people, trained to arms, is the proper, natural, and safe defence of a free state ; that standing armies, in time of peace, should be avoided, as dangerous to liberty ; and in all cases, the military should be under strict subordination to, and governed by, the civil power.

XIV. That the people have a right to uniform government ; and therefore, that no government separate from, or independent of, the government of Virginia, ought to be erected or established within the limits thereof.

XV. That no free government, or the blessing of liberty, can be preserved to any people but by a firm adherence to justice, moderation, temperance, frugality, and virtue, and by frequent recurrence to fundamental principles.

XVI. That religion, or the duty which we owe to our Creator, and the manner of discharging it, can be directed only by reason and conviction, not by force or violence, and therefore all men are equally entitled to the free exercise of religion, according to the dictates of conscience ; and that it is the mutual duty of all to practise Christian forbearance, love, and charity towards each other. [1]

[1] Laws of Virginia. Acts since 1768 in Force, folio, Richmond, 1785.

THE BILL OF RIGHTS.

The Speaker laid before the House the following communication from the Governor :

"EXECUTIVE DEPARTMENT,
"February 15, 1844.

" To the General Assembly :

" I have received from General John Mason of Fairfax County, an 'autograph copy of the first draught of the Bill of Rights of Virginia,' together with a letter from that gentleman to your honorable body, both of which I have now the gratification, at his request, to place in your hands. If the Bill of Rights and the body of our first Constitution are too well authenticated at present as the production of George Mason, and the Preamble as that of Mr. Jefferson, to give to this autograph the high interest which the doubtful authorship of that instrument might have attached to it, it is, nevertheless, full of historical and personal interest, as a rich and cherished record of a great work and a great man, and is well entitled, as such, to be passed from amongst the memorials of a family to those of a State. It has long been preserved for the sake of the Father by the Son, who now in the decline of life, when his care of it cannot be greatly prolonged, offers it to you as its best depositary, and asks that the State, which that Father so illustriously contributed to serve, will consent to receive and to save it. This you will no doubt consider as much a privilege as a duty to do. Of the political documents belonging to our country, there is none more justly the subject of profound veneration than the very 'Bill' the first draught of which is now offered to your acceptance, and the Constitution—the first defined and written one, it is believed, of modern times—which is founded upon it. Not only has this 'Bill' the remarkable merit of having been adopted unanimously at two successive periods of our government, fifty years apart, and that at each period by a body of statesmen amongst the wisest and best of mankind, but it has the farther merit of having led the way for our sister States, and been to them the model for similar declarations of rights and similar constitutions. Thus it is, that it stands the foremost in that series of events which have placed our united country at the head of the popular principle of the world, and have made it, of all other instruments, the chief one of this age, for enlarging the basis and advancing the triumphs of civil and religious freedom. In this light—in every light—the noble encomium pronounced by Mr. Jefferson upon its author is true of his work, that it is not only truly great, but the first in the order of greatness. It is an honor to Virginia to have had them both as products of her own, and this cherished sentiment of the State, I rejoice, as one of her functionaries, to have with you so happy an occasion to express.

"With every consideration of respect,

"I am your most obedient servant,

"JA. McDOWELL."

General Mason's letter transmitted with the Governor's communication.

"To the Honorable, the General Assembly of Virginia :

"As the only surviving son of the late George Mason of Gunston, I respectfully offer to the acceptance of the General Assembly, the *first draught* of the Bill of Rights of Virginia in the form in which it was reported by the author to the Convention of 1776. It is believed to be the only original draft of that instrument now extant ; none being found in the archives of the Commonwealth. Besides the historic interest connected with it, as the first written declaration of popular rights and the principles of popular government to which the times gave birth, with the fact that it was closely followed by the other States of the Confederacy in modelling their republican forms of government, it may be of value at some future day as an authentic memorial of the fundamental law. The evidences of its authenticity are clear and undoubted. It came into my possession from the papers of the author soon after his death ; more than half a century since. It is throughout in his own handwriting. And its character as the first draft reported to the Convention is declared, as well by the memoranda with his initials prefixed as by the note at the foot of the manuscript. Should the General Assembly deem it worthy of acceptance by the State, I shall be gratified and honored by their making such order for its future preservation as to them shall seem proper. And I am with very great respect their most humble servant,

"JOHN MASON.

"CLERMONT, FAIRFAX CO., Jan. 23, 1844."

After these documents were read, Mr. Lacy offered the following resolutions, which were unanimously adopted : "Whereas the Governor of this Commonwealth hath this day communicated to this House a MS. copy of the admirable Bill of Rights, prefixed to the first Constitution of Virginia and hence adopted into the present Constitution, and this copy is in the handwriting of its illustrious author George Mason, whose Revolutionary services, inflexible principles, and eminent talents are held in reverence by every citizen of Virginia ; And the original Constitution emanating in the greater part from the pen of the same author is perhaps the first written Constitution that was ever adopted in America or established by a free people :

"*Resolved,* That this very interesting document be thankfully received by the Legislature of Virginia and deposited with the archives of our government.

"*Resolved, also,* That the Governor of this Commonwealth be requested to communicate to the family of George Mason, by whom it was presented, the warm acknowledgments of the Legislature for the patriotic spirit which has prompted them to transfer this precious relic from their own family to their country."

Mr. Lacy was deputed to convey the letters and resolutions to the Senate. The Senate, having first inserted the word " written " before the word Constitution so that it would read " first written Constitution that was ever adopted," &c. (as corrected above), at once concurred in the Resolutions of the House.

TABLE ON WHICH GEORGE MASON WROTE THE BILL OF RIGHTS

Table of black walnut, 20 x 30 inches surface ; height 24 inches —with drawer. Edges of the table moulded, legs below the drawer rounded, terminating in knobs.

Silver plate 3 x 4½ inches, in the shape of a shield. Mason crest and motto and below it this inscription :

" The Writing Table of
George Mason
Gunston Hall, Fairfax County, Va.
upon which he wrote the
Virginia Bill of Rights
Adopted in Convention June 12th, 1776.
Presented to the
Virginia Historical Society
by his Great-grandson
George Mason
of
Alexandria, Virginia."

FIRST DRAFT OF CONSTITUTION, OR PLAN OF GOVERNMENT, LAID BEFORE SELECT COMMITTEE.

1. Let the legislative, executive, and judicative departments be separate and distinct, so that neither exercise the powers properly belonging to the other.

2. Let the legislative be formed of two distinct branches, who together shall be a complete legislature. They shall meet once or oftener, every year, and shall be called the General Assembly of Virginia.

3. Let one of these be called the Lower House of Assembly, and consist of two delegates or representatives, chosen for each county annually, by such men as have resided in the same for a year last past, are freeholders of the county, possess an estate of inheritance of land in Virginia of at least one thousand pounds value, and are upwards of twenty-four years of age.

4. Let the other be called the Upper House of Assembly, and consist of twenty-four members; for whose election, let the different counties be divided into twenty-four districts, and each county of the respective district, at the time of the election of its delegates for the Lower House, choose twelve deputies or sub-electors, being freeholders residing therein, and having an estate of inheritance of lands within the district of at least five hundred pounds value. In case of dispute, the qualifications to be determined by the majority of the said deputies. Let these deputies

choose by ballot one member of the Upper House of Assembly, who is a freeholder of the district, hath been a resident therein for one year last past, possesses an estate of inheritance in lands in Virginia of at least two thousand pounds value, and is upwards of twenty-eight years of age. To keep up this assembly by rota_tion, let the districts be equally divided into four classes, and numbered. At the end of one year after the general election, let the six members elected by the first division be displaced, ren_dered ineligible for four years, and the vacancies be supplied in the manner aforesaid. Let this rotation be applied to each division according to its number, and continued in due order annually.

5. Let each House settle its own rules of proceeding, direct writs of election for supplying intermediate vacancies ; and let the right of suffrage, both in the election of members of the Lower House and of deputies for the districts, be extended to those having leases for land in which there is an unexpired term of seven years, and to every housekeeper who hath resided for one year last past in the county, and hath been the father of three children in this country.

6. Let all laws originate in the Lower House, to be approved or rejected by the Upper House, or to be amended with the consent of the Lower House, except money-bills which in no instance shall be altered by the Upper House, but wholly approved or rejected.

7. Let a governor or chief magistrate be chosen annually by joint ballot for both Houses, who shall not continue in that office longer than three years successively, and then be ineligible for the next three years. Let an adequate but moderate salary be settled on him, during his continuance in office ; and let him, with the advice of a council of state, exercise the executive powers of government, and the power of proroguing or adjourning the General Assembly, or of calling it upon emergencies, and of granting reprieves or pardons, except in cases where the prosecution shall have been carried on by the Lower House of Assembly.

8. Let a privy council, or council of state, consisting of eight members, be chosen by joint ballot of both Houses of Assembly, promiscuously from their own members or the people at large, to

assist in the administration of government. Let the governor be president of this council ; but let them annually choose one of their own members as vice-president, who, in case of the death or absence of the governor, shall act as lieutenant-governor. Let three members be sufficient to act, and their advice be entered of record in their proceedings. Let them appoint their own clerk, who shall have a salary settled by law, and take an oath of secrecy in such matters as he shall be directed by the board to conceal, unless called upon by the Lower House of Assembly for information. Let a sum of money, appropriated to that purpose, be divided annually among the members, in proportion to their attendance ; and let them be incapable during their continuance in office, of sitting in either House of Assembly. Let two members be removed, by ballot of their own board, at the end of every three years, and be ineligible for the three next years. Let this be regularly continued, by rotation, so as that no member be removed before he hath been three years in the council ; and let these vacancies, as well as those occasioned by death or incapacity, be supplied by new elections, in the same manner as the first.

9. Let the governor, with the advice of the privy council, have the appointment of the militia officers, and the government of the militia, under the laws of the country.

10. Let the two Houses of Assembly, by joint ballot, appoint judges of the supreme court, judges in chancery, judges of admiralty, and the attorney-general, to be commissioned by the governor, and continue in office during good behaviour. In case of death or incapacity, let the governor, with the advice of the privy council, appoint persons to succeed in office *pro tempore,* to be approved or displaced by both Houses. Let these officers have fixed and adequate salaries, and be incapable of having a seat in either House of Assembly, or in the privy council, except the attorney-general and the treasurer, who may be permitted to a seat in the Lower House of Assembly.

11. Let the governor and privy council appoint justices of the peace for the counties. Let the clerks of all the courts, the sheriffs and coroners, be nominated by the respective courts, approved by the governor and privy council, and commissioned by the governor. Let the clerks be continued during good

behaviour, and all fees be regulated by law. Let the justices appoint constables.

12. Let the governor, any of the privy councillors, judges of the supreme court, and all other officers of government, for mal-administration, or corruption, be prosecuted by the Lower House of Assembly (to be carried on by the attorney-general, or such other person as the House may appoint), in the supreme court of common law. If found guilty, let him or them be either removed from office, or forever disabled to hold any office under the government, or subjected to such pains or penalties as the laws shall direct.

13. Let all commissions run in the name of the *Commonwealth of Virginia,* and be tested by the governor, with the seal of the Commonwealth annexed. Let writs run in the same manner, and be tested by the clerks of the several courts. Let indictments conclude, *Against the peace and dignity of the Commonwealth.*

14. Let a treasurer be appointed annually, by joint ballot of both Houses.

15. In order to introduce this government, let the representatives of the people, now met in convention, choose twenty-four members to be an upper House ; and let both Houses, by joint ballot, choose a governor and privy council; the Upper House to continue until the last day of March next, and the other officers until the end of the succeeding session of Assembly. In cases of vacancies, the president to issue writs for new elections.[1]

THE CONSTITUTION OR FORM OF GOVERNMENT AGREED TO AND RESOLVED UPON BY THE DELEGATES AND REPRESENTATIVES OF THE SEVERAL COUNTIES AND CORPORATIONS OF VIRGINIA.

I. Whereas George the third, King of Great Britain and Ireland, and Elector of Hanover, heretofore entrusted with the exercise of the kingly office in this government, hath endeavoured to pervert the same into a detestable and insupportable tyranny, by putting his negative on laws the most wholesome and necessary for the public good : By denying his Governors permission

---

[1] " Life of Madison," vol. i., Appendix C.

to pass laws of immediate and pressing importance, unless suspended in their operation for his assent, and, when so suspended, neglecting to attend to them for many years : By refusing to pass certain other laws, unless the persons to be benefited by them would relinquish the inestimable right of representation in the Legislature : By dissolving Legislative Assemblies repeatedly and continually, for opposing with manly firmness his invasions of the rights of the people : When dissolved, by refusing to call others for a long space of time, thereby leaving the political system without any Legislative head : By endeavouring to prevent the population of our country, and, for that purpose, obstructing the laws for the naturalization of foreigners : By keeping among us, in time of peace, standing armies and ships of war : By affecting to render the military independent of, and superior to, the civil power : By combining with others to subject us to a foreign jurisdiction, giving his assent to their pretended acts of Legislation : For quartering large bodies of armed troops among us : For cutting off our trade with all parts of the world : For imposing taxes on us without our consent : For depriving us of the benefits of trial by jury : For transporting us beyond seas, to be tried for pretended offences : For suspending our own Legislatures, and declaring themselves invested with power to legislate for us in all cases whatsoever : By plundering our seas, ravaging our coasts, burning our towns, and destroying the lives of our people : By inciting insurrections of our fellow subjects, with the allurements of forfeiture and confiscation : By prompting our negroes to rise in arms among us, those very negroes whom, by an inhuman use of his negative, he hath refused us permission to exclude by law : By endeavouring to bring on the inhabitants of our frontiers, the merciless Indian savages, whose known rule of warfare is an undistinguished destruction of all ages, sexes, and conditions of existence : By transporting, at this time, a large army of foreign mercenaries, to complete the works of death, desolation, and tyranny, already begun with circumstances of cruelty and perfidy unworthy the head of a civilized nation : By answering our repeated petitions for redress with a repetition of injuries : And finally, by abandoning the helm of government, and declaring us out of his allegiance and protection. By which several acts of misrule, the government of this country, as formerly exercised under the crown of Great Britain, is totally dissolved.

II. We therefore, the Delegates and Representatives of the good people of Virginia, having maturely considered the premises, and viewing with great concern the deplorable condition to which this once happy country must be reduced, unless some regular, adequate mode of civil polity is speedily adopted, and in compliance with a recommendation of the General Congress, do ordain and declare the future form of government of Virginia to be as followeth :

III. The Legislative, Executive, and Judiciary departments shall be separate and distinct, so that neither exercise the powers properly belonging to the other ; nor shall any person exercise the powers of more than one of them at the same time, except that the Justices of the county courts shall be eligible to either House of Assembly.

IV. The Legislative shall be formed of two distinct branches, who, together, shall be a complete Legislature. They shall meet once or oftener, every year, and shall be called the General Assembly of Virginia.

V. One of these shall be called the House of Delegates, and consist of two Representatives to be chosen for each county, and for the district of West Augusta, annually, of such men as actually reside in and are freeholders of the same, or duly qualified according to law, and also one Delegate or Representative to be chosen annually for the city of Williamsburg, and one for the borough of Norfolk, and a Representative for each of such other cities and boroughs as may hereafter be allowed particular representation by the Legislature ; but when any city or borough shall so decrease as that the number of persons having right of suffrage therein shall have been for the space of seven years successively less than half the number of voters in some one county in Virginia, such city or borough thenceforward shall cease to send a Delegate or Representative to the Assembly.

VI. The other shall be called the Senate, and consist of twenty-four members, of whom thirteen shall constitute a House to proceed on business, for whose election the different counties shall be divided into twenty-four districts, and each county of the respective district, at the time of the election of its Delegates,

29

shall vote for one Senator, who is actually a resident and freeholder within the district, or duly qualified according to law, and is upwards of twenty-five years of age ; and the sheriffs of each county, within five days at farthest after the last county election in the district, shall meet at some convenient place, and from the poll so taken in their respective counties return as a Senator the man who shall have the greatest number of votes in the whole district. To keep up this Assembly by rotation, the districts shall be equally divided into four classes, and numbered by lot. At the end of one year after the general election, the six members elected by the first division shall be displaced, and the vacancies thereby occasioned supplied from such class or division, by new election, in the manner aforesaid. This rotation shall be applied to each division, according to its number, and continued in due order annually.

VII. That the right of suffrage in the election of members of both Houses shall remain as exercised at present, and each House shall choose its own Speaker, appoint its own officers, settle its own rules of proceeding, and direct writs of election for supplying intermediate vacancies.

VIII. All laws shall originate in the House of Delegates, to be approved or rejected by the Senate, or to be amended with the consent of the House of Delegates ; except money bills, which in no instance shall be altered by the Senate, but wholly approved or rejected.

IX. A Governor, or Chief Magistrate, shall be chosen annually, by joint ballot of both Houses, to be taken in each House respectively, deposited in the conference room, the boxes examined jointly by a Committee of each House, and the numbers severally reported to them, that the appointments may be entered (which shall be the mode of taking the joint ballot of both Houses in all cases), who shall not continue in that office longer than three years successively, nor be eligible until the expiration of four years after he shall have been out of that office. An adequate but moderate salary shall be settled on him during his continuance in office ; and he shall, with the advice of a Council of State, exercise the executive powers of government according to the laws of this commonwealth ; and shall not, under any pretence, exercise any power or prerogative, by virtue of any law,

statute, or custom, of *England*. But he shall, with the advice of
the Council of State, have the power of granting reprieves or pardons, except where the prosecution shall have been carried on by
the House of Delegates, or the law shall otherwise particularly
direct ; in which cases, no reprieve or pardon shall be granted,
but by resolve of the House of Delegates.

X. Either House of the General Assembly may adjourn themselves respectively. The Governor shall not prorogue or adjourn
the Assembly during their sitting, nor dissolve them at any time ;
but he shall, if necessary, either by advice of the Council of
State, or on application of a majority of the House of Delegates,
call them before the time to which they shall stand prorogued or
adjourned.

XI. A Privy Council or Council of State, consisting of eight
members, shall be chosen by joint ballot of both Houses of Assembly, either from their own members or the people at large, to
assist in the administration of government. They shall annually
choose out of their own members a President, who, in case of the
death, inability, or necessary absence of the Governor from the
government, shall act as Lieutenant Governor. Four members
shall be sufficient to act, and their advice and proceedings shall
be entered of record, and signed by the members present (to any
part whereof any member may enter his dissent), to be laid before
the General Assembly, when called for by them. This Council
may appoint their own clerk, who shall have a salary settled by
law, and take an oath of secrecy in such matters as he shall be
directed by the Board to conceal. A sum of money appropriated
to that purpose shall be divided annually among the members,
in proportion to their attendance ; and they shall be incapable,
during their continuance in office, of sitting in either House of
Assembly. Two members shall be removed by joint ballot of
both Houses of Assembly at the end of every three years, and be
ineligible for the three next years. These vacancies, as well as
those occasioned by death or incapacity, shall be supplied by new
elections in the same manner.

XII. The Delegates for *Virginia* to the Continental Congress
shall be chosen annually, or superseded in the meantime by joint
ballot of both Houses of Assembly.

XIII. The present militia officers shall be continued, and vacan-

cies supplied by appointment of the Governor, with the advice of
the Privy Council or recommendations from the respective county
courts ; but the Governor and Council shall have a power of suspending any officer, and ordering a court-martial on complaint
of misbehaviour or inability, or to supply vacancies of officers
happening when in actual service. The Governor may embody
the militia, with the advice of the Privy Council, and when embodied, shall alone have the direction of the militia under the
laws of the country.

XIV. The two Houses of Assembly shall, by joint ballot,
appoint Judges of the Supreme Court of Appeals, and General
Court, Judges in Chancery, Judges of Admiralty, Secretary, and
the Attorney General, to be commissioned by the Governor, and
continue in office during good behaviour. In case of death, incapacity, or resignation, the Governor, with the advice of the
Privy Council, shall appoint persons to succeed in office, to be
approved or displaced by both Houses. These officers shall
have fixed and adequate salaries, and, together with all others
holding lucrative offices, and all Ministers of the Gospel of every
denomination, be incapable of being elected members of either
House of Assembly, or the Privy Council.

XV. The Governor, with the advice of the Privy Council, shall
appoint Justices of the Peace for the counties ; and in cases of
vacancies, or a necessity of increasing the number hereafter, such
appointments to be made upon the recommendation of the respective county courts. The present acting Secretary in *Virginia*,
and clerks of all the county courts, shall continue in office. In
case of vacancies, either by death, incapacity, or resignation, a
Secretary shall be appointed as before directed, and the clerks by
the respective courts. The present and future clerks shall hold
their offices during good behaviour, to be judged of and determined in the General Court. The Sheriffs and Coroners shall be
nominated by the respective courts, approved by the Governor,
with the advice of the Privy Council, and commissioned by the
Governor. The Justices shall appoint constables, and all fees of
the aforesaid officers regulated by law.

XVI. The Governor, when he is out of office, and others
offending against the State, either by mal-administration, corruption, or other means by which the safety of the State may be en-

dangered, shall be impeachable by the House of Delegates, such impeachment to be prosecuted by the Attorney General, or such other person or persons as the House may appoint in the General Court, according to the laws of the land. If found guilty, he or they shall be either for ever disabled to hold any office under government, or removed from such office *pro tempore*, or subjected to such pains or penalties as the law shall direct.

XVII. If all, or any of the Judges of the General Court, shall, on good grounds (to be judged of by the House of Delegates), be accused of any of the crimes or offences before-mentioned, such House of Delegates may, in like manner, impeach the Judge or Judges so accused, to be prosecuted in the Court of Appeals ; and he or they, if found guilty, shall be punished in the same manner as is prescribed in the preceding clause.

XVIII. Commissions and grants shall run *In the name of the* COMMONWEALTH OF VIRGINIA, and bear test by the Governor with the seal of the commonwealth annexed. Writs shall run in the same manner, and bear test by the clerks of the several courts. Indictments shall conclude, *Against the peace and dignity of the commonwealth.*

XIX. A Treasurer shall be appointed annually, by joint ballot of both Houses.

XX. All escheats, penalties, and forfeitures, heretofore going to the king, shall go to the commonwealth, save only such as the Legislature may abolish, or otherwise provide for.

XXI. The territories contained within the charters erecting the colonies of Maryland, Pennsylvania, North and South Carolina, are hereby ceded, released, and for ever confirmed to the people of those colonies respectively, with all the rights of property, jurisdiction, and government, and all other rights whatsoever which might at any time heretofore have been claimed by *Virginia*, except the free navigation and use of the Rivers *Potowmack* and Pokomoke, with the property of the Virginia shores or strands bordering on either of the said rivers, and all improvements which have been or shall be made thereon. The western and northern extent of *Virginia* shall in all other respects stand as fixed by the charter of King *James* the first, in the year one thousand six hundred and nine, and by the public treaty of peace between the Courts of *Great Britain* and *France* in the year one thousand seven hundred and sixty-three ; unless, by act of Legislature, one or more territories shall hereafter be laid off, and governments established westward of the *Allegheny* mountains. And no purchase of lands shall be made of the *Indian* natives but on behalf of the public, by authority of the General Assembly.

XX. In order to introduce this government, the representatives of the people met in Convention shall choose a Governor and Privy Council, also such other officers directed to be chosen by both Houses as may be judged necessary to be immediately appointed. The Senate to be first chosen by the people, to continne until the last day of *March* next, and the other officers until the end of the succeeding session of Assembly. In case of vacancies, the Speaker of either House shall issue writs for new elections.

END OF VOLUME I.

Made in the USA
Lexington, KY
13 December 2019